It is essential to our true understanding of the triune God that we be clear about the biblical and dogmatic basis for our confession. This book brings together an impressive array of world-class theologians whose Scholarship is matched by their godliness addressing one of the key components of that task; the basis of our knowledge of relations in God.

Dr. Liam Goligher, senior minister, Tenth Presbyterian Church, Philadelphia, PA

The creedal doctrine that the Son of God was "begotten of the Father before all worlds" is a notion that is often misunderstood or else maligned by many contemporary theologians. In this context, Swain and Sanders have brought together an impressive collection of essays from across the theological disciplines in order to elucidate and defend this linchpin Trinitarian doctrine. The book's coherence lies not only in the sum of its parts but also in the synthetic nature of its individual chapters. This is retrieval theology at its best—careful in its treatment of the historical sources and relevant in its theological import.

R. Lucas Stamps, assistant professor of Christian studies, Anderson University

PRAISE FOR *RETRIEVING ETERNAL GENERATION*

The Christian teaching of the eternal generation of the Son has from the beginning engendered detailed scrutiny and fierce opposition, and again in the present, the doctrine is causing great controversy. By way of response, Swain and Sanders have gathered together for this volume a range of experts from the fields of biblical exegesis, church history, and systematic theology to consider this teaching in detail. The result is a powerful and dynamic defence of the doctrine, insisting vigorously upon its scriptural, traditional, and dogmatic importance. At a time of much doctrinal diversity and uncertainty, this book lucidly sets out a salutary and welcome account of this venerable teaching and of its central significance for faithful Christian belief.

> PAUL T NIMMO, King's Chair of Systematic Theology,
> University of Aberdeen

Retrieval is an important part of the task systematic theology faces today. In *Retrieving Eternal Generation*, Scott Swain and Fred Sanders, along with their fellow contributors, render a great service to the church and theology. In the midst of a fierce and sometimes confused debate over the doctrine of the Trinity, this excellent collection of essays provides a careful biblical, historical, and conceptual analysis that helps uncover the profound richness of the classic understanding of the Son's eternal generation from the Father. *Retrieving Eternal Generation* brings together some of the best of biblical, patristic, and doctrinal theology in a convincing case for a doctrine that is unjustly accused of being overly metaphysical or Greek, among other deprecating terms. It shows that, to the contrary, this doctrine is vital for proper confession of the triune God.

> DOLF TE VELDE, assistant professor of systematic theology,
> Theological University Kampen

This is the best single study examining one of the most important yet neglected aspects of the Christian doctrine of God, namely, the idea of the Son's eternal begottenness, that singular procession of the Son that grounds the Son's earthly mission (incarnation), and hence the ultimate basis ("before the foundation of the world") of Christmas. The authors display the wisdom of retrieving theological light from the patristic past, light that is just as valuable and vital today as it was in early Christianity.

Retrieving Eternal Generation is an encouraging display of how biblical studies, church history, and systematic theology can work together to the glory of God, recovering from the past and commending for today the confession of Jesus Christ as the "only begotten" Son of the Father, Light from Light, very God from very God.

> KEVIN J. VANHOOZER, research professor of systematic
> theology, Trinity Evangelical Divinity School

In contemporary Trinitarian theology, conservative Christians have all too often been moving in one of two directions: either inadvertently undermining the full divinity of the Son—thereby turning Christianity into a unitarianism—or inadvertently distinguishing the divine persons in ways that are logically tritheistic. In response, Swain and Sanders have put together an important and profound volume whose timing simply could not be better.

> MATTHEW LEVERING, James N. and Mary D. Perry Jr.
> Chair of Theology, Mundelein Seminary

Retrieving Eternal Generation is a vital gift to evangelical theology. The various authors provide stimulating biblical exegesis, hermeneutical breadth, historical expertise, and theological depth. Respectfully but courageously engaging the challengers of this classic doctrine, they transcend polemics to contribute fresh dogmatic insight. I will be referring to several of these essays again and again.

> DANIEL J. TREIER, Knoedler Professor of Theology,
> Wheaton College Graduate School

The heart of the doctrine of the Trinity is not the puzzle of the one and the three, but the eternal relationship between Father and Son. Such is, quite rightly, Sanders and Swain's basic claim in the introduction to this book. The stellar essays that follow cogently argue that the doctrine of the eternal generation of the Son constitutes the bedrock of the Christian confession of the triune God. This book presents a compelling and timely retrieval of Nicene Christianity.

> HANS BOERSMA, J. I. Packer Professor of Theology,
> Regent College

RETRIEVING ETERNAL GENERATION

FRED SANDERS AND SCOTT R. SWAIN,
EDITORS

Z ZONDERVAN®

ZONDERVAN

Retrieving Eternal Generation
Copyright © 2017 by Fred Sanders and Scott R. Swain

ISBN 978-0-310-53787-8 (softcover)

ISBN 978-0-310-53788-5 (ebook)

Requests for information should be addressed to:
Zondervan, *3900 Sparks Dr. SE, Grand Rapids, Michigan 49546*

Scripture quotations are taken from The Holy Bible, New International Version®,
NIV®. Copyright © 1973, 1978, 1984, 2011 by Biblica, Inc.® Used by permission of
Zondervan. All rights reserved worldwide. www.Zondervan.com. The "NIV" and
"New International Version" are trademarks registered in the United States Patent and
Trademark Office by Biblica, Inc.®

Any internet addresses (websites, blogs, etc.) and telephone numbers in this book are
offered as a resource. They are not intended in any way to be or imply an endorsement
by Zondervan, nor does Zondervan vouch for the content of these sites and numbers for
the life of this book.

No part of this publication may be reproduced, stored in a retrieval system, or
transmitted in any form or by any means—electronic, mechanical, photocopy,
recording, or any other—except for brief quotations in printed reviews, without the
prior permission of the publisher.

Cover design: Studio Gearbox
Cover photo: Erich Lessing / Art Resource, NY

Printed in the United States of America

17 18 19 20 21 22 23 24 25 26 27 /DHV/ 15 14 13 12 11 10 9 8 7 6 5 4 3 2 1

To the Evangelical Theological Society,
in gratitude and hope

CONTENTS

Acknowledgments 11
Contributors. 13
Abbreviations 15
Introduction—Fred Sanders and Scott R. Swain 17

PART I:
BIBLICAL REASONING

1. THE RADIANCE OF THE FATHER'S GLORY: Eternal
   Generation, the Divine Names, and Biblical Interpretation . . 29
   Scott R. Swain

2. THE ROLE OF PROVERBS 8: Eternal Generation
   and Hermeneutics Ancient and Modern. 44
   Matthew Y. Emerson

3. ETERNAL GENERATION AND THE OLD TESTAMENT:
   Micah 5:2 as a Test Case 67
   Mark S. Gignilliat

4. JOHN 5:26: *Crux Interpretum* for Eternal Generation. 79
   D. A. Carson

5. A LEXICAL DEFENSE OF THE JOHANNINE
   "ONLY BEGOTTEN" 98
   Charles Lee Irons

6. HEBREWS I AND THE SON BEGOTTEN "TODAY" 117
   Madison N. Pierce

7. *Generatio, Processio Verbi, Donum Nominis*:
   Mapping the Vocabulary of Eternal Generation 132
   R. Kendall Soulen

PART II:

HISTORICAL WITNESSES

8. At the Origins of Eternal Generation: Scriptural Foundations and Theological Purpose in Origen of Alexandria 149
   Lewis Ayres

9. Eternal Generation in the Trinitarian Theology of Augustine........................ 163
   Keith E. Johnson

10. Post-Reformation Trinitarian Perspectives 180
    Chad Van Dixhoorn

11. Jonathan Edwards and Eternal Generation..... 208
    Christina N. Larsen

12. Eternal Generation after Barth 226
    Michael Allen

PART III:

CONTEMPORARY STATEMENTS

13. Philosophical Models of Eternal Generation .. 243
    Mark Makin

14. Eternal Generation and Soteriology........... 260
    Fred Sanders

15. Eternal Generation: Pro-Nicene Pattern, Dogmatic Function, and Created Effects 271
    Josh Malone

Subject Index.. 286
Scripture Index...................................... 292
Author Index.. 298

ACKNOWLEDGMENTS

THE EDITORS WOULD LIKE TO THANK the other members of the Trinitarian Theology Consultation of the Evangelical Theological Society. Since first convening in 2012, the members of the steering committee have planned strategically and worked diligently to retrieve the doctrine of eternal generation and to commend it to the present generation. This set of essays is the direct result of that planning and work. That steering committee consisted of the editors, along with Jeff Bingham, Keith E. Johnson, Josh Malone, and Ben Rhodes. It was Malone and Rhodes who pulled the consultation together in the first place, had many of the key ideas, did most of the work, and kept the project moving toward the goal of publication. Most of the chapters in this volume began as papers presented at the Consultation during the years devoted to the doctrine of eternal generation. We would also like to thank Oliver Crisp, Dan Treier, and Michel Barnes for presenting papers in that Consultation that were important in shaping our scholarly dialogue. Two of the chapters in this volume (those by Emerson and Irons) were presented at the Far West Region of the Evangelical Theological Society in 2014, in response to a call for papers on the Trinity and the Bible. The final two chapters, by Makin and Pierce, were solicited specifically for this volume.

CONTRIBUTORS

Michael Allen—is John Dyer Trimble Professor of Systematic Theology and academic dean, Reformed Theological Seminary, Orlando, Florida.

Lewis Ayres—is professor of Catholic and historical theology in the Department of Theology and Religion, University of Durham.

D. A. Carson—is research professor of New Testament, Trinity Evangelical Divinity School.

Matthew Y. Emerson—is Dickinson Assistant Professor of Religion, Oklahoma Baptist University.

Mark S. Gignilliat—is professor of divinity, Beeson Divinity School, Samford University.

Charles Lee Irons—is senior research administrator, Charles R. Drew University of Medicine and Science, Los Angeles, and adjunct professor, California Graduate School of Theology, Garden Grove, California.

Keith E. Johnson—is director of theological education and development at Cru and guest professor of systematic theology at Reformed Theological Seminary.

Christina N. Larsen—is a member of the theology faculty, Grand Canyon University.

Mark Makin—is assistant professor of philosophy in the Torrey Honors Institute, Biola University.

Joshua Malone—is assistant professor of theology, Moody Bible Institute, Spokane, Washington.

Madison N. Pierce—is assistant professor of biblical studies and theology, Tyndale University College & Seminary, Toronto, Canada.

Fred Sanders—is professor of theology in the Torrey Honors Institute, Biola University.

R. Kendall Soulen—is professor of systematic theology, Candler School of Theology, Emory University.

CONTRIBUTORS

Scott R. Swain—is president and James Woodrow Hassell Chair of Systematic Theology, Reformed Theological Seminary, Orlando, Florida.
Chad Van Dixhoorn—is chancellor's professor of historical theology and associate professor of church history, Reformed Theological Seminary.

ABBREVIATIONS

ANF	*Ante-Nicene Fathers*
Ant.	Josephus, *The Antiquities of the Jews*
C. Ar.	Athanasius, *Orationes contra Arianos* (*Orations Against the Arians*)
CD	Karl Barth, *Church Dogmatics*
Trin.	Augustine, *De trinitate* (*On the Trinity*)
EurJTheol	*European Journal of Theology*
GCS	Die Griechischen Christlichen Schriftsteller
Inst.	John Calvin, *Institutes of the Christian Religion*
JBL	*Journal of Biblical Literature*
JETS	*Journal of the Evangelical Theological Society*
JTS	*Journal of Theological Studies*
LCL	Loeb Classical Library
NPNF[1]	*Nicene and Post-Nicene Fathers*, series 1
NPNF[2]	*Nicene and Post-Nicene Fathers*, series 2
NTS	*New Testament Studies*
Or. Bas.	Gregory of Nazianzus, *Oratio in laudem Basilii*
Princ.	Origen, *On First Principles*
SC	Sources Chrétiennes
ST	Thomas Aquinas, *Summa Theologiae*
TLG	Thesaurus Linguae Graecae
Tract.	Augustine, *In Johannis evangelium tractatus*
TrinJ	*Trinity Journal*
VT	*Vetus Testamentum*
WJE	*The Works of Jonathan Edwards*
ZNW	*Zeitschrift für die neutestamentliche Wissenschaft und die Kunde der älteren Kirche*

INTRODUCTION

FRED SANDERS AND SCOTT R. SWAIN

THE TRIUNE GOD IS NOT COMPOSED of parts, but the doctrine of the Trinity has parts. There are a number of discrete theological commitments that go together to compose the fully developed, properly functioning doctrine of the Trinity. When any of them are removed or underdeveloped, Trinitarian theology suffers and, in the worst cases, comes apart.

One of the most widespread ways of considering the parts of the doctrine of the Trinity is to chart the three persons in their relations to each other and to divinity. The resulting logical diagram shows the Father, Son, and Holy Spirit each specified as being God but not being each other. At a bare minimum, the doctrine of the Trinity can be stated as the teaching that the one God is three persons who are each God but are not each other.

But this common schematic account of Trinitarianism focuses too much on the three-one dynamic at the expense of the character of the relations among the three persons. Leading with the three-one dynamic of the doctrine of the Trinity tends to suppress the crucial insight that first led to the formulation of Trinitarianism at all. That insight is that the Son is eternally begotten (or generated) from the Father. It is not enough to say that the Son is God; we must see that he is God the Son, not just God in general. Sonship, or eternal generation, is what gives both form and content to the relation between the Father and the Son: the relation has the form of fromness and the content of filiality. Whenever the nature of that relation is left unspecified, any articulation of Trinitarian theology becomes brittle and disconnected. Without eternal generation, the constellation of truths that compose the doctrine of the Trinity remain just so many points of stellar light; they are stars that fail to constellate. They remain strangely isolated facts about threes and ones, essences and persons, in the cold vacuum of theologoumenal abstraction. In modern times, the doctrine of the Trinity is often taught in this misconfigured, unconstellated

17

way: set forth as a teaching about one God in three persons as if that were the main business of the doctrine, with the possibility left open that the actual relations of the persons do not need to be specified, but could be as a matter of detail. But this rough-and-ready approach is clean contrary to the systematic needs of a coherent doctrine of the Trinity. It is not how the great, central tradition of Christian teaching has presented the doctrine. Nor is it how we first encounter the reality of the Trinity in Scripture. The goal of *Retrieving Eternal Generation* is to make three cases in adequate detail: that this classic piece of theological confession is in fact biblically, traditionally, and systematically satisfying. It is our hope that these three are one persuasive argument for retrieving the doctrine of eternal generation and recognizing its central importance for the doctrine of the Trinity.

THE NEED FOR RETRIEVAL

Nearly all the chapters gathered in this volume begin with a brief report on why the doctrine has fallen on hard times in recent decades and what kind of recovery is needed. The fact that this set of biblical scholars, historical theologians, and contemporary constructive theologians can all recognize the same problem from their various angles is telling. In cases where the doctrine has been actually rejected, the following chapters engage those arguments on the appropriate grounds (especially exegetical, hermeneutical, and philosophical). But even where the doctrine has not been rejected, it has been neglected. A few years ago Kevin Giles identified the need for a defense of eternal generation, and in 2012 he published a volume with that goal.[1] Giles certainly filled a gap in the literature. In fact, it is hard to say when the doctrine had been given a book-length treatment prior to his study, perhaps not since James Kidd's 1823 *Dissertation on the Eternal Sonship of Christ*, in which he said, "The doctrine of the Eternal Sonship of Jesus Christ has been received by the Orthodox Church in all ages. Of late years, however, its truth has been questioned."[2] Like Kidd in 1823, Giles in 2012 was roused to defend the doctrine when he noted defections from it taking place. In Giles's case, he was worried about developments in American evangelical theology that tend toward subordinationism, and he threw everything he had at the task of rescuing eternal generation from that error.

---

1. Kevin Giles, *The Eternal Generation of the Son: Maintaining Orthodoxy in Trinitarian Theology* (Downers Grove, IL: IVP Academic, 2012).

2. James Kidd, *Dissertation on the Eternal Sonship of Christ* (Philadelphia: Alexander Towar, 1823), 1.

INTRODUCTION

While the gratitude toward Giles felt by several authors in this volume is evident in their chapters, the goal of this book is considerably different from his. These chapters have been gathered in the conviction that eternal generation secures Trinitarian theology against a broad array of disorders, scleroses, and deflections. Subordinationism is only one of the errors against which a clear confession of eternal generation secures Christian doctrine.[3] As is evident from the scope and range of the chapters gathered here, the task of retrieving eternal generation is a wide-ranging project that requires the cooperation of theological collaborators from across the full range of theological disciplines. Eternal generation needs to be retrieved from Scripture and from classic Christian formulations so that it can be planted in contemporary theological work where it will bear fruit.

SURVEY OF THE CHAPTERS

The chapters follow the conventional sequence of the theological curriculum. After we begin with biblical studies (chapters 1–7), we move through historical theology (chapters 8–12) and finally reach contemporary systematic formulation (chapters 13–15, which include philosophical theology, spirituality, and dogmatics).

However, the integral nature of the doctrine under examination seems to have exerted a beneficent pressure on each of our authors. While plying the specialized tools of their respective guilds, each of them has taken their bearings from outlying disciplines to an unusual degree. Each of the chapters in the biblical section of the book is informed by acute awareness of the hermeneutical situation in which exegetical decisions are embedded, and several of them analyze that situation at length. Each of these exegetical chapters is already informed by the history of interpretation and by the dogmatic consequences of exegetical decisions. The chapters covering historical witnesses pivot from biblical interpretation on the one hand (because each historical figure under consideration was directly concerned with the interpretation of Scripture) to constructive doctrinal moves on the other hand (partly because most of the authors are in fact systematic theologians by training and partly because retrieval entails handling historical theology

---

3. This volume as a whole is not conceived as a response to developments within the evangelical debates about gender roles, as the work of Giles quite explicitly was. Several chapters do allude to the controversy when appropriate, according to each author's judgment. But the editors believe those controversies to be regionally contained and short lived. Our reasons for retrieving eternal generation are part of a broader project of restoring classical wisdom to contemporary systematic theology.

19

FRED SANDERS AND SCOTT R. SWAIN

as more than reportage). By the time we reach the final section, on contemporary statements of the doctrine of eternal generation, the synthetic task has already been engaged repeatedly; so the final three chapters do not have to gather up fragments and see how they might combine for a constructive project. Instead, each of them can survey a broad field of maneuvers that have already been synthesized and constructed in various ways. The ampleness of theological scope by such a diverse array of authors, it seems to us, can be credited to the doctrine under consideration. The doctrine of the Son's eternal generation calls forth the most comprehensive and well-connected thinking of practitioners who turn to the task.

The unity and the diversity of the chapters in this volume are worth noting. As already mentioned, the attentive reader will see that most chapters include a brief report of the way eternal generation has come to be questioned, marginalized, or even rejected in modern scholarship. But as our respective authors cite representative examples from the literature they have engaged, it is striking that no two authors cite the same evidence. The reason for this is that the trend toward marginalizing or rejecting eternal generation has been pervasive. It would not be possible to catalogue it exhaustively, but we hope that the differentiated agreement among the authors in this volume may count as the testimony of many witnesses from many points of view. To collate all their evidence in one list, here in this introduction for example, would still fail to be comprehensive and would lose the virtue of presenting testimonies without collusion. On the other hand, alert readers will note that our authors disagree with each other on a few points. They construe evidence differently and build their cases in ways that are incompatible with each other. There is even some diversity in how they identify the core terms and concerns of the doctrine of eternal generation.

In chapter 1, Scott Swain provides the orientation for the entire book by calling to mind the great tradition's witness to eternal generation, noting recent demurrals, and introducing the properly theological task of retrieval. Under the title "The Radiance of the Father's Glory: Eternal Generation, the Divine Names, and Biblical Interpretation," Swain correlates two different ways Scripture names God: as the one divine Being, and as the Father, Son, and Holy Spirit identified by their relational, personal names. Because he is outlining a comprehensive program of biblical interpretation centered on a theology of the divine names, Swain does not set out to provide biblical warrant for eternal generation (though he does deliver some). Instead, he shows how eternal generation is integral to the kind of biblical reasoning that takes Scripture seriously as a guide to knowing God's identity.

INTRODUCTION

Matthew Emerson continues the necessarily broad hermeneutical considerations with chapter 2, "The Role of Proverbs 8: Eternal Generation and Hermeneutics Ancient and Modern." One of the most striking contrasts between patristic and modern Trinitarianism is that in the early church orthodox and heretics alike agreed that Proverbs 8 was about the Son of God; what they disagreed about was whether it considered him a creature or the Creator. Modern Trinitarians almost never consider an appeal to the wisdom figure of Proverbs 8 as anything but a fanciful illustration. If they do treat Proverbs 8 as evidence for the Trinity, the focus is narrowly on the character of Wisdom, or at best on the hypostatization of this divine attribute as a glimpse of distinct personhood. Instead, Emerson attends not to Wisdom but to the way Wisdom proceeds from God while remaining in him. Here we have the movement of thought necessary for confession of eternal generation.

In chapter 3, Mark S. Gignilliat takes up another passage that was dear to the church fathers but highly suspect under the modern regime: Micah 5:2. This text's prophecy that from Bethlehem would come one "whose origins are from of old, from ancient times" is an especially clear instance of a text from which no support for Trinitarian theology can be coaxed by conventional grammatical-historical analysis. But Gignilliat, by attending closely to the way the words run, shows that the prophet does provide instruction about what lies behind the predicted or predetermined birth of the Messiah in Bethlehem. Something has happened in primal days in the divine council, and this something is the mysterious aspect of a going-forth behind the Messiah's coming-forth. In this chapter Gignilliat only takes up one text that played a role in patristic Trinitarian reading of the Old Testament, but he intends the single demonstration to be an example of the way to approach much of the Old Testament's particular witness to Trinitarianism.

In chapter 4, D. A. Carson identifies John 5:26 as a *crux interpretum* for the doctrine of eternal generation. This is an interesting observation because neither the vocabulary of eternality nor of generation/begetting is even present in this passage. Instead, the terminology of John 5:26 trades on categories of giving, receiving, and having "life in oneself." Nevertheless, as Carson shows, the relation of the Father and the Son is worked out in this passage in ways that are normative for understanding their eternal relations of origin. Modern scholarship has often failed to recognize the broad biblical foundation for the doctrine of eternal generation because its research has been misdirected by a large-scale instance of the word-concept

21

FRED SANDERS AND SCOTT R. SWAIN

fallacy, as if eternal generation can only be present where the words eternal and generation are present. Carson redirects our attention to the subject matter itself by expounding the Johannine theology of gift and life in the context of the being of God; the benefit is a biblical doctrine of eternal generation that operates with one of the alternative vocabularies provided by Scripture itself.[4]

In chapter 5, Charles Lee Irons argues that the Johannine word *monogenēs*, contra the strong modern consensus that renders it "unique," ought to be translated "only begotten." Irons introduces an innovative lexical argument that reconsiders the way the word (and other compounds using the same root) started from a literal biological meaning and extended to various metaphorical senses. Readers who think this case was decisively settled in the last century will want to attend to the way Irons queries the entire database of extant Greek sources because his superior search strategy has introduced new evidence that contributes to a compelling case for reconsidering "only begotten." As Irons notes, his argument is about a single word that occurs only five times in only one biblical author. The doctrine of eternal generation has a much broader foundation than *monogenēs*, as Irons and several other authors in this volume agree. Nevertheless, if the argument of this chapter were to win the day (or even just demote the consensus translation from its current reputation of being self-evident rather than a relatively defensible option), the plausibility of eternal generation would be greatly increased even in the popular mind by the rehabilitation of one of its most eloquent terms.

Madison Pierce, in chapter 6, interprets the classic text "You are my son, today I have begotten you," which bestrides the two testaments with one foot in Psalm 2 and the other in Hebrews 1. Ancient interpreters read it as powerful support for the doctrine of eternal generation; in modern times it began to be urged instead as an objection to the doctrine. Much depends on the meaning of the word "today" in the psalm, and even more depends on its appropriation within the theology of Hebrews. Attending to the interpretive moves made by the author of Hebrews, Pierce argues that if "today" sets a beginning point for the begetting of this royal son, it is the today of God's own eternity. This chapter gives the volume's closest attention to the New Testament's own strategies for reading the Old Testament and handling its claims. Because the apostolic way of handling

---

4. The other vocabularies that Scripture uses to teach eternal generation include image, radiance, word, and wisdom. Each of these make appearances throughout this volume.

INTRODUCTION

the prophets underlies theological interpretation of Scripture in our own day, the observations of this chapter are foundational for the historical and constructive moves in the rest of the book.

Chapter 7 rounds out the biblical section of the volume with Kendall Soulen's investigation of the giving of the divine name. Indeed, the theology of divine self-naming presented here provides the bookend to Scott Swain's opening chapter, rightly framing the entire task of Trinitarian exegesis as an exercise in understanding God's name. Soulen's essay investigates the various ways that Scripture speaks of the relation of the Father and the Son and draws conclusions about the total message of Scripture about the nature of God. The Father gives the name above all names to the Son; Soulen invites us to think of this giving of the divine name as an eternal event that takes place between the Father and the Son. It is a striking proposal that makes sense of much biblical language. Soulen goes on to exploit a set of "happy correspondences" between biblical language on the one hand and later technical Trinitarian terms on the other, an illuminating use of his argument, which also marks our volume's transition to the historical elaboration of eternal generation.

In Chapter 8, Lewis Ayres examines the earliest surviving patristic development of eternal generation, that of Origen of Alexandria. Though Origen's program included elements that later generations would recognize as heterodox, his biblical reasoning about eternal generation has the status of a theological classic. Ayres traces Origen's interpretive strategies closely, paying special attention to the way Origen took up multiple biblical texts at once and then established a web of implications from reading them all simultaneously as implicating each other. Origen is also instructive, according to Ayres, because of the way eternal generation is deeply embedded in the core of his ideas about God and Christ. Since Origen, eternal generation has had a special rank among doctrines and has been recognized as uniquely integral to any coherent Christian teaching on God.

While much could be said about several figures of earlier pro-Nicene theology, our selective survey leaps to the fifth century with chapter 9, Keith E. Johnson's study of Augustine. Augustine focuses on the Johannine theology of sending, and he connects the sending of the Son into the world quite directly to the prior procession or generation of the Son in the life of God. Having established these long, solid lines that unite mission to procession, Augustine's display of biblical interpretation is masterful. There is probably no theme in this entire volume that is not in one way or another worked out by Augustine as he takes on the project of interpreting Scripture in a

Trinitarian fashion. Johnson's careful analysis of Augustine's interpretation showcases Augustine at his holistic, synthesizing best.[5]

The Reformed tradition has a complex history of various ways of handling the doctrine of eternal generation. To this day, there are persistent rumors that some of the Reformers and the Protestant Orthodox theologians were interested in reimagining the Son's relation to the Father along less Nicene lines. While the Reformed tradition at large has taught the eternal generation of the Son quite vigorously, it has also included some persistent minority reports that are worth considering. In chapter 10, Chad Van Dixhoorn examines the broader Reformed trajectories on eternal generation by focusing on the Westminster Assembly's history and documents. It is an illuminating example because of the way various competing concerns were brought into alignment by the work of the Westminster Assembly. The tensions and balances worked out in Westminster's Trinitarian theology have long deserved the kind of closer attention that Van Dixhoorn applies to them here.

In chapter 11, Christina N. Larsen explores the theology of Jonathan Edwards, who published robustly traditional affirmations of eternal generation but who also worked out (mostly in documents not published during his lifetime) some idiosyncratic ways of talking about the doctrine. Among Edwards's theological gains in this area are the implications of eternal generation for God's single essence and its attributes. In particular, eternal generation provided the foundation for Edwards's confession of God as happy, or infinitely pleased in himself with himself. Edwards, according to Larsen's account, provides a strong example of a thinker for whom eternal generation held a central role.

In chapter 12, Michael Allen traces a number of trajectories in modern theology after Barth. In addition to clarifying some interpretive controversies that have drawn much attention in Barth scholarship in recent years, Allen uses Barth to show how modern theology as a whole has grappled with the doctrine of eternal generation and identifies a number of temptations for modern theologians that a firm doctrine of eternal generation would provide protection against.

---

5. Perhaps the most obvious omission from this lineup of historical figures is Thomas Aquinas. We have three excuses to offer. First, the book needed to be kept to a reasonable size. Second, excellent analysis of Aquinas on eternal generation is widely available in recent scholarship by Gilles Emery (*The Trinitarian Theology of St. Thomas Aquinas* [Oxford University Press, 2010]) and Matthew Levering (*Scripture and Metaphysics: Aquinas and the Renewal of Trinitarian Theology* [Wiley-Blackwell, 2004]). And third, Johnson presents Augustine as so comprehensive a thinker on this point that he covers much of the ground we might normally assign to Aquinas as master synthesizer.

INTRODUCTION

Mark Makin turns our attention to philosophical theology in chapter 13, "Philosophical Models of Eternal Generation." Makin reports on various philosophical construals of eternal generation, explains how philosophers have dealt with them, and identifies their strengths and weaknesses. Makin then picks a favorite and devotes considerable attention to what the model makes of the metaphysics of essential dependence. Readers familiar with the conventions of analytic theology and the philosophy of religion will find in this chapter a careful specification of alternatives and a willingness to offer a hypothetical account in service of giving a responsible account of what faith affirms.

In chapter 14, Fred Sanders argues, in a somewhat homiletic register, that the doctrine of eternal generation and the doctrine of salvation enjoy mutual fittingness. Eager to ensure that the doctrine of God has priority over the doctrine of salvation, Sanders does not recommend this fit as a ground for affirming eternal generation; instead Sanders argues the other way around, showing that eternal generation is a doctrine that is fruitful for an understanding of salvation and the Christian life. If one of the objections urged against retrieving the doctrine of eternal generation is that the doctrine is simply too abstract and speculative to be relevant to Christian experience, to soteriology that argument is a good defense. Eternal generation is the reality in the life of God that unfolds in the life of the redeemed as adoptive sonship based on eternal sonship.

The volume ends with Joshua Malone's chapter 15, the most explicitly systematic of the chapters, which offers a wide-ranging survey of the place of eternal generation in dogmatics. Malone explores the patterns of thought implicit in affirming eternal generation. These patterns are pro-Nicene, but Malone is speaking constructively rather than merely historically or descriptively. What previous chapters (including this introduction) have assumed, Malone makes explicit: the dogmatic function of eternal generation is to secure Trinitarianism more broadly. The grammar of eternal generation is what allows Trinitarians to recognize God's essential unity, personal distinctions, and relational order. Finally, Malone turns his attention from this center point of the doctrine of God to what he identifies as a few of the "created effects" of the incarnate Son's eternal generation. He finds these effects in creation and in new creation, in adoption and in the resurrection.

One way to approach *Retrieving Eternal Generation* is as a series of counter-arguments against recent rejections of the doctrine of eternal generation. That is, if in some quarters the doctrine of eternal generation has been subjected to critique designed to defeat its cogency or relevance,

25

the chapters assembled here offer defeaters for those defeaters. We hope it functions that way, because defeaters need defeating. But this volume should also contribute to a vigorous retrieval of classic Christian doctrine for contemporary theology and the church in a deeper and broader way. Eternal generation may be one of the parts of which Trinitarian theology is composed, and Trinitarian theology may in turn be one of the parts of which Christian doctrine is composed. But the doctrine of the Trinity is also the entirety of Christian doctrine seen from the angle of the identity of God. And eternal generation is in its own way the entire Christian doctrine of God and salvation seen from the angle of the Son's relation to the Father. Recognizing this crucial role of the doctrine is an urgent task in our time. The eternal generation of the Son, wherever it is confessed, ought to be celebrated; wherever it is not confessed, ought to be established; and wherever it is attenuated or marginalized, ought to be retrieved.

PART I

BIBLICAL REASONING

CHAPTER 1

THE RADIANCE OF
THE FATHER'S GLORY:
Eternal Generation, the Divine
Names, and Biblical Interpretation

SCOTT R. SWAIN

INTRODUCTION

The doctrine of the eternal generation of the Son from the Father is a particularly beautiful element of Christian teaching. The doctrine concerns one who is in person the radiance of the Father's glory (Heb 1:3): light of light, true God of true God. This one proceeds as light from "the Father of lights" (Jas 1:17), but he does not proceed from God as creatures proceed from God.[1] He proceeds as one "begotten, not made," as one "consubstantial with the Father." In terms of dogmatic location, the doctrine of eternal generation belongs to the constellation of Trinitarian doctrine. Specifically, it is one of the eternal processions that constitutes the eternal persons. The rays of this doctrine extend themselves far beyond the realm of Trinitarian theology proper, however, shedding light upon the entire economy of God's works *ad extra*, from creation to incarnation, from sanctification to the beatific vision. In contemplating the eternally begotten Son of God, we behold "the king in his beauty" (Isa 33:17).

The doctrine of the Son's eternal generation from the Father is not among the truths revealed to created reason through "the things that have been made" (Rom 1:20). Although "the true light" of the Word shines

---

1. Unless noted otherwise, Scripture quotations in this chapter come from the ESV.

29

SCOTT R. SWAIN

in all creatures and is the condition of created reason's enlightenment (John 1:4, 9), created reason does not perceive this light through creation but only as the Word manifests himself in his incarnate mission and by means of those witnesses who beheld his glory—the glory of the μονογενής from the Father, full of grace and truth (John 1:14). Our fellowship *with* the Word of life is a fellowship obtained only *through* the testimony of his authorized emissaries in Holy Scripture (1 John 1:1–3). Because of this, the doctrine of eternal generation emerges as an article of Christian confession solely as a consequence of biblical reasoning within "the glorious company of the apostles" and "the goodly fellowship of the prophets."

Between the time of the fourth and eighteenth centuries, it would be difficult to find a Christian theologian—Catholic, Orthodox, or Protestant—who would not affirm the preceding assertions. There is a small witness of theologians who believed that the doctrine of eternal generation could be perceived apart from scriptural revelation by reflecting upon the nature of divine perfection. Moreover, a "minority report" of Reformed theologians going back to John Calvin expressed reservations about certain formulations of the doctrine, particularly among the church fathers. These reservations notwithstanding, Calvin and this Reformed minority report continued to affirm the broad ecumenical consensus that the doctrine of eternal generation is true, theologically meaningful, and biblical.[2]

Much has changed. Leaving aside the many revisionist programs in Trinitarian theology that have occupied the Christian theological imagination since the nineteenth century, a scan of recent evangelical systematic theologies and biblical commentaries reveals that evangelicals have not warmly embraced the aforementioned ecumenical consensus on eternal generation. Many are not convinced that the doctrine of eternal generation is true. Even among those who continue to affirm the doctrine, some wonder whether it is theologically meaningful. Still others question the doctrine's basic intelligibility as a concept. For all their variety, evangelical critics of eternal generation agree on one thing: the doctrine of eternal generation is unbiblical.

Along with the other contributors to the present volume, I believe the doctrine of eternal generation is worth retrieving: for the good of the church and theology and for the glory of the triune God. As I and others understand the enterprise, retrieval involves drawing upon resources from

---

2. Brannon Ellis, *Calvin, Classical Trinitarianism, and the Aseity of the Son* (Oxford: Oxford University Press, 2012).

the past for the sake of theological renewal in the present.[3] Retrieval is not repristination, nor is it disinterested reception history. Retrieval is a spiritual and theological attempt to reconnect to a vital root, to recover lost vision, to relearn a forgotten grammar. As such, retrieval calls for careful attention to texts and their reception, patient historical description, and, perhaps above all, discriminating judgments about how past resources might open up "new points of departure"[4] for contemporary theological reflection. As the preceding discussion suggests, one of the most important challenges to address in retrieving the doctrine of eternal generation concerns the doctrine's status as biblical teaching. Is the doctrine of eternal generation biblical? And, if so, what does it mean to say that it is biblical? These are the types of questions that the present volume addresses.

For my own part, I wish to address the issue through recourse to the theology of the divine names.[5] I believe this theology—part hermeneutics, part metaphysics, part ascetics—opens an illuminating window on what it means to say that the doctrine of eternal generation is a biblical doctrine. As we will see, the doctrine of eternal generation is a biblical doctrine in that it reflects a faithful interpretation of the divine names revealed in Holy Scripture, specifically, the names that signify the relation between the First and Second Persons of the Trinity. The argument will unfold in three steps. First, we will consider three levels of analysis that belong to responsible biblical interpretation in order to orient ourselves to the interpretation of the divine names. Second, we will introduce in broad strokes the theology of the divine names. Third, and finally, we will consider the divine names that signify the Father–Son relation and that establish the biblical basis for the doctrine of eternal generation.

On Biblical Interpretation

In order to appreciate the argument that follows, it will be helpful to clarify how the interpretation of the divine names fits within the larger program of biblical interpretation. As I understand it, responsible interpretation of any biblical text involves three levels of analysis.[6] The first level of analysis

---

3. See Michael Allen and Scott R. Swain, *Reformed Catholicity: The Promise of Retrieval for Theology and Biblical Interpretation* (Grand Rapids: Baker Academic, 2015).

4. Lewis Ayres, "In the Cloud of Witnesses: Catholic Trinitarian Theology Beyond and Before Its Modern 'Revivals,'" in *Rethinking Trinitarian Theology: Disputed Questions and Contemporary Issues in Trinitarian Theology*, ed. Giulio Maspero and Robert Wozniak (London: T&T Clark, 2012), 23.

5. I discuss this topic more broadly in "On Divine Naming," in *Aquinas among the Protestants*, ed. Manfred Svensson and David VanDrunen (Oxford: Wiley, forthcoming).

6. For a complementary perspective on the task of biblical interpretation to what I sketch here,

involves the exegesis of discrete texts qua texts. Here we consider texts in their semantic and grammatical particularities as well as in their distinctive historical and literary forms. The second level of analysis involves the interpretation of texts in light of their intertextual relations to other texts. How does *this* biblical text and its teaching relate to *that* biblical or extrabiblical text and its teaching? This level of analysis includes but is not exhausted by the important work of "biblical theology," which traces patterns and themes across authorial and canonical corpora and along the line of redemptive historical development. There are historical and literary dimensions to this level of analysis as well. The third level of analysis concerns the agents and activities of interpretation, theologically and philosophically considered. At this level of analysis we reflect upon the ways in which our assumptions about authors, texts, and readers shape and are shaped by the interpretive process. Who is the author(s) of these texts? And how do our answers to this question shape the way we read these texts? What is the nature of these texts? Are they "inspired"—and what does that mean? Is the relationship we perceive to exist between this text and that text (i.e., intertextuality) merely a matter of cultural process or convention, or is there some deeper basis for this perception? Do we as readers require aids in interpretation? If so, are these aids academic, spiritual, liturgical, ecclesiastical? "Theological interpretation of Scripture," at least as I understand it, is largely though not exclusively concerned with the third level of interpretive analysis.

Note well: These three levels do not represent three rival interpretive options. The conflict of the faculties we commonly witness at this point is a spiritual problem, not a metaphysical one. Much less do these three levels represent three "steps" in the interpretive process. All three levels are in constant play in any healthy approach to biblical interpretation. For reasons of disciplinary focus or scholarly prudence, it is legitimate for individual interpreters to direct their energies to one or two of these levels. Nevertheless, it is important to remember that interpretive malfunction inevitably follows when any of the levels are ignored, for example, when it is assumed that the biblical basis of eternal generation can be determined solely at the first level of analysis—that is, based merely upon the lexical semantics of μονογενής.

What is the upshot for our present discussion? The interpretation of the divine names may strike us as an esoteric topic, reminiscent of mystical

---

see Al Wolters, "Confessional Criticism and the Night Visions of Zechariah," in *Renewing Biblical Interpretation*, ed. Craig Bartholomew, Colin Greene, and Karl Möller (Grand Rapids: Zondervan, 2000), 90–117.

theology and medieval speculation—and thus useless for establishing the biblical basis of anything. I want to suggest that this is not the case. One way of helping us appreciate the point is by noting analogies between an exercise we more commonly engage in at level two of biblical interpretation (i.e., biblical theology) and an exercise we less commonly engage in at level two of biblical interpretation (i.e., interpretation of the divine names). Two analogies between these two interpretive exercises are worth noting.

The first analogy lies in the fact that *both interpretive exercises presuppose the unity of Scripture.* In the case of biblical theology, the major operative presupposition is *the unity of the biblical story line.* The assumption is that because the Bible is a unified story, we may expect the various themes and trajectories of Scripture to be heading in the same direction, and indeed to find a common and coherent resolution in the gospel of Jesus Christ. In the case of the divine names, the major operative presupposition is *the unity of the Bible's main character,* the triune YHWH. The assumption is that because YHWH is one God, we may expect that the various names and descriptions ascribed to him in Scripture refer to the same agent and paint a coherent (albeit finally unfathomable) portrait of his identity and character.

The second analogy lies in the fact that *both interpretive exercises are occupied primarily with tracing analogous patterns.* In the case of biblical theology, we are concerned with tracing analogous patterns along a redemptive-historical axis: How does the theme of temple or seed or messiah unfold and develop throughout the course of redemptive history? How do these themes progress? How are they enriched? What mysterious surprises do they hold? In the case of the divine names, we are not concerned primarily with tracing analogous patterns that unfold along a *historical* axis. Rather, we are concerned primarily with tracing analogous patterns—"family resemblances"—across three *ontologically* distinct relational registers: the relation of creature to creature, the relation of Creator to creature, and the relation of divine Father to divine Son. When it comes to interpreting both kinds of analogies—the historical and the ontological—context is king. Just as failure to appreciate historical context leads to failure in interpreting the analogies operative in biblical theology, so too failure to appreciate ontological context leads to failure in interpreting the analogies operative in the divine names.

With this clarification in view, we turn to the interpretation of the divine names.

On the Divine Names

The Christian doctrine of God is that species of biblical reasoning devoted to the prayerful contemplation and commendation of the divine names revealed in Holy Scripture. Due to the divine largesse, Holy Scripture furnishes us with a "surplus of description"[7] that we may draw upon in articulating the doctrine of God. The biblical writers praise God by "many names."[8] God is identified as "Lord," "Almighty," "one," and "good." He is also identified as "Father," "Son," and "Holy Spirit." God is the one who created heaven and earth, who cut a covenant with Abraham, Isaac, and Jacob, and who rescued Israel from Egypt and caused them to possess the land of Canaan as an inheritance. He is the one who delivered over Jesus because of our transgressions and raised him up because of our justification, who poured out his Spirit on all flesh, and who promises to make all things new. Because the biblical naming of God is so very "great," the Christian doctrine of God is afforded with resources that are truly "unsearchable" (Ps 145:3).

As it seeks to fathom the wealth of resources available to it, the Christian doctrine of God must be aware of several challenges intrinsic to the task of interpreting the divine names.[9] Not only is there the issue of scope (to what extent has Christian teaching about God faithfully borne witness to the fullness of biblical revelation?), there is also the issue of fidelity in conceptual paraphrase—that is, which words count as faithful repetitions of the biblical witness, and which words count as betrayals of that witness? For example, does predicating divine immutability and divine impassibility of God faithfully render the biblical claim that with God "there is no variation or shadow due to change" (Jas 1:17)? Or do these predications distort the biblical presentation of divine constancy? Finally, there is the more complex issue of interpreting the logical status of the various biblical descriptions of God: Does naming God "creator of heaven and earth" or "the one who brought Israel out of Egypt" carry the same significance for God's identity as naming him "the Father of our Lord Jesus Christ"? If not, what is the difference between these kinds of naming and these kinds of relations? As these questions suggest, the doctrine of God is a proposal

---

7. Denys Turner, "On Denying the Right God: Aquinas on Atheism and Idolatry," *Modern Theology* 20 (2004): 148.

8. Dionysius, *The Divine Names*, in *Pseudo-Dionysius: The Complete Works*, trans. Colm Luibheid (New York: Paulist, 1984), 1.6.

9. For fuller discussion, see Stephen Holmes, "The Attributes of God," in *The Oxford Handbook of Systematic Theology*, ed. John Webster, Kathryn Tanner, and Iain Torrance (New York: Oxford University Press, 2009), 54–71.

THE RADIANCE OF THE FATHER'S GLORY

not only regarding which descriptions are "necessary and appropriate" to faithful speech about God but also regarding how various descriptions of God "work."[10]

For the sake of space, let me summarize five points regarding the way various biblical descriptions of God work in order to prepare us for interpreting the divine names relevant to eternal generation. Here I follow Thomas Aquinas's discussion of the divine names in question 13 of the *prima pars* of the *Summa theologiae*.[11] (1) Because God is the "Father of all" (Eph 4:6), "from whom every family in heaven and on earth is named" (Eph 3:15), there are "family resemblances" between God and his creatures. These family resemblances are the ontological basis of the divine names. (2) *In terms of the order of being*, these family resemblances flow *from* God the Father of all *to* his creaturely offspring, and not vice-versa. Creatures are like God because God created them; however, God is not like creatures.[12] (3) *In terms of the order of naming*, the order is reversed. God names himself in our language using names originally applied to creatures. This is true whether it is said that God is good or whether it is said that God is a rock: in both instances the creature provides our primary context for understanding that which is good and that which is a rock.[13] (4) These two different orders (the order of being and the order of naming) explain the difference between *proper* and *metaphorical* names of God. (a) Some names apply properly and primarily to creatures and only metaphorically and secondarily to God. God is a rock, to be sure, but God is not *literally* a rock. When we say that God is not literally a rock, however, we are not denying his steadfast nature or strength in relationship to his helpless people. We understand that even rocks reflect something of God's greatness and therefore that their characteristics are susceptible to secondary, metaphorical application to God, the one who birthed the mountains (Ps 90:2). (b) Other names apply properly and primarily to God and only secondarily to creatures: God alone is wise; God alone is good—not in the sense that creatures cannot be wise or good but in the sense that they cannot be supreme and simple wisdom and goodness. God alone is wise and good in that sense, and all gifts of creaturely wisdom and goodness proceed from him (Jas 1:5, 17). (5) These two

---

10. Stephen Holmes, "Divine Attributes," in *Mapping Modern Theology: A Thematic and Historical Introduction*, ed. Kelly M. Kapic and Bruce L. McCormack (Grand Rapids: Baker Academic, 2012), 48. This and the previous paragraph are slightly modified from Scott R. Swain, *The God of the Gospel: Robert Jenson's Trinitarian Theology* (Downers Grove, IL: IVP Academic, 2013), 78–79.

11. For further exposition of this topic, see Rudi te Velde, *Aquinas on God: The 'Divine Science' of the* Summa Theologiae (Burlington, VT: Ashgate, 2006), ch. 4.

12. Dionysius, *Divine Names* 9.6; Thomas Aquinas, *De veritate*, 2.11, ad. 11.

13. The order of naming also explains why we have many names for God.

different orders (the order of being and the order of naming) also explain the epistemological and linguistic "grammar" whereby we interpret the family resemblances that exist between God and his creatures, the Dionysian *threefold way* (*triplex via*). Because God is the Father of all creatures and their perfections (*via causalitatis*), we understand and assert that he prepossesses all perfections that appear in the creature in their primary and supreme form (*via excellentiae*) without any creaturely limitation (*via negativa*).[14]

This understanding of the family resemblances that exist between God and his creatures will help us better appreciate how the divine names that signify the Father–Son relation and that constitute the biblical basis of the doctrine of eternal generation.

ON ETERNAL GENERATION

The pro-Nicene exegetical tradition identifies two broad categories of divine names within Scripture that are especially pertinent to the development of Trinitarian theology (along with a third category, undiscussed here, that is of special importance to Christology). With respect to the first category of divine names, the Bible identifies each person of the Trinity as the one true and living God. The three persons share *the single divine "name"*—"the name of the Father and of the Son and of the Holy Spirit" (Matt 28:19). The Father is the one Lord God (e.g., Matt 11:25); the Son is the one Lord God (e.g., John 20:28; 1 Cor 8:6); and the Spirit is the one Lord God (e.g., Acts 5:3–4; 2 Cor 3:17–18). Furthermore, the Bible identifies each person as an agent of *God's unique actions* (Gen 1:1–2; Ps 33:6; John 1:1–3; Gal 4:4–6; etc.) and as a bearer of *God's unique attributes* (John 5:26; 1 Cor 2:10–11; etc.). These *"common names"* reveal that the multiplication of persons in the Trinity does not amount to the multiplication of gods. For us there is "one Spirit . . . one Lord . . . one God and Father of all" (Eph 4:4–6). The doctrine of the Trinity is a species of monotheism (compare Deut 6:4 with 1 Cor 8:6). To borrow creedal terminology, the Son and the Spirit are "consubstantial" with the Father. With respect to the second category of divine names, the Bible indicates that each person is nevertheless irreducibly distinct from the other persons. How is this distinction indicated? The distinction does not involve the deity of the persons—these three are one Lord God. Nor does it involve a distinction in power, wisdom, or will—in God all these things are "one" (Deut 6:4). The distinction between the

---

14. For further discussion, see Swain, "On Divine Names."

THE RADIANCE OF THE FATHER'S GLORY

persons is indicated by their *"personal names"*: "Father," "Son," and "Holy Spirit." And these names signify *relations*. The Father is Father to the Son ("paternity" is thus his unique personal property); the Son is Son to the Father ("filiation" is thus his unique personal property); the Spirit is the Spirit of the Father and the Son ("spiration" is thus his unique personal property). These personal properties are not interchangeable. The Father is not the Son. The Son is not the Father. And the Spirit is not the Father or the Son. The Bible identifies God as irreducibly three in one, and so with all the saints we confess and adore the holy Trinity.[15]

The doctrine of eternal generation is an interpretation of the personal names that characterize the Father–Son relation. In order to appreciate how this works, I would like to trace three analogous patterns of father–son relations across three ontologically distinct relational registers: that of creature to creature, of creator to creature, and of divine Father to divine Son. I will do so through a brief analysis of three texts: Genesis 5:1–3; James 1:17; and Hebrews 1:3. Given the previous discussion, we should expect to see family resemblances across each register. Given the previous discussion, we should also expect to see these family resemblances modulated according to their diverse ontological contexts. The doctrine of eternal generation emerges as we perceive how the Bible's "transgeneric predication"[16] of father–son relations works across these three different but related ontological registers.

Genesis 5:1–3: Creature to Creature

It is not uncommon for Scripture to draw analogies from father–son relations that exist between creature and creature to the father–son relation that exists between Creator and creature. For example, in Luke 11:13 Jesus asks, "If you then, who are evil, know how to give good gifts to your children, how much more will the heavenly Father give the Holy Spirit to those who ask him?" Similarly, Hebrews 12:9 states, "We have had earthly fathers who disciplined us and we respected them. Shall we not much more be subject to the Father of spirits and live?" Note in each instance that the analogy is not directly drawn from earthly fathers to our heavenly Father (A:B as C:B). The analogy is between how earthly fathers relate to earthly sons and how the heavenly Father relates to his creaturely children (A:B as C:D).

The same pattern appears in Genesis 5:1–3, which states, "When God

---

15. This paragraph is slightly modified from Scott R. Swain, "The Mystery of the Trinity," in *The Essential Trinity: New Testament Foundations and Practical Relevance*, ed. Brandon D. Crowe and Carl R. Trueman (London: Apollos, 2016), 194.

16. Te Velde, *Aquinas on God*, 112.

created man, he made him in the likeness of God. Male and female he created them, and he blessed them and named them Adam when they were created. When Adam had lived 130 years, he fathered a son in his own likeness, after his image, and named him Seth." Notice three features regarding the Adam–Seth relation in verse three. (1) We have *two relatives*: Adam, the father, and Seth, the son. (2) We have the *action* of one relative that establishes the relationship between the two relatives: "Adam *fathered* Seth." (3) We have a resulting *similarity* between these two relatives: Seth is in Adam's likeness, after his image.

The remarkable thing, of course, is that this text draws an analogy between what happens between Adam and Seth in verse 3 and what happens between God and Adam in verse 1. Here too three features regarding the God-Adam relation are worth noting. (1) We have *two relatives*: God, the creator, and Adam, the creature. (2) We have the *action* of one relative that establishes the relationship between the two relatives: "God *created* Adam." (3) And we have a resulting *similarity* between these two relatives: Adam is created "in the likeness of God."

While there is analogy between the God-Adam relation and the Adam-Seth relation (A:B as C:D), there is disanalogy as well. *Creating* is not *fathering*. God is Adam's creator. Adam is Seth's father. For this reason too the creature's likeness to the creator must be distinguished from a son's likeness to his father. And yet this is not the whole story. As commentators point out, Luke 3:38 identifies Adam not as the *creature* of God but as the *son* of God, and Luke appears to draw this identification on the basis of Genesis 5:1–3. So we need to put the matter like this: while creating is not, *properly speaking*, fathering, creating, Luke seems to suggest, is *a kind of* or *analogous to* fathering.

We may find help for making sense of this by looking at our next text, James 1:17.

James 1:17: Creator to Creature

James 1:17 identifies God as "the Father of lights, with whom there is no variation or shadow due to change." Based upon comparisons with Jewish literature, the description "Father of lights" probably intends to identify God as the Father/Creator of the heavenly lights.[17] The identification of creating as an act of "fathering" is not without precedent in the Old Testament (see, e.g., Deut 32:18; Job 15:7; Ps 90:2).

---

17. Douglas J. Moo, *The Letter of James* (Grand Rapids: Eerdmans, 2000), 78–79.

THE RADIANCE OF THE FATHER'S GLORY

Following this reading, note three features of the father–son relation between creator and creature according to James 1:17. (1) We have *two relatives*: "the Father of lights" and his children, the heavenly lights. (2) We have (by implication) the *action* of one relative that establishes the relationship between the two relatives: God has *fathered* the heavenly lights (recall Luke 3:38). (3) We have a resulting *similarity and dissimilarity* between these two relatives: Both the creator Father and his creaturely children are *lights*. But the *Father* and creative cause of the heavenly lights is himself light *without variation and without change*—one cannot help but think here of 1 John 1:5: "God is light, and in him is no darkness at all," whereas the heavenly lights are characterized by *variation and change*—like all creatures, "they will all wear out like a garment. You will change them like a robe, and they will pass away" (Ps 102:26). Here we have similarity between relatives, a similarity that flows from the fatherly relation between the luminous God and his created lights. But we also have dissimilarity between relatives: the heavenly lights are only a mutable reflection of God's immutable divine light.

From the discussion thus far, we may draw several interesting observations. First, the father–son analogy is capable of doing quite a lot of work across different ontological registers. Second, the different kinds of work the analogy is capable of doing are not, for the most part, related to different terminology: Seth is the "likeness" of Adam; Adam is the "likeness" of God; but "likeness" means something different in each case. Adam "fathered" Seth; God "fathered" the heavenly lights; but "fathering" means something different in each case. Third, different senses of "likeness" and "fathering" are determined by the ontological context of the father–son relation in view. God's "fathering" Adam and the heavenly lights is, properly speaking, an act of creation—the *production of being* out of nothing. God's "fathering" Adam and the heavenly lights is only metaphorically (or analogically) speaking an act of begetting.[18] Adam's "fathering" Seth is, properly speaking, an act of fathering—a *communication of nature* from parent to offspring.[19]

This leads us to our last text and to our last ontological register: the relation between divine Father and divine Son according to Hebrews 1:3.

---

18. On issues related to metaphorical/analogical naming in describing the Father-creature relation, see John Baptist Ku, *God the Father in the Theology of St. Thomas Aquinas* (New York: Peter Lang, 2013), 339n13.

19. I am not aware of any case where the Bible applies a metaphorical sense of "creating" to the action of a creature fathering a creature: Seth too is "begotten, not made."

SCOTT R. SWAIN

Hebrews 1:3: Divine Father to Divine Son

Standing at the center of a series of splendid descriptions of the Son through whom the Father has spoken to us in these latter days, Hebrews 1:3 declares, "He is the radiance of the glory of God and the exact imprint of his substance [ὃς ὢν ἀπαύγασμα τῆς δόξης καὶ χαρακτὴρ τῆς ὑποστάσεως]."[20] In a manner similar to John 1:1–18 (where the title "Son" is amplified by the title "Word") and Colossians 1:15–20 (where the title "beloved Son" is amplified by the title "Image"), we see the father–son relation in this text amplified through the use of language and imagery associated with Old Testament and Jewish reflection on divine wisdom: the Son is the "radiance" or "effulgence" [ἀπαύγασμα] of the Father's glory (compare with Wis 7:26). The Son is here identified as the Father's glory shining forth, as the divine filial brightness of the divine paternal light.[21]

In keeping with our tracing of family resemblances above, note three features of the Father–Son relation according to Hebrews 1:3. (1) We have *two relatives*: God and "his Son." (2) We have the *activity* of one agent that describes the relationship between the two relatives: the Father is glorious; the Son is the effulgence of the Father's glory shining forth. (3) We have a description regarding the nature of the *similarity* that obtains between these two relatives: the Son is "the exact imprint of his substance." Although the precise sense of the latter phrase is not perhaps clear in itself, the broader context of Hebrews clarifies the nature of the Son's similarity to the Father. The radiant Son shares his Father's "name" (Heb 1:8, 10). He shares his Father's eternal and immutable life (Heb 1:11–12). He shares in his Father's unique divine actions of creation and providence (Heb 1:2–3). He shares his Father's throne (Heb 1:8, 13). The one who is the radiance *of* God the Father is one God *with* his Father, "the exact imprint of his substance."

What does this mean for the doctrine of eternal generation? Having traced various father–son relations across various ontological registers, we are now prepared to address this question.

First, we have noted a series of "family resemblances" across each ontological register. In each register, we have seen (1) two relatives, (2) the

---

20. Though descriptions such as this one (may) speak of the Son *in* his incarnate state, they do not speak *of* his incarnate state. They speak of the Son's *relation* to his Father.

21. For further discussion of how the author of Hebrews transforms the title "son" vis-à-vis God, human beings, and angels, see Madison Pierce's chapter in the present volume. For theological commentary on Heb 1:1–4, see John Webster, "One Who Is Son: Theological Reflections on the Exordium to the Epistle to the Hebrews," in *The Epistle to the Hebrews and Christian Theology*, ed. Richard Bauckham, Daniel R. Driver, Trevor A. Hart, and Nathan MacDonald (Grand Rapids: Eerdmans, 2009), 69–94.

THE RADIANCE OF THE FATHER'S GLORY

activity of one relative that defines the relationship between the two relatives, and (3) a similarity that obtains between the two relatives.

Second, looking more closely at these family resemblances, we may observe a couple of common features that obtain across the various ontological registers. In each case, there is a discernible *order* in relation to the *action* or *activity* that defines the relationship between the two relatives: God *makes* Adam (not vice versa); Adam *fathers* Seth (not vice versa); God *radiates* his Son (not vice versa). The first relative is the principle of the action that constitutes the relationship between the two relatives. Furthermore, in each case the *likeness* between the two relatives follows a discernible *order* as well: Adam is like God; Seth is like Adam; the Son is the exact imprint of his Father's substance. Here too the order is not reversible.

Third, while each ontological register bears family resemblances, each ontological register operates according to a distinct logic that determines our understanding of the father–son relation described within that register. *Properly speaking*, Adam fathers Seth. He communicates his nature to Seth with the result that Seth is in the likeness of Adam. *Metaphorically speaking*, God "fathers" Adam and the heavenly lights. *Properly speaking*, God *creates* them out of nothing with the result that there is a distinct but distant similarity between the divine "father" and his creaturely "children." What about the relationship between divine Father and divine Son? Unlike the imagery of James 1:17, where clear lines of discontinuity are drawn between the immutable Father of lights and his mutable creaturely offspring, the imagery of Hebrews 1:3 suggests that the Father should be understood as the *natural principle* of the Son—as light naturally radiates its brightness, so too God naturally radiates his Son. "Light and its splendour are one."[22] The rest of Scripture, I believe, confirms this interpretation. The First Person of the Trinity is, *properly speaking*,[23] fatherly principle to the Second Person of the Trinity with the result that the two relatives share a common name (John 17:11–12)[24] and a common nature (see, e.g., John 5:26).

Fourth, *the relation between the divine Father and the divine Son whereby the Father naturally radiates the Son and consequently the Son is the exact imprint of the Father's substance is in essence all that the doctrine of eternal generation seeks to identify.* The doctrine of eternal generation does not seek to *explain* this

---

22. Webster, "One Who Is Son," 85.
23. For example, see John 5:18 and Rom 8:32, which identify God as Jesus's "proper" Father and Jesus as God's "proper" Son.
24. On which, see R. Kendall Soulen, *The Divine Name(s) and Holy Trinity*, vol. 1, *Distinguishing the Voices* (Louisville: Westminster John Knox, 2011), 201–6.

relationship. Indeed, Gregory of Nazianzus instructs us that the eternal generation of the Son "must be honored by silence." He states, "It is a great thing for you to learn that he was begotten. But the manner of his generation we will not admit that even angels can conceive, much less you. Shall I tell you how it was? It was in a manner known to the Father who begot, and to the Son who was begotten. Anything more than this is hidden by a cloud, and escapes your dim sight."[25] The doctrine of eternal generation does not seek to explain this relationship; it only seeks, in the words of Bonaventure, to "believe simply" and to "contemplate with penetrating gaze . . . that from that Eternal Light which is at the same time measureless and most simple, most brilliant and most hidden, there emerges a coeternal, coequal and consubstantial splendor, who is the power and wisdom of the Father."[26]

CONCLUSION

Had we more space, we could trace other titles, images, and actions whereby the Father–Son relation is named in Holy Scripture.[27] In each instance, we would discover patterns similar to what we have traced above. In terms of the various titles and images used by the New Testament to amplify the Father–Son relation, we would discover, along with the divine glory that radiates a divine effulgence, a divine speaker who utters a divine word (John 1:1–18) and a divine exemplar who produces a divine image (Col 1:15–18). In terms of the various actions that amplify the nature of the Father–Son relation, we would discover a Father who has life in himself and who has granted his Son to have life in himself (John 5:26), and we would discover a Father who possesses the unique divine name and who has granted his

---

25. Gregory of Nazianzus, *Or. Bas.* 29.8 (*Christology of the Later Fathers*, ed. Edward R. Hardy [Louisville: Westminster John Knox, 1954], 165). Similarly, Francis Turretin states, "The similitudes usually employed to explain this mystery (drawn either from the mind, which by understanding itself, excites the idea and image of itself in itself, which always remains in the mind whence it may emanate; or from the sun from which rays simultaneously emanate as was neither before nor without them) can in some measure serve to illustrate this mystery, and the more because Scripture sometimes alludes to them when it calls the Son of God, *Logon*, 'Wisdom,' 'the image of God' and 'the brightness of the Father's glory' (*apaugasma doxēs*). But they cannot set forth a full and accurate determination of the mode of this generation. Hence here (if anywhere) we must be wise with sobriety so that content with the fact (*tō hoti*) (which is clear in the Scriptures), we should not anxiously busy our thoughts with defining or even searching into the mode (which is altogether incomprehensible), but leave it to God who alone must perfectly know himself" (*Institutes of Elenctic Theology*, ed. James T. Dennison, trans. George Musgrave Giger [Phillipsburg, NJ: P&R, 1992–94], 1:302).

26. Bonaventure, *The Tree of Life*, in *Bonaventure: The Soul's Journey into God, The Tree of Life, The Life of St. Francis*, trans. Ewert Cousins (New York: Paulist, 1978), 126 (1).

27. See Scott R. Swain, "Divine Trinity," in *Christian Dogmatics: Reformed Theology for the Church Catholic*, ed. Michael Allen and Scott R. Swain (Grand Rapids: Baker Academic, 2016), 87–90.

THE RADIANCE OF THE FATHER'S GLORY

Son to possess the unique divine name (John 17:11–12). Would this breadth of divine naming lead us away from the label "eternal generation," perhaps inviting us to find new labels such as "the eternal radiating of the Son," "the eternal uttering of the Son," or "the eternal granting of the divine name to the Son"? Probably not. But it would help us appreciate more fully that Christian theology is heir to an embarrassment of riches when it comes to the divine names that signify the Father–Son relation in Holy Scripture and therefore that establish the biblical basis of the doctrine of eternal generation. Scripture affords us many opportunities to consider the eternal begetting of the Son and thus many opportunities to contemplate "the king in his beauty."

CHAPTER 2

THE ROLE OF PROVERBS 8:
Eternal Generation and Hermeneutics Ancient and Modern

MATTHEW Y. EMERSON

INTRODUCTION

The doctrine of the eternal generation of the Son has come under fire in modernity.[1] Detractors argue that eternal generation is an imposition of Greek philosophical categories onto the text rather than a doctrine derived from the biblical data. Contemporary interpreters argue this position especially vigorously in the exposition of Proverbs 8. Even when scholars defend the doctrine, Proverbs 8 is, at worst, passed over as an unfortunate incident of proof texting by the patristic and medieval theologians or, at best, seen as containing the language needed for the doctrine ("begotten") without actually teaching it explicitly.[2]

This chapter seeks to explore and compare the hermeneutical presuppositions and methods of early Christian interpreters who saw the doctrine taught in Proverbs 8 and of modern interpreters who do not see eternal generation

---

1. I use "eternal generation" synonymously with "eternal begottenness" throughout this chapter.

2. See the otherwise excellent work of Kevin Giles, *The Eternal Generation of the Son: Maintaining Orthodoxy in Trinitarian Theology* (Downers Grove, IL: IVP Academic, 2012), 78–87. Giles believes that eternal generation is a biblical doctrine, but he also thinks that it is not taught explicitly but only "suggested" in Prov 8:22–31 (p. 78). Especially curious is his statement about a related passage, Ps 2:7, on which he says, "It is true that Psalm 2:7 *read critically and historically* does not speak of *the eternal begetting of the Son of God.* . . . However, we learn from . . . New Testament appeals to Psalm 2:7 that the apostolic authors read this psalm christologically. They did not assume that the words of Psalm 2:7 were limited to or constrained to their historical meaning and application" (p. 79). The reader can presume that this same sort of conclusion can be made about Prov 8, dealt with by Giles in the following paragraph. It seems to me that more nuance and exegetical precision is needed to say that Prov 8 supports eternal generation.

THE ROLE OF PROVERBS 8

in this text.[3] What makes the difference in interpretation? It is surely not exegetical rigor—both premodern and modern interpreters have rigorously explored the text with every available interpretive tool.[4] And if one assumes modern exegesis is more rigorous and scientific than premodern interpretation, it should be noted here that modern commentators cannot come to an agreement on the passage's meaning, either as a whole or in determining what specific verbs mean (e.g., *qanah* in v. 22). This is in spite of a general commitment to a method (historical-critical, or its younger evangelical brother, historical-grammatical) and a conclusion (the passage does not teach eternal generation).[5] In other words, the issue has to lie elsewhere, and I propose here that the difference between those who affirm eternal generation, both in Proverbs 8 and elsewhere, and those who deny it, is their theological and hermeneutical foundations. This chapter will compare the aforementioned interpreters' approaches in order to demonstrate that this is indeed the case.

The chapter begins with a brief explanation of eternal generation, including its historical importance to the fourth- and fifth-century Trinitarian debates and its conceptual outline. It then compares the hermeneutical assumptions of early Christian theologians and modern interpreters. To anticipate the conclusion, premodern Trinitarian interpreters tended to focus on the textual interconnectedness, narrative economy, and christological nature of all Scripture, while modern interpreters tend to isolate Proverbs 8 (and other passages) from the rest of the Bible and focus narrowly on individual words in their immediate literary context. Ironically, this latter approach appears in some ways like that of Arius, Eusebius of Nicomedia, and Asterius, even if some modern interpreters do not share these anti-Nicene theologians' dogmatic conclusions.[6]

---

3. By "modern" I mean post-Enlightenment, which includes both modern and postmodern readers. Modern readers tend to eschew the objectivism and scientific positivism with which moderns approach the text, and postmodern readers still tend to retreat to modernistic exegetical methods in their interpretation.

4. Thus this chapter is not primarily an exegetical defense of eternal generation from Prov 8, but rather, by means of historical comparison, it is an argument that those who see the doctrine taught here have legitimate theological and interpretive rationales for doing so. For a recent essay that reaches similar conclusions, see Daniel J. Treier, "Proverbs 8: Hearing Lady Wisdom's Offer Again," in *Theological Commentary: Evangelical Perspectives*, ed. Michael Allen (Edinburgh: T. & T. Clark, 2011), 57–72. Treier's work here, and in his 2011 commentary on Proverbs (*Proverbs and Ecclesiastes*, Brazos Theological Commentary on the Bible [Grand Rapids: Brazos, 2011]), constitutes an exception to the rule that modern commentators refuse to see the connection between Prov 8 and eternal generation.

5. One notable exception is Richard M. Davidson, "Proverbs 8 and the Place of Christ in the Trinity," *Journal of the Adventist Theological Society* 17, no. 1 (2006): 33–54, but even here it should be noted that he does not use the language of eternal generation but only hypostatization. His focus is more on the incarnation language in the passage than on the relationships between the persons of the immanent Trinity. See also Roland E. Murphy, O. Carm., "Wisdom and Creation," *JBL* 104, no. 1 (1985): 3–11.

6. See Sarah Parvis's description of these three interpreters' methods in "Christology in the Early Arian Controversy: The Exegetical War," in *Christology and Scripture: Interdisciplinary Perspectives*, ed. Angus Paddison and Andrew T. Lincoln (London: T&T Clark, 2007), 120–37.

What Is Eternal Generation?

The doctrine of eternal generation was a linchpin for pro-Nicene theology. It was, as Kevin Giles notes, "hugely important because it grounds divine self-differentiation in the inner life of God in eternity, as does the doctrine of the eternal procession of the Spirit."[7] Given the pro-Nicene affirmation that there is one God in three persons, the question becomes how to differentiate these three hypostases without falling into subordinationism on the one hand or modalism on the other. For the patristic and medieval theologians, and indeed for most of the church's theological reflection, the eternal processions have grounded divine unity together with divine threeness.[8] The three persons of God are thus distinguished by their relations of origin: The Father is unbegotten, the Son is begotten of the Father, and the Spirit proceeds from the Father and the Son (in the Western tradition).[9]

Social Trinitarianism is a recent departure from classic Trinitarianism and provides an alternative answer to how God is one in essence and three in person:[10] the three persons are distinguished not by their relations of origin but by relation*ships*. That is, the three persons of God each possess what we would call a personality, including a distinct volitional will, and how these relate to one another is what distinguishes Father, Son, and Spirit. Typically, both the economic roles *and* the volitional relationships that bind them (e.g., eternal subordination) distinguish Father, Son, and Spirit. As Giles and Stephen Holmes (among others) have noted, though, this social Trinitarianism is purely a twentieth-century phenomenon and does not reflect the classic orthodoxy of the ecumenical councils and creeds.[11] Further, because of their rejection of eternal generation, social Trinitarians typically do not affirm the early Christian interpreters' reading of Proverbs 8. Thus while the early Christian theologians read Proverbs with reference to Christ and his relationship to the Father, modern interpreters

---

7. Giles, *The Eternal Generation of the Son*, 20, 258.

8. Ibid., 92.

9. While this chapter focuses on the hermeneutical issues involved, it should be noted here that some deny eternal generation based on an assumption that "generation" and "procession" imply ontological subordination. As Johnson points out, though, *eternal* generation is the timeless communication of the divine essence from Father to Son, not a generation in time in which the Son becomes divine. In other words, if generation is not eternal, it is Arian subordinationism. Keith Johnson, "Augustine, Eternal Generation, and Evangelical Trinitarianism," *TrinJ* 32 (2011): 142n1, 142n2, 148–49.

10. For an introduction to this view that also discusses eternal generation, see J. Scott Horrell, "The Eternal Son of God in the Social Trinity," in *Jesus in Trinitarian Perspective: An Introductory Christology*, ed. Fred Sanders and Klaus Issler (Nashville: B&H Academic, 2007), 44–79.

11. Giles, *The Eternal Generation of the Son*, 91–204; Stephen R. Holmes, *The Quest for the Trinity: The Doctrine of God in Scripture, History, and Modernity* (Downers Grove, IL: IVP Academic, 2012).

THE ROLE OF PROVERBS 8

do not. What, then, caused many premodern interpreters to read Proverbs 8 christologically and in support of eternal generation, and what causes many modern theologians to reject that interpretation? We turn now to discerning the hermeneutical and theological foundations displayed during these two periods in the history of interpretation.

HERMENEUTICAL AND THEOLOGICAL FOUNDATIONS IN INTERPRETIVE HISTORY
The Nature of Theological Reflection
One initial clarification is that theological reflection, and the language used to articulate its conclusions, is not a mere repetition of biblical terms. Rather, as David Yeago argues, it is using a conceptual term (e.g., *homoousios*) to render accurate judgments about the patterns of Scripture, and specifically its talk of God.[12] Further, these conceptual terms and the judgments they render should be a reflection of what is *in* the text of Scripture, not merely *from* it.[13] In other words, simply because a conceptual term is not found in Scripture or does not have a specific proof text does not necessarily mean that the doctrine to which it refers is not biblical. Thus, the argument that eternal generation is invalid because the term is absent in Scripture or because it does not have a proof text does not accurately recognize the nature of the theological task. Nor does it recognize what the early Christian theologians were doing in using the phrase.

Early Christian Interpretation
Justin Martyr
Reading Proverbs 8 christologically is a tradition that begins very early in Christian interpretation.[14] While the apostolic fathers did not reflect on the intricacies of the intra-Trinitarian relations, when the apologists begin to write, we find Proverbs 8 used to explain the relationship between Father and Son. Justin Martyr, for instance, identifies Jesus with Wisdom in Proverbs 8 at least three times in his *Dialogue with Trypho* (61.1–5; 126.1;

---

12. David Yeago, "The New Testament and Nicene Dogma," in *The Theological Interpretation of Scripture: Classic and Contemporary Readings* (Oxford: Blackwell, 1997), 93.

13. Ibid., 87.

14. I am not here attempting to provide a comprehensive survey of the history of interpretation of Prov 8 but instead to highlight the interpretation of prominent figures in the Trinitarian debates, which in turn will allow us to draw conclusions about their hermeneutical and theological foundations. On the patristic interpretation of Prov 8, see the classic study of Manlio Simonetti, "Sull'interpretazione patristica di Proverbi 8, 22," in *Studi sull'Arianesimo* (Rome: Editrice Studium, 1965), 9–87. For a much briefer summary, see Davidson, "Proverbs 8 and the Place of Christ in the Trinity," 34–37.

MATTHEW Y. EMERSON

129.3).[15] In these passages Justin refers to Christ as begotten and "as a beginning before all creatures" (61.1),[16] although Justin's language is expectedly less nuanced and precise than the later christological debates would be. It also appears that Justin mainly uses the term "begotten" to refer to Christ's incarnation. Nevertheless, with Justin we see early interpretations of identifying the preexistent Son, as Logos, with Wisdom in Proverbs 8. And while, unsurprisingly, Justin does not articulate a clear hermeneutical method, we can discern at least one of the theological foundations for his interpretation: Christ is referent of all Scripture and, particularly for this apologetic work against Judaism, the referent of all the Old Testament.[17] The other apologists shared this foundational commitment to seeing Christ as Scripture's ultimate referent and therefore the particular referent of Proverbs 8.

Irenaeus

With Irenaeus there is a far more explicit picture of his foundational interpretive assumptions.[18] The first of these is the stark divide between Creator and creature; there is no space for a mediating being. The second is that Irenaeus assumes the unity of the Scriptures—a product of its inspiration by one divine author—and that unity manifests itself in a variety of ways. There is a textual unity, so that Irenaeus feels justified in connecting disparate passages that use the same words or phrases; there is a conceptual unity, which he calls the "hypothesis" of Scripture, where the overarching theme or point of the Bible is Jesus; and there is a narrative unity to Scripture, called the "economy," that shows how the Bible structurally fits together. Additionally, Irenaeus believes that every part of Scripture, whether person, event, or concept, is summed up in Christ. Irenaeus calls this interpretive strategy "recapitulation." Irenaeus's *The Demonstration of the Apostolic Preaching* is, essentially, a typological and narratively recapitulative reading of the entire Bible that demonstrates its inherent christological character. Irenaeus uses both close textual readings and narrative parallels to make his point that the Bible is a unified story centered on Christ. While it is possible to simply assume, based on Irenaeus's extensive use of typology,

---

15. St. Justin Martyr, *Dialogue with Trypho*, rev. ed., trans. Thomas B. Falls, ed. Michael Slusser (Washington, DC: Catholic University of America Press, 2003).

16. As William G. Rusch notes, the apologists used the language of generation to hold together the unity of the divine substance with the identity of the Logos with the Father. See the introduction to *The Trinitarian Controversy*, ed. and trans. William G. Rusch (Minneapolis: Fortress, 1980), 5.

17. Ibid., 4–5.

18. This paragraph is primarily a summary of John O'Keefe and R. R. Reno, *Sanctified Vision: An Introduction to Early Christian Interpretation of the Bible* (Baltimore: Johns Hopkins University Press, 2005), 33–44.

THE ROLE OF PROVERBS 8

that he would conclude that Christ is the referent of personified Wisdom in Proverbs 8, Irenaeus makes that assumption even more likely through a probable allusion to the passage.[19] Finally, Irenaeus distinguishes between the intrinsic (immanent) and extrinsic (economic) life of God and insists that the distinctions between the persons of the Godhead are revealed in the economy but nevertheless fully existent from eternity.[20] With these principles, Irenaeus laid the foundations for future orthodox Trinitarianism. Later pro-Nicene theologians would continue to assume the christological unity of Scripture, its economic structure, and the Creator–creature divide. They would also build on Irenaeus's distinction between the intrinsic and extrinsic relations between the persons of the Godhead.

With the rise of Monarchianism and Sabellianism in the third century, the christological and Trinitarian discussions began to intensify, and thus, with each new challenger, implicit Trinitarian formulations had to be explicitly worked out with more precise language. Additionally, Origen's and Clement of Alexandria's contributions to the topic, while not necessarily heretical, were nevertheless mulled over as possibly heterodox. Finally, the christological and theological controversy came to a head in the fourth century with the arrival of the subordinationists, including Arius, Eusebius of Nicomedia, and Asterius.

The Nicene Controversy

As Khaled Anatolios has helpfully articulated, both the anti-Nicene and pro-Nicene theologians shared several theological convictions that necessarily influenced their hermeneutical method.[21] They agreed that the Bible was normative for theology, that apostolic tradition bore authority in debates, and that arguments were based on a rationally articulated faith. They also shared the conviction that the Father, Son, and Spirit were the "object of Christian faith and worship," that God created all things from nothing, and that Christ is lord, the way of salvation for the whole world, preexistent creator, and worthy of worship. Finally, all parties clearly distinguished themselves from Manichaeism, gnostic emanationism, the adoptionism associated with Paul of Samosata, and Sabellianism. Particularly important

---

19. See section 43 of *The Demonstration of the Apostolic Preaching*, trans J. Armitage Robinson (New York: Macmillan, 1920), 108: "Because, for God, the Son was (as) the beginning before the creation of the world."

20. William G. Rusch, *The Trinitarian Controversy*, ed. and trans. Rusch (Minneapolis: Fortress, 1980), 7.

21. This paragraph is a summary of Khaled Anatolios, *Retrieving Nicaea: The Development and Meaning of Trinitarian Doctrine* (Grand Rapids: Baker Academic, 2011), 38–40.

here are the common confessions of Christ as preexistent Creator and the object of Christian worship; these factors especially prompted the questions about the place of Christ in relation to the Father.

Thus in many ways the interpretive controversy over Proverbs 8 stems from that common confession about Christ as well as from recognition that the New Testament identifies the Logos with Wisdom (see 1 Cor 1:24; Rev 3:14) and particularly with Wisdom personified in Proverbs 8. The interpretive history of this passage therefore serves as a helpful test case for the different hermeneutical approaches taken by the parties involved in the Nicene controversy. For the Arians, two fundamental principles were involved.[22] The first was distinguishing between the undivided monad and all other beings. For Arius especially, this Platonic view of the deity led him to distinguish God the Father, as the monad, from what was derived from him. The idea of a triune deity unified in essence is therefore antithetical to Arius's and others' fundamental beliefs about the nature of the divine being. For the anti-Nicenes, therefore, the Father exists as monad, while the Son (or Logos) and Spirit exist as mediatory beings between Creator and creation who were nevertheless worshiped as divine. This philosophical presupposition resulted in the anti-Nicenes searching for texts that demonstrated a clear separation between the Father, Son, and Spirit. Proverbs 8 certainly seemed to the anti-Nicenes to be an airtight case for their position, and their focus on it resulted in part from their commitment to this first philosophical principle.

The second important methodological strategy was a commitment to find texts that supported the distinction between the Father and Son and to cite them together. Anatolios notes that, according to Alexander, "Arius and his supporters made extensive use of scriptural texts that support their doctrine of ontological inferiority of the Son, particularly texts that pertain to his suffering humanity."[23] Indeed, "his project is fundamentally concerned with integrating a strict definition of divine transcendence with a relativized but, in his view, scripturally adequate conception of the primacy of Christ."[24]

The pro-Nicene theologians also had their own precommitments of course; particularly important for them is the Creator–creature divide. Anything that is uncreated is God, while anything that is created is not God. This necessarily excludes any sense of a divine but created mediatorial

---

22. Sarah Parvis notes that while "Arians" may be anachronistic, it is still helpful in providing workable categories (Parvis, "Christology in the Early Arian Controversy," 120).

23. Anatolios, *Retrieving Nicaea*, 43.

24. Ibid., 52.

THE ROLE OF PROVERBS 8

being.[25] Both sides, in other words, interpreted scriptural passages within the bounds of their own version of monotheism.[26] As we will see, though, the pro-Nicene interpreters did not approach this task by isolating texts from their narrative and canonical context, while the anti-Nicenes seemed to be more comfortable simply compiling texts without much reference to their literary contexts.

Proverbs 8, especially Proverbs 8:22–25, is particularly important for Arius. The passage provides him with the linguistic precedent for speaking of Christ as "created," "founded," and "begot," and thus as "an event in time, or at least just before time, but with a 'before' of its own."[27] Eusebius of Nicomedia and Asterius follow Arius's pattern here, although Eusebius attempts to widen the divide between unbegotten and begotten, and Asterius seeks to close the gap using the idea of image. In any case, all three focus on individual scriptural verses that support their presuppositions about monotheism while maintaining the Trinitarian nature of Christian confession in worship. There is not, in these theologians' work, a sense of the economic unity of Scripture or an attempt to place biblical data within the larger pattern of the scriptural narrative. Instead, "a narrow-minded literalism prevented [Arius] from a creative reading which would have orchestrated Lady Wisdom's speech by calling on the symphonic trends of all scriptures."[28]

The pro-Nicene interpreters, on the other hand, used the economic argument as a primary strategy against Arius and other subordination-ists. Perhaps beginning with Marcellus of Ancyra, and seemingly echoing Irenaeus, this argument took those passages that Arius and others use to demonstrate that Christ is a subordinate being to the Father and applied them instead "to the incarnate Christ."[29] In other words, it takes into consideration the *oikonomia* of Scripture—its narrative pattern—which is decisively centered on the incarnation of the Logos in the fourfold Gospel corpus. Therefore, when exegeting passages pertaining to Christ, the interpreter

---

25. See, for instance, Gregory of Nazianzus, *Or. Bas.* 29.4, 14; Basil of Caesarea, *On the Holy Spirit*, 16.37, 20.51, 24.55; Augustine, *Trin.* 1.2.9. It should also be noted that this commitment was for these writers thoroughly scriptural. While Arius seems to have taken his precommitments from Platonic philosophy, Athanasius et al. are at pains to show that this sharp Creator–creature divide is taught in Scripture.

26. Aloys Grillmeier, *Christ in Christian Tradition I: From the Apostolic Age to Chalcedon (451)*, 2nd ed., trans. John Bowden (Louisville: John Knox, 1975), 222.

27. Parvis, "Christology in the Early Arian Controversy," 123.

28. Charles Kannengiesser, "Lady Wisdom's Final Call: The Patristic Recovery of Proverbs 8," in *Nova Doctrina Vetusque: Essays on Early Christianity in Honor of Fredric W. Schlatter, S.J.*, ed. Douglas Kries and Catherine Brown Tkacz (New York: Peter Lang, 1999), 72.

29. Parvis, "Christology in the Early Arian Controversy," 130, 135. In addition, I am not arguing that Marcellus is fully Nicene, but he is a vital influence on Athanasius's interpretive approach and thus worthy of noting here.

must discern whether it is speaking of the preincarnate or incarnate Word. Athanasius uses this argument prolifically in his *Discourse Against the Arians*, and the Cappadocians and Augustine followed suit.[30] Additionally, in this reading strategy, Proverbs 8 proved important, both because of its use by the anti-Nicenes and because it provided these theologians with a passage that spoke of both Christ's humanity and divinity. This is perhaps one of the most fundamental hermeneutical moves that the pro-Nicene theologians make, although there are a number of other important methodological features of their exegesis.

A second important methodological tactic was the use of divine names to understand the nature of God. Both Basil of Caesarea, in his first volume of *Contra Eunomium,* and later Gregory of Nyssa in his *Contra Eunomium* and *Refutatio Confessionis Eunomii*, develop a "theology of the divine names."[31] For Basil and Gregory, because Father, Son, and Spirit are "named with the same divine names" and "perform the same divine actions," we must find a way to speak adequately of one God with one essence but existing in three persons. Further, the three different names for the three persons also speak theologically about their distinguishing features, and for these early Christian theologians that difference lies in the relations of origin (e.g., unbegotten, begotten, proceeding), *not* in the relations of personality or volition. The latter was the argument of Eunomius that was thoroughly rejected by both Greek and Latin pro-Nicene theologians.[32] For Basil and Gregory of Nyssa, the terms "Father" and "Son" imply a relation of origin, or more specifically a relation of begetting. In other words, eternal generation (and subsequently eternal procession) distinguishes the Son from the Father (and subsequently the Spirit from both Father and Son). Furthermore, this argument was, for many of the pro-Nicene theologians, one of the primary keys for proving the Son's divinity. When a father begets a son, the son is always of the same nature as the father, and so to call the Logos "Son" and the First Person of the Trinity "Father" is to imply a unity of essence. Additionally, the names assigned to the Son, especially Wisdom and Power (cf. 1 Cor 1:24), were crucial in arguing that the Father is never without his word, wisdom, or power and therefore that there never was a time that the Son, who is the Wisdom, Word, and Power of God, was not. Names again demonstrate the unity of essence in Father and Son. This was absolutely central for Athanasius in his argument against Arius, and for

---

30. See *C. Ar.* especially bk. 2.
31. Holmes, *The Quest for the Trinity*, 101–11.
32. Ibid., 109.

THE ROLE OF PROVERBS 8

Basil and both Gregorys in their arguments against Eunomius.[33] And for all three Proverbs 8 was a central text. The use of names led these theologians to understand the Son's full divinity and therefore also to affirm his eternal generation as the Son of the eternal Father. In these arguments Proverbs 8 is, again, crucial for the early Christian theologians, as it provides them an understanding of the Son's divinity and humanity, as well as the distinction of relations between the Father and Son.

In addition to the economy of Scripture and reflection on the divine names, Athanasius, the Cappadocians, and then later Augustine consid-ered genre a significant feature of particular biblical books. Each of these interpreters saw that the genre of Proverbs makes it especially important to be careful in exegeting individual passages and words. While some books of the Bible are more straightforward in their language, Athanasius, for instance, following Marcellus, argues "that what has been said in the book of Proverbs also has a proper sense (*ortē dianoia*). The key to understanding it is the Greek title of the book of Proverbs, *paroimiai.—paroimia* has two meanings: proverb, so *proverbium*, and likeness."[34] To read Proverbs, then, means to take care not to take statements too concretely when they are, in fact, using language that is metaphorical or figurative.

A fourth common hermeneutical method is demonstrated by these early interpreters' employment of both Greek and Hebrew linguistic tools to understand the meaning of individual words. Departing from Athanasius's decisive statements on the meaning of ἔκτισέν με in Proverbs 8:22, Basil uses Hebrew and Greek to argue for his interpretation of the verse, noting that the language of both the Hebrew *Vorlage* and the LXX translation are ambiguous. Further, Basil notes that the phrase "he created me from the beginning" is a *hapax legomenon* and should not be used to promote any major doctrine; rather, it should be interpreted in light of other biblical teaching.[35] Athanasius, on the other hand, argues from the Greek text for a particular interpretation of the phrase ("he acquired me"), noting verbal parallels for κτιζεῖν (e.g., Prov 9:1) that do not speak of "creating" and

---

33. Athanasius, *C. Ar.* bk. 1–4 (on Prov 8, see especially 2.19ff). See also Gregory of Nazianzus, *Or. Bas.*, and Gregory of Nyssa, *Against Eunomius.*

34. Luise Abramowski, "Das Theologische Hauptwerk Des Athanasius: Die Drei Bücher Gegen Die Arianer (Ctr. Arianos I–III)," *Communio Viatorum* 42, no. 1 (2000): 17. Abramowski's original German is "daß das in den Proverbien Gesagte auch einen richtigen Sinn hat (ὀρτή διάνοια). Der Schlüssel zum Verständnis ist ihm der griechische Titel des Proverbienbuches, παροιμίαι.—παροιμία hat zwei Bedeutungen: Sprichwort, also proverbium, und Gleichnis."

35. Mark DelCogliano, "Basil of Caesarea on Proverbs 8:22 and the Sources of Pro-Nicene Theology," *JTS* 59, no. 1 (2008): 183–90. See also Eugen J. Pentiuc, "A Self-Offering God and His Begotten Wisdom (Proverbs 8:22–24)," *Greek Orthodox Theological Review* 46, no. 3–4 (2001): 259–60.

employing what Matthew Bates has termed "prosopological exegesis."[36] This tactic identifies the New Testament speaker of particular Old Testament verses; thus for Athanasius the incarnate Christ speaks in Proverbs 8:22, while the eternal Logos speaks in 8:25. Basil disagrees, saying that we cannot determine definitively the speaker in Proverbs 8:22 (while of course still maintaining a pro-Nicene position).[37] Thus, while Basil and Athanasius disagree on some of the details, we find them, along with other pro-Nicene theologians, using similar exegetical methods: an understanding of genre, a close reading of textual details, a willingness to read individual passages in light of the entirety of Scripture, an awareness of intertextual links, and the assumption of a prosopological element in passages where different persons speak.[38]

For Proverbs 8:22 and 25, therefore, the pro-Nicene theologians read a proverbial text, connected closely to New Testament Wisdom Christology passages, that speaks of "begot" and "created" as referring to two different periods in the economy of salvation: verse 22 refers to the incarnation (especially for Athanasius) while verse 25 refers to the eternal Logos. This latter point led them to attempt to clearly articulate how divine Wisdom, as the Second Person of the Trinity, could be "begotten" of the Father while also being eternally and equally God. For the early Christian theologians, eternal generation is the answer to this question. Further, it is a thoroughly textual answer, grounded in clear hermeneutical methods and theological commitments.

Augustine likewise uses these methods and comes to the same conclusions, and again preeminent for him is the New Testament's identification of Wisdom with the Logos and the shape of the biblical narrative. For the latter, he applies what Keith Johnson refers to as "canonical rules," or ways of reading the biblical text that pay attention to its narrative contours. In this regard there are two: the "form of God" rule and "form of servant" rule.[39] That is, it is important for the interpreter to know when the text is speaking of the eternal Logos and when it is speaking of the incarnate

---

36. Abramowski, "Das Theologische Hauptwerk Des Athanasius," 18. On the basic approach of prosopological exegesis, see Matthew W. Bates, *The Hermeneutics of Apostolic Proclamation: The Center of Paul's Method of Interpretation* (Waco: Baylor University Press, 2012), 183–222.

37. DelCogliano, "Basil of Caesarea on Proverbs 8:22," 187.

38. For a short overview of Athanasius's hermeneutics, in addition to Abramowski, "Das Theologische Hauptwerk," see Kannengiesser, "Lady Wisdom's Final Call." For a fuller treatment that also includes an assessment of Athanasius's philosophical presuppositions, see Peter J. Leithart, *Athanasius* (Grand Rapids: Baker Academic, 2011), esp. 57–88, 117–46. On the Cappadocians, in addition to DelCogliano, "Basil of Caesarea," see Michel Van Parys, "Exégèse et Théologie Trinitaire: Prov 8,22 Chez Les Pères Cappadociens," *Irénikon* 43, no. 3 (1970): 362–79.

39. *Trin.* 1.3–4. English trans. from Augustine, *The Trinity*, 2nd ed., ed. John E. Rotelle, trans. Edmund Hill, O.P. (New York: New City, 2012).

THE ROLE OF PROVERBS 8

Christ. But in addition to these two rules, Augustine has a third: the "from another" rule. This rule states that there are passages which do not speak either of the Logos as eternal or Christ as incarnate but instead of relations of origin between the Son and the Father (e.g., John 5:19, 26). For these passages, the first two rules cannot help, but the third allows the interpreter to understand the relationship between Father and Son no longer only economically but now metaphysically.[40] This third rule is used in support of the doctrine of eternal generation, and it clarifies and strengthens the earlier pro-Nicene theologians' position on the doctrine.

For the early Christian theologians, then, the Second Person of the Trinity is (a) the object of Christian worship and (b) identified with Wisdom in the NT. Because of the language it uses and its assumed christological referent, Proverbs 8:22–31 was a critical passage for understanding the Trinity. In interpreting these verses, the anti-Nicenes, on the one hand, worked from the philosophical assumption of God as a monad and sought texts to support that notion. In doing so they isolated passages from the rest of Scripture and focused on a limited literalistic meaning. The pro-Nicenes, on the other hand, followed Jewish monotheism in recognizing a sharp Creator–creature divide that did not allow for the mediating role;[41] saw the Father, Son, and Spirit spoken of as unified in essence and operation throughout Scripture; and therefore argued for what has become known as the *homoousion* position. Thus, in their interpretation of Proverbs 8, they followed the following hermeneutical principles:

1. They assumed that the New Testament identifies the Son as Wisdom.
2. The narrative of Scripture must be given attention when the text speaks of Christ. Specifically, the climax of the incarnation provides the reference point for the entire story and for all language about Jesus.
3. The divine names give insight into the Father–Son relationship, both metaphysically and relationally.
4. Anachronistically, we can use Augustine's "form of God" vs. "form of a servant" distinction to summarize this point.
5. The genre of each biblical book—and, for our purposes, of Proverbs—must be given consideration when interpreting words, phrases, and whole passages.

---

40. See Johnson, "Augustine, Eternal Generation, and Evangelical Trinitarianism," 149–50.
41. Richard Bauckham, *Jesus and the God of Israel: God Crucified and Other Studies on the New Testament's Christology of Divine Identity* (Grand Rapids: Eerdmans, 2008), esp. 1–59.

MATTHEW Y. EMERSON

6. The individual words of Scripture are important, and thus a study of their meaning in the original language, their connection to other parts of Scripture, and their prosopological referent are all necessary components of exegeting a text.

7. Following Augustine, Proverbs 8:25 must follow the "from another" rule; it does not speak of Christ's incarnation, but neither is it speaking of a subordinated, temporal creation of the Logos. It must, then, like John 5:19 and 26, be referring to the eternal relations between the Father and the Son.

Thus the patristic interpreters had clear exegetical and theological grounds for interpreting Proverbs 8:22–31 as both referring to Christ and as teaching the eternal generation of the Son. This doctrine did not arrive based on a suprabiblical philosophical structure or metaphysical reflection; rather, it arose through a careful engagement with the biblical text that sought to reflect an accurate judgment about scriptural patterns regarding talk of Father and Son. The conceptual term used to make this judgment, taken from Proverbs 8:25, is "eternal generation." To conclude, therefore, that there is no biblical warrant for the doctrine of eternal generation seems a step too far at best and seems to ignore the evidence while misconstruing patristic interpretation at worst.

After Augustine, Christian interpreters continued to reflect on the person of Christ and the Trinitarian relations *ad intra*, and they continued to operate with these basic theological and hermeneutical presuppositions.[42] The support for eternal generation on both exegetical and dogmatic grounds continued virtually unabated until the early post-Reformation period, and even then its detractors were few.[43] Not until the late nineteenth and early twentieth century did it begin to lose widespread support.[44]

---

42. This is not to say that the Christian tradition remained unchanging; on the contrary, both foundations and method changed dramatically in the late medieval period. Unfortunately, space does not permit an exploration of these changes. For a detailed explanation of how interpretive foundations and methods shifted in the last few centuries prior to the Reformation, see G. R. Evans, *The Language and Logic of the Bible: The Earlier Middle Ages* (New York: Cambridge University Press, 1984); Evans, *The Language and Logic of the Bible: The Road to the Reformation* (New York: Cambridge University Press, 1985); and Henri de Lubac, *Medieval Exegesis: The Four Senses of Scripture*, vol. 3, trans., E. M. Macierowski (Grand Rapids: Eerdmans, 2009).

43. On what many would consider the height of medieval theological reflection, and particularly Trinitarian doctrine, in Thomas Aquinas, see Gilles Emery, *The Trinitarian Theology of St. Thomas Aquinas*, trans. F. A. Murphy (Oxford: Oxford University Press, 2010); and for an examination of John Calvin's questions about eternal generation's relationship to aseity, see Brannon Ellis, *Calvin, Classical Trinitarianism, and the Aseity of the Son* (Oxford: Oxford University Press, 2012), 64–102.

44. Giles, *The Eternal Generation of the Son*, 91–204.

Modern Interpretation of Proverbs 8
Proverbs 8 in Biblical Studies

To say that the interpretive landscape looks quite different today than it did in the second, third, fourth, and fifth centuries would be an extreme understatement. Modern interpreters continue to reflect on Proverbs 8, but their methods and theological foundations are quite different. The typical approach is to study the passage in its immediate literary and historical context. Interpreters tend to focus on ancient Near Eastern parallels, such as Egyptian and Ugaritic articulations of wisdom's relationship with the gods,[45] as well as on the meaning of particular Hebrew words given conclusions about historical background.[46] Most commentators do not see here either a reference to Christ or to eternal generation.[47] Instead, interpreters see in this passage Lady Wisdom as (1) a personification of an abstract concept[48] or (2) a created being that is with Yahweh during creation.[49] For the second option, there are two additional choices, as some say that Wisdom assists Yahweh in the creative act, while others say she is merely present. Further, many point to Wisdom here as the pattern of creation.[50] One notable exception is Richard Davidson, who finds evidence for the hypostatization of the Godhead. He does not, however, explore how that hypostatization relates to Yahweh, nor does he discuss eternal generation.[51]

---

45. For example, Jean de Savignac's claim that the background for *'amon* (v. 30) lies in Egyptian checkerboards. J. De Savignac, "La sagesse en Proverbs VIII 22–31," *VT* 12, no. 2 (1962): 211–15.

46. For a survey of possible ancient Near Eastern backgrounds, including Gen 1–2, as well as a critique of the definitive conclusions some interpreters make about which background is correct, see R. N. Whybray, "Proverbs VIII 22–31 and Its Supposed Prototypes," *VT* 15, no .4 (1965): 504–14. Mitchell Dahood also lists several possible ancient Near Eastern backgrounds in "Proverbs 8,22–31: Translation and Commentary," *Catholic Biblical Quarterly* 30, no. 4 (1968): 512–21.

47. R. P. C. Hanson has even characterized both parties' reading of Proverbs 8 as referring to Christ and their subsequent exegetical arguments as "two blindfolded men trying to hit each other." See P. R. Ackroyd and C. F. Evans, eds., *The Cambridge History of the Bible* (Cambridge: Cambridge University Press, 1970), 1:440.

48. See, for example, Stuart Weeks and Gale Yee, who both argue that Wisdom is merely a literary device, not an actual person or being. Stuart Weeks, "The Context and Meaning of Proverbs 8:30a," *JBL* 125, no. 3 (2006): 433–42; Gale A. Yee, "The Theology of Creation in Proverbs 8:22–31," in *Creation in the Biblical Traditions*, ed. Richard J. Clifford and John J. Collins (Washington, D.C.: Catholic Biblical Association of America, 1992).

49. E.g., along with the aforementioned de Savignac, Whybray, and Dahood articles, Shimon Bakon, "Two Hymns to Wisdom: Proverbs 8 and Job 28," *Jewish Bible Quarterly* 36, no. 4 (2008): 222–30; William P. Brown, "Proverbs 8:22–31," *Interpretation* 63, no. 3 (2009): 290–92; Michael V. Fox, "'Amon Again," *JBL* 115, no. 4 (1996): 699–702; Alan Lenzi, "Proverbs 8:22–31: Three Perspectives on Its Composition," *JBL* 125, no. 4 (2006): 687–714; Cleon L. Rogers III, "The Meaning and Significance of the Hebrew Word אמון in Proverbs 8,30," *Zeitschrift für die alttestamentliche Wissenschaft* 109, no. 2 (1997): 208–21; Bruce Vawter, "Prov 8:22: Wisdom and Creation," *JBL* 99, no. 2 (1980): 205–16; and Daniel H. Williams, "Proverbs 8:22–31," *Interpretation* 48, no. 3 (1994): 275–79.

50. For a survey of contemporary interpretive conclusions, see Davidson, "Proverbs 8 and the Place of Christ in the Trinity," 37–41.

51. Davidson, "Proverbs 8 and the Place of Christ in the Trinity."

MATTHEW Y. EMERSON

Absent in these interpretations, including Davidson's, is any reflection on either the New Testament's appropriation of the passage as referring to Christ or how Wisdom relates to Yahweh in Jewish monotheism. The former lacuna is a product of their methodological limitation of study to the immediate literary and historical context. But for evangelical interpreters, this ignores Scripture's divine authorship and its interconnectedness, both textually and conceptually. Interpreters who do not affirm an evangelical understanding of the Bible's divine inspiration are not off the hook in this regard either; dismissing the New Testament's appropriation of the passage still ignores the reception history of the text. Although there are a variety of later interpretations of Wisdom (e.g., Sirach and the Wisdom of Solomon), the New Testament is one of those, and as these interpreters are studying the Christian Bible, it seems necessary at least to deal with that issue rather than ignoring it completely. Reception history also brings to mind an important conclusion, or rather lack thereof, about the meaning of the passage and the verbs used in it. Modern scholarship has not arrived at any type of consensus regarding the meanings of, for instance, *qanah* (v. 22) or *'amon* (v. 30), resulting in the variety of interpretations of Wisdom's nature noted above.[52] Thus it is not at all clear that the New Testament's, and later the early Christian interpreters', assumption that Proverbs 8 has a christological referent is an aberrant eisegetical reading.

Even more troubling than the lack of reflection on the New Testament's christological reading, though, is the omission of any reflection on how a preexistent, mediating, created being fits into a Jewish worldview. It is not at all clear that the Jewish monotheism either of premonarchical or postexilic Israel would have accepted a reading of Proverbs 8 that postulates a mediating divine being between Yahweh and creation.[53] In fact, this interpretation sounds strikingly like Arius's, and yet no modern biblical commentator notes that peculiar parallel. More importantly, this lack of engagement with the New Testament's reception is coupled with a dismissal of the patterns of scriptural language about the relationship of Logos/Wisdom with the Father, a pattern that continually speaks of the Son as "from" the Father, one with the Father, creator with the Father, and so

---

52. For the variety of modern interpretations of the passage, see note 49. For an example of an argument that the Hebrew of Prov 8 is ambiguous, see R. B. Y. Scott, "Wisdom in Creation: The *'āmôn* of Proverbs VIII 30," *VT* 10, no. 2 (1960): 419–27. Scott notes that because of this ambiguity, the variety of interpretations of Prov 8 cannot be decided upon by mere historical-critical exegesis. Instead, reception history plays a major role. It is for this reason that the Christian interpretation of the text must seriously consider the New Testament's reading.

53. See e.g. Bauckham, *Jesus and the God of Israel*, 1–59.

on. To ignore this language is to ignore completely the theological task of all readers of Scripture, which is, again, to provide conceptual terms that render accurate judgments about the patterns of language in the text.

Proverbs 8 in Theology

Kevin Giles has helpfully summarized the (typically American evangelical) contemporary questioning of eternal generation's validity as a biblical doctrine. After surveying contemporary evangelical systematic theologies and their comments on the subject, he lists the following as the basic rationales for rejecting, or at least questioning, eternal generation:

1. It has no "biblical warrant." This is their first and most important objection.
2. It reflects Neo-Platonic thinking about God more than Christian thinking.
3. It makes no sense.
4. Nothing theologically important is lost if it is abandoned.
5. There are better ways to eternally differentiate the Father and the Son.
6. It implies or necessarily involves the eternal subordination of the Son, even the Arian heresy.[54]

While a complete defense of the doctrine of eternal generation should include a response to each of these, here we are concerned primarily with the first, as it is the most often used and directly contributes to the other objections on the list. More specifically, we are concerned primarily with *why* these theologians believe there is no biblical warrant for eternal generation.

One of the main reasons that theologians question the biblical basis for the doctrine is that they do not agree with the early theologians' assessment that the New Testament identifies Christ as the personified Wisdom of

---

54. Giles, *The Eternal Generation of the Son*, 36–37. This list is based on Giles's reading of Wayne Grudem, Bruce Ware, Paul Helm, William Lane Craig, and John Feinberg, among others. Feinberg's analysis contains most of the points listed by Giles and can be used by readers unfamiliar with the parties involved. See John S. Feinberg, *No One Like Him: The Doctrine of God* (Wheaton, IL: Crossway, 2001), 489–92. Note also that Feinberg misreads the fathers and their supposed reliance on *monogenēs* as one of the biblical cruxes for the doctrine. Grudem also mistakenly reads the early Christian theologians' position as reliant on translating the word *monogenēs* as "only begotten" instead of "only." See Wayne Grudem, *Systematic Theology: An Introduction to Biblical Doctrine* (Grand Rapids: Zondervan, 1994), 1233–34. For evidence of Grudem's and Feinberg's misreading of the patristic theologians, see Giles, *The Eternal Generation of the Son*, 63–66. See also Johnson's summary of objections in "Augustine, Eternal Generation, and Evangelical Trinitarianism," 143–46.

the Old Testament.[55] Daniel Ebert provides one of the primary exegetical attempts to defend this position, and he argues that 1 Corinthians 1:24, 30 does not speak of Christ as the personification of preexistent Wisdom but as the personification of the Wisdom of the gospel.[56] He also rejects the idea that any of the other identifications of Jesus as Wisdom draw on the Old Testament personification of Wisdom, especially as found in Proverbs 8.

While Ebert's attempt at an exegetical understanding of the relationship between Jesus and Wisdom is laudable, there are three problems with his argument. The first is that one wonders if that background is so easily dismissed, given the New Testament's constant reliance on the Old Testament for its understanding of Christ and given the development of the personification of wisdom over the course of the Old Testament. A second and related problem is that identifying Christ as the personification of the wisdom of the gospel apart from any reference to the Old Testament material strips the passage of its Old Testament background and thus leaves it standing alone without impetus, warrant, or explanation. To say that Christ as Wisdom refers to the Wisdom of the cross or of the gospel makes no sense apart from an Old Testament background—and the Old Testament personifies Wisdom.

Third, as the early Christian theologians frequently point out, it is illogical to posit that, in the case of Proverbs 8, there are two Wisdoms: Christ as Wisdom and then another attribute of God called Wisdom that is created, the latter of which is the only referent in Proverbs 8. If the Wisdom referenced in Proverbs 8 is not Christ but one of God's attributes, does this mean that wisdom as an attribute did not exist in God from eternity? This introduces complexity into the nature of God and diminishes his wisdom. The early Christian theologians were at pains to show that God never gains any attribute but is eternal in his essence, and to call Wisdom in Proverbs 8 something other than Christ suggests that wisdom does not exist for God until he creates it. Perhaps some will say that Wisdom in Proverbs 8 is not brought into being, as was just suggested, but instead that it is brought forth to be present and active in creation. This is no solution either: it only suggests that there are two Wisdoms present at creation, the Son and this impersonal wisdom, and that both Wisdoms are active agents in the act of creation.

---

55. This in and of itself should be astounding to those familiar with the historical development of the doctrine of the Trinity, as the development of this preeminent Christian doctrine "was decisively shaped by the use of Proverbs 8:22–31 (LXX) as a passage dealing with the relation between the preexistent Logos and the Father." Jaroslav Pelikan, *The Emergence of the Christian Tradition (100–600)*, vol. 1, *The Christian Tradition: A History of the Development of Doctrine* (Chicago: The University of Chicago Press, 1971), 61.

56. Daniel J. Ebert IV, *Wisdom Christology: How Jesus Becomes God's Wisdom for Us*, ed. Robert A. Peterson (Phillipsburg, NJ: P&R, 2011), 12–15, 64–66.

THE ROLE OF PROVERBS 8

Fourth and perhaps most important, rejecting the link between New Testament talk about Christ as Wisdom with the Old Testament personification of Wisdom ignores the textual links between New Testament passages and Proverbs 8 (see John 1:1–3;[57] 1 Cor 1:24, 30; Heb 1:1–4; and, perhaps most notably, Rev 3:14). In Revelation 3, the phrase ὁ Ἀμήν appears to be a direct transliteration of the Hebrew word 'amon of Proverbs 8:30, and the rest of the verse may well be a presentation of Christ in light of that word. Further, both Colossians 1:15–17 and Revelation 3:14 identify Christ as the beginning of creation (with Paul using πρωτότοκος and John using ἀρχὴ), a phrase that has its only possible Old Testament background in Proverbs 8.[58] Finally, with respect to the preexistent power and creative work of Christ in John 1 and Hebrews 1, we are once again left in a position to find an alternative Old Testament background for these ideas if it is not found in Proverbs 8. To put it simply, for each of these New Testament texts Proverbs 8 provides the most appropriate and explicit, and probably the sole, Old Testament background for talk of the Logos as preexistent, holding creation together, and taking part in the act of creation. To reject it as such is to leave these New Testament texts without an Old Testament branch on which to stand. Using Yeago's terms, we are left without biblical warrant for judgments that need to be rendered about the language of the Son as preexistent Creator.

An additional supposed biblical warrant for the dismissal of eternal generation comes from Wayne Grudem and John Feinberg, who argue that, because Proverbs 8:25 can be read as "he acquired me," there is no biblical support for the language of eternal begetting.[59] The problem with this argument is

---

57. Davidson notes that this passage is a combined reading of Gen 1:1 and Prov 8:23. "Proverbs 8 and the Place of Christ in the Trinity," 34. On the textual relationship between Gen 1 and Prov 8, see Michaela Bauks and Gerlinde Baumann, "Im Anfang war . . . ? Gen 1,1ff und Prov 8,22–31 im Vergleich," *Biblische Notizen* 71 (1994): 24–52.

58. Scott, "Wisdom in Creation," 218. Scott also sees a possible reference to 'amon in John 7:5. For the Rev 3:14 parallel, see also Kannengiesser, "Lady Wisdom's Final Call," 65–66. While Scott focuses on the transliteration of 'amon, Kannengiesser sees the explicit parallel more so in the phrase *hē archē tēs ktiseōs tou theou*. The 4th ed. of the UBS GNT lists Rev 3:14 as a textual quotation of or allusion to Prov 8:22.

59. Grudem, *Systematic Theology*, 229–30. Grudem also argues that we are justified and even compelled to reject a reading of Prov 8:22–31 as referring to an actual person because there are other personified concepts in Proverbs (e.g., Lady Folly in 9:13–18) that are not taken as actual persons. While we should appreciate here Grudem's detailed inspection of the surrounding text, the logic is nevertheless faulty. Lack of reference to an actual person for one personification does not *a priori* rule it out for another. Further, and as noted above, the New Testament seems to make clear reference to this passage as referring to Christ.

A similar interpretation comes from Daniel Ebert, who prefers to see Wisdom's role in creation "as a type of Christ's role in creation" instead of as a reference to the eternal Logos (Ebert, *Wisdom Christology*, 70). But one wonders how this makes any sense of either Wisdom or typology. In regards to Wisdom, if she is a part of creation, what part does she play? How does that reading interact with Jewish monotheism? If she is merely a type and not an actual reference to the Logos, does this accurately reflect the nature of Old Testament typology? Old Testament types are always

MATTHEW Y. EMERSON

at least threefold. First, Grudem and Feinberg have ignored the ambiguity of the Hebrew, as noted above, which provides at least permission for the reading of "he begot me." Second, Athanasius had no problem seeing this verb translated as "he acquired me" and at the same time teaching that the Son is eternally begotten. Third, Grudem's argument for "he acquired me" provides simply another set of questions rather than a solution. If this is the correct reading, what exactly does it mean? Is the reference still to Christ? If so, what does it mean for him to be "acquired from the beginning"? If the reference is not to Christ, are we then rejecting the readings of the entire history of the church for the first eighteen centuries of its existence? This may be an option for those such as Feinberg,[60] but should evangelicals be so quick to dismiss the ecumenical conclusions of the Christian tradition? The reading of Proverbs 8 as teaching eternal generation has been virtually codified in the Nicene Creed. To reject the Creed's language is to implicitly reject this interpretation of Proverbs 8, and vice versa, and I for one am not comfortable with so easily dismissing either. Perhaps most important, if we reject or question the usefulness of eternal generation, what biblical warrant are we left with to distinguish the three persons of the Trinity?[61]

Grudem, Ware, and others choose to answer this vexing question with the doctrine of eternal functional subordination. Arguing from texts such as 1 Corinthians 11:3, 15:28, and the "sent" passages in John, Ware believes that these passages, as well as the names Father and Son, teach that the Second Person of the Trinity (and, by implication, the Third Person as well) is eternally subjected to without becoming ontologically subordinate from the Father.[62] Again, there are a number of problems with this position. First, the texts Ware cites do not clearly teach the subordination of the Son in the Trinitarian life *ad intra*, but rather all refer to the Trinitarian work of salvation, the Trinity as it is made known *ad extra*.

---

rooted in actual events and never literary inventions; does this mean Wisdom and the Logos are both involved in the creation event?

Derek Kidner makes exactly this point when he argues that "the personifying of wisdom, far from overshooting the literal truth, was a preparation for its full statement, since the agent of creation was no mere activity of God, but the Son, His eternal Word, Wisdom, and Power (see also John 1:1–14; 1 Cor 1:24, 30; Heb 1:1–4)." In other words, the typological reading of Prov 8 does not negate the actuality of Wisdom's personhood but instead only strengthens it, based on the NT's appropriation of the passage and assertion that the Logos is the agent of creation. See Derek Kidner, *Proverbs: An Introduction and Commentary* (Downers Grove, IL: InterVarsity, 1964), 79.

60. Feinberg, *No One Like Him*, 492.

61. We should note here that Grudem and Ware have both publicly affirmed eternal generation at the 2016 annual meeting of the Evangelical Theological Society in San Antonio, Texas. They have not yet done so in a professional publication.

62. Bruce Ware, *Father, Son, and Holy Spirit: Relationships, Roles, and Relevance* (Wheaton, IL: Crossway, 2005), 76–83.

THE ROLE OF PROVERBS 8

While the economic Trinity certainly reflects the immanent Trinity, we need to be careful not to read all aspects of the economic back into the immanent. As the fathers were at pains to note, the narrative of Scripture, the economy of salvation, is distinct from the life of God from eternity. The incarnation is a unique event that changes the way we talk about the Second Person of the Trinity, namely, as taking on flesh and submitting to the Father. It is in this sense, the sense Augustine calls "form of a servant," that the texts cited by Ware speak of the Second Person of the Trinity. 1 Corinthians 11:3 and the Johannine "sent" passages clearly refer to the incarnate Christ, while 1 Corinthians 15:28 in context is referring to the man Christ Jesus handing over his kingdom to the Father.[63] This is not the life of God as it existed prior to creation but the life of God as it exists in the economy of salvation. Further, it is not clear at all that we should read the Johannine sending passages as teaching subordination. Instead, we see here the order, or *taxis*, of Trinitarian activity in the salvific economy. While the Son's coming is fitting, it does not imply or necessitate subordination in the immanent Trinity. Eternal functional subordination therefore cannot be relied upon to provide a fitting and biblical distinction between Father and Son. We are thus left again with the question of how to distinguish the three persons of the Godhead without lapsing into tritheism or modalism.

One final problem with doubting or rejecting the biblical basis for eternal generation lies in the names given to the First and Second Persons of the Trinity. Surely the biblical authors, under the inspiration of the Spirit, could have chosen different names that implied both ontological unity and relational differentiation without implying begetting. And yet they did not, and so we must deal with the theological implications of the divine names. As Alan Gomes notes in his description of W. G. T. Shedd's method,

> The Bible describes the members of the Trinity by the titles *Father, Son*, and *Spirit*, and it follows that there must be something about these persons that warrants such designations. Now, *it is impossible to conceive of the father/son relationship apart from some concept of generation*. And if there is generation and if the Son is the same ontological being as the Father, who is eternal, then the generation must be an eternal generation.[64]

---

63. As Augustine rightly argues in *Trin.* 1.3.15–17.

64. Alan W. Gomes, "A Historical and Theological Introduction to W. G. T. Shedd and His *Dogmatic Theology*," in William G. T. Shedd, *Dogmatic Theology*, 3rd ed., ed. Alan W. Gomes (Phillipsburg, NJ: P&R, 2003), 29n60 (emphasis added).

What, then, are we to conclude about modern biblical scholars' and theologians' rejection of the biblical basis for eternal generation, especially in Proverbs 8? First, there seems to be a lack of engagement with the unity of Scripture conceptually, textually, and narratively. Conceptually, these interpreters reject the unity of the descriptions of Wisdom throughout the canon, including the New Testament's identification of Christ as Wisdom. Textually, the links between, for instance, Proverbs 8:30 and Revelation 3:14, which provide clear warrant for the previous conceptual link, are either dismissed or ignored. Narratively, the economy of Scripture is minimized as a factor, either by affirming eternal subordination from texts that do not support it or by ignoring the culminating typological fulfillment of all Old Testament figures, including Lady Wisdom, in Christ.

This dismissal or minimalization of the biblical narrative and its conceptual and textual unity is seen not only in the rejection of eternal generation but also more broadly in the contemporary theologian's approach as a whole. For biblical scholars, the basic approach is to isolate a passage from the larger biblical context, both narratively and textually. For theologians, the tendency is toward a stark biblicism, where we have doctrines in search of a verse or a collection of disparate verses in search of a doctrine.[65] For the biblical scholars, they cannot see how Proverbs 8 in its historical context is a description of the Logos who took on flesh. Systematicians like Grudem and Ware cannot find their verse, and so they question eternal generation's biblical warrant. Both approaches are effectively the same in that they isolate texts from their larger narrative and textual context, which is ultimately all of Scripture.

As mentioned above, Ware and Grudem have affirmed eternal generation in public (at the 2016 ETS annual meeting) if not yet in publication. Grudem's change of mind was prompted by a prepublication version of Lee Irons's chapter in this volume. But the methodological problem remains—only a stark biblicism, one which only affirms those doctrines for which can find a proof text, would shift so dramatically based on the translation

---

65. See Grudem's explanation of his method in *Systematic Theology*, 35–37. For a similar approach with more detailed explanation, see Millard Erickson, *Christian Theology*, 2nd ed. (Grand Rapids: Baker Academic, 1998), 70–82. Erickson also rejects eternal generation. See Millard Erickson, *God in Three Persons: A Contemporary Interpretation of the Trinity* (Grand Rapids: Baker, 1995), 305–6, 309–10. Interestingly, Erickson (and others) continue to rely on the economic argument advanced by the fathers to explain language about the Son that refers to his incarnation versus language about the Son that refers to his relationship with the Father *ad intra* (see Erickson, *Christian Theology*, 713–14). The problem is that while they use the fathers' arguments about the humanity of the incarnate Son, they do not then adequately explain exactly how the Father and Son (and Spirit) can be one God and yet three distinct persons using biblical language and taking into account the "from another" passages. In other words, Erickson here uses part of the logic of the early Christian theologians' arguments without referencing, and indeed while rejecting, the other crucial half of that same logic.

The Role of Proverbs 8

of one word (μονογενής). While I am grateful for Grudem's and Ware's very recent, clear affirmation of eternal generation, I see no reason to assume that this shift is due to a change in method but rather is actually another example of the method described here.

Furthermore, the questioning and/or rejection of eternal generation is reliant on and contributes to social Trinitarianism, a seemingly modern innovation and one lacking in biblical warrant.[66] The early Christian theologians were not satisfied with finding unity between the Trinitarian persons in three separate wills. In other words, they were not comfortable saying that what distinguishes the three persons of the Trinity are three separate volitional wills, precisely because, along with being unconvinced by the biblical data, the anti-Nicenes used that argument (not to mention the metaphysical problems that arise from such an affirmation).[67] While some, like Bruce Ware, deny trithelitism, it is hard to imagine how the persons can be distinguished as personal agents, two of whom submit to others in the case of eternal functional subordination (or eternal relations of authority and submission), without an implicit trithelitism. Again, while these theologians rightly affirm *homoousios*, they do so in such a way that was foreign to the pro-Nicene theologians who coined the term. In other words, their approach is in many ways divergent from the approach taken by the pro-Nicene theologians. Strikingly, therefore, the approach of some modern theologians is very similar to the anti-Nicenes' approach to the Bible, where the idea is to collect all the disparate data and make a conclusion based on the sum of the parts. I am of course not arguing here that Ware, Grudem, Feinberg, and others are anti-Nicene; rather, in spite of their orthodox conclusions about the *homoousios* nature of the three persons of God, their (at least previous) questioning of the corollary doctrine of eternal generation reveals a *hermeneutic* that finds more in common with the anti-Nicenes than with the pro-Nicenes.

CONCLUSION

The early Christian interpreters' belief in the eternal generation of the Son was based on theological and hermeneutical foundations such as recognizing Christ as the referent of all Scripture; paying attention to the narrative

---

66. E.g., reading Trinitarian language about the three different persons of God as implying a difference in *personality*, that is, three separate seats of consciousness that are nevertheless united in their will. Ironically, this "unity of will" is precisely what Arius and other Monarchians argued united Father, Son, and Spirit rather than unity of being (*homoousios*). Anatolios, *Retrieving Nicaea*, 41–79.

67. Ibid.

contours of the canon, and especially its climax in the life and work of Christ; noticing textual links between passages; reflecting on the implications of the divine names; understanding the importance of genre and textual details; and using conceptual terms to render accurate judgments about the patterns of the biblical text. For them, therefore, Proverbs 8 was read both as about the Second Person of the Trinity, both as he exists *ad intra* (v. 25) and *ad extra* (v. 22), and thus as supporting the doctrine of the eternal generation of the Son via verse 25. Their support of that doctrine is thus robustly founded in biblical reflection, and to say that there is no biblical warrant for eternal generation is to deny the profundity of biblical interpretation, including interpretation of Proverbs 8, in the patristic and medieval periods.

Modern scholarship, on the other hand, has tended to read texts in a more isolated fashion, separating them from their narrative and textual canonical context. Their methods, therefore, appear more like that of Arius than of Athanasius. This has even produced interpretations of Proverbs 8 that mirror Arius's, with Wisdom seen as a mediating semidivine being. Even when that latter interpretation is not taken, as it is not in evangelical systematicians' works, Proverbs 8 is still rejected as a reference to Christ or to eternal generation. Subsequently, these theologians question or reject the doctrine and prefer eternal functional subordination as a means to distinguish between the three persons of the Trinity. Their case for eternal subordination, though, is also plagued by the same methodological problems that caused them to reject eternal generation in the first place (namely, a method akin to proof texting), as well as by the thorny problem of departing from the classic doctrine of the Trinity in favor of the twentieth-century innovation of social Trinitarianism. For these reasons, I suggest that we, first, continue to affirm eternal generation as a crucial doctrine for maintaining Trinitarian orthodoxy and, second, affirm Proverbs 8 as a supporting text for that doctrine. The eternal generation of the Son is the doctrine that allowed the pro-Nicene theologians to speak of the one God in three persons *with biblical warrant*, including warrant from Proverbs 8.

CHAPTER 3

ETERNAL GENERATION AND THE OLD TESTAMENT:
Micah 5:2 as a Test Case

MARK S. GIGNILLIAT

INTRODUCTION

"The church's struggle with the Trinity was not a battle *against* the Old Testament, but rather a battle *for* the Old Testament."[1] This is certainly one of Brevard Childs's more memorable quotes and presses on a subject matter of continued importance. What is the material relationship between the givenness of Scripture in human language *ante Christum natum* and Christian dogmatic claims about God's triune character? In what way does biblical language refer and to whom? As I often remind my students and myself, early church struggles to come to terms with the unity of God in a shared divine essence, conjoined with the distinctions within this same God—distinctions of person or hypostasis, not essence—took place on the battlefield of biblical exegesis. And in this exegetical war, the Old Testament is Gettysburg.

Increasingly, I am impressed by the efforts made by the early church fathers to come to terms with Scripture's total witness, giving the Scripture's straightforward claims an ordered account to avoid crashing on Arian or Sabellian rocks. Micah 5:2 (5:1 in the Masoretic Text) remains an important text in the larger mosaic of Trinitarian reflection, particularly as this text relates to the eternal generation of the son. In other words, theological and

---

1. Brevard S. Childs, *Biblical Theology of the Old and New Testaments: Theological Reflections on the Christian Bible* (Minneapolis: Fortress, 1992), 376.

exegetical instincts of the patristic kind are in order when coming to terms with this text. "But you, Bethlehem Ephrathah, though you be least among the tribes, from you to me a ruler shall go forth, whose goings forth are from of old, even from eternity."[2]

So as not to bury my lede, I will make a few hermeneutical comments on the front end of this chapter. These hermeneutical reflections will take the form of a modest interaction with two important interlocutors, namely, Thomas Aquinas and John Owen. I do so because these two figures from the tradition bear materially on the theological subject matter at hand and the place of Micah 5:2(1) on it. From these hermeneutical comments, I will then turn toward a brief account of Micah 5:2(1) in the history of interpretation and current scholarship. I'll conclude with reflections on a theological account of grammar and sense-making in light of Micah 5.2(1)'s verbal character.

A Word about Aquinas and the Hermeneutical Role of Speculative Theology

Gilles Emery's impressive account of Thomas's Trinitarian theology makes much of the shared goal between Thomas's biblical commentary and speculative theology: the elucidation of God's truth. Similar comments may be made about many of the best theological voices from the tradition, Catholic and Protestant: Calvin and Barth come to mind as more well-known figures, but lesser figures do so as well. Emery makes a significant point about Aquinas and the hermeneutical role speculative theology made in his engagement with the biblical text.

Aquinas's John commentary provides Emery with the tools necessary to make the following claim: Thomas resists too brittle a distinction between Trinitarian theology of the biblical and speculative types. "It is the same theology," writes Emery.[3] The synthetic character of speculative theology and the close reading of the biblical text in commentary both have the same purpose: "the reflective explanation of Scripture."[4] Emery's conclusion is worth repeating in full: "In every case, speculative theology

---

2. My translation.
3. Gilles Emery, *The Trinitarian Theology of St. Thomas Aquinas* (Oxford University Press, 2010), 19.
4. Ibid., 19. Emery comments on the means by which Aquinas brought the speculative work to bear on textual commentary, to wit, a deployment of Hugh of St. Victor's three levels of literal exposition: *littera* (textual analysis with reference to grammar and linguistics, an overview of the words' meaning in their immediate context), the *sensus* (the analysis of the signification of each member), and the *sententia* (a genuine understanding of the text, which draws out its theological and philosophical meaning) (ibid., 20). The *sententia* allows speculative theology its hermeneutical role in establishing the text's letter.

is not superimposed on or juxtaposed with the biblical text, but is *part and parcel* of the biblical reading."[5]

I wish to highlight the terms "part and parcel" here because the substantive point of this collocation is straightforward. The literal sense of Scripture is not devoid of theological sense-making, nor can the literal sense of the text in its Christian, canonical form be established when verbal signs are disjointed from their theological subject matter. This hermeneutical instinct can be traced in practice to apostolic figures such as Paul, and in time it was given a formal character in works such as Augustine's *De Doctrina*. Aquinas's Augustinian hermeneutic is in full gear at this point, with the necessary dialectic between sign and thing signified remaining intact.[6] I wish to return to this matter at the end of the chapter in conversation with the modern literary and intellectual historian George Steiner.

MICAH 5:2 IN THE TRADITION: JOHN OWEN AS EXEMPLAR

Our attention turns to John Owen's reading of Micah 5:2(1) as an example of this Augustinian hermeneutic brought to bear on the Socinian crisis in England in the early seventeenth century.

Socinianism made its tyrannical march from Italy in the late sixteenth century into Poland during the early seventeenth century, where its roots settled deeply. The Racovian Catechism emerged from Poland's Socinian movement, and in time, Socinian doctrine made its way into England via an Oxford don by the name of Mr. John Biddle—a Dickensian name if there ever was one. Mr. Biddle translated the Racovian Catechism into English, and the publication of this non-Trinitarian form of Christianity prompted Owen the polemicist into action. Owen produced a counter attack to this catechism, line by line, in his *Vindiciae Evangeliae* (Defense of

---

5. Ibid., 20 (emphasis mine).

6. The use of analogical language, like *ousia* and *hypostasis*, by no means diminishes the mystery of the divine Godhead. This abstract language provides a rational account of God's triune identity (Emery refers to this as the "far-reaching goal"), and more modestly, "the theologian carries out a contemplative exercise in order to grasp a droplet of the divine knowledge communicated by revelation, without losing sights of the limits of our knowledge" (Emery, *The Trinitarian Theology of St. Thomas Aquinas*, 35). George Hunsinger distinguishes Barth's use of analogical reasoning from Aquinas's precisely at this point. For Aquinas, our analogical language breaks down regarding the knowledge of God *in se* with God's identity in himself remaining a mystery. Whereas for Barth, in line with the Reformed tradition, God's revelation of himself truly corresponds with God's actual identity and provides the epistemic possibility for real knowledge of God, accommodated as this revelation is. While at the same time, comprehensive knowledge of God's eternal identity remains beyond the purview of human knowledge, thus the linguistic appeal to analogy in opposition to univocal and equivocal: apprehensive knowledge vs. comprehensive knowledge. George Hunsinger, *Disruptive Grace: Studies in the Theology of Karl Barth* (Grand Rapids: Eerdmans, 2000), 220–21 n12.

the Gospel). Some 589 pages of English prose later, Owen completed his task. The denial of Trinitarian faith was of massive moral consequence for Owen. Nothing less than our salvation hangs in the balance.

As one might anticipate, Owen's counter to Mr. Biddle's Socinian views focuses much on the relation of the Second Person, the Logos, to the Father in an attempt to provide biblical and theological support for Nicene orthodoxy. Central to the concerns are the full divinity of the Son with attention given to the notion of the Son's eternal generation by means of the Father's eternal act of generating, language familiar to fourth-century Trinitarian debates.

Mr. Biddle's catechism denies the eternal generation of the Son because, in his terms, "If Christ were begotten of the essence of his Father, either he took his whole essence or but part. Part of his essence he could not take, for the divine essence is impartible; nor the whole, for it being one in number is incommunicable."[7] Owen's immediate comment after quoting Biddle cuts straight: "And this is the fruit of measuring spiritual things by carnal, infinite by finite, God by ourselves, the object of faith by corrupted rules of corrupted reason."[8]

What fascinates about this section in Owen, and for that matter Mr. Biddle's catechism too, relates to the location of the exegetical debate: the Old Testament. Mr. Biddle raises the question, where do they argue for the eternal generation of the Son? Answer: "From these chiefly, Mic v. 2; Ps. ii. 7; cx. 3; Prov. viii. 23." From the identification of these texts, Mr. Biddle argues against their validity concerning the eternal generation of the Son by various and sundry means. For example, Micah 5:2, our text of study, does not refer to the eternal generation of the Son. This is a misunderstanding of the lexical data, according to Mr. Biddle. The language refers quite simply to days of antiquity, and the use of the term "day" removes us from the sphere of eternity. The reference to days of antiquity conjoined with the identification of Bethlehem as the place of nativity refers simply to David and his progeny, the line from which Christ would come—a reading conspicuously like most current approaches to the same text. Owen counters with his theological/exegetical armor strapped on for battle. The whole of chapter 9 in Owen's *Defense of the Gospel* is an exegetical debate regarding the eternal generation of the son and the Old Testament. Micah 5:2 registers as the first text under critical scrutiny.

---

7. Also from the *Racovian Catechism*, as cited in John Owen, *The Gospel Defended*, in *The Works of John Owen* (Edinburgh: Banner of Truth, 1966), 12:237.

8. Ibid., 237.

ETERNAL GENERATION AND THE OLD TESTAMENT

The exchange between Owen and Biddle remains instructive, especially in the realm of evangelical hermeneutics, because Owen and Biddle formally agree when it comes to their doctrine of Scripture. In fact, Owen says little against Biddle's catechetical statements concerning Scripture—a point of some interest. As Carl Trueman's work on John Owen explains,

> When Owen tackles Biddle's text proper, he starts with a surprisingly brief comment on the *Twofold Catechism's* doctrine of scripture, with which he has little disagreement. The very brevity of the chapter, along with its somewhat petulant *ad hominem* nature, indicates the problem: the Socinians appear to hold to a basic scripture principle in a formally similar manner to the orthodox. The differences, in fact, are significant, and go straight to the heart of why Owen can see scripture as teaching the doctrine of the Trinity and the Socinians reject such a conclusion: the point at issue is not simply whether scripture is the authoritative noetic foundation for theology, but how that scripture is to be interpreted, a point which draws in matters of logic, of metaphysics, and of how individual passages of scripture are mutually related in the act of interpretation.[9]

Biddle's claim strikes at the heart of our evangelical sensibility. "I'm only interested in what the Bible claims and nothing more." And while this kind of appeal has a pedestrian cache, with interpretive instincts heading in the right direction—we seek to order our thoughts and prayers in accord with Scripture's norming voice—the surreptitious character of the statement remains. For Biddle is not devoid of a metaphysic in his sole interest in the Bible and what it claims, namely, it is logically impossible to hold to a sharing in the divine essence between a plurality of personae in the Godhead. The divine essence is indivisible, and the eternal generation of the Son from the Father's divine essence does not follow this indivisibility. This *a priori* notion of the divine essence functions as a hermeneutical cipher for Biddle. Owen identifies this Socinian metaphysic as "rationalistic reductionism."[10]

As an aside, Spinoza's interpretive outline in his *Tractatus* makes similar claims. "I'm only interested in coming to terms with what Scripture claims and nothing more," to paraphrase Spinoza. Starting afresh with Cartesian

---

9. Carl R. Trueman, *John Owen: Reformed Catholic, Renaissance Man* (Aldershot: Ashgate, 2007), 48.

10. Richard A. Muller, *Post-Reformation Reformed Dogmatics: The Rise and Development of Reformed Orthodoxy, ca. 1520 to ca. 1725*, vol. 4, *The Triunity of God* (Grand Rapids: Baker Academic, 2003), 283.

modes of inquiry fully deployed, Spinoza sets himself to the task. But the indubitable foundation of Spinoza's hermeneutic was the natural light of reason, a claim he repeats enough to register it as a central leitmotif in the *Tractatus*. This "neutral" hermeneutic led to the necessary sequestering of metaphysical truth claims from Scripture into the specialized world of philosophy. Owen's response to Spinoza would be similar to Biddle's, I imagine: "rationalistic reductionism."

Why? Because Owen is steeped enough in the church's exegetical tradition to recognize the necessary two-way street between the engagement with the biblical texts themselves and the confession regarding the identity of the one God witnessed to therein. In David Yeago's formulation, Trinitarian language, while extrabiblical, is deployed as an act of *hermeneia* for the sake of coming to terms with Scripture's total witness regarding its naming of the persons of the Trinity: naming related to the divine essence at times and to eternal relations or processions at others. Owen certainly strives to give a rational and ordered account of Christian orthodoxy (an understatement if there ever was one), but he does so in an effort to come to terms with Scripture's total witness. For Mr. Biddle, the distinction between *essence* and *person* is patently false. For Owen, on the other hand, this distinction maintains Scripture's unity while at the same time comes to terms with its diverse modes of expression concerning divine unity and plurality. Again, the Bible's own self-witness demands such an account.

As far as Micah 5:2 is concerned, Owen finds Biddle's philological analysis lacking. For Owen, the מוֹצָאֹת refers unquestionably to the Son's eternal generation. He complains Biddle takes no account of מקדם, which for Owen refers to eternity. And despite the temporal *nomen regens* (construct noun), given the subject matter, Owen understands מימי עולם as a reference to pretemporal eternity as well, much in the same way as the Aramaic Ancient of Days in Daniel 7:9 makes use of "days" in reference to eternity.

Owen perhaps overreaches in his downplaying of the Davidic context. He finds Hugo Grotius's identification of Zerubbabel as the immediate fulfillment of this text problematic. Owen appeals to the Targum's paraphrastic rendering of the text as a reference to the coming Messiah, undercutting Grotius's reading—not to mention Zerubbabel is born in Babylon, not Bethlehem. Of interest, Theodore of Mopsuestia understands this text as having an immediate reference to Zerubbabel, though not at the expense of its ultimate christological referent: a double-literal fulfillment, one might say, or perhaps a figural reading that takes into account multiple referents?

What are we to make of all of this? One, Biddle's (and Grotius's) reading

ETERNAL GENERATION AND THE OLD TESTAMENT

of this text shares much in common with current scholarship on Micah 5:2, a point I will turn to next. Two, Owen's reading of the text is not a close philological analysis of the words themselves but the words in light of the subject matter of Christian Scripture. As his snarky response to Grotius intimates, "That it [Mic 5:2] properly belongs to Christ we have a better interpreter to be sure than Grotius or any of his rabbis, Matt. ii. 4–6."[11] For Owen, the exegetical deck is stacked because Scripture itself speaks clearly about this text's final referent. Because this is so, the literal sense of the text can only be made sense of in a close reading of the verbal/grammatical character of the text in shared relation with its Triune subject matter. Owen's reading is standard fare in the tradition.

Excurses: Snapshots from the Tradition

- Cyril of Alexandria understands the "going forth" of Micah 5:2 as either (1) eternal generation or (2) the emergence in time of the Logos's incarnation (logos incarnatus).[12]
- Theodoret of Cyrus understands Micah 5:2 as relating substantially to the prologue of John's Gospel and cannot be reduced to immediate fulfillment in Zerubbabel.[13]
- Aquinas states the objection: "Further, nothing that has come out from another is within it. But the sone from eternity came out from the Father, according to Micheas v. 2. . . . Therefore the Son is not in the Father" (ST 1.42.5, arg. 2). To which Aquinas replies, "The Son's going forth from the Father is by mode of the interior procession whereby the word emerges from the heart and remains therein. Hence this going forth in God is only by the distinction of the relations, not by any kind of essential separation" (ST 1.42.5, co. 2). Again, Aquinas is drawing on the metaphysical tradition of the church fathers in distinguishing between essence and persons. As Gilles Emery claims, "The sole distinction in the Godhead is between the persons, but there is no distinction between the persons and the divine nature."[14]

---

11. Owen, The Works of John Owen, 12:240.

12. St. Cyril of Alexandria, Commentary on the Twelve Prophets, vol. 2, trans. Robert C. Hill, The Fathers of the Church 116 (Washington, DC: Catholic University of America Press, 2008), 235.

13. Theodoret of Cyrus, Commentaries on the Prophets, vol. 3, Commentary on the Twelve Prophets, trans. Robert C. Hill (Brookline, MA: Holy Cross Orthodox, 2006), 164.

14. Gilles Emery, Trinity, Church and the Human Person: Thomistic Essays (Naples: Sapientia, 2007), 106. See Lewis Ayres, Nicaea and Its Legacy: An Approach to Fourth-Century Trinitarian Theology (Oxford: Oxford University Press, 2004), 236. McCormack's interaction with Levering and Emery emphasizes the overlap between Barth and Aquinas on this matter. Emery prefers the categories of

- Luther too sees the correspondence between Micah 5:2 and John's prologue regarding the eternal generation of the Son from the father.[15]
- Philip Melanchthon states, "Although this testimony is brief, yet it asserts that the Messiah existed before the creation of the world. Therefore He is eternal and God."[16]
- Calvin's exegetical instincts are similar, but he goes in a pastoral direction, encouraging hearers in their suffering to recognize the eternal character of Christ's kingdom in his sermons on Micah.[17] His commentary makes the strange statement that though he is willing to grant this text refers to the eternal generation of the Son, he prefers reading the text more simply as a reference to the long-before determination of God to bring Christ into the world. Why the simple reading? "This will never be allowed by the Jews."[18]

While the chord may be struck with different cadence and emphasis in the tradition, by and large the Trinitarian referent of Micah 5:2 is assumed. The phrase "whose origin is from of old, from ancient days" refers not simply to the eternal plan of God to perpetuate David's throne, though it should be added the text does not say less than this. Rather, the text, whose theological referent is God's triune revelation of himself in the redemption of humankind, refers to the coming Davidic ruler who does indeed perpetuate David's throne but does so as one whose eternal identity is in procession from the Father in a shared divine essence.

MICAH 5:2 IN CURRENT SCHOLARSHIP

The dominance of historicist approaches to textual and philological analysis in the modern period comes as no surprise. And the fruits of modern textual analysis in historical guise remain a towering contribution to our understanding of the biblical text. The challenge, however, relates to fitting

---

procession and mission as proceeding from the one pretemporal eternal act rather than economic and immanent because the latter language runs the risk of speaking of two trinities. McCormack sees that the only difference between Barth and Aquinas is the latter's willingness to allow metaphysical speculation a more substantive role. But in the Trinitarian reflections proper, there is much overlap.

15. Martin Luther, *Minor Prophets I: Hosea-Malachi*, Luthers Works American Edition, trans. R.J. Dinda, ed. H.C. Oswald (Saint Louis: Concordia, 1975), 248.

16. Melanchthon, *Loci Communes 1543*, trans. J. A. O Preus (St. Louis: Concordia, 1992), 26.

17. John Calvin, *Sermons on the Book of Micah*, trans. and ed. B. W. Farley (Phillipsburg: P&R, 2003), 275–76.

18. John Calvin, *Commentary on Jonah, Micah, and Nahum*, trans. John Owen (Grand Rapids: Baker, 2005), 299.

ETERNAL GENERATION AND THE OLD TESTAMENT

historical referentiality within an ontological frame regarding the one God of the two Testaments. Micah 5:2(1) is a case in point.

While not wanting to weary readers with an exhaustive taxonomy of current readings on Micah 5:2(1), a few matters are worth highlighting. One, the syntactical notion of "from you to me [לִי]" remains a challenge simply because the first-person referent comes from nowhere. The form is odd. Nevertheless, despite efforts to correct the text in various ways, there is no textual variant (except perhaps the Micah fragment at Qumran which has a לֹא after the לִי). The LXX and Vulgate read the text as "to me," *moi* or *mihi*. The figure who will emerge as a ruler in Zion is *from you to me*, with the referent implicitly understood as Adonai.[19]

Micah 5:2(1) begins as a contrastive to the moment of judgment Judah is currently experiencing (4:14): "But you." A ruler will come forth to lead God's people into peace. In fact, he is peace (a likely intertextual referent to Isa 9:6). From Judah's midst will emerge a ruler who will be the means of overturning wrath with peace—contextually, this figure is the means by which Micah 4:1–4 is actualized.

The next line of the prophetic utterance receives the spotlight of our attention and the focus of this text's history of interpretation. "And his going forth is from of old, even from days of eternity or days long ago." The term "going forths" or "origins" מוֹצָאֹת is in effect a *hapax legomenon*. The only other use is 2 Kings 10:27, and there it means "latrine." So we are safe to assume that is not the sense here. Hans Walter Wolff understands the plural use—interesting to note "going forths" or "origins"—as giving the expression a heightened sense of feeling.[20] A great deal depends on settling the meaning of "going forth." Mays describes this term in the following suggestive way: "Origin echoes the verb 'come forth' and thinks of children originating in the loins of their father."[21] This phraseology is unique in the Old Testament, and as such, our philological instincts should be on guard about making immodest claims about what the rest of the text can or can't mean.

Can *miqedem* refer to a distant time in the past, thus limiting its potential? Yes it can (cf. Amos 9:11). Can a similar claim regarding *'olam* be made, especially given the fact that it is preceded by a temporal absolute noun,

---

19. Wolf understands the strange syntax as stemming for the use of a Davidic tradition and its preference for the verbal phrase יָצָא; cf. Isa 11:1 and 2 Sam 7:13.

20. Hans Walter Wolff, *Micah: A Commentary*, trans. G. Stansell (Minneapolis: Augsburg Fortress, 1990), 140.

21. James Luther Mays, *Micah: A Commentary* (Philadelphia: Westminster, 1976), 115.

MARK S. GIGNILLIAT

"days"? Yes it can. And many, if not most, modern commentators go this route. But must it? Are we forced lexically to nod in the affirmative with *NIDOTTE*'s conclusion regarding Micah 5:2? "While it is tempting to see here a reference to the eternal preexistence of the Messiah, no such an idea is found in biblical or postbiblical Jewish literature before the Similitudes of Enoch (1 En 48:2–6)." Does such a philological instinct make good on a historical referent or potentially even the intention of the author (however such is conceived) while at the same time divorcing the linguistic character of Scripture from its divine referent in a two-testament frame?

Linguistically speaking, the terms *qedem* and *'olam* can individually and collectively refer to the eternal character of God (Deut 33:27, "The eternal God [אלהי קדם] is your refuge, and underneath are the everlasting arms ['*olam*]," and Ps 90:2, "from everlasting to everlasting"). Even Hillers in the Hermeneia commentary suggests that *qedem* has a mythical quality to it, "primeval, from the beginning, as an order of creation."[22] Jörg Jeremias believes the connotative force of *qedem* refers to "*mythische Urzeit*," a time properly referred to as "*Gottes Zeit*." Why is this God's time? Because in it, claims Jeremias, the primeval saving will of God (*Heilswille*) originates there.[23] *The highlighting of Bethlehem and not Jerusalem is itself significant because God makes clear his future purposes have to do with something new regarding the Davidic line rather than the current Davidic line in place in Jerusalem.* A new David is anticipated. Moreover, the use of "days" does not necessarily limit *'olam* (cf. Dan 7:9—the ancient of Days, or the long of days). In other words, a strictly governed historical account of this text's philological sense may attenuate its canonical intentionality.

The question here is a modest one. Given the unique character of this text, should its referent be limited to its undeniable Davidic context? The text is certainly not less than this, but is it more? Even Anderson and Freedman in their Anchor Bible commentary claim, "At the least the language suggests that the birth of the Messiah has been determined, or predicted in the divine council, in primal days. . . . Even if *mosa'ot* means no more than an oracle expressing the divine determination, it does not require a great shift in conceptuality to move to the Son of Man figure of

---

22. Delbert R. Hillers, *Micah* (Philadelphia: Fortress, 1984), 66.

23. Jörg Jeremias, *Die Propheten Joel, Obadja, Jona, Micha* (Göttingen: Vandenhoeck & Ruprecht, 2007), 185. This reading shares much in common with Calvin, who places going forth in the divine will. Again, speculative theology helps here because the divine will is one with the various personae of the Trinity sharing in it.

ETERNAL GENERATION AND THE OLD TESTAMENT

the later apocalypses—the *Urmensch*. . . . So Christians did not abuse the text when they found Jesus in it."[24]

I would like to press the matter further and suggest that not only have Christians not abused this text when allowing it a substantive role in the doctrine of the eternal generation of the Son, but they in fact are reading the text well in light of the Trinitarian subject of Scripture, a matter itself that not only provides a hermeneutic for all of Scripture but is in fact the retina (to borrow Gerhard Sauter's memorable phrase) that allow us to see the text's ontological relation to its subject matter.

A THEOLOGICAL ACCOUNT OF GRAMMAR

For Augustine the *signa* of the text mediate divine instruction. As such, the words of Scripture are laden with metaphysical weight when the subject matter, as properly identified in the various and sundry voices of Scripture, is God's own self and expressed will to redeem. Words mean something given the formal character of language in its phonetic and syntactical arrangement. But as George Steiner says, "A sentence always means more."[25] As Steiner, with his own Augustinian hermeneutical instincts engaged, warns, "The absolute decisive failing occurs when such approaches seek to formalize *meaning*, when they proceed upward from the phonetic, the lexical and the grammatic to the semantic and aesthetic."[26] Why, we might ask Steiner, is this a problem? He answers, "There is always, as Blake taught, 'excess' of the signified beyond the signifier."[27]

---

24. Francis I. Andersen and David Noel Freedman, *Micah: A New Translation with Introduction and Commentary* (New Haven: Yale University Press, 2000), 468.

25. George Steiner, *Real Presences* (Chicago: University of Chicago Press, 1989), 82.

26. Ibid, 81. Similarly, Michael Polanyi claims, "Much less can we control in advance the myriads of arrangements in which nouns, adjectives, verbs, and adverbs can be meaningfully combined to form new affirmations or questions, thus developing, as we shall see, the meaning of the words themselves ever further in these new contexts. Verbal speculation may therefore reveal an inexhaustible fund of true knowledge and new substantial problems, just as it may also produce pieces of mere sophistry" (*Personal Knowledge: Towards a Post-Critical Philosophy* [Chicago: University of Chicago Press, 2015], 94–95).

27. Steiner, *Real Presences*, 84. Steiner's metaphysical understanding of the semantic potential of words relates to Origen's understanding of figures in the Old Testament and the two-fold potential of words. Word have their basic referent (the literal) but are also symbolic of some other referent—literal and allegorical interpretation. See Peter Martens, *Origen and Scripture: The Contours of the Exegetical Life* (Oxford: Oxford University Press, 2012), 66. See Erich Auerbach, "Figura," in *Selected Essays of Erich Auerbach: Time, History, and Literature*, ed. J. I. Porter, trans. J. O. Newman (Princeton: Princeton University Press, 2014): "Even if Augustine decisively rejects abstract allegorical spiritualism and develops his entire interpretation of the Old Testament out of its concrete reality in worldly historical time, he nevertheless continues to endorse a kind of idealism that removes the concrete event from time as *figura*—even though it also remains entirely real—and places it into the perspective of timeless eternity. Such ideas were implicit in the very fact of the incarnation" (p. 88).

How much more so when the signified is God in his triune processions and missions? Such a confession releases the philological clutch, allowing words in their given morphological and syntactic form a fuller frame of reference when the associated field-mapping brought to bear in textual analysis is the God Christians confess as triune. *He is before all things*, Paul reminds.

Such a theological account of biblical language seeks to do justice to Scripture's literal sense and its ability to swell into the subject matter of Scripture's referent, namely, the triune God's procession and mission—the theological field-map for the terrain of Scripture. It also resists an anemic linguistic approach to biblical language by minimizing the potential referent to the hermetic moment of original utterance or writing (the distinction between the two is itself an interesting thought experiment regarding the canonical intentionality of language once embedded in particular books and quarters of the canon). Such a move cuts the Gordian knot that separates sign and reality, or scriptural language and its divine subject matter.

A Trinitarian hermeneutic resists a sclerotic tendency to leave language in the past, unencumbered by the metaphysical underpinnings of language in general and biblical language in particular. Can Micah 5:2(1) be read in different ways than the traditional reading that links it to the eternal generation of the son? Certainly. But given the subject matter of Scripture and its canonical function as a continued means by which the Father reveals himself in the Son by the Spirit, must it be read in an overly historicist fashion? Not if the text of Micah 5:2(1) and the New Testament canon share in the same triune subject matter. For his processions are indeed from eternity.

CHAPTER 4

JOHN 5:26: *Crux Interpretum* for Eternal Generation

D. A. CARSON

WE ARE NOT THE FIRST GENERATION to reflect on this text and this theme, of course. From the patristic period on, the theological rubric under which the Father–Son relationship within the Trinity has been commonly discussed is the eternal generation of the Son. Certain biblical words, texts, and themes have often been adduced in support of this doctrine, and of what it is said to bring to the doctrine of the Trinity. In this chapter, I shall focus on John 5:26 before briefly integrating other bits of evidence into the discussion, all in the hope of engaging some contemporary Trinitarian debates.

THE INTERPRETATION OF JOHN 5:26

"For as the Father has life in himself, so he has granted the Son also to have life in himself."[1] If the clause "the Father has life in himself" refers to God's independence and self-existence—that is, the Father, unlike everything in the created order, is dependent on no one and nothing for his life, because he has "life-in-himself"—then the passage is more than a little strange. If it said that just as the Father has life in himself, so the Son also has life in himself, this would be an extraordinarily strong affirmation of the Son's deity, his unqualified equality with God. On the other hand, it would suggest the Son is a second God. What would be affirmed is a form of ditheism. Alternatively, if the text said that just as the Father has life in himself, so he has granted the Son to have life, the logic of the passage would remain less

---

1. Unless otherwise indicated, the English Bible cited in this chapter is NIV 2011.

79

than straightforward, because the exact force of "just as" would be less than transparent (a point to which I shall return), but in any case the Son would be diminished: he would no longer be said to be on a par with God. The life the Son would enjoy, under such a reading of the passage, would not be the life of independence and self-existence, but derived life received at a concrete moment. In reality, the wording of our passage makes its interpretation very difficult: "For as the Father has life in himself, *so he has granted* (ἔδωκεν) the Son also to have life in himself." If it is a "grant" or a gift, how is it "life in himself," that is, self-existent life? If the Son has such life-in-himself, how can it be said to have been received as a grant or a gift from the Father?

Although scholars have advanced many subtle interpretations of this text, in the end there are three that control the discussion. *First*, probably a majority of biblical scholars today deny that "life in himself" has anything to do with divine self-existence. That stance is well represented by J. Ramsey Michaels, who argues that this passage has nothing to do with God's self-existence and therefore nothing to do with the eternal generation of the Son.[2] What the Father has is ζωὴν ἐν ἑαυτῷ; what he grants the Son is ζωὴν ἐν ἑαυτῷ. But what does that expression mean? In the bread of life discourse, Michaels points out, Jesus tells his hearers that unless they eat his flesh and drink his blood they cannot enjoy ζωὴν ἐν ἑαυτοῖς (6:53). This surely does not mean "self-existent life" or the like; indeed, the parallel in the next verse is ζωὴν αἰώνιον. In other words, the "life-in-oneself" expression does not in John 6 refer to self-existent life but to the eternal life that the believer receives from Christ. So on Michaels's showing, the Father has life, the Father grants life to the Son, and the Son grants life to believers (cf. 6:57). This does not affirm the eternal generation of the Son any more than the eternal life granted to believers indicates that they have been eternally generated. On this showing, there is no hint of the unique eternal generation of the Son in 5:26.

Of course, for Michaels to be right in his understanding of John 5:26 would require that the expression ἐν ἑαυτοῖς in reference to the life of believers must have exactly the same force as ἐν ἑαυτῷ in reference to the life of God and of the Son—a kind of *terminus technicus*. But we must ask if that is the most likely reading.

Marianne Meye Thompson's commentary is similar, but hints at the differences between what "life in him" might mean for God, for Jesus, and for believers:

---

2. Michaels, *The Gospel of John* (Grand Rapids: Eerdmans, 2010), 318.

JOHN 5:26

In the statement "Even as the Father has life in himself, so he has granted the Son to have life in himself" (5:26), we find the epitome of John's Christology. God, the living Father, has no prior and external cause; now the Son is similarly said to "have life in himself." The Son has life as God does, but he has it because God has granted (or, "given," *edōken*) it to him. The first formulation ("life in himself") points to independence; the second formulation ("for the Father has granted him") points to dependence. The Father gives his own kind of life to the Son; the Son in turn gives life to the world.[3]

Thus, applied to God, "life in himself" signals "independence," but the same expression cannot be read the same way with respect to the Son, precisely because that life has been "granted" to him, and the Son in turn gives life to the world. So the tension has been deftly removed, and there is little ground for the patristic developments that tie this passage to the eternal generation of the Son. As Raymond Brown puts it, "The common possession of life by Father and Son was used in patristic times as an anti-Arian argument. However, 'life' here does not refer primarily to the internal life of the Trinity, but to a creative life-giving power exercised toward men."[4]

Second, some commentators tightly tie "life in himself" used of God to "life in himself" used of Jesus, and differentiate that reality from any notion of "life" experienced by believers. Rudolf Bultmann observes that both the Father and the Son raise the dead and give life: that is, "the Revealer is identified with God," and a similar identification takes place in v. 26. "ζωὴν ἔχειν can, of course, also be said of men who believe; but the latter have life 'in him' [3:16; 20:31; cf. 16:33], while God and the Revealer have life 'in themselves.'" In other words, "They [i.e., the Father and the Son] possess the creative power of life; whereas the ζωή which man can enjoy is the kind of life proper to the creature."[5] The sense of identity that Bultmann finds between God and Jesus the Revealer is very strong: "In a certain sense v. 26 goes a step further behind the statement in v. 21, and so gives grounds for it: the Son exercises the office of Judge because he shares the divine nature."[6] But Bultmann feels under no constraint to explain how

---

3. Marianne Meye Thompson, *John: A Commentary* (Louisville: Westminster John Knox, 2015), 130.
4. Raymond E. Brown, *The Gospel According to John I–XII* (New York: Doubleday, 1966), 251.
5. Rudolf Bultmann, *The Gospel of John* (Oxford: Blackwell, 1971), 260. Somewhat similarly, George R. Beasley-Murray, *John*, 2nd ed. (Nashville: Thomas Nelson, 1999), 77.
6. Bultmann, *John*, 260.

this "sharing" of the "divine nature" (since it can be said that the Father has "life in himself" and that the Son has "life in himself") is to be squared with the notion that in the case of the Son, but obviously not the Father, it was something given to him. Thus what Bultmann means by Jesus sharing the "divine nature" does not seem to include eternality.

Third, the reference to the Father's "life in himself" is, in this context, that life that God alone experiences. It is bound up with his divine nature, his independence, his self-existence. The same "life in himself" is possessed by the Son, who shares the Father's divine nature, independence, and self-existence. And yet John's Gospel tells us that the Father granted to the Son to have this life in himself. How can both perspectives be simultaneously true?

The best response remains that adopted by Augustine and other fathers of the church: this is an eternal grant.[7] It is not as if there was a moment when God granted to the Son to have life in himself, before which the Son did not have life in himself. If such were the case, then whatever it was that the Son was granted could not have been divine, independent, self-existent life. In other words, this grant does not establish a certain time in chronological sequence when the grant took place; rather, if it is an eternal grant, it establishes the nature of the Father–Son relationship. In short, this is a way of establishing the eternal generation of the Son.

The Reformers tended to adopt a similar interpretation.[8] The assumption that this is the faithful and orthodox interpretation of the passage continues to surface at the end of the nineteenth century in the recently discovered and incomplete commentary on John by J. B. Lightfoot. Lightfoot's total preserved comment on John 5:26 reads, "ζωὴν ἔχειν ἐν ἑαυτῷ compared to ἔδωκεν αὐτῷ expresses the whole doctrine of the Person of Christ, derived from and yet subservient to the Logos doctrine, the eternal generation of the Son."[9]

---

7. Augustine, *Trin.* 1.5.26; 1.5.30; 2.2.3; cf. also Ambrose, *On the Christian Faith* 3.16.133 (*NPNF²* 10:261); Hilary of Poitiers, *De trinitate* 7.27 (*NPNF²* 9:130).

8. Cf. Aegidius Hunnius, *Commentarius in Joannem*, 336–37, trans. Craig S. Farmer, in *John 1–12*, Reformation Commentary on Scripture (Downers Grove, IL: InterVarsity, 2014), 178: "In two ways the Father gives to the Son to have life in himself. First, by the eternal, ineffable generation through which he essentially shared with the Son all his life, divinity, essence, majesty, power and glory. . . . Second, he gave to the Son this same life or power to make alive at the 'fullness of time,' when he assumed that human nature." On Calvin's development of patristic Christology, see the superb volume by Brannon Ellis, *Calvin, Classical Trinitarianism, and the Aseity of the Son* (Oxford: Oxford University Press, 2012).

9. J. B. Lightfoot, *The Gospel of St. John: A Newly Discovered Commentary*, ed. Ben Witherington III and Todd D. Still (Downers Grove, IL: InterVarsity, 2015), 146.

JOHN 5:26

ADJUDICATION

How shall we adjudicate among these three major interpretations of John 5:26? We must begin by reflecting on the immediate context of the verse.

(1) Both Jesus's healing of the man who had been paralyzed for thirty-eight years (5:1–9) and his instruction to the man to pick up his mat and go (5:8–13), taking place as they do on the Sabbath, arouse the sensitivities of the Jewish leaders regarding Sabbath observance (5:16).[10] Jesus might have replied by inviting his interlocutors to engage in halakhic discussion, but instead he defends himself, here as often in the Gospels, by making a christological claim: "My Father is always at his work to this very day, and I too am working" (5:17). The Jewish leaders take this as a blasphemous claim. In their view, Jesus is "even calling God his own Father, making himself equal with God" (5:18). From the perspective of the Fourth Evangelist, Jesus's opponents are curiously right and wrong: Jesus *does* make himself equal with God, but they imagine that he is doing so in such a way as to claim to be an alternative God, a second God. What they have in mind is apparently ditheism, and this side of the exile they are painfully aware that God stands implacably opposed to all forms of polytheism, including ditheism. As they see it, monotheism is being challenged before their eyes, and they are enraged.

(2) But what Jesus has in mind is rather different. The following verses (5:19–30) find Jesus articulating and defending what would become in time the distinctively *Christian* understanding of monotheism. Jesus most emphatically insists that he is not a separate deity, an independent deity—far from it. He insists that "the Son can do nothing by himself; he can do only what he sees his Father doing" (5:19). Here is dependence of the most thorough kind, a form of subordination (there is certainly no reciprocity in the relationship)—yet it immediately turns out to be a subordination carefully qualified. The Son can do only what he sees his Father doing, we are told, "because whatever the Father does the Son also does" (5:19).

Two elements in this clause are striking. (a) The Son's activities are co-extensive with those of the Father. Has the Father created all things? So also has the Son, as God's Word—God's own agent in creation (1:1–5). Is it the Father's prerogative to give resurrection life, raise the dead, and exercise final judgment? So also is it the prerogative of the Son (5:24–30).

---

10. It is well known that οἱ Ἰουδαῖοι in John's Gospel has a variety of referents, depending on the context: all Jews, Jews of Judea (i.e., Judeans), Jewish leaders, and yet other options. As such variations have little effect on the interpretation of our passage, I shall opt for whatever English equivalent seems best to me, without pausing to argue the case.

83

This co-extensiveness of the activities of the Father and the Son is expressed in functional categories: they both *do* the same things. Nevertheless, it is difficult not to perceive some ontological implications behind the descriptions of common function.

(b) The word "because" (γάρ) demands explanation. In what way does the truth that "whatever the Father does the Son also does" provide the ground or the explanation (surely the force of γάρ in this context) of the truth that the Son "can do only what he sees his Father doing"? The second clause explains the first, on the assumption that the Son sees *everything* that the Father does, *for* "whatever the Father does the Son also does." Once again we have the sweeping coextensiveness of the actions of the Father and the Son coupled with the utter dependence of the Son upon the Father in the discharge of those coextensive actions. In fact, this γάρ-clause at the end of verse 19 is succeeded by three more γάρ-clauses, each one grounding or explaining what immediately precedes it, all four of these clauses having a bearing on our discussion. Observe the sequence of these four "for" clauses. The first, at the end of verse 19, asserts that the Son can do only what he sees the Father doing, *for* "whatever the Father does, the Son also does"—*for* "the Father loves the Son and shows him all he does" (v. 20), which grounds the coextensiveness of the actions of Father and Son in the Father's love for the Son. (In passing, note that the Father's love for the Son is demonstrated in his placing everything in the hands of the Son, 3:35, or, as here, in his "showing" all he does to the Son so that the Son may do exactly the same things. By contrast, the Son's love for the Father is demonstrated in his perfect obedience to the Father, 14:31.) There is more the Father "shows" the Son so that the Son may carry out his Father's will and amaze the disciples (5:20), *for* "just as the Father raises the dead and gives them life, even so the Son gives life to whom he is pleased to give it" (5:21): the raising of the dead, accomplished by Father and Son alike, grounds the promise that more is coming, enough to amaze Jesus's disciples. *For* "the Father judges no one, but has entrusted all judgment to the Son" (5:22)—that is, the Son exercises judgment and raises the dead precisely because the Father has entrusted such work to him (5:22).

In short, Jesus both repudiates and accepts the charge that he makes himself equal with God (5:18): he repudiates it in that he strenuously avoids any suggestion that he is an independent God, a second God, or an alternative God, since all that he does is utterly dependent on the Father; and he accepts the charge that he makes himself equal with God in that whatever the Father does he also does, to the end that he should receive the same

JOHN 5:26

glory as the Father. In other words, the flow of the argument sounds very much like an unpacking of the traditional interpretation of 5:24.

(3) Some thought must be devoted to the ὥσπερ . . . οὕτως ("as . . . so") construction in John 5:26. The comparison cannot be between two "givings," as if the Father and the Son each gives "life in himself" to the other. Rather, the construction ensures that whatever "life in himself" means in the Father's existence, it means the same thing in the Son's existence. The parallel is so tight that it would be difficult to avoid suspicion of ditheism were it not for the assertion that the Father has given this to the Son. "This means that if we are to understand the kind of life that the Son has, we must look to the kind of life the Father has."[11]

(4) This block of material (5:19–30) continues with the same tension voiced in various ways: the tension between, on the one hand, coextensive action and existence between the Father and the Son, and, on the other, the assertion of the utter dependence of the Son on the Father. On the one hand, the Father gives the authority to act as final judge to the Son (5:27), and the Son's judgment on the last day is never independent of the Father's will, for the Son never seeks to please himself but only the one who sent him (5:30; cf. 8:16). On the other hand, one of the reasons why the Father has entrusted all judgment to the Son is precisely so "that all my honor the Son just as they honor the Father. Whoever does not honor the Son does not honor the Father, who sent him" (5:23).

To summarize, the context of 5:26 describes what God alone does, yet insists that the Son does it, too. This can be cast in universal terms ("*whatever* the Father does the Son also does," 5:19, and thus can include things mentioned elsewhere, such as creation) or in the specifics of particular actions that only God can do (exercise final judgment; raise the dead on the last day). In such a context, the "life in himself" terminology of John 5:26 is likely referring to what is exclusively God's: namely, what we call self-existent life, life that God has because he is God and dependent on no one and nothing, life that is his before creation. If *such* life is "granted" to the Son, the conclusion of Augustine—that this is an eternal grant—is the only one that makes sense of the text.

(5) This interpretation is readily supported by an array of texts in John that depict the Son coming from the Father and the like—texts to which Augustine readily appealed. The same pattern of tension between bold

---

11. Michael J. Ovey, *Your Will Be Done: Exploring Eternal Subordination, Divine Monarchy and Divine Humility* (London: Latimer Trust, 2016), 84.

D. A. CARSON

affirmations of the Son's deity and unapologetic affirmations of the Son's dependence upon and submission to his Father permeates the entire Gospel. On the one hand, the Word that becomes flesh is in fact God (1:1, 14), and can affirm, "Before Abraham was born, I am" (8:58)—apparently more than a claim of mere preexistence. This same Jesus unhesitatingly tells his followers, "Anyone who has seen me has seen the Father" (14:9). After Jesus's resurrection, Thomas's confession, "My Lord and my God" (20:28), far from being rebuked, is something Jesus approves. On the other hand, the dependence of Jesus upon his Father, and his submission to his Father, surface not only here in John 5:19–30 but in 8:29 ("The one who sent me is with me; he has not left me alone, for I always do what pleases him") and in 14:31 (the world must learn "that I love the Father and do exactly what my Father has commanded me").[12] None of these pairings is reciprocal. It makes most contextual sense to read our text, John 5:26, as comfortably nestling within this larger Johannine matrix.

(6) "Son" terminology in the Bible is remarkably rich and diverse. Even if we restrict our focus from "son" to "son of God" (excluding, for example, "son of Man," "son of David," "son of Belial" and a host of other "son"-expressions that don't make it through the barrier of translation into English), we soon discover that "son of God" can refer to angels (even fallen angels), the first human being, the people of Israel collectively, individual Israelites, the Davidic king, and individual Christians—as well as to Jesus. And when the expression *does* refer to him, it can refer to him as the Son of God by virtue of his role as the true Israel, or it can refer to him as the Son of God by virtue of his role as the ultimate Davidic, messianic king, without any necessary eternal and "Trinitarian" association. Indeed, a few have argued that sonship terminology is suitably applied only to the human existence of the Second Person of the Godhead—that is, "Father, Son, and Holy Spirit" are terms appropriately applicable only to the economic Trinity. Yet "son" is clearly sometimes attested in Scripture to refer to the Son *before* he becomes a human being: for example, God sends his Son into the world (John 3:17). The text does not mean to say that God sends the one who would become his Son into the world. That immediately raises the question of how we are to understand Father–Son language applied to the immanent Trinity.[13]

---

12. Other examples in John's Gospel where Jesus unilaterally submits to his Father include 6:38; 7:16, 28; 10:29; 12:49–50; 14:28; 17:4; 20:17. Cf. the discussion of Randy Rheaume, "John's Jesus on Life Support: His Filial Relationship in John 5:26 and 6:57," *TrinJ* 33 (2012): 49–75.

13. I have discussed many of these things at greater length in my *Jesus the Son of God: A Christological Title Often Overlooked, Sometimes Misunderstood, and Currently Disputed* (Wheaton, IL: Crossway, 2012).

JOHN 5:26

Unlike other New Testament writers, John reserves ὁ υἱός for Jesus; his followers are τὰ τέκνα τοῦ θεοῦ or the like. Other New Testament writers have other ways of distinguishing the sonship of Jesus from the sonship of believers (in Paul, for example, only the latter are sons "by adoption"), but John's way of doing so brings sharp focus on the word "son." The eternal Word, who was with God and who was God from the beginning (John 1:1), is clearly designated the Son of God, not the Brother of God, still less the Cousin of God—the biblical authors display considerably more discipline than in William P. Young's fanciful depiction of the Trinity in *The Shack*. In other words, "Son" language tied to "Father" language is one of the unavoidable hints that the relationship between the "Father" and the "Son" is rightly conceived of in terms of generation—indeed, of eternal generation. More broadly, of course, the Fathers spoke of the generation of the Son and the procession of the Spirit, fastening on specific Johannine words. Augustine's stress on "not three brothers" remains vital not only for our reflection on the biblical data themselves but also for our attempts at Trinitarian formulation. To obliterate biblical distinctives among the persons of the Godhead "may create individuations [among] the Persons that are our inventions."[14] Hilary rightly perceives that John 5:26 is crucial in combating Arianism because it affirms that both the Father and the Son have the same kind of life.[15] To understand what kind of life the Son enjoys, one need only study the life of the Father. As different as Arianism and Sabellianism may be, both heresies have this in common: they both deny the true sonship of the Son, as Hilary saw. The former teaches that he is a creature rather than a son; the latter teaches that he is the same person as the Father and therefore not a genuine son.[16] The eternal generation of the Son, rightly understood, effectively rebuts both heresies.

(7) Some writers, both ancient and modern, focus on the word μονογενής. God so loved the world that he gave τὸν υἱὸν τὸν μονογενῆ (John 3:16), translated, in the KJV, "his only-begotten Son." Most contemporary English-language translations render the expression "his only Son" or "his one and only Son" or "his unique Son." Etymologically, the former in effect read μονογενής as deriving from μόνος + γεννάω, and the latter read μονογενής as deriving from μόνος + γένος. Of course, nowadays we all know that etymology is a horribly unreliable way to determine the meaning of words, best reserved for rare words that show up so infrequently we have

---

14. This is a comment by the late Mike Ovey in a personal communication, dated April 12, 2014.
15. Hilary, *De trinitate* 2.11.
16. Ibid., 1.16–17.

too few contexts to help determine their meaning. Across the centuries the common understanding of μονογενής (and of its Latin equivalents, *unicus filius* or *unigenitus*; Jerome opted for the latter in the five Johannine occurrences) was that it meant "only begotten," that is, in a biological sense, "without a sibling," with various extensions in meaning. This consensus was powerfully challenged by Dale Moody in an article published in 1953,[17] supported by Longenecker and others.[18] The new consensus dispensed with "only begotten," opting for "only," "unique," or "one and only," and swept along the overwhelming majority of New Testament scholars, myself included.

One of the things that convinced us was that the New Testament, quite apart from extrabiblical sources, provides one instance where the meaning simply *cannot* be "only begotten": in Hebrews 11:17, the author tells us that Abraham was about to sacrifice τὸν μονογενῆ—that is, "his one and only [son]." Isaac certainly wasn't Abraham's "only begotten" son: Abraham was also the father of Ishmael and became the father of a packet of progeny by Keturah (Gen 25:1–2). But Isaac was Abraham's unique son, his only-one-of-a-kind son. Of course, the precise meaning of words can change with context, so the fact that this *must* be the meaning in Hebrews 11:17 does not establish that the word must have the same meaning in, say, John 3:16, or in the four other instances in the Johannine writings where Jesus is referred to as the μονογενής (1:14, 18; 3:18; 1 John 4:9). What we *can* say from the use of μονογενής in Hebrews 11:17 is that it is seriously mistaken to hold that μονογενής *must* mean only begotten in any particular passage. Like many others, I was inclined to think that μονογενής never means more than "one and only" or "unique" anywhere in John, whatever it might mean elsewhere.

But now an important series of excellent papers by Charles Lee Irons has challenged the modern consensus and urged us to return to the rendering "only begotten." This represents one of the best parts of a flurry of hundreds of exchanges on the Trinity that have lit up the digital world during the last couple of years.[19] Irons's five digital papers[20] are especially strong in

---

17. Moody, "God's Only Son: The Translation of John 3:16 in the Revised Standard Version," *JBL* 72 (1953): 213–19. The RSV committee had opted for "only" in the light of the unpublished Ph.D. dissertation by Francis Marion Warden, "ΜΟΝΟΓΕΝΗΣ in the Johannine Literature" (Southern Baptist Theological Seminary, 1938). It is important to recognize that this understanding of the word was anticipated by Westcott, who argued for "unique, only one of its kind": see Brooke Foss Westcott, *The Epistles of St. John* (Cambridge and London: Macmillan, 1886), 169–72.

18. Richard N. Longenecker, "The One and Only Son," in *The NIV: The Making of a Contemporary Translation*, ed. Kenneth Barker (Grand Rapids: Zondervan, 1986), 119–26.

19. The most comprehensive list of these exchanges, as far as I know, is being tracked by Books at a Glance: see their "Twenty-sixth Updated Edition of the Trinity Debate Bibliography" at http://www.booksataglance.com/blog/twenty-sixth-updated-edition-trinity-debate-bibliography/.

20. Not to mention his contribution to this volume, which, at this writing, I have not seen.

JOHN 5:26

their survey of the uses gathered from TLG across several centuries: if Irons is right to assert that "only begotten" is the most common meaning of the Greek word when a responsible synchronic study is undertaken, the default assumption ought to rest with the older interpretation, not with the modern consensus. Nevertheless, three observations might not be out of place.

First, Irons himself (unlike some of his supporters and cheerleaders) is careful to say, "My claim is not that *monogenes* always means 'only begotten' and never means 'only one of its kind' in biblical and extrabiblical Greek." I confess that "only" seems to be a perfectly adequate understanding of μονογενής in such passages as Luke 7:12; 8:42; and 9:38.

Second, even if μονογενής really should be rendered "only begotten" in all five of its Johannine occurrences, a reasonable conclusion, by itself that would not establish the *eternal* generation of the Son but only the *unique* generation of the Son. "The ancient Arians were very ready to call the Son ὁ μονογενὴς θεός; this appellation, in their view, happily distinguished him from the Father, who alone was God in the highest sense, as unbegotten, uncaused, and without beginning."[21] The Arian Eunomius, according to Gregory of Nyssa, appealed to the "only begotten" label as part of the evidence that shows the Son is not divine, for God alone is "ungenerate" (*Expositio Fidei*, c. AD 383).[22] The point is that both the Arians and the orthodox appealed to the "only begotten" understanding of μονογενής but came away with diametrically opposed conclusions.[23] In other words, even if someone holds that, on balance of probabilities, μονογενής in John means "only begotten," one must recognize that the expression itself is an exceedingly weak reed to support the *eternal* generation of the Son. It needs the support of John 5:26 and other passages. Conversely, if it were decided that μονογενής in its Johannine occurrences is best rendered by "one and only" or the like, it would not rule out the generation of the Son. "It is fundamentally misguided to move from isolated exegetical discoveries, such as *monogenes* in texts like John 1:18 not necessarily denoting 'begotten,' toward denying eternal generation."[24]

Third, it must be said that Irons's treatment of Hebrews 11:17, referenced above, is less than satisfactory. He points to the passage where Josephus

---

All my references to his work are drawn from his digital contributions.

21. Ezra Abbot, *The Authorship of the Fourth Gospel and Other Critical Essays* (Boston: George H. Ellis, 1888), 285.

22. Gregory of Nyssa, *Answer to Eunomius' Second Book*, in NPNF[2] 5:252–55.

23. On Athanasius's response to the Arians on this and related matters, see the treatment by Peter J. Leithart, *Athanasius* (Grand Rapids: Baker Academic, 2011).

24. Daniel J. Treier, "Incarnation," in *Christian Dogmatics: Reformed Theology for the Church Catholic*, ed. Michael Allen and Scott R. Swain (Grand Rapids: Baker Academic, 2016), 228.

explains the love of Monobazus for one of his sons: "He had an elder son by Helene . . . and other children by his other wives; but it was clear that all his favour was concentrated on Izates *as if* he were an only child (ὡς εἰς μονογενῆ)."[25] Irons, then, argues that in a similar way Hebrews 11:17 presents Isaac *as if* he were the only begotten son, since in Genesis 21:10–12 Abraham, compelled by Sarah, disowns Ishmael. But this really will not do. The passage in Josephus deploys ὡς (rendered "as if," above); Hebrews 11:17 has no similar construction. More importantly, Abraham sired not only Ishmael and Isaac but several others by Keturah (Gen 25:1–2), as we have seen. Hebrews 11:17 makes perfectly good sense if it is *not* saying that Isaac was the "only begotten" son but the unique son, the son of promise, the son of the covenant.

To summarize, the recent work of Irons is important and thought-provoking and may in time change some "default" assumptions about the meaning of μονογενής, but like all ground-breaking work, it needs further testing. His actual exegesis of the five Johannine passages that deploy the word (which I do not have space to discuss) calls for careful and respectful probing. Under the most optimistic reading of his work, the restoration of the meaning "only begotten" drives reflection on the generation of the Son, but not, by itself, on the *eternal* generation of the Son. It may thus provide tacit confirmation of a doctrine established on other grounds, but it cannot itself establish the doctrine.

FURTHER EVIDENCE AND REFLECTIONS

The following points either support the interpretation of John 5:26 offered in this chapter or provide some theological reflection flowing out of that interpretation.

(1) Numerous biblical scholars and theologians have gathered other biblical passages together, not least drawn from John's Gospel, that are said to support the eternal generation of the Son.[26] There is no space to survey their work here, except for a couple of representative instances.

(2) Many point to the prologue of Hebrews. In these last days, the writer avers, God has spoken to us ἐν υἱῷ (1:2)—this Son who is immediately described as "the radiance of God's glory and the exact representation of his

---

25. Josephus, *Ant.* 20.20 (emphasis added by Irons).
26. E.g., Keith E. Johnson, "Augustine, Eternal Generation, and Evangelical Trinitarianism," *TrinJ* 32 (2011): 141–63.

JOHN 5:26

being" (1:3).[27] The Son, as it were, is the shining of the Father's shining. Even though this imagery is not immediately tied to notions of generation, nevertheless the passage is pretty compelling as a picture where Son-language is used, where, as it were, both God and the Son shine, where nevertheless the Son's shining is somehow derived from the Father's shining, and where, in context, the Son, as also the Word in John's prologue, is one with God in creation.

(3) Some church fathers, not least Augustine, point to Psalm 2:7 as a place where the eternal generation of the Son is affirmed. Here God says to the Davidic king, "You are my son; today I have become your father." This interpretation is a misreading of the passage. For this verse to support the weight of the eternal generation of the Son, the "today" would have to be an eternal "today." This is most unlikely. The imagery used here is first established at the time of God's establishment of the Davidic dynasty (2 Sam 7:14), when God announces, with respect to Solomon, "I will be his father, and he will be my son." As I have argued elsewhere, "sonship" is often a functional category in Scripture.[28] Insofar as one makes peace, for instance, one is acting like God the supreme peacemaker, so along the axis of peacemaking one shows oneself to be a son of God (like Jesus in the beatitudes, Matt 5:9). Again, insofar as one tells lies and kills, so along the axis of lies and murder one shows oneself to be a son of the devil, who has been a murderer and a liar from the beginning (John 8:44). Similarly, when a Davidide becomes king, he is to act like the King *par excellence*, God himself. Ideally, the Davidide reigns with justice and integrity, defending the covenant and protecting the people, thereby showing himself along the axis of kingship to be a son of God. So also in Psalm 2:6: the day when God says, "I have installed my king on Zion, my holy mountain" (2:6a), labelled "the LORD's decree," is the day when the Davidide steps up to the throne. God pronounces, "You are my son; today I have become your father." In other words, in this context the "son of God" terminology is connected with the ascension of a particular Davidide to the throne; it is not obviously being used in the same way as in John 3:17 or Hebrews 1:2. Elsewhere I have argued that in Hebrews 1:5ff., the sonship terminology, including the citation of both Psalm 2:7 and 2 Samuel 7:14 in verse 5, makes reference to the Davidic kingship. Yet at the same time, the sonship terminology in verse 2, which cannot be said to focus on Davidic kingship but

---

27. See Scott Swain, "The Radiance of the Father's Glory: The Hermeneutical Basis of the Doctrine of Eternal Generation," ETS paper, November 21, 2013.

28. Carson, *Jesus the Son of God*.

has overtones of the eternal generation of the Son, is certainly referring to the same person as the sonship terminology in verse 5; probably the two different meanings of "son" are intentionally confused, or better, merged. But I remain unpersuaded that Psalm 2:6 itself can be said to support, exegetically, the eternal generation of the Son.

(4) Note carefully how in the relationship between the Father and the Son, the relationship between command and obedience, plays out between sending and going, between showing and doing, and between standard and comparison: it is always in one direction, from the Father to the Son. In *none* of these cases is the action reciprocal. The Father sends the Son, and the Son goes, never the reverse. The Father loves the Son and insists that all must honor the Son as they honor the Father: the reverse standard is not argued. The Father demonstrates his love for the Son by "showing" the Son all he does, such that the Son does everything the Father does; nowhere do we read that the Son demonstrates his love for the Father by showing him all that the Son does, such that the Father does everything the Son does. In fact, the Son displays his love for the Father by obeying him perfectly; we are not told that the Father displays his love for the Son by a kind of reciprocal obedience. The Father entrusts all judgment to the Son, while of the Son we are told that he judges only as he hears, for he seeks not to please himself but rather him who sent him. Along exactly the same lines, our verse, John 5:26, asserts that as the Father has life in himself, so he has granted the Son also to have life in himself; it does not assert that as the Son has life in himself, so he has granted to the Father to have life in himself. The pattern is starkly persistent, unidirectional, without exception, and will not be denied. Indeed, although it is true that the doctrine of the eternal generation of the Son by the Father is designed not only to explain certain biblical passages, and within that framework to uphold the ontological equality of the Father and the Son, the raw fact remains that although the church has long confessed the eternal generation of the Son by the Father, it has nowhere confessed the eternal generation of the Father by the Son. For a start, this would be horrendously incongruous with the Father–Son terminology of Scripture.

(5) Without wanting in this chapter to enter the lists in the frequently heated debates between egalitarians and complementarians, nevertheless some of the issues raised by both sides in that controversy intersect with our exegesis of John 5:26, and therefore we cannot ignore them. We have observed that the eternal generation of the Son, expressed in John 5:26 (assuming our exegesis is correct), simultaneously preserves, indeed asserts,

JOHN 5:26

the full deity of the Son (measured not least by the fact that the actions of
the Father and the Son are coextensive and that the Son is to receive the
same honor as the Father) and the dependence of the Son upon the Father.
This dependence of the Son upon the Father is not a casual or indifferent
detail; it is intrinsically bound up with the very notion of eternal generation, which is not a reciprocal operation. The question then becomes:
Is there some measure of the Son's submission (subordination? obedience?)
to the Father that reaches back into preincarnation eternity? Or is such
terminology locked into the incarnation? Often the debate is cast in terms
of the relationships among the persons in the immanent Trinity versus the
relationships among the persons in the economic Trinity.[29] Is the appeal to a
headship distinction between God and Christ (1 Cor 11:3) restricted to the
Son in his incarnate state, or is there an "eternal functional subordination"
(inevitably abbreviated EFS) of the Son to the Father?

The lines are strongly drawn. On the one hand, Kevin Giles may be
taken as a representative of those who insist that the doctrine of the eternal
generation of the Son reflects subordination neither in the economic Trinity
nor in the immanent Trinity, neither in the incarnate Son nor in the preincarnate Son.[30] Whatever subordination is found in the incarnate Son is
restricted to his incarnate existence, and in any case is not enmeshed in his
eternal generation. For Giles, the *only* distinction between the Father and
the Son in the immanent Trinity has to do with their respective origins, not
with differences in authority, obedience, functional roles, or anything else.
To allow any exceptions is to jeopardize the full deity of the Son, which the
doctrine of the eternal generation of the Son was designed to defend, for,
according to Giles, it is unavoidably the case that all forms of subordination
presuppose some kind of inferiority. On the other hand, Randy Rheaume
may be taken as representative of those who insist that the biblical texts,
especially John's Gospel, consistently portray the Son both as the Father's
equal and as the Father's subordinate, both in time and in eternity, both in
the incarnation and in eternity past.[31] Between the polarities of these two
opinions, there are of course many variations, but to set out the polarities

---

29. As a way of setting the egalitarian/complementarian debate to one side, I should say that
the strongest biblical model for husband-wife relationships is the relationship between Christ and
his church (Eph 5) rather than the relationships among the persons of the Godhead (notwithstanding
1 Cor 11:3).

30. Kevin Giles, *The Eternal Generation of the Son: Maintaining Orthodoxy in Trinitarian Theology*
(Downers Grove, IL: IVP Academic, 2012).

31. Cf. Rheaume, "John's Jesus on Life Support"; Rheaume, *An Exegetical and Theological Analysis
of the Son's Relationship to the Father in John's Gospel: God's Equal and Subordinate* (Lewiston: Edwin
Mellen, 2014).

D. A. Carson

has the advantage of making clear not only what is at stake but what the fundamental issues are on which the polarized positions turn.

How, then, shall we think our way through the interaction of our exegesis of John 5:26 (and, implicitly, other texts supporting the eternal generation of the Son) with the issues of what we have (sometimes rather glibly) referred to as the Son's submission or dependence or subordination? Five reflections follow:

First, all sides ought to agree that one may distinguish certain personal properties among the persons: in particular, the Father's paternity (specifically, his unbegottenness), the Son's filiation (or generation), and the Spirit's procession. It is therefore appropriate to speak of a certain *taxis* in the immanent Trinity. Nicaea affirms that the only distinctions to be drawn among the eternal persons are their relations of origin: unbegotten Father, eternally begotten Son, and the eternally proceeding Holy Spirit; similarly, Augustine asserts that the divine persons *ad intra* are one in substance, distinguished only according to their relations of origin. But Augustine adds that the divine persons are also united *ad extra* (i.e., in their Trinitarian operations) even though they are distinguished in their operations in terms of their respective economic missions (viz., the sending of the Son and the Spirit), which missions in some sense reflect the immanent relations.[32] One recalls the influential assertion of Rahner, still debated, that the economic Trinity, the Trinity as God is revealed in redemptive history, *is* the immanent Trinity.[33] At the very least we must conclude that the immanent Trinity does not abolish or contradict itself in the outworking of the economic Trinity. "I believe that there is something about the persons of the Father, Son, and Spirit that made it *appropriate* for them to take on the economic roles they did. This does not involve ontological subordination."[34]

Second, not a few have drawn attention to the terminology and argumentation in 1 Corinthians 15:20–28.[35] All the Son's authority between his ascension and his return has been granted to him by his Father: it is a mediated authority. Christ "must reign until he has put all his enemies

---

32. Cf. the important discussion of Keith E. Johnson, "Trinitarian Agency and the Eternal Subordination of the Son: An Augustinian Perspective," in *The New Evangelical Subordinationism? Perspectives on the Equality of God the Father and God the Son*, ed. Dennis W. Jowers and H. Wayne House (Eugene: Pickwick, 2012), 108–32.

33. Karl Rahner, *The Trinity*, trans. J. Donceel (London: Burns and Oates, 1970), 22. Cf. Robert Shillaker, "Rahner's Axiom and the Hermeneutic Foundation of Thomas Weinandy's *Reconceiving the Trinity*," *EurJTheol* 25 (2016): 33–43.

34. John Frame, "John Frame on the Trinity," http://frame-poythress.org/john-frame-on-the-trinity/, accessed April 5, 2017.

35. See especially Craig S. Keener, "Subordination Within the Trinity: John 5:18 and 1 Cor 15:28," in *The New Evangelical Subordinationism?*, 39–58.

JOHN 5:26

under his feet" (15:25): all of God's authority is mediated through him (15:27; cf. also Matt 28:20). But once he has destroyed the last enemy, he "hands over the kingdom to God the Father" (1 Cor 15:24), and "then the Son himself will be made subject to him who put everything under him, so that God may be all in all" (15:28). The most natural reading of these verses is that the Son, the exalted God-man, remains, after the consummation, eternally subject to his Father, no longer the exclusive mediator of the Father's sovereignty—though the final clause, "so that God [not the 'Father'] may be all in all," lays the emphasis on (the Trinitarian) God. If being "made subject to" the Father does not entail some kind of intrinsic inferiority (which is at this juncture almost unthinkable), then why should any sort of functional submission among the persons of the Godhead be thought to entail ontological inferiority?

Third, John's Gospel asserts that the *Paraklētos*, variously designated "the Spirit" or "the Spirit of truth," will be sent or given by the Father (John 14:16, 26) or by Jesus (15:26)—"the Spirit of truth who goes out [proceedeth in the KJV, or ἐκπορεύεται] from the Father" (15:26). As in the case of the sending of the Son and in the generation of the Son, so in the case of the "sending" or the "procession" of the Spirit: there is a certain *taxis* that spills over into the Trinity's economic mission. What is worth pondering in the case of the Spirit, however, is that the obedience of the Spirit cannot be cast in terms of his human nature since he has no human nature: arguments relevant in the case of the incarnate Son cannot be relevant in the case of the Spirit, yet there is demonstrable *taxis*, with the Father (and the Son) sending or giving the Spirit and the Spirit going and being given. It is hard to know what can wisely be made of this observation, but the least that must be inferred is that within the Trinity, being at the "receiving" end of a relationship—the end that receives commands and obeys, the end that is commissioned to go and proceeds, the end that is sent, the end that is "shown" what the Father does and does the same thing—cannot be said to betray any sort of inferiority.

Fourth, why should this surprise us? In the light of the Jesus who insists that proper stances of rule are characterized less by authoritative rights and more by self-sacrificing service for the good of those ruled, in a way that leads directly to the cross (Matt 20:20–28), to discuss the relationships among the persons of the Godhead in terms of authority structures (as we have been taught by our culture to think of authority structures) might be hugely misleading. Clearly we are running into trouble with our terminology. It is difficult to read John's Gospel and avoid the language of the obedience of the Son, the language of his subordination to the Father; indeed, it is difficult to avoid such terminology of the Son within the immanent Trinity, as we have seen. If we review once again all the ways in which the Son in John's Gospel obeys, speaks as he is given words to say, comes and goes on the Father's command, performs the Father's will not only in coming into the world through the incarnation but also in going to the cross and in securing those whom the Father has given him, what term shall we use to describe his relation to the Father in all of its unidirectional obedience and dependence (another word on the edge of saying too much), if not subordination? Yet if in our culture "subordination" is corrupted by the tincture of inferiority, it is not a happy term to use. Again, if there is a certain *taxis* in the Trinity, then in some highly qualified ways it may not be inappropriate to speak of the obedience and subordination of the Son even while we robustly insist that he is in no way inferior to his Father in essence, glory, power, majesty, perfections, and holiness, which of course is what the eternal generation of the Son is designed to protect while still depicting him as the *Son* of God.[36] Indeed, John 5:26 celebrates that the Son has the same "life in himself" as the Father, which implicitly denies dependence and contingency, at least in the immanent Trinity, while the same verse in making such "life in himself" an eternal grant surely bespeaks some kind of dependence, however carefully we wish to guard the expression. Or is part of the problem that we know too little about eternity, with the result that while we read John 5:26 and blithely affirm that "life in himself" is an eternal grant made by the Father to the Son, although we have very little idea of what "eternal grant" means?[37]

---

36. See the thoughtful explorations of Scott R. Swain and Michael Allen, "The Obedience of the Eternal Son: Catholic Trinitarianism and Reformed Christology," in *Christology Ancient and Modern: Explorations in Constructive Dogmatics*, ed. Oliver D. Crisp and Fred Sanders (Grand Rapids: Zondervan, 2013), 74–95. To begin to deal with this more adequately, it would be necessary to double the length of this chapter and explore what John's Gospel might contribute to debates about Monarchianism and the monothelite/dyothelite controversy. For competent introductions to the topic, which adopt somewhat different conclusions, see D. Glenn Butner Jr., "Eternal Functional Subordination and the Problem of the Divine Will," *JETS* 58 (2015): 131–49; and Michael J. Ovey, *Your Will Be Done*. The classical understanding is that while Jesus Christ the incarnate Son of God had two wills (the two wills tied respectively to the divine and human natures of the incarnate Son, united by the hypostatic union in one person; monothelitism was formally condemned in the Council of Constantinople in 680), nevertheless in eternity past the persons of the Godhead exercised one will only, for otherwise God's rule would be in some sense divided (hence the connection with discussions over Monarchianism). For a summary of the historical developments in brief compass, including the important role played by Maximus the Confessor, see Gerald Bray, *God Has Spoken: A History of Christian Theology* (Wheaton, IL: Crossway, 2014), 384–93. Yet here too our overly crisp definitions are in danger of domesticating contributing evidence. The one will of the triune God in eternity past must be articulated in such a way that allowance is made, for example, for the fact that the Father loves the Son and the Son loves the Father.

37. Cf. Scott R. Swain, "The Mystery of the Trinity," 195: "Eternal Generation is not something our minds can comprehend, so determined is our thinking by the categories of time and finitude.

JOHN 5:26

In short, even though we affirm that the doctrine of the Trinity is warranted by Scripture and rightly affirmed in the ecumenical creeds, it remains, at numerous junctures, impenetrably mysterious, at many points beyond our comprehension. All of us must own that Scripture gives us little more than glimpses of the relations among the Persons, and certainly not a well-elaborated depiction of those relations. Of no part of the discussion is this observation more relevant than of the eternal generation of the Son. Tim Keller recently reminded me of an oft-repeated adage of the late Reformed theologian Roger Nicole, who liked to say that, with respect to the doctrine of the Trinity, it is much easier to be precise about what we are denying than about what we are affirming.

According to Martin Luther, the doctrine of eternal generation 'is not even comprehensible to the angels', and 'those who have tried to grasp it have broken their necks over it' [Martin Luther, *The Three Symbols or Creeds of the Christian Faith*, in *LW* 14.216–18.]. Nevertheless, Luther also insists, eternal generation is a doctrine 'given to us in the gospel' and glimpsed 'by faith.' The doctrine is, furthermore, beautiful teaching, for it indicates the kind of perfection that characterizes the Father as an eternally radiant, communicative perfection, and it indicates the kind of perfection that characterizes the Son: when we see the Son, we see deity shining forth in its full brilliance, supreme over all creaturely lights."

97

CHAPTER 5

A LEXICAL DEFENSE OF THE JOHANNINE "ONLY BEGOTTEN"

CHARLES LEE IRONS

THE TWO PROCESSIONS—the eternal generation of the Son and the eternal procession of the Spirit—are an essential component of Trinitarian orthodoxy. They function as the linchpin for maintaining the distinctions among the three persons without compromising the unity and simplicity of God. The nineteenth-century Southern Presbyterian theologian Robert Lewis Dabney put it this way:

> In a word, the generation of the Son, and procession of the Spirit, however mysterious, are unavoidable corollaries from two facts. The essence of the Godhead is one; the persons are three. If these are both true, there must be some way, in which the Godhead multiplies its personal modes of subsistence, without multiplying its substance.[1]

But one of the puzzles of the doctrine of eternal generation is the apparent disjunction between how it was developed and formulated in the history of the church, particularly in the context of the Arian controversy in the fourth century, and how it is to be justified biblically today. The church fathers appealed to a number of passages in support of the eternal generation of the Son that would be understood rather differently by many modern exegetes. But if modern exegetes no longer find the patristic proof

---

1. Robert Lewis Dabney, *Systematic Theology* (Edinburgh: Banner of Truth Trust, 1985), 209.

A LEXICAL DEFENSE OF THE JOHANNINE "ONLY BEGOTTEN"

texts for the eternal generation of the Son convincing, where does that leave the doctrine? This chapter is an attempt to bridge the gap between patristic and modern exegesis with respect to one particular point, namely, the use of the word *monogenēs*, which is applied to the Second Person of the Godhead five times in the New Testament—four times in the Gospel of John (1:14, 18; 3:16, 18) and once in the Epistles of John (1 John 4:9).

SKETCH OF THE HISTORY OF INTERPRETATION

Traditionally, the five verses that speak of the Second Person of the Godhead as *monogenēs* were understood as having reference to the uniqueness of the Son's relationship to the Father, as one who is the "only begotten" Son of the Father. This word was one of the favorite designations for the Son in the Greek fathers of the East, sometimes adjectivally in the phrase, "the only begotten Son" or "the only begotten God," but very often substantivally, "the Only Begotten" (ὁ Μονογενής). A search of the digital library of Greek literature Thesaurus Linguae Graecae (TLG)[2] turns up some startling statistics on the usage of this term in the church fathers. Here are the most important Greek fathers and other ecclesiastical writers by the number of times they use this term:[3]

Ecclesiastical Writer	Μονογενής	Dates
Cyril of Alexandria	981	d. 444
Gregory of Nyssa	643	c. 330–395
John Chrysostom	465	c. 347–407
Theodoret of Cyrrhus	351	c. 393–460
Didymus the Blind	346	c. 313–398
Eusebius of Caesarea	340	c. 260–340
Epiphanius of Salamis	304	c. 315–403
Athanasius	287	c. 296–373
Basil of Caesarea	281	c. 330–379

2. According to the website, "The Thesaurus Linguae Graecae (TLG) is a research center at the University of California, Irvine. Founded in 1972 the TLG has collected and digitized most literary texts written in Greek from Homer to the fall of Byzantium in AD 1453. Its goal is to create a comprehensive digital library of Greek literature from antiquity to the present era" (www.tlg.uci.edu).

3. Dates from F. L. Cross and E. A. Livingstone, eds., *The Oxford Dictionary of the Christian Church*, 3rd ed. (Oxford: Oxford University Press, 1997).

CHARLES LEE IRONS

Ecclesiastical Writer	Μονογενής	Dates
Origen	126	c. 185–254
Cyril of Jerusalem	89	c. 315–387
Gregory Nazianzen	27	329–389

Perhaps we would not have been surprised to find the term used dozens of times, but that many hundreds of times? This term seems to have had special significance for the Greek fathers.

In the Latin West, the Johannine *monogenēs* was carried over into theological Latin in two main ways: either as *unicus filius* or as *unigenitus*. The first rendering is found in the (pre-Vulgate) Old Latin of John 1:14, 18.[4] The Old Latin renders *monogenēs* not as *unicus* ("unique") but as *unicus filius* ("only son"), which suggests the *-genēs* stem was taken as communicating the notion of sonship or offspring. In the Vulgate, Jerome translated the five Johannine occurrences as *unigenitus* ("only begotten"), which clearly indicates his understanding. The Vulgate probably influenced Tyndale, who rendered the word "only begotten" in three out of five of its Johannine occurrences.[5] The King James Version continued this rendering in all five Johannine occurrences so that it became the standard interpretation in the English-speaking world for the next three centuries.

However, in the last decades of the nineteenth century, the rendering "only begotten" was called into question, and in its place the rendering "only" became the reigning consensus among biblical scholars. It was argued that *monogenēs* is derived from μόνος + γένος (rather than μόνος + γεννάω) and therefore it had the meaning "only one of its/his kind," "unique." In 1886, B. F. Westcott included a three-page excursus on *monogenēs* in his commentary on the Epistles of John in which he argued that the word originally meant "unique" and that the transition in meaning to "only begotten" was prompted by the dogmatic concerns of the pro-Nicene church fathers reacting against Arianism,[6] concerns that were given final

---

4. "[The] Word became flesh and lived among us and we beheld his glory, glory as of [the] only Son from [the] Father (*sicut unici filii a patre*), full of grace and truth. . . . No one has ever seen God except [the] only Son (*unicus filius*), alone in [the] side of [the] Father, he has made him known" (translation mine). Francis A. Gasquet, ed., *Codex Vercellensis* (Rome: F. Pustet, 1914). Codex Vercellensis (ca. 350), which contains only the Gospels, is our most ancient witness to the Old Latin text of the New Testament.

5. At John 1:14, 18; 1 John 4:9, Tyndale has "only begotten" (3x), but at John 3:16, 18 he has "only" (2x). N. Hardy Wallis, ed., *The New Testament Translated by William Tyndale 1534* (Cambridge: Cambridge University Press, 1938).

6. I use the term "pro-Nicene" in the sense articulated by Lewis Ayres, to refer to the consolidation of the orthodox position after the Council of Nicaea in 325 and culminating in the First

creedal expression at the First Council of Constantinople in 381.[7] In a 1938 dissertation written at the Southern Baptist Theological Seminary, Francis Marion Warden expanded upon Westcott's argument in much greater detail.[8] His dissertation was never published, but the substance of it was picked up by the translation committee of the Revised Standard Version, which published the New Testament in 1946, followed by the whole Bible in 1952. In 1953 the Southern Baptist theologian Dale Moody forcefully defended the RSV's rendering ("only"), appealing to Warden's dissertation as the scholarly basis for it.[9] Moody dismissed the traditional translation "only begotten" as a simple error that the RSV finally corrected after fifteen centuries.

A shift in the scholarly consensus seems to have occurred at this point, for after the RSV nearly all modern English versions follow the RSV's lead. The first to do so was the first edition of the New International Version in 1978, which rendered the word "one and only." This rendering has been retained in all subsequent editions of the NIV, including the most recent 2011 edition. The NIV's rendering was defended by Richard Longenecker in a 1986 article.[10] As a consequence of this scholarly shift, the renderings "only" (CEV, ESV, NAB, NRSV, RSV) and "one and only" (HCSB/CSB, NIV, NLT) have become entrenched across a wide spectrum of modern English versions. Even scholars who maintain the traditional doctrine of the eternal generation of the Son in most respects do not appeal to *monogenēs* in support of it.[11]

Council of Constantinople in 381. See Lewis Ayres, *Nicaea and Its Legacy: An Approach to Fourth-Century Trinitarian Theology* (Oxford: Oxford University Press, 2004).

7. Brooke Foss Westcott, *The Epistles of St. John* (Cambridge and London: Macmillan, 1886), 169–72. See also his briefer comments in his commentary on the Fourth Gospel: Westcott, *The Gospel According to St. John* (Grand Rapids: Eerdmans, 1954), 1:23, 28. Interestingly, Westcott's colleague, F. J. A. Hort, apparently did not follow Westcott and continued to defend the "only begotten" interpretation. Hort, *Two Dissertations: I. On ΜΟΝΟΓΕΝΗΣ ΘΕΟΣ in Scripture and Tradition; II. On the 'Constantinopolitan' Creed and Other Eastern Creeds of the Fourth Century* (London: Macmillan, 1876), 16–18. However, Westcott's excursus made an impact, for not long after, in 1908, the article on "Only Begotten" in the Hasting's *Dictionary of Christ and the Gospels* followed Westcott in arguing for "only, unique" over "only begotten." Ferdinand Kattenbusch, "Only Begotten," in James Hastings, ed., *A Dictionary of Christ and the Gospels* (New York: Scribner's Sons, 1908), 2:281–82.

8. Francis Marion Warden, *ΜΟΝΟΓΕΝΗΣ in the Johannine Literature* (PhD diss., Southern Baptist Theological Seminary, 1938). He also summarized his work in "God's Only Son," *Review and Expositor* 50 (April 1953): 216–23.

9. Dale Moody, "God's Only Son: The Translation of John 3:16 in the Revised Standard Version," *JBL* 72 (1953): 213–19.

10. Richard N. Longenecker, "The One and Only Son," in *The NIV: The Making of a Contemporary Translation*, ed. Kenneth Barker (Grand Rapids: Zondervan, 1986) 119–26.

11. E.g., Kevin Giles, *The Eternal Generation of the Son: Maintaining Orthodoxy in Trinitarian Theology* (Downers Grove, IL: IVP Academic, 2012), 64–69, 81, 144–48. Giles makes the incredible claim that the Greek-speaking fathers "do not use [*monogenēs*] or the texts in which it is found as textual support for the eternal generation of the Son. For them . . . the word was understood to mean 'unique' or 'only'" (81n44).

Did "Only Begotten" Develop in Response to Arianism?

Before I go on to defend the translation "only begotten," I think it will first be useful to interact briefly with the argument of Westcott, Warden, and Moody that the interpretation of *monogenēs* as "only begotten" began with Jerome soon after the First Council of Constantinople in order to combat Arianism. As James M. Bulman and John V. Dahms showed in a series of articles in the 1980s, this argument is undercut by two salient facts.[12]

The first fact is that *monogenēs* in the sense of "only begotten" (or *unigenitus*) was used long before Jerome's Vulgate and long before the Arian controversy. This usage is found in the writings of two well-known *second-century* Christian authors, one who wrote in Greek (Justin Martyr) and one who wrote in Latin (Tertullian). Justin Martyr uses *monogenēs* in reference to the Son without clearly quoting any one of the five Johannine texts, but presumably echoing all of them. He writes, "I have already proved that He was the only-begotten of the Father of all things (μονογενὴς γὰρ ὅτι ἦν τῷ πατρὶ τῶν ὅλων οὗτος), being begotten (γεγεννημένος) in a peculiar manner Word and Power by Him, and having afterwards become man through the Virgin."[13] Note the use of the perfect passive participle of γεννάω in apposition to and explaining the meaning of *monogenēs*.

When we come to our Latin writer, Tertullian, the same picture emerges. He quotes John 1:18 (as well as 1:14) and renders the word *unigenitus*.[14] If one has any doubt as to how he understands the term, attend to his explanation earlier in the same treatise: "Thus does He make Him equal to Him: for by proceeding from Himself He became His first-begotten Son, because begotten before all things; and His *only-begotten* also, because alone begotten of God, in a way peculiar to Himself, from the womb of His own heart."[15] The last line is key: Tertullian parses *unigenitus* as "alone begotten of God" (*solus ex deo genitus*). The first salient fact, then, is that we have two second-century Christian authors, well before the fourth-century Arian controversy, who, on the basis of the Johannine *monogenēs* passages, affirmed that the Son was "only begotten."[16]

---

12. James M. Bulman, "The Only Begotten Son," *Calvin Theological Journal* 16 (1981): 56–79; John V. Dahms, "The Johannine Use of *monogenēs* Reconsidered," *NTS* 29 (1983): 222–32; Dahms, "The Generation of the Son," *JETS* 32, no. 4 (1989): 493–501.

13. Justin Martyr, *Dialogue with Trypho* 105, in *ANF* 1.251.

14. Tertullian, *Against Praxeas* 15, in *ANF* 3.611.

15. Tertullian, *Against Praxeas* 7, in *ANF* 3.601. "*Exinde eum patrem sibi faciens de quo procedendo filius factus est primogenitus, ut ante omnia genitus, et unigenitus, ut solus ex deo genitus, proprie de vulva cordis.*"

16. In addition, there are three passages in Irenaeus where he quotes John 1:18, and in each case

A LEXICAL DEFENSE OF THE JOHANNINE "ONLY BEGOTTEN"

The second fact undercutting the anti-Arian theory of Westcott, Warden, and Moody is that taking *monogenēs* as "only begotten" would not have been sufficient, by itself, to refute Arianism. The dispute between the Arians and the pro-Nicenes was not primarily over whether *monogenēs* expressed the idea that the Son was begotten.[17] The dispute centered on whether the Father's begetting of the Son was temporal or eternal and, concomitantly, whether the begetting was to be understood as an act of creation out of nothing so that there was a time when the Son did not exist (as the Arians thought) or as his being begotten from the essence of the Father so that the Son is not a creature but the Father's true and eternal offspring (as the pro-Nicenes taught). The claim that the word *monogenēs* first began to be understood in the sense of "only begotten" in the fourth century as a weapon against Arianism runs aground on the shoal of the historical facts.

ETYMOLOGY OF *Monogenēs*

Next, we must examine the etymological argument against translating *monogenēs* as "only begotten." The etymological argument is that *monogenēs* is derived from μόνος + γένος ("kind"), understood as deriving from γί(γ)νομαι ("be, become") rather than γεννάω ("beget"), with the result that it means "only one of its/his kind."

First, this appeal to etymology fails to recognize that γεννάω and γί(γ)νομαι are related and derive from the same Indo-European root, *genh* ("beget, arise").[18] The word γί(γ)νομαι itself can mean "be born," the first meaning listed in *Liddell and Scott* (hereafter *LSJ*), in addition to its more

---

the text as we have it has *unigenitus* (*Against Heresies* 3.11.6; 4.20.6, 11). We may also add Origen from the third century: "We have always held that God is the Father of His only-begotten Son (*unigeniti Filii sui*), who was born (*nati*) indeed of Him, and derives from Him what He is, but without any beginning" (*Princ.* 1.2.2, in *ANF* 4.246). However, we should be cautious about this evidence, since the Greek originals of both Irenaeus and Origen have been lost and come down to us in later Latin translations.

17. "The ancient Arians were very ready to call the Son ὁ μονογενὴς θεός; this appellation, in their view, happily distinguished him from the Father, who alone was God in the highest sense, as unbegotten, uncaused, and without beginning" (Ezra Abbot, *The Authorship of the Fourth Gospel and Other Critical Essays* [Boston: George H. Ellis, 1888], 285, cf. 267). The extreme Arian, Eunomius, in his *Expositio Fidei* (published in 383) appealed to the appellation seeking to prove that the Son cannot be divine, since God's essential attribute is that he is "ungenerate" (according to Gregory of Nyssa, *Answer to Eunomius' Second Book*, in *NPNF²* 5:252–55). This "indicates that [the phrase μονογενὴς θεός] by no means necessitates an entirely Nicene Christology" (Benjamin J. Burkholder, "Considering the Possibility of a Theological Corruption in Joh 1,18 in Light of its Early Reception," *ZNW* 103 [2012]: 80).

18. Hjalmar Frisk, *Griechisches etymologisches Wörterbuch* (Heidelberg: Carl Winter, 1954), 1:296–97, 306–8; Pierre Chantraine, *Dictionnaire étymologique de la langue grecque: histoire des mots*, new ed. (Paris: Librairie Klincksieck, 2009), 212–15; and Robert Beekes, *Etymological Dictionary of Greek* (Leiden: Brill, 2010), 1:266, 272–73.

CHARLES LEE IRONS

common meanings, "be, become, occur."[19] Sometimes scholars will try to drive a wedge between γεννάω and γί(γ)νομαι by pointing to the additional ν in γεννάω. But no significance should be attributed to the geminate ν in γεννάω versus the single ν in γί(γ)νομαι, since the doubling of ν, as well as spelling variants confusing the two, is a common feature of Greek.[20] In addition, the word γένος, which has only one ν, can mean "descendant" (e.g., Rev 22:16). The history of the Greek language will not allow us to exclude notions of birth and generation from *monogenēs* on the ground that it derives from γένος or γί(γ)νομαι.

Second, there is a wealth of lexemes in Greek that are built upon the *-genēs* stem. The word list of TLG reveals that there are at least 145 such words in the ancient Greek vocabulary.[21] In the vast majority of instances, the glosses given in *LSJ* contain such words as "born" and "produced." Examples include θαλασσογενής ("sea-born"), κογχογενής ("born from a shell," picture the Birth of Venus by Botticelli), μοιραγενής ("favored by destiny at birth, child of destiny"), νεογενής ("new-born, newly produced"), πατρογενής ("begotten of the father"), προτερηγενής ("born sooner, older"), and πυριγενής ("born in or from fire"). Fewer than 12 of the 145 *-genēs* words involve meanings related to "kind" (e.g., ὁμογενής means "of the same genus"), and there are a few with miscellaneous meanings (e.g., διγενής, "of doubtful sex").

Another piece of etymological evidence is to be found in the *Lexicon of Greek Personal Names* (hereafter *LGPN*), which has catalogued nearly 36,000 Greek personal names from all ancient sources (literature, inscriptions, graffiti, papyri, coins, vases, and other artefacts).[22] According to the online *LGPN* database, there are at least 166 ancient Greek proper names based on the *-genēs* stem.[23] The most common examples include names like *Diogenēs*

---

19. *LSJ* s.v. γίγνομαι I.1: "of persons, *to be born*." For example, Agamemnon and Menelaus were "born from the same father (πατρὸς ἐκ ταύτοῦ γεγώς)" (Euripides, *Iphigenia in Aulis*, 406). Chantraine says the original meaning of γίγνομαι was "to be born" and that it generated several lexemes pertaining to concepts of birth, race, etc. (*Dictionnaire étymologique de la langue grecque*, 212).

20. G. L. Prestige, *God in Patristic Thought* (London: SPCK, 1952), 37–52.

21. Ancient Greek includes Archaic, Classical, and Hellenistic (Koine) Greek, and excludes Byzantine (Medieval) and Modern Greek.

22. Peter M. Fraser et al., eds., *LGPN*, vols. I, II, III.A, III.B, IV, V.A, V.B (Oxford: Oxford University Press, 1987–2013). Each volume covers a different geographical area. The project aims "to collect and publish with documentation all known ancient Greek personal names (including non-Greek names recorded in Greek, and Greek names in Latin), drawn from all available sources (literature, inscriptions, graffiti, papyri, coins, vases and other artefacts), within the period from the earliest Greek written records down to, approximately, the sixth century A.D." (http://www.lgpn.ox.ac.uk/project/index.html).

23. Number of occurrences in *LGPN*, summing all occurrences in the seven volumes published thus far. There are two more volumes forthcoming. Search conducted at http://www.lgpn.ox.ac.uk/database/lgpn.php.

("offspring of Zeus"), *Hermogenēs* ("offspring of Hermes," cf. 2 Tim 1:15), *Epigenēs* ("born after"), and *Theogenēs* ("offspring of the god," "born of God"). Naturally, when used in personal names, the *-genēs* stem ordinarily communicates the concept of biological birth or begetting, indicating something special about the offspring's parentage or circumstances of birth. Of course, we cannot assume that every child named *Diogenēs* was believed to be literally the offspring of Zeus. Yet that is what the name means, and it invites the interpretation that parents thought the giving of such a name would enhance the child's good fortune in life. It is conceivable that in some cases the *-genēs* stem in a proper name could communicate the abstract notion of species or kind apart from the biological notion of offspring or birth, but I have not been able to identify any *-genēs* names that would lend themselves to such an interpretation.

Of course, it is a well-known principle of lexical semantics that the meanings of words are to be determined by usage rather than etymology. I have reviewed the etymological evidence not to prove that *monogenēs* means "only begotten" but to answer those who appeal to etymology in the attempt to prove that it cannot mean "only begotten." The etymological evidence suggests that *monogenēs* could very well mean "only begotten."

THE LEXICAL ARGUMENT

Having cleared away two of the principal objections, we come now to the positive lexical argument. My claim is not that *monogenēs* always means "only begotten" and never means "only one of its/his kind" in biblical and extrabiblical Greek. John Dahms tries to make that claim, and he has to strenuously explain away a number of difficult passages where *monogenēs* plausibly does mean "only one of its/his kind."[24] On the other hand, Gerard Pendrick attempts to argue the opposite position against Dahms— that *monogenēs* always means "only one of its/his kind" with the notion of begetting never present.[25] He is equally wrong. Neither extreme is correct.

The earliest meaning of *monogenēs* was biological, in reference to an only child.[26] For example, Hesiod advises, "Let there be a single-born (μουνογενής) son to nourish the father's household: in this way wealth is

---

24. John V. Dahms, "The Johannine Use of *monogenēs* Reconsidered," *NTS* 29 (1983): 222–32.
25. Gerard Pendrick, "ΜΟΝΟΓΕΝΗΣ," *NTS* 41 (1995): 587–600.
26. "Without siblings" is the gloss given for μουνογενής in Michael Meier-Brügger, ed., *Lexicon des frühgriechischen Epos* (Göttingen: Vandenhoeck & Ruprecht, 1993), 15:258. Compare the German glosses "einzig geboren, einziges Kind" in Adolf Kaegi, ed., *Benselers griechisch-deutsches Schulwörterbuch* (Leipzig and Berlin: B. G. Teubner, 1904), 592.

CHARLES LEE IRONS

increased in the halls."[27] If a man has more than one son, the inheritance will get divided. The fourth-century Greek-speaking church fathers understood this, for when discussing the term they glossed its meaning as "the only one begotten," "having no brother," or "lacking siblings."[28] To provide a definition of the sort one might find in *A Greek-English Lexicon of the New Testament and Other Early Christian Literature* by Frederick Danker et al. (BDAG), my claim is that *monogenēs* is used most basically and frequently in reference to an only child begotten by a parent, with the implication of not having any siblings. A base/profile analysis puts the term in a biological familial context.[29] It presupposes a biological relationship between a parent and his or her only son or daughter.

Querying the TLG database reveals that *monogenēs* is an ordinary word quite common in extrabiblical Greek. Its earliest use is in Hesiod (3x), but after that it is found in the Aesopica (2x), Aeschylus (1x), Herodotus (2x), Plato (4x), Theophrastus (3x), Diodorus Siculus (2x), Dionysius of Halicarnassus (3x), Septuagint (10x), Josephus (4x), Plutarch (8x), Arrian (1x), and many others. The word is used most frequently as an adjective modifying the nouns "son," "daughter," and "child." This can be seen in the ordinary, non-Johannine, non-Christological uses in the New Testament (Luke 7:12; 8:42; 9:38).[30] If the word meant "only," then we would expect to find it used to modify many other nouns that do not involve the concept of being begotten or being an offspring, for example, "only wife," "only brother," "only friend," "only slave"; or "only eye," "only foot," "only hand"

---

27. Hesiod, *Opera et dies* 376–77 (LCL 57).

28. Athanasius: "The term μονογενής is used where there are no brethren, but πρωτότοκος because of brethren" (*C. Ar.* 2.62, in *NPNF²* 4.382). Cyril of Jerusalem: "On hearing of a 'Son,' think not of an adopted son but a Son by nature, an Only-begotten Son, having no brother" (*Catechetical Lectures* 11.2, in *NPNF²* 7.64). Basil of Caesara: "In common usage μονογενής does not designate the one who comes from only one person [as Eunomius claimed], but the one who is the only one begotten (ὁ μόνος γεννηθείς). . . . If your [Eunomius's] opinions were to prevail, it would be necessary for the entire world to re-learn this term, that the name 'only-begotten' does not indicate a lack of siblings but the absence of a pair of procreators" (St. Basil of Caesarea, *Against Eunomius*, trans. Mark DelCogliano and Andrew Radde-Gallwitz, The Fathers of the Church 122 [Washington, DC: Catholic University of America Press, 2011], 159, 161 [2.20–21; PG 29:616–17]). Gregory of Nyssa: "Who does not know how great is the difference in signification between the term μονογενής and πρωτότοκος? For πρωτότοκος implies brethren, and μονογενής implies that there are no other brethren. Thus the πρωτότοκος is not μονογενής, for certainly πρωτότοκος is the first-born among brethren, while he who is μονογενής has no brother; for if he were numbered among brethren he would not be only-begotten" (*Against Eunomius* 2.7–8, in *NPNF²* 5.112; *Refutatio confessionis Eunomii* §76 in *Gregorii Nysseni Opera*, vol. 2, ed. Werner Jaeger [Leiden: Brill, 1960]).

29. Ronald W. Langacker, *Foundations of Cognitive Grammar*, 2 vols. (Stanford: Stanford University Press, 1987, 1991); Langacker, *Concept, Image, and Symbol: The Cognitive Basis of Grammar* (Berlin: Mouton de Gruyter, 1991); William Croft and D. Alan Cruse, *Cognitive Linguistics* (Cambridge: Cambridge University Press, 2004).

30. Hebrews 11:17 should also be mentioned to complete the list of New Testament uses, but here it is a substantive adjective (τὸν μονογενῆ).

A LEXICAL DEFENSE OF THE JOHANNINE "ONLY BEGOTTEN"

(for a person missing one eye, foot, or hand); or a man's "only garment," "only house," "only sword," and so on. But such collocations are completely absent in extrabiblical Greek. This suggests that the literal meaning, which is by far the most common usage in extrabiblical Greek, is the straightforward biological meaning: "only begotten," that is, "without siblings."

This biological meaning is explicitly present when accompanied by the verb γεννάω, for instance, when Diodorus Siculus informs us that the god Ares slept with Harpinē and begat Oenomaüs, "who, in turn, begat a daughter, an only child (οὗτος δὲ θυγατέρα μονογενῆ γεννήσας), and named her Hippodameia."[31] The biological meaning, "only begotten," is the basic and original meaning of the word.[32]

But as is common in language, this basic meaning gets gradually extended in ever new nonliteral, metaphorical directions. As linguists recognize, such nonliteral extensions of meaning are rooted in the prototypical, embodied experiential meaning and radiate outward from there.[33] Consider, for example, the sentence, "foolish, ignorant controversies . . . beget quarrels (γεννῶσιν μάχας)" (2 Tim 2:23). This is clearly a nonliteral or metaphorical use of the verb γεννάω. The word has not shed its original meaning "beget."[34] It would be quite illegitimate for a lexicographer to argue, "We know that controversies don't literally 'beget' quarrels; therefore, the word here must have a fundamentally different meaning, perhaps 'give rise to.'" Even in this instance, γεννάω retains the meaning "beget," but its meaning has been extended by being used as a metaphor. The metaphorical usage depends on the literal picture of begetting in order for the metaphor to be successful. So it is with *monogenēs*. Its fundamental biological meaning

---

31. Diodorus Siculus, *Bibliotheca historica* 4.73.1–2 (LCL 375).

32. The biological usage is found in the following occurrences: Hesiod, *Theogonia* 426, 448; *Opera et dies* 376; *Corpus fabularum Aesopicarum*, ed. Hausrath and Hunger, Fable 279; *Aesopi fabulae*, ed. Chambry, Fable 296 ; Aeschylus, *Agamemnon* 898; Herodotus, *Historiae* 2.79; 7.221; Plato, *Leges* 691e; *Critias* 113d; Eudemus of Rhodes, *Fragmenta*, ed. Wehrli, frag. 150 line 41; Arrian, *Historica Indica* 8.6 (quoting Megasthenes); Apollonius Rhodius, *Argonautica* 3.847; 3.1035; Posidonius, *Fragmenta*, ed. Theiler, frag. 398 line 15; Diodorus Siculus, *Bibliotheca historica* 4.73.2; 6.7.2; Dionysius of Halicarnassus, *Antiquitates Romanae* 2.45.2; 3.1.2–3; Septuagint (Judges 11:34; Tobit 3:15; 6:11, 15; 8:17); Josephus, *Ant.* 1.222; 2.182; 5.264; 20.20; Apion, *Fragmenta de glossis Homericis* 75.101.15; Plutarch, *De fraterno amore* 480E; *Fragmenta*, ed. Sandbach, frag. 57; Lycurgus 31.4; *De facie in orbe lunae* 943B; Apollonius, *Lexicon Homericum* 152.18; Antoninus Liberalis, *Mythographi Graeci* 32.1; *Pseudo-Clementina: Homiliae* 12.21.5; *Orphic Hymns* 29.2; Hippolytus, *Refutatio omnium haeresium* 8.9.3 (*ANF* 8.2); Epiphanius, *Panarion* (or *Adversus haereses*) 2.287.2.

33. Croft and Cruse, *Cognitive Linguistics*, 111, 193–221; Alan Cruse, *Meaning in Language: An Introduction to Semantics and Pragmatics*, 2nd ed. (Oxford: Oxford University Press, 2004), 195–214; Dirk Geeraerts, *Diachronic Prototype Semantics: A Contribution to Historical Lexicology* (Oxford: Clarendon, 1997); Geeraerts, *Theories of Lexical Semantics* (Oxford: Oxford University Press, 2010), see ch. 5, "Cognitive Semantics," and esp. 233–34.

34. Bulman, "The Only Begotten Son," 60.

CHARLES LEE IRONS

"only begotten" has been extended in a variety of nonliteral applications, but the nonliteral or metaphorical applications do not negate, and in fact depend on, the primary or literal meaning. A careful study of *monogenēs* in the Septuagint, the Greek New Testament, and extrabiblical Greek literature suggests at least three nonliteral extensions of the word *monogenēs* in ever-widening concentric circles.

The First Nonliteral Extension: Only Legitimate Child or Heir

The first nonliteral extension is in biblical contexts shaped by the concern for an heir. This is most clearly seen in the case of Isaac, who is called *monogenēs* even though Abraham had another son, Ishmael (Gen 22:2, Aquila; Gen 22:12, Symmachus; Heb 11:17; Josephus, *Ant.* 1.222).[35] In this case, an "only begotten" son may actually have siblings and yet be his father's only legitimate son or heir and so it is *as if* he were an "only begotten" son. This is how Josephus explains the love of Monobazus, king of Adiabene, for one of his sons: "He had an elder son by Helena . . . and other children by his other wives; but it was clear that all his favour was concentrated on Izates *as if* he were an only child (ὡς εἰς μονογενῆ)."[36] Why might Isaac be regarded as if he were an only son? The answer is ready at hand. In Genesis 21:10–12, Sarah compels Abraham to disown Ishmael so that he is no longer an heir in competition with Isaac. In spite of Abraham's affection for Ishmael, God sides with Sarah and tells Abraham to do as Sarah said, "for through Isaac shall your offspring be named."[37] The point is clear: although Ishmael is also Abraham's biological son, he is no longer Abraham's heir, leaving Isaac alone in that position. Philo captures this by saying that Isaac was Abraham's "only legitimate son" (*Abr.* 194). It is this context that explains the use of *monogenēs* as a descriptor for Isaac, a descriptor that clearly involves a slight shift from a literal biological sense to a related sense of being the only legitimate son or heir. The explanation for this shift comes from that fact that even in the literal usage of *monogenēs*,

---

35. The LXX has "beloved" (ἀγαπητός) at Gen 22:2, 12, 16. The likely reason the LXX avoids μονογενής in these three verses is to resolve the apparent problem that Isaac is not the "only begotten" son of Abraham, since he has a half-brother, Ishmael. This is all the more noteworthy given that μονογενής is the standard Greek equivalent for יָחִיד (as in Symmachus and Aquila). The LXX's intentional avoidance of μονογενής provides further evidence that μονογενής was understood to mean "only begotten."

36. Josephus, *Ant.* 20.20 (LCL 456).

37. "So [Sarah] said to Abraham, 'Cast out this slave woman with her son, for the son of this slave woman shall not be heir with my son Isaac.' And the thing was very displeasing to Abraham on account of his son. But God said to Abraham, 'Be not displeased because of the boy and because of your slave woman. Whatever Sarah says to you, do as she tells you, for through Isaac shall your offspring be named'" (Gen 21:10–12 ESV).

A LEXICAL DEFENSE OF THE JOHANNINE "ONLY BEGOTTEN"

the concern for an heir is present, a concern that is heightened if there is any danger that the parent may lose his or her *monogenēs* child.

This concern can be seen in the apocryphal book of Tobit. The story concerns Sarah, daughter of Raguel, who had been married to seven husbands, but the demon Asmodeus had killed each of them before the marriage was consummated. Sarah was weeping and about to hang herself, but she changed her mind since she did not want to bring reproach on her father. So she prayed to God and asked him to take her life. In her prayer she said, "I am my father's only begotten (μονογενής εἰμι τῷ πατρί μου), and he has no other child to be his heir" (Tobit 3:15 NETS).[38] If a father or a mother has only one child, then the loss of that child would be especially tragic since it would mean losing one's heir. This, then, is why Isaac can be called "only begotten" (*monogenēs*) even though he is not literally the sole offspring of Abraham.

This is the answer to those who appeal to Hebrews 11:17, "He who had received the promises was offering up his only begotten *son* (τὸν μονογενῆ)" (NASB). Moody triumphantly claims, "No passage illustrates the meaning of *monogenēs* more clearly than Heb 11:17. . . . It is impossible to say Isaac was the only son begotten by Abraham."[39] If users of language are limited to literal meanings only, then it would be impossible. But language is more flexible than Moody thinks. We see the same thing in classical usage. For example, in the play by Aeschylus, *Agamemnon*, Clytemnestra speaks on the occasion of Agamemnon's return from the Trojan war, just before she murders him for sacrificing their daughter Iphigenia to propitiate the goddess Artemis to let his ships sail to Troy. She sarcastically hails her returning lord as "the watchdog of the fold, the savior forestay of the ship, firm-based pillar of the lofty roof, only-begotten son unto a father (μονογενὲς τέκνον πατρί)."[40] This cannot be taken literally, since Agamemnon and his brother, Menelaus, were both sons of Atreus. "Agamemnon is not, of course, an only son; this phrase, like the previous three, metaphorically describes him as one on whom depends the whole safety of the house and/or the city."[41]

Under this first nonliteral extension we may include a related usage that is quite rare and only exists in translation. It has to do with the idea

---

38. NETS is *A New English Translation of the Septuagint*, ed. Albert Pietersma and Benjamin G. Wright (Oxford: Oxford University Press, 2007).

39. Moody, "God's Only Son," 217.

40. Aeschylus, *Agamemnon*, trans. Herbert Weir Smyth, LCL 146 (London: Heinemann, 1926), 75 (898).

41. Aeschylus, *Agamemnon*, trans. Alan H. Sommerstein, LCL 146 (Cambridge: Harvard University Press, 2009), 103n185.

of being alone and in danger of death. It occurs only three times—all of them in the Greek Psalter (Pss 21:21; 24:16; 34:17 LXX).[42] The translator felt obligated to translate the Hebrew word יָחִיד literally. *monogenēs* in these cases is related to the previous meaning because of the biblical concern for an heir, having someone provide for one in old age, and having someone to bury one upon one's death. If a person has only one child, then losing that child would be an unbearable loss. One has lost everything. See the passages in the prophets about "mourning as for an only son/child" (Jer 6:26; Amos 8:10; Zech 12:10). One's life is like that, too. To lose one's "precious" life is to lose everything.

The Second Nonliteral Extension: Metaphorical Only Begotten

Our circle of nonliteral extended meanings expands further. The second nonliteral extension arises when the act of "begetting" is no longer biological but metaphorical, and yet the begetting metaphor is still very much alive. This can be seen in the way Greek philosophical literature deals with the physical universe as if it were God's "only begotten" offspring. Plato twice affirms that God did not make two universes or an infinite number of universes, but only this one *monogenēs* universe.[43] The Loeb Classical Library translates the word "unique (or sole) of its kind," which is certainly legitimate, although it conceals the metaphor of the universe as God's offspring. Since God's act of creating the universe is being viewed as a "begetting" of sorts, the term is still related to ordinary biological begetting by way of analogy. Plutarch, who was influenced by Plato, says the same thing, calling the present universe "only begotten," since it is the only universe that God created.[44]

A related case is Wisdom of Solomon 7:22, where Solomon is presented as praising Wisdom and listing off her many attributes, one of which is *monogenēs*. Although two modern versions render this as "unique" (NETS and NRSV), it is probably to be interpreted as containing the notion of Wisdom's being begotten of God due to the influence of Proverbs 8:25 in the Septuagint: "Before the mountains were established and before all the hills, he begets me (γεννᾷ με)" (NETS).

---

42. Pss 22:20; 25:16; 35:17 in the English Bible.

43. Plato, *Timaeus* 31b3; 92c9.

44. Plutarch, *De defectu oraculorum* 423A10 and C12; *Fragmenta*, ed. Sandbach, frag. 279, line 64 (quoting Parmenides). Calling the cosmos *monogenēs* seems to have been a commonplace in the Platonic and Neoplatonic tradition: Timaeus, *Fragmenta et titulus*, ed. W. Marg, 207 line 1; Cornutus, *De natura deorum*, ed. Lang, 49 line 13; Clement of Alexandria, *Stromata* 5.11.74.3; Joannes Philoponus, *De aeternitate mundi* 18.2; 512.27; 534.10; 549.9.

A LEXICAL DEFENSE OF THE JOHANNINE "ONLY BEGOTTEN"

The Third Nonliteral Extension: Only One of Its Kind

This brings us to the third nonliteral extension, which finally severs any link with begetting, even as a metaphor. We may call this the scientific usage of *monogenēs*, although it is not limited to scientific literature. In the scientific usage, the relationship between a genus and a species is viewed on the analogy of a father and his offspring. In these cases, the word clearly does mean "only one of its kind," the relationship being no longer genealogical but purely notional or conceptual. Aristotle's successor as the head of the Peripatetic School, Theophrastus, uses the term three times in his treatise, *Enquiry into Plants*. Throughout the book, Theophrastus describes the various "kinds" of each tree. For example, he says that certain types of trees, such as the beech tree, the yew, and the alder exist in only one kind (*monogenēs*), as opposed to other trees, like the maple or the ash, which exist in two kinds.[45] It is interesting to note that in some cases, he uses the synonym μονοειδής, which means "one in kind" (*LSJ*) without any connotation or hint of the begetting metaphor.

Another example of the scientific usage is 1 Clement 25:2, which refers to the phoenix as *monogenēs*, "the only one of its species."[46] In the context there is no thought of the phoenix being begotten. Clement simply means that this strange eagle-like creature, which goes through a cycle of death and rebirth every five hundred years, each one rising from the ashes of its predecessor, is utterly unique. There is nothing like it in all creation. We now see that in this scientific usage of the term, the original meaning "only begotten" has been extended and stretched so far that the begetting metaphor has dropped out of sight. However, the biological metaphor is still lurking in the background insofar as the scientific "kind" (meaning "species") is conceptualized on the analogy of biological kinship.[47]

My argument is that there is a directional flow from a literal biological meaning ("only begotten, not having any siblings") to various metaphorical extensions in ever-increasing circles that get further and further away from the original biological context so that the notion of begetting ultimately

---

45. Theophrastus, *Historia plantarum* 3.10.1–2; 3.14.3.

46. Michael W. Holmes, ed., *The Apostolic Fathers: Greek Texts and English Translations* (Grand Rapids: Baker, 1999), 57.

47. Other examples of the scientific usage of μονογενής ("only one of its kind") include the following: the liver as a "unique" organ (Galen, *De placitis Hippocratis et Platonis* 6.9.31); the Decalogue designating sins by means of "an elementary principle, simple and of one kind (ἁπλῷ καὶ μονογενεῖ ... στοιχείῳ)" (Clement of Alexandria, *Paedagogus* 3.12.89.1); a church building "unparalleled" in size and beauty (Eusebius, *Vita Constantini* 3.50.2); the sun, called "unique" because it is alone (Ammonius, *Fragmenta in Joannem*, ed. Reuss, frag. 86); and each of the stars is "unique" (Joannes Philoponus, *De aeternitate mundi* 549.13–14). Most of these are cited by Pendrick, "ΜΟΝΟΓΕΝΗΣ."

111

CHARLES LEE IRONS

drops from view. The directionality of this flow from biological to metaphorical to scientific is the best explanation for all the data. On the one hand, the earliest instances of *monogenēs* are plainly biological, and on the other hand, there are occurrences where the literal biological meaning does not fit, and a more abstract meaning such as "only one of its kind" or "unique" fits much better. It is precisely backward to start with the latter set of data and attempt to reinterpret the former set of data so that it fits into a nonbiological mold. One can only do this by getting rid of the notion of "begetting." But the fundamental biological concept of "begetting" is surely present in the word when used in literal or metaphorical familial contexts.[48]

The scientific meaning, "only one of his kind," is the meaning that modern scholars and English versions attempt to find in the five Johannine passages. But the five Johannine passages clearly do not fit under the third nonliteral extension. The genre and context are not scientific. The Gospel of John is dealing with the relationship between the Father and the Son, not botany. We are not dealing, like Theophrastus, with genus/species analysis. The father–son analogy is very strongly attested in these contexts, as opposed to the scientific usage, where this analogy has dropped from view.

"Only Begotten" in John 1:14, 18

With the lexical evidence and my lexical argument in mind, then, I would like to turn our attention to the first two of the five Johannine occurrences of *monogenēs*—John 1:14, 18. These two verses provide compelling evidence that *monogenēs*, when applied to the Son in the Johannine literature, is not being used in a scientific sense to mean "only one of his kind" but in a metaphorical biological sense meaning "only begotten."

We will look at John 1:14 first: Καὶ ὁ λόγος σὰρξ ἐγένετο καὶ ἐσκήνωσεν ἐν ἡμῖν, καὶ ἐθεασάμεθα τὴν δόξαν αὐτοῦ, δόξαν ὡς μονογενοῦς παρὰ πατρός, πλήρης χάριτος καὶ ἀληθείας. It is difficult to see how the meaning "only" or "one and only" fits in a meaningful way unless the notion of sonship or begottenness is part of the meaning of the word. Indeed, many of the modern English versions (like the Old Latin—see note 4 above) bring back the supposedly banished concept of begetting by adding the word "Son"

---

48. For the sake of completeness, it should be noted that there are at least two technical uses of μονογενής among the ancient Greek grammarians. Philoxenus, Apollonius Dyscolus, and Aelius Herodianus use the term as a descriptor of words "having one form for all genders" (*LSJ* s.v. μονογενής 4), and Hephaestio uses it as the name of a metrical foot (*LSJ* s.v. μονογενής 5).

112

A Lexical Defense of the Johannine "Only Begotten"

even though it is not present in Greek: "And the Word became flesh and dwelt among us, and we have seen his glory, glory as of the only Son from the Father, full of grace and truth" (ESV), and "the glory of the one and only Son, who came from the Father" (NIV). Both these English versions, though refusing to see "begetting" as part of the meaning of *monogenēs*, nevertheless cannot avoid inserting the word "Son," even though it is not present in Greek. In like manner, C. H. Dodd—though taking *monogenēs* as "only of his kind"—recognized that "one who is μονογενής relatively to a πατήρ can be no other than the only *son*."[49] The context is pushing the translators and the commentators in the right direction, almost against their will. But why not go the whole way? Barnabas Lindars does just that when he notes that while *monogenēs* can mean "unique in kind," the added phrase "from the Father" here in John 1:14 is decisive for "only-begotten."[50] He adds that it is not just the phrase "from the Father" but the entire clause that is significant: "We have seen his glory, glory as of the Only Begotten from the Father" (translation mine). Lindars points out that "glory" here carries the added connotation of "reflection." "Thus Jesus reflects the glory of God as a son reflects the aspect of a father on account of family likeness."[51] The concept that the son bears the father's family likeness or image and reveals who the father is further reinforces the biological metaphor of begetting.

Let us now turn to John 1:18 and the second Johannine occurrence of *monogenēs*: Θεὸν οὐδεὶς ἑώρακεν πώποτε·μονογενὴς θεὸς ὁ ὢν εἰς τὸν κόλπον τοῦ πατρὸς ἐκεῖνος ἐξηγήσατο. As is well known, there is a text-critical issue with this verse. Although the Majority Text has ὁ μονογενὴς υἱός, since the time of Westcott and Hort, the reading [ὁ] μονογενὴς θεός has been thought more likely on both external and internal grounds.[52] This is also the reading presented the main text of Nestle-Aland in all editions.[53] Objectively, either reading comports with taking *monogenēs* in the sense of "only begotten," but I argue that the superior reading, μονογενὴς θεός, requires that *monogenēs* be taken in the sense of "only begotten."

---

49. C. H. Dodd, *The Interpretation of the Fourth Gospel* (Cambridge: Cambridge University Press, 1958), 305n1; cf. C. K. Barrett, *The Gospel According to St. John*, 2nd ed. (Philadelphia: Westminster, 1978), 166.

50. Barnabas Lindars, SSF, *The Gospel of John* (London: Marshall, Morgan & Scott, 1972), 96.

51. Barnabas Lindars, SSF, *John* (Sheffield: JSOT, 1990), 17.

52. The Bodmer Papyri (P⁶⁶ and P⁷⁵), Sinaiticus, and Vaticanus have μονογενὴς θεός. The reading μονογενὴς υἱός appears to be secondary, due to assimilation to John 3:16, 18; 1 John 4:9. See Bruce M. Metzger, *A Textual Commentary on the Greek New Testament*, 2nd ed. (Stuttgart: Deutsche Bibelgesellschaft, 1994), 169.

53. Nestle-Aland, *Novum Testamentum Graece* (Stuttgart: Deutsche Bibelgesellschaft). The reading μονογενὴς θεός goes back at least to the 24th edition (1960) and continues in every subsequent edition, including the 28th (2012).

Interestingly, the NIV adopts the μονογενὴς θεός reading, and yet, as in verse 14, it inserts the notion of "Son" in its rendering: "No one has ever seen God, but the one and only Son, who is himself God and is in closest relationship with the Father, has made him known." The NIV renders *monogenēs* as "the one and only Son" and takes *theos* in apposition to it, "who is himself God." Again, as we saw in verse 14, the context is pushing the translators to recognize that the concept of sonship is present in the pregnant word *monogenēs*.

By contrast, the ESV avoids inserting the word "Son," but the resulting translation is, in my view, extremely problematic: "No one has ever seen God; the only God, who is at the Father's side, he has made him known." Presumably the ESV translation committee was attracted to what seemed to them a powerful affirmation of the deity of Christ. Not only is the predicate "God" attributed to him (as in John 1:1), but even more power- fully, the predicate "the only God." There is only one true and living God. Jesus is therefore not a lesser divine being distinct from the only God; he *is* the only God.

However, there are three problems with the ESV's handling of this verse. In my view, the problems are so serious that they are fatal. First, perhaps without fully realizing it, the ESV translators have removed this one occurrence of *monogenēs* out of the frame of reference of the other four Johannine occurrences, in all of which *monogenēs* is used in reference to the uniqueness of the person of the Son: "the only Son from the Father" (John 1:14 ESV), "his only Son" (John 3:16; 1 John 4:9 ESV), or "the only Son of God" (John 3:18 ESV). On the ESV's rendering of John 1:18 ("the only God"), the adjective "only" is an attributive modifying God (generic deity) rather than the Son.

The second problem with the ESV's translation of John 1:18 is that it could easily be misused as a proof text for modalistic monarchianism or the "Jesus only" heresy of Oneness Pentecostalism. The New Testament nowhere else calls Jesus "the only God" or "the one true God." Instead, it consistently calls him "the Son of [the one true] God." Of course, that means he is fully divine, since the Son is everything that the Father is as to his essential nature. But he is fully divine, not because he just is the one God but because he is the one God's eternal Son.

Third, the ESV's rendering produces an unintended result. Here is the ESV again: "No one has ever seen God; the only God, who is at the Father's side, he has made him known." If "the only God" is a person who is "at the Father's side," then "the only God" is distinct from the Father.

A LEXICAL DEFENSE OF THE JOHANNINE "ONLY BEGOTTEN"

That seems to place the Father outside of "the only God." The point of the affirmation that Jesus is "the only God" is to make clear that he is fully divine. But no sooner has the ESV put the Son within the ontological deity than it proceeds (unwittingly, no doubt) to place the Father outside of it.[54]

It would seem that these two things—translating *monogenēs* as "only" and adopting the μονογενὴς θεός reading at John 1:18—do not comport with one another. Interpreters and translators have to tie themselves up in pretzels in order to harmonize them. It is better to choose one or the other. If interpreters are convinced that *monogenēs* means "only" rather than "only begotten," then they ought to follow the RSV and adopt the Majority Text reading, ὁ μονογενὴς υἱός, to maintain the inner coherence and logic of the verse: "No one has ever seen God; the only Son, who is in the bosom of the Father, he has made him known." On the other hand, if we are convinced (as I am) that μονογενὴς θεός is the earliest and best reading, then the only way to make coherent sense of the text is to take *monogenēs* in the traditional sense: "No one has seen God at any time; the only begotten God who is in the bosom of the Father, He has explained *Him*" (NASB).

Thus, John 1:14 and 18 are of crucial importance for demonstrating that the Johannine *monogenēs* cannot be reduced to "only of his kind" but must have a metaphorical biological meaning, "only begotten." John views Christ as the only begotten Son of God in the sense that he is the Father's only proper offspring deriving his divine being from the Father. The fact that John 1:18 adds that he "is" (ὤν, present participle) in the bosom of the Father (ὁ ὢν εἰς τὸν κόλπον τοῦ πατρός) underscores that his sonship transcends time and is not to be interpreted as a temporal event like ordinary human begetting. The phrase εἰς τὸν κόλπον reinforces this by emphasizing the profound intimacy and love between the Father and his only begotten Son. We may conclude that, for John, the Son is eternally generated by or begotten of the Father.

Of course, the concept of a human father begetting a human son is an analogy or metaphor that is being used by John as a way of pointing to the eternal Son's relationship with the Father. It is a relationship of love, intimacy, and delight. When the Son is sent into the world, he comes in

---

54. The ESV provides an alternate rendering in a footnote: "No one has ever seen God; the only One, who is God, who is at the Father's side, he has made him known." In one sense, this construction, which takes *monogenēs* as a substantive ("the only One"), and θεός in apposition to it, is an improvement insofar as it keeps *monogenēs* as an attribute of the Son (consistent with the rest of Johannine usage) rather than of generic deity. However, in this case, the attempt to hold on to the premise that *monogenēs* means "only" and not "only begotten" becomes even less tenable, for the postulated christological title, "the only One," is without example elsewhere in the New Testament and has no definite significance.

115

obedience to his Father's will. Ultimately the Son reveals the Father because, by being the offspring begotten of the Father's divine nature, he possesses the same divine nature as the Father. Therefore, like all metaphors, there are notable points of discontinuity: unlike a human begetting, this begetting (1) had no beginning, (2) did not occur in time, (3) does not grant the Father chronological priority over the Son, and (4) lacks the involvement of a mother. But there is an analogy between human biological begetting and intra-Trinitarian begetting. The main points of continuity are: (1) the Father is the source or cause of the Son, (2) the Son possesses the same nature (*homoousios*) with the Father who begat him, (3) the Father delights in his Son and calls him "beloved," and (4) it is fitting that the Son is the one sent on a mission from the Father to do the Father's will.

CONCLUSION

In spite of the modern consensus that the Johannine *monogenēs* ought to be rendered "only" or "one and only," thereby eliminating the notion of begottenness, the lexical evidence for "only begotten" is actually quite compelling. The five occurrences of the term in the Gospel and first Epistle of John thus provide part of the exegetical basis for the traditional doctrine of the eternal begetting or generation of the Son, which is in turn a crucial linchpin for the pro-Nicene doctrine of the Trinity. This is not to say that patristic exegesis relied solely on the Johannine *monogenēs*. Many other important texts informed their thinking on this issue.[55] Nevertheless, the importance of the Johannine *monogenēs* for the construction of the doctrine of the eternal generation of the Son cannot be underestimated. While modern exegetes may need, in some cases, to provide legitimate correctives to elements of patristic exegesis, this may turn out to be one case where the church fathers had it right all along.

---

55. See Charles Lee Irons, "Begotten of the Father before All Ages: The Biblical Basis of Eternal Generation according to the Church Fathers," *Christian Research Journal* 40, no. 1 (2017): 41–47.

CHAPTER 6

HEBREWS 1 AND THE SON BEGOTTEN "TODAY"

MADISON N. PIERCE

"YOU ARE MY SON; today I have begotten you."[1] The Epistle to the Hebrews quotes this text from Psalm 2:7 near the opening of the Epistle, but what does the author mean that the Son was begotten *today?* Is Hebrews advocating an adoptionist Christology? If so, then how does that cohere with the author's depiction of the Son in the rest of the Epistle? If not, then what does he mean by the word "today?" There are two noteworthy yet divergent views on this verse: (1) the "day" is the day of Jesus's enthronement and exaltation, and (2) the "day" is eternity—the span of Jesus's existence.

This chapter will argue that even though this quotation is sometimes used in service of an adoptionist Christology, the author of Hebrews intends to use this quotation of Psalm 2:7 in Hebrews 1:5 to claim that Jesus is the Son of God eternally. This reading supports the doctrine of "eternal generation," which teaches that the Father by necessity generated the Son in eternity past. To support this thesis, I will first outline Hebrews 1:1–5 and show how 1:5 in particular fits within the chapter as a whole. Second, I will discuss some representative modern readings that offer a helpful contrast to my own. Then, I will show how the Old Testament context does and does not relate to the use of Psalm 2:7 in Hebrews and connect this context with the author's exegetical method. Finally, I will draw these threads together in order to offer my own explanation of the passage and show how it reasonably supports reading "today" as a metaphorical temporal designation. Before I proceed to a summary of Hebrews 1, let me summarize this issue further.

---

1. Unless noted otherwise, Scripture translations are original to the author.

117

MADISON N. PIERCE

In the Nicene Creed, the summary of orthodox teaching about Jesus is succinct and yet holds together the humanity and divinity of God's Son in a way that, to borrow the Creed's syntax, is thorough, not erudite, and simple, not simplistic. The slightly expanded version from AD 381 reads:

> We believe . . . in one Lord Jesus Christ, the only-begotten Son of God, begotten of the Father before all worlds, *Light of Light, very God of very God, begotten, not made*, being of one substance with the Father, by whom all things were made, who for us, humanity, and for our salvation came down from heaven, *was incarnate by the Holy Ghost of the Virgin Mary*, and was made human [emphasis added].

That Jesus is God of God and Light of Light means that he is wholly God, that he is fully one with the Father—he is as it were "like from like." Yet another crucial part of his identity is the fact that he was mothered by the Virgin Mary. He is eternal and yet lived a human life in which he was born and died. He is eternal and "begotten, not made"—a teaching referred to by many theologians as the doctrine of eternal generation, which in this chapter will be primarily referred to in terms of "eternal begetting"—is thought to be a part of orthodox theological instruction; however, it has become common among biblical scholars to insist that these ideas cannot be found explicitly within our Bible.[2] The biblical authors, they claim, had only a rudimentary understanding of God, and it was not for several hundred years—until the Council of Nicaea in AD 325—that people *really* took an interest in some of these more complex theological distinctives. I am not thoroughly convinced. This chapter considers the use of Hebrews 1:5 as test case to illustrate how some interpretations take more complex routes in hopes of arriving at a less complex theological conclusion.

---

2. For example, L. D. Hurst cautions against the "tendency to homogenize the thinking of the New Testament writers and to read later theological concerns into their statements." This must be "resisted," he says, if the "purity of the discipline is to be preserved" ("The Christology of Hebrews 1 and 2," in *The Glory of Christ in the New Testament: Studies in Christology*, ed. L. D. Hurst and N. T. Wright [Oxford: Clarendon, 1987], 163). Among many other proponents of a separation between "biblical studies" and "theology" are: John Barton, *The Nature of Biblical Criticism* (Louisville: Presbyterian, 2007), esp. 177; Michael V. Fox, "Bible Scholarship and Faith-Based Study: My View," *SBL Forum*, February 2006, http://sbl-site.org/Article.aspx?ArticleID=490; G. F. E. William Wrede, "The Tasks and Methods of 'New Testament Theology,'" in *The Nature of New Testament Theology* (London: SCM, 1973), 68–116. This is in contrast to Francis Watson, for example, who writes, "Biblical interpretation should no longer neglect its theological responsibilities," in *Text, Church and World: Towards a Theological Hermeneutic for Biblical Studies* (Edinburgh: T&T Clark, 1994), vii.

SUMMARY OF PASSAGE

Though biblical scholars are encouraged to set aside their theological biases and approach the text "critically," it is sometimes the case that avoiding supposedly anachronistic theology might actually damage a plain—or at least plainer—reading of some texts. One passage that offers a helpful example is Hebrews 1. The author opens his Epistle with this grand summary: "At many times and in various ways, God, who formerly spoke to our ancestors through the prophets, in these last days speaks to us through the Son, whom he appointed heir of all things and through whom also he made the universe. The Son is the radiance of God's glory and the exact representation of his being" (Heb 1:1–3a). The Son is a secondary agent of creation and heir of all things. He likewise emanates or radiates God's glory and replicates his very essence.

This section of Hebrews has since fueled many theological treatises. Athanasius, one example among many, writes of the first description of the Son in Hebrews 1:3: "As the apostle, writing to the Hebrews, says, 'who being the brightness of his glory and the stamp of his nature.' . . . For when did anyone see light without the brightness of its radiance that one may say of the Son, 'There was once when he was not,' or 'Before his generation he was not'?"[3] Light and brightness can be distinguished, but they cannot be separated. Athanasius implies that this image clearly depicts the relationship between the Father and Son. Likewise, at another point in his *Orations against the Arians*, Athanasius also explicates the next description of the Son as the "exact representation of his being" (χαρακτὴρ τῆς ὑποστάσεως αὐτοῦ): "He is true God, existing consubstantially (*homoousios*) with the true Father. . . . For he is the 'very stamp' of the Father's 'being,' and 'light' from 'light,' and the 'power' and true 'image' of the Father's substance."[4] Athanasius interprets χαρακτήρ as "stamp" and/or "image." This language is also used in the minting of coins.[5] The Father is seen via the Son (cf. John 1:18)—he is imprinted upon his likeness. For Athanasius, Hebrews offers a substantive glimpse of something in accord with later Nicene theology. Early readers, especially but not only Athanasius, found these verses in Hebrews to be influential in their understanding of God.

---

3. *C. Ar.* 1.4.12. This translation and the next are updated from *NPNF²* vol. 4 by Erik M. Heen and Philip D. W. Krey, eds., *Hebrews* (Downers Grove, IL: InterVarsity, 2005).

4. *C. Ar.* 1.3.9.

5. Michael P. Theophilus, "The Numismatic Background of Χαρακτήρ in Hebrews 1.3," *Australian Biblical Review* 64 (2016): 69–80; cf. Walter Bauer et al., eds., *A Greek-English Lexicon of the New Testament and Other Christian Literature* (Chicago: University of Chicago Press, 1999), 1077–78.

MADISON N. PIERCE

The author of Hebrews begins with his own summary of who the Son is, but, as we shall see, he does not stop there. Rather than having his readers take his word on the matter, the author then goes on to quote God's words—not as a written text but as God's spoken communication about the Son. Since the Son later responds to the Father's words in Hebrews 2, some even refer to this as an "inner-Trinitarian conversation."[6] For the author, grounding these claims in God's words makes them authoritative. The author does not call Jesus "Son"—God does.

In addition to this speech, to make clear just how remarkable the Son is, the author of Hebrews compares him with God's prior mediators—the angels. They are not worthy recipients of God's speech, even though they are powerful divine beings. Even so, the Son is of course superior:

> For to whom among the angels did God ever say,
>   "You are my Son;
>   *today I have begotten you*"
>
> and again,
>   "I will be his Father;
>   he will be my Son." (1:5)

In each of these quotations from Scripture, first Psalm 2:7 and then 2 Samuel 7:14, the author of Hebrews capitalizes on an ambiguity or tension within the text or its subsequent interpretation in order to identity the addressee of the speech as Jesus.[7] But modern interpreters have of course found ambiguity in the author of Hebrews's work as well. In the next section I will summarize some representative views of Hebrews 1:5 that I find problematic. These views will offer a helpful contrast to my own, which I will offer at the close.

---

6. Markus Barth, "Old Testament in Hebrews: An Essay in Biblical Hermeneutics," in *Current Issues in New Testament Interpretation* (New York: Harper, 1962), 62; Hans Hübner, *Biblische Theologie des Neuen Testaments* (Göttingen: Vandenhoek & Ruprecht, 1990), 3:24, 28; cf. Michael Theobald, "Vom Text zum 'lebendigen Wort' (Hebr 4,12): Beobachtungen zur Schrifthermeneutik des Hebräerbriefs," in *Jesus Christus als die Mitte der Schrift: Studien zur Hermeneutik des Evangeliums*, ed. Christof Landmesser, Hans-Joachim Eckstein, and Hermann Lichtenberger (Berlin: de Gruyter, 1997), 774.

7. This technique is now formally referred to as "prosopological" (or "prosopographic" or "prosoponic") exegesis. For a recent discussion of this technique and its use in the NT, see Matthew W. Bates, *The Hermeneutics of Apostolic Proclamation: The Center of Paul's Method of Interpretation* (Waco: Baylor University Press, 2012), ch. 4; Matthew W. Bates, *The Birth of the Trinity: Jesus, God, and Spirit in New Testament and Early Christian Interpretations of the Old Testament* (Oxford: Oxford University Press, 2015). For the origins of this discussion, see Carl Andresen, "Zur Entstehung und Geschichte des trinitarischen Personbegriffes," *ZNW* 52 (1961): 1–39; Marie-Josèphe Rondeau, *Les commentaires patristiques du Psautier (IIIe-Ve siècles)*, vol. 2., *Exégèse prosopologique et théologie* (Rome: Institutum Studiorum Orientalium, 1985).

Modern Readings

The primary view of Hebrews 1:5 among biblical scholars is that this verse takes place at the exaltation of Jesus. Though the author does not quote Psalm 110:1, "sit at my right hand," until the end of these seven quotations about the Son's superiority, an allusion to this verse first appears in Hebrews 1:3. The author says that "after [Jesus] provided purification for sins, he sat down at the right hand of the Majesty on High." With this allusion and the subsequent quotation of Psalm 110:1 in Hebrews 1:13, the author brackets the series of quotations inside references to the Son sitting at the right hand of the Father. Some contend that this frame is put in place so that readers envision the throne room throughout the seven quotations, seeing the Son firmly at rest in his heavenly session.[8] Many interpreters locate the Father's part of the conversation between the Father and Son precisely in that setting—in the heavens at the exaltation.

Nevertheless, the key question is whether all the acts and events depicted in the quotations occur in this setting as well, as so many claim. Victor Rhee, for example, states that "Christ was begotten as the Son [at] the same time that he was appointed as high priest"—which for Rhee is at the exaltation.[9] L. D. Hurst likewise claims, "The author's *main* interest was not in a uniquely privileged, divine being who becomes man; it is in a human figure who attains to an exalted status."[10] For some, such as Kenneth Schenck, Christ was always the Son because someday he would function as such.[11] In other words, Christ always had the *potential* to sit at the Father's right hand. This understanding upholds the sonship of Jesus throughout his life but implies that the Son is superior to the angels and worthy of the worship described in Hebrews 1:6 based on what he *becomes*, not on what he *was*—and of course always *is*.

Others avoid the issue of the "begetting" and what it entails by relying upon the time and place at which the declaration is spoken. They explicitly

---

8. For example, Gareth Lee Cockerill, *The Epistle to the Hebrews* (Grand Rapids: Eerdmans, 2012), 96–97; Joshua W. Jipp, "The Son's Entrance into the Heavenly World: The Soteriological Necessity of the Scriptural Catena in Hebrews 1.5–14," *NTS* 56, no. 4 (2010): 559.

9. Rhee, "The Role of Chiasm for Understanding Christology in Hebrews 1:1–14," *JBL* 131, no. 2 (2012): 360–61.

10. Hurst, "The Christology of Hebrews 1 and 2," 163. The line of interpretation fits with interpretations of Jesus's baptism as the moment that the Father "adopts" or "appoints" Jesus as Son. When the heavens open, the Father speaks a combination of Psalm 2:7 and Isaiah 42:1. See, e.g., James D. G. Dunn, *Christology in the Making: A New Testament Inquiry into the Origins of the Doctrine of the Incarnation,* 2nd ed. (Grand Rapids: Eerdmans, 1996), 35–36.

11. Schenck, "Keeping His Appointment: Creation and Enthronement in Hebrews," *Journal for the Study of the New Testament* 19, no. 66 (1997): 104.

MADISON N. PIERCE

state that their view is incompatible with reading Psalm 2:7 in Hebrews 1:5 in terms of the Son's eternal generation, even though their primary aim is simply to locate the speech at the exaltation.[12] I will argue in what follows that locating this speech at the exaltation is compatible with an "eternal" interpretation of the begetting. Those interpreters are right: it happened *today*.

CONTEXT OF OLD TESTAMENT QUOTATIONS

Since readings of Hebrews 1:5 need to take the context of Hebrews's quotations into account, let us turn briefly to the Old Testament. In Hebrews 1:5, the author quotes two verses from the Greek version of the Old Testament: Psalm 2:7 and 2 Samuel 7:14. In the former, the speaker tells his audience how the Lord bestowed upon him an inheritance—the nations (2:8)—and vowed to be his Father (2:7). Traditionally, this psalm was associated with David or another ruler in the Davidic line, primarily due to the messianic language, which is often linked to the Davidic monarchy.[13] The next verse, 2 Samuel 7:14, has a more concrete historical setting; these are words spoken to David via the prophet Nathan about his descendent (τὸ σπέρμα) being called "son" by YHWH, often thought to be Solomon. In both Psalm 2 and 2 Samuel 7, the texts portray a metaphorical father–son relationship between God and the human king,[14] which according to Joseph Fitzmyer entails "divine sponsorship, support, or assistance for the king, and by implication the dynasty."[15] This assumes that the verse does not necessitate that the Son is truly the Son of God—one who is "like from like." As for the setting, the "today" of the proclamation is thought to be the coronation

---

12. For example, Cockerill, *Epistle to the Hebrews*, 103–4; Rhee, "The Role of Chiasm," 360–61.

13. Eric F. Mason, "Interpretation of Psalm 2 in 4QFlorilegium and in the New Testament," in *Echoes from the Caves: Qumran and the New Testament*, ed. Florentino G. Martínez (Leiden: Brill, 2009), 67–82; Joseph A. Fitzmyer, *The Dead Sea Scrolls and Christian Origins* (Grand Rapids: Eerdmans, 2000), esp. 74–75. For a more thorough summary of the history of interpretation for this passage, see Tryggve N. D. Mettinger, *King and Messiah: The Civil and Sacral Legitimation of the Israelite Kings* (Lund: CWK Gleerup, 1976). Some additional (particularly recent) material can be found in Gert Jacobus Steyn, *A Quest for the Assumed LXX Vorlage of the Explicit Quotations in Hebrews* (Göttingen: Vandenhoeck & Ruprecht, 2011), 34–36.

14. Tryggve N. D. Mettinger claims the use of the prefixed preposition -לֹ also confirms a metaphorical interpretation in 2 Sam 7:14 (*King and Messiah*, 61). The Greek tradition translates the phrase: ἐγὼ ἔσομαι αὐτῷ εἰς πατέρα, καὶ αὐτὸς ἔσται μοι εἰς υἱόν.

15. Fitzmyer, *The Dead Sea Scrolls and Christian Origins*, 66. For an argument in favor of a more literal divine begetting, see Gard Granerød, "A Forgotten Reference to Divine Procreation? Psalm 2:6 in Light of Egyptian Royal Ideology," *VT* 60, no. 3 (2010): 323–36. Luke Timothy Johnson also points to the fact that "Both speak of a Son who is also a king" (*Hebrews: A Commentary* [Louisville: Westminster John Knox, 2006], 77).

for the king.[16] This statement conferring sonship language to the human king is a "performative utterance" that "adopts" the person as God's son.[17]

Thus two elements to bear in mind as we progress are (1) the timing of these passages and by extension the setting at the enthronement and (2) the quality or type of sonship they imply. If one or both elements are intended to carry over into the use of these passages in the New Testament, then Jesus too might be God's metaphorical offspring who is praised as Son only at his exaltation and not in his preexistence or earthly life.

Were this imposition of the broader interpretive framework to be stressed, the consequences for the otherwise well-developed Christology of Hebrews would be significant.

EXEGETICAL STRATEGIES IN HEBREWS 1

But is this what the author of Hebrews is trying to communicate by these quotations? Explicitly he tells his readers that he is comparing the Son and the angels, but what other comparisons arise through his reading of these passages in this way? The author is taking portions of Jewish Scripture and identifying one of its characters as Jesus. This character- or person-centered exegesis, often referred to as "prosopological" or "prosoponic" exegesis,[18] relates to an ancient literary method that can be traced to Greco-Roman rhetorical education. Although the interpretive move of reading Jesus into Old Testament texts may seem rather natural to us now due to its frequency in the New Testament and early Christian literature, it still requires further discussion and evaluation in light of its Jewish context.

This technique found throughout Hebrews is also found in at least one episode from Jesus's teaching in the Synoptic Gospels. In Matthew 22:42–45, Jesus asks the Pharisees,

---

16. William Hugh Brownlee, "Psalms 1–2 as a Coronation Liturgy," *Biblica* 52, no. 3 (1971): 321–36.

17. Mettinger, *King and Messiah*, 266–67. Here Mettinger also lists some Assyrian parallels for adoption and marriage taking place as a result of similar declarations.

18. Fred Sanders prefers "prosoponic" exegesis and has a useful discussion of the phenomenon and its implications for Trinitarian theology (*The Triune God* [Grand Rapids: Zondervan, 2016], 224–37). In earlier studies, Carl Andresen uses the term "prosopographic exegesis" ("Zur Entstehung und Geschichte des trinitarischen Personbegriffes"), but Marie-Josèphe Rondeau, whose study remains the most comprehensive with regard to patristic exegesis, suggests that "prosopological exegesis" should be preferred since "prosopographic" already has an established meaning. See Rondeau, *Les commentaires patristiques*, 2:8, no. 7. Matthew Bates goes a step further by arguing that "prosopological exegesis presupposes the divine *Logos* . . . as the ultimate author" (Bates, *Hermeneutics of the Apostolic Proclamation*, 218). See also Matthew W. Bates, "Justin Martyr's Logocentric Hermeneutical Transformation of Isaiah's Vision of the Nations," *JTS* 60, no. 2 (2009): 538–55.

"What do you think about the Messiah? Whose son is he?" They reply, "The son of David." "How then," Jesus asks, "is it that David, speaking by the Spirit, calls him 'Lord'? For he says,

'The Lord said to my Lord:
"Sit at my right hand
    until I put your enemies under your feet."'

If then David calls him 'Lord,' how can he be his son?"

Jesus points to a tension in the common interpretation of this text that sees the "lord" as a son of David. David is, after all, a great king, and to call his descendant or child "lord" is a bit strange if something is not truly significant about the individual. Though none of the Gospels end up explicitly identifying the "Lord" of the psalm, the clear implication is that it is Jesus. This interpretation of Psalm 110 attempts to resolve the potential tension of David referring to his child as "lord."

Hebrews 1:5 likewise seeks to address a tension found in the common identification of the "son" begotten today as one within the Davidic line. Even though this psalm is distinctive in its lack of connection to David in the Greek version of Scripture, it does contain a reference to the Christ—the Messiah or the anointed one. But who is the anointed one? Hebrews identifies him with Jesus. Likewise, who is the one among David's offspring that 2 Samuel 7:14 says will be a king *forever*? Only one among David's many, many descendants—Jesus.

These quotations are used by the author in a creative way to establish the superiority of the Son over the angels. The author, as we shall see, shows that the Son is the only one truly qualified to be called "Son" by God. While the author uses his quotations to assert who the Son is, he uses the introductory formula, "for to whom among the angels did God ever say," to make a point about who the Son is not. In Hebrews 1:5, the addressee—the Son—and the nonaddressees—the angels—are both of great importance. The author makes clear that this speech is exceptional; however, even though part of the author's purpose is to elevate the Son over the angels, by calling him "Son" he actually introduces a correlation rather than a contrast. This is because the angels sometimes are called "sons of God" in Scripture,[19] as

---

19. In the Greek text, this phrase occurs in Gen 6:2, 4, as well as Pss 28:1, 88:7—sometimes likely referring to angels or other divine beings (Gen 6:2, 4; Ps 88:7) and sometimes to humans (Ps 28:1). In the Hebrew, three additional references in Job also contain this phrase (1:6; 2:1; 38:7),

HEBREWS I AND THE SON BEGOTTEN "TODAY"

in Genesis 6:1–4 (LXX): "Then humans began to become numerous on
the earth, and daughters were born to them, and the sons of God, seeing
that the human daughters were beautiful, took for themselves wives from
all whom they chose . . . when the sons of God had intercourse with the
human daughters, they gave birth."

Interpreters typically identify the "sons of God," and their sin of gigan-
tic proportions, with the angels.[20] If the angels are sons, then how is this
Son distinct? While the author of Hebrews does not explicitly acknowledge
this potential counterpoint for his readers, a few clues in the text answer
the hypothetical objection. First, no *singular* angel is ever called "son,"
just as the author suggests with his introductory formula. Further, Jesus is
not simply Son; he is the "firstborn" (Heb 1:6).[21] With this more specific
designation, the author minimizes any lingering counterarguments about
another "son of God." Even if one claimed that the references to the angels
as "sons of God" in Scripture suggest a multiplicity of sons, this Son has
supremacy.

Even though no single angel was called "son," a single human is, namely,
the Davidic king. He bears this title in Psalm 2:7 and 2 Samuel 7:14.[22]
Further, in Psalm 89:27, the king is called the firstborn (πρωτότοκος),
which is likely referenced in the next introductory formula in Hebrews 1:6:
"but again when he brings the firstborn (πρωτότοκον) into the world, he
says . . ."[23] Within the Psalms, these texts can plausibly be applied to someone within the Davidic line, but the author of Hebrews has made certain

---

but the Greek tradition translates בני as ἄγγελοι in each instance. These alterations in LXX Job may
suggest a growing reticence among some to refer to the angels in this way. Ps 88:7, conversely, reads
"holy ones" in the Hebrew, but υἱοί θεοῦ in the Greek.

20. Sven Fockner and others have challenged the identification of these sons with angels
("Reopening the Discussion: Another Contextual Look at the Sons of God," *Journal for the Study
of the Old Testament* 32, no. 4 [2008]: 435–56); however, this potential misinterpretation does not
account for the texts in Job and the Psalms or later "Watcher" traditions. If it is a misreading of the
Hebrew text, then it is an influential one.

21. For a discussion of the author's later reference to humanity as an "assembly of the firstborn"
(ἐκκλησία πρωτοτόκων) in Heb 12:23, Amy L. B. Peeler, *You Are My Son: The Family of God in the
Epistle to the Hebrews* (London: T&T Clark, 2014), 168–72.

22. Compare also parallels in 1 Chr 17:13; 22:10. One additional text to note is 4Q246, which
refers to the "Son of God" and the "Son of the Most High." While the text is traditionally interpreted
to be messianic, it is fragmentary and could, with more material, reveal a possible exception. For
more, see John J. Collins, *Scepter and the Star* (New York: Doubleday, 1996).

23. This additional messianic king text is likely in view since if not only fits the author's argument but is also the only context in which πρωτότοκος is used of an individual firstborn of God in
the LXX. For more on this reading, see Peeler, *You Are My Son*, 52–55. See also George B. Caird,
"Son by Appointment," in *The New Testament Age: Essays in Honor of Bo Reicke*, ed. William C.
Weinrich (Macon, GA: Mercer University Press, 1984), 1:75; Ardel B. Caneday, "The Eschatological
World Already Subjected to the Son: The Οἰκουμένη of Hebrews 1.6 and the Son's Enthronement,"
in *A Cloud of Witnesses: The Theology of Hebrews in Its Ancient Contexts*, ed. Richard Bauckham et al.
(London: T&T Clark, 2008), 33.

125

that his readers know the words are about the exalted Son. The author has reinterpreted them by identifying Jesus as a character within these texts.[24]

As I have suggested, this technique often takes place when an interpreter finds a tension with a common reading. In this case, the author of Hebrews, perhaps in line with a previous tradition,[25] proposes that nearly every text that refers to a human king as the "son of God" (or "firstborn") should instead be read exclusively christologically. In other words, his cognitive framework suggests that an ordinary human cannot be the Son of God, so he looks for another character behind these texts. What he finds is the Christ.[26] As a result, the author suggests that something is distinct about God's bestowal of the title son here—it is unfit for a (human) king.

If the author of Hebrews is not using every element of the Old Testament context, and is perhaps even creating some distance between his reading and common readings of Psalm 2, then the assumption that numerous elements of Psalm 2 obviously influence other elements for Hebrews 1 requires further evaluation. This is especially true for the two facets of these texts that I mentioned previously—the timing and the type of sonship in view.

Delaying our discussion of the timing momentarily, let us consider the type of Father–Son relationship depicted elsewhere in Hebrews. Is it purely metaphorical and/or spiritual in nature? In one sense, this is a difficult question to answer because an integral part of Hebrews's theology points to the one Son Jesus extending salvation, his inheritance, and other blessings as Son of God to his brothers and sisters. So how might we determine that Hebrews envisions a distinct relationship between Jesus and God the Father when the author so often connects Jesus to humanity? Here, the theological discussions of the fourth century assist us again. For Jesus to be a distinct and actual Son of God, he needs to be one with God, connected and coherent with him in ways that we are not—in ways that Hebrews 1 says Jesus is indeed connected. He is the exact representation of God's being—his ὑπόστασις (1:3). He has inherited a name from his Father that makes him superior to the angels (1:4). He is called God by God in Hebrews 1:8–9 and Lord, the Greek equivalent to the Divine Name,

---

24. One text that the author cannot reinterpret is 1 Chr 28:6: "He said to me, 'Solomon, your son, will build my house and my courts, for I chose him as my son, and I will be his father.'" This text does not diminish the author's argument, as he does not say, "To whom among the humans?" but it does complicate his mission to present this son as wholly unique.

25. Even setting aside the question of Hebrews's use of a *testimonia*, which most now reject, 4QFlorilegium demonstrates that a number of texts similar to those Hebrews uses (e.g., Ps 89:23; 2 Sam 7:11–14; Isa 8:11) were being read as messianic.

26. This seems even more likely with the introduction of Ps 89:26–29, which provides an allusion to (or citation of) every necessary text (except 1 Chr 28:6; see n24 above).

YHWH, in Hebrews 1:10–12. Jesus is Son of God, God himself, and Lord. His depiction early in Hebrews is consistent with God the Father. He is indeed "like from like."

It seems, therefore, that the author of the Epistle to the Hebrews is indeed aware of the broader context of Psalm 2 and 2 Samuel 7, but that he finds a rationale within these texts to think that the extraordinary king discussed is none other than Jesus. By reading the text in this way, he not only introduces a comparison between Jesus and the great King David, but also suggests that no mere mortal could be spoken of in this way. The true Son of God is not a son like the angels or David, but is one who is coeternal and divine.

"Today" and Eternity in Hebrews

Turning to my own reading of Hebrews 1:5, I find a number of compelling reasons that, particularly when taken together, suggest that the author could have the eternal generation of the Son in view. The first relates to the relationship between the timing of the speech and that of the begetting. In the psalm itself, the depiction of the "enthroned one," who is installed on Mount Zion, certainly supports a view that locates Hebrews 1 at the exaltation of the Son to the Father's right hand. But it is from the throne that the Anointed One says,

> I will tell of the decree of the Lord: He said to me,
> "*You are my son;*
> > *today I have begotten you.*
> Ask of me, and *I will make the nations your inheritance,*
> > and the ends of the earth your possession."

This is reported speech from the past.[27] By the time the speaker speaks, he has already been proclaimed Son, but when this decree takes place is not further specified by the author. In the psalm, it *is* contemporaneous with his appointment, but neither Hebrews nor the psalm indicates when that appointment happens. What we do know is at the time of the decree the promise to make the nations the king's inheritance remains in the future. Psalm 2:8 is of course not quoted in Hebrews 1:5; however, Hebrews 1:2

---

27. For a more thorough discussion of the reported speech in Ps 2, see Bates, *The Birth of the Trinity*, 62–71.

contains a likely reference to it: the Son is the one "whom [God] appointed heir of all things."

While this initially suggests that the Son has indeed received his inheritance, other elements in Hebrews suggest a tension. After showing how Psalm 8 ties to the future of humanity (as brought about by Jesus), Hebrews 2:9 says, "But we do not yet see all things in subjection to him." Here the marriage of Psalm 2 and Psalm 110 found in Hebrews 1 remains key to the author's understanding of the Son, and this combination of texts recurs when the author discusses Christ's priesthood in Hebrews 5 as well, confirming the likely link in the author's conceptual framework. What Hebrews 2 suggests is that the full inheritance for the Son is the subjection of all things, and that remains unfulfilled. This may mean that the promise of the inheritance and the reception of the inheritance itself are separate. This is certainly the case for Abraham and others in Hebrews 11—since theirs is a promise not yet obtained (11:39). Returning to Hebrews 1, this sequence is somewhat challenging to untangle with multiple texts in view, but the sequence of events appears to be as follows: the Son was said to be begotten and appointed heir, he reported the Father's speech, and then he fully inherited all things.

But, we may ask, if the day of the speech is not the day of the begetting, then why has the author chosen a quotation that apparently locates the begetting "today" when he quotes the text? After all, if he desired to avoid this complication, then he could have quoted only 2 Samuel 7:14 and not Psalm 2:7. But seeing Psalm 2 as an avoidable complication is a flawed hypothetical assumption that misses the point. For this author, "today" is far more than a twenty-four-hour timespan. Using Psalm 2:7 allows him the opportunity to say something particular about the Son.

Let us turn now to the author's other uses of this word "today" to explore this strategy further. Among the eight uses of this language in Hebrews, perhaps the most recognizable is Hebrews 13:8: "Jesus Christ is the same yesterday, today, and forever." For our purpose, the most helpful occurrences are found in Hebrews 3–4. There the author quotes Scripture yet again, but this time the speaker is the Holy Spirit. With the words of Psalm 95:7–11, the Spirit exhorts the community:

> Today if you hear his voice,
>   do not harden your hearts as in the rebellion,
>   on the day of testing in the wilderness
>   where your ancestors tested [me] with scrutiny

HEBREWS 1 AND THE SON BEGOTTEN "TODAY"

and saw my works for forty years.
Therefore, I became angry with that generation and said,
"They always go astray in their hearts,
and they do not know my ways."
As I swore in my wrath,
"They shall never enter my rest."

The psalmist says, "Today if you hear his voice, do not harden your hearts." Although this quotation is directed to the audience with second-person plural language, the author's discussion moves beyond implicit address to explicit imperatives in the exhortation that follows. Beginning in Hebrews 3:13, the author says, "Encourage one another each day, as long as it is called 'today,' so that none among you becomes hardened by the deceit of sin." For the author to command this behavior each day that is called "today" assumes that it will continue forever because on no known occasion will this day not be "today."

Thus, the author draws upon the relative dimension of the word "today," which is always in the present, so that the words of the psalm and his subsequent exhortation are valid forever. This is likewise in effect in Hebrews 13:8. The fact that "Jesus is the same yesterday, today, and forever" of course means that in our past, present, and future Jesus is eternal and consistent.[28] It would be enough to say that Jesus is the same *forever*, but the author uses "today" and "yesterday" for effect. In more colloquial terms, Jesus is the same forever and ever and ever.

Saint Augustine also reads the "today" in this way. In his Psalms commentary, he writes of this passage:

> The word today denotes the actual present, and as in eternity nothing is past as if it had ceased to be, nor future as if it had not yet come to pass, but all is simply present, since whatever is eternal is ever in being, the words, "Today I have begotten you," are to be understood of the divine generation. In this phrase, the orthodox catholic [i.e., universal] belief proclaims the eternal generation of the Power and Wisdom of God who is the only-begotten Son.[29]

---

28. "Forms of a formula indicating that God was, is, and will be appear in various sources . . . so that Heb 13:8 implies Jesus' divinity" (Craig Koester, *Hebrews* [New York: Doubleday, 2001], 559).

29. *Enarrat. Ps.* 2:6. This is a more modern version of the translation offered here: Augustine, *St. Augustine on the Psalms*, ed. Scholastica Hebgin and Felicitas Corrigan (New York: Paulist, 1960), 1:27.

129

Similarly, in the *Confessions* when he comments on Psalm 102:27, also spoken about Jesus in Hebrews 1:12, Augustine says to God, "Your years are but a day, and your day is not recurrent, but always today. Your 'today' yields not to tomorrow and does not follow yesterday. Your 'today' is eternity. Therefore, you did generate the Co-eternal to whom you said, 'Today I have begotten you.'"[30] For Augustine, God's day lasts forever.

This is likewise the case for Philo of Alexandria, a well-educated Jewish author who was roughly contemporary with the Apostle Paul and perhaps also contemporary with the author of Hebrews. Commenting on Deuteronomy 4.4, Philo writes, "[Moses] adds, 'You are alive to this day'; and this day is interminable eternity, from which there is no departure . . . the unerring proper name of eternity is 'today'"[31] Philo's comment is particularly salient for understanding Hebrews since he and the author both show the influences of similar traditions, even to the point that some have claimed the author of Hebrews draws upon Philo's work.

Whether or not this is the case, Philo attests to the possibility of a metaphorical and eternal understanding of "today" in the first century, as does Augustine in later centuries. These writers corroborate the author of Hebrews's reading of Psalm 2:7 as an eternal event, as though he says: "You are my Son; *forever* I have begotten you." This corresponds with his teaching elsewhere in Hebrews. Jesus is one whose throne is forever in Hebrews 1:8–9. His priesthood and priestly ministry is forever in Hebrews 7, but especially Hebrews 7:24. Jesus is indeed the same yesterday, today, and forever.

Conclusion

This chapter began with a concern regarding claims that Hebrews contains an adoptionist Christology. After summarizing the issue at hand, I proceeded through a discussion of modern interpreters who mistakenly argue that all the events of Hebrews 1 take place at the enthronement. This led into an analysis of the original contexts of the Old Testament quotations and the reading strategy of the author of Hebrews. I then transitioned to my own reading of Hebrews 1:5 within its context in the Epistle as a whole.

---

30. Augustine, *Confessions and Encheiridion*, ed. Albert Cook Outler, rev. ed. (Louisville: Westminster John Knox, 2006), 12.16 (p. 254).

31. See Philo, *On Flight and Finding. On the Change of Names. On Dreams.*, trans. F. H Colson and G. H. Whitaker, LCL 275 (Cambridge, MA: Harvard University Press, 1934), 56–57 (pp. 40–41). This translation is primarily based upon C. D. Yonge, ed., *The Works of Philo: Complete and Unabridged* (Peabody, MA: Hendrickson, 1993), 326.

HEBREWS 1 AND THE SON BEGOTTEN "TODAY"

Casting some doubt on traditional understandings of the timing in Psalm 2 and showing other places in Hebrews and in the works of others that view "today" as a metaphorical timespan, I think we are in a position to conclude that Hebrews 1:5 supports the eternal generation of the Son and that it may even be the preferred reading of the verse. This suggests that theologians of the third and fourth centuries could likewise draw these conclusions from Hebrews and that this and other theological positions attributed to them could therefore be traced to the New Testament. Hebrews 1:5 and its support of eternal generation serve as a mere test case, but I hope it encourages other biblical scholars to reevaluate their conclusions about the Bible's support for other doctrinal positions as well. "You are my Son; today I have begotten you" is not just a claim about Jesus reaching an exalted status. It is a declaration of his eternal relationship with the Father that is always in effect.

CHAPTER 7

GENERATIO, PROCESSIO VERBI, DONUM NOMINIS:
Mapping the Vocabulary of Eternal Generation

R. KENDALL SOULEN

"All musick is but three parts vied and multiplied."
George Herbert

CONTEMPORARY THEOLOGIANS often discuss the mystery of eternal generation using the vocabulary of Father and Son, as though this were self-evidently the most appropriate available, or at any rate the least inappropriate. Karl Barth thought this was a mistake. He argued that Christians speak least inadequately about the mystery when they alternate between two different scriptural idioms: the Father's generation of the Son, or *generatio*, on the one hand, and the Word's procession from God, or *processio verbi*, on the other. Barth writes,

> Assuredly *generatio* and *processio verbi* must be regarded as describing the same material content. But not in such a way that one of these concepts may simply be reduced to the other. . . . The two figures, that of the Son and that of the Word of God, point to an object for which they are not appropriate. But for that very reason each of them must be taken seriously for itself, and neither of them should be dispensed with because the other is suggested.[1]

---

1. Karl Barth, *CD* I/1, ed. Geoffrey W. Bromiley and Thomas F. Torrance, trans. Geoffrey W. Bromiley (Edinburgh: T&T Clark, 1975), 493.

GENERATIO, PROCESSIO, VERBI, DONUM NOMINIS

Readers familiar with Barth will recognize here one of his most beloved rhetorical figures: signaling a single inexpressible truth by affirming two incomplete truths in its place. Interestingly, though, Barth's analysis of the vocabulary of eternal generation quickly bursts the bonds of this familiar trope. Examined more closely, the apparently singular image of *processio verbi* leads to a larger family of images from Scripture and tradition, such as "Light from Light," "God from God," Thinker and Thought, *Urbild* and *Abbild*, and so on. After reviewing—and approving!—a number of such images, Barth draws an interesting conclusion. Christians, he proposes, speak least inadequately of Christ's eternal origin when they employ—not two, three, or four images—but *all* available figures of speech (*alle Bildreden*).[2]

Stimulating as it is, Barth's conclusion raises an obvious question. What are all the ways the Bible prompts Christians to speak about the mystery of eternal generation? Is it possible to map the linguistic terrain, as it were? In this chapter, I want to draw such a map, although it will be closer to a back-of-the-envelope sketch than a detailed fold-out. It will include the patterns of speech that Barth identified—the kinship vocabulary of *generatio* and the multifaceted language of *processio verbi*. But it will also include a pattern of scriptural speech that Barth did not mention, which I will call the gift of the Name, or (to invent a fancy Latin expression) the *donum nominis*.

SCRIPTURE'S THREEFOLD VOCABULARY FOR GOD

To start our investigation, let us bracket the question of eternal generation for a moment and simply ask what kind of nouns the Bible uses to refer to the one God. We get the rudiments of an answer from the following verse:

> You O LORD are our Father,
> our Redeemer from of old is your name. (Isa 63:16)[3]

Here the prophet invokes the living God by using three different kinds of nouns: a personal proper name, a kinship term, and a common noun. The nouns signify the same divine subject, of course, but each does so in a distinctive way that is determined by the *kind* of noun it is.

---

2. Barth, *CD* I/1 (501).
3. Unless otherwise indicated, Scripture quotations in this chapter come from the NRSV.

- The personal proper name YHWH (represented by the surrogate "LORD") signifies God with an exclusivity of reference that the other two kinds of nouns cannot match. Though void of conventional meaning, YHWH is, as the logicians say, a rigid signifier that denotes but one reality: the living God of the Bible. Moreover, it has the peculiarity of exhausting the set to which it belongs: according to the Old Testament, the living God has but one personal proper name, the Tetragrammaton.
- "Father" belongs to a small set of kinship terms that the Old Testament applies to God, including husband and, at least by implication, mother (cf. Isa 54:5; Deut 32:18). Like kinship terms generally, it lacks the referential rigidity of a proper name (many individuals answer to the title "father"), but it denotes relation to a personal counterpart who bears the corresponding kinship term, in this case, "son" or "sons."
- Finally, "Redeemer" belongs to a very large pool of common nouns that the Bible applies to God, each of which has its own special shade of meaning and each of which stands ready to be called upon at need, such as "God," "Light," "Shepherd," "King," "Shield," and so on.

In one way, our verse from Isaiah is unusual, since Scripture does not often predicate all three kinds of nouns of God in such close proximity. In another way, though, the verse is paradigmatic: all the nouns that the Old Testament predicates of God belong to one of these three classes: personal proper name, kinship term, or common noun.

Turning from Old Testament to New, we may at first get the impression that God's personal proper name has vanished, leaving the work of denominating God to the remaining two patterns of speech. In reality, the Tetragrammaton is as prominent as ever, but the New Testament writers signify it in a new way, in keeping with the conventions of Second Temple Judaism. Rather than employ God's personal proper name *directly*, they invoke it *indirectly*, by employing one or another *surrogate* in its place (e.g., "Lord," "Name," "Power," "Blessed," "Holiness," etc.).[4] Once we recognize this, we quickly see that the New Testament writers continue the Old Testament practice of portraying God by using three different kinds of nouns. Consider, for example, this verse from 2 Peter: "For he [Jesus Christ]

---

4. Sean M. McDonough, *YHWH at Patmos: Rev. 1:4 in Its Hellenistic and Early Jewish Setting* (Tübingen: Mohr Siebeck, 1999) offers an excellent overview of beliefs and practices connected with the Divine Name in Second Temple Judaism. Julius Boehmer, *Die neutestamentliche Gottescheu und die ersten drei Bitten des Vaterunsers* (Halle: Richard Mühlmann Verlagsbuchhandlung, 1917), provides an inventory of every word and phrase in the New Testament reflecting the impact of reserve before the name of God, totaling many hundreds of instances.

received honor and glory from *God the Father* when that voice was conveyed to him by *the Majestic Glory*" (1:17, emphasis added). The author identifies the one who spoke to Jesus on the Mount of Transfiguration by means of a common noun ("God"), a kinship term ("the Father"), and a proper name, here designated by the circumlocution "the Majestic Glory," leaving the Tetragrammaton itself reverently unspoken.

Significantly, the Bible's threefold vocabulary for God continues to form the bedrock of subsequent Christian tradition. Consider, for example, the opening words of the Nicene Creed: "We believe in one God, the Father, the Almighty." Superficially, we may again seem to have only common nouns and kinship terms. But first impressions can be misleading. The literary backbone of the Nicene Creed—"We believe in one God, the Father, . . . and in one Lord Jesus Christ"—derives *verbatim* from St. Paul's confession in 1 Corinthians 8:6: "For us there is one God the Father . . . and one Lord, Jesus Christ." Paul's confession, in turn, is a carefully composed literary riff on the *Shema*, which Jews of Paul's day prayed daily to magnify God's (no longer routinely spoken) name: "Hear O Israel, the LORD our God, the LORD is one" (Deut 6:4 ESV). With supreme calculation, Paul has taken all the *Shema's* key theononyms ("YHWH/LORD," "God," "one") and reformulated them so as to place Jesus Christ *inside* Israel's primordial confession of faith. Understood in light of its scriptural antecedents, therefore, the Nicene Creed's confession of "one God the Father" and "one Lord Jesus Christ" is more than an aggregation of kinship terms and common nouns. It is also a carefully crafted echo of the *Shema's* confession of the deity who bears the name YHWH.[5]

Now let us return to the subject of eternal generation. The task we set ourselves was to sketch a map of the biblically authorized ways of speaking of this mystery. Does the threefold vocabulary we have just described provide a clue? I think it does. While Scripture speaks of eternal generation in many concrete ways, these can all be distinguished into three chief domains according to the *kind* of nouns in play: personal proper name, kinship term, or common noun.

In the rest of this chapter, I want to substantiate this claim by reviewing some evidence from Scripture and tradition, and then offer a brief systematic reflection on the significance of the threefold vocabulary.

---

5. For a recent discussion of 1 Cor 8:6 and the *Shema*, see Erik Waaler, *The "Shema" and the First Commandment in First Corinthians: An Intertextual Approach to Paul's Re-reading of Deuteronomy* (Tübingen: Mohr Siebeck, 2008).

Scripture and Tradition's Threefold Vocabulary for Eternal Generation

Eternal Generation as Processio Verbi: *Common Nouns in the Apologists*

The first Christian theologians to reflect extensively on God's pretemporal relation to Christ were the second-century apologists, and they had a preferred vocabulary for doing this: common nouns drawn from the vocabulary of the wisdom tradition. As Maurice Wiles has pointed out, for the apologists "the ideas of God and his Word or God and his Wisdom" were much more important than "the idea of God the Father and his Son."[6] Tatian, for example, never uses the concept of Son in his *Address to the Greeks*, and Theophilus does so only rarely in *Apology to Autolycus.* Instead, both theologians prefer to speak of Christ as the first-begotten Word or Wisdom of God.

This fact is fairly well known, and indeed it accounts for another name by which the apologists are commonly known: Logos theologians. The apologists' choice of conceptuality is often chalked up to the fact that they were seeking to make Christian faith intelligible and attractive to contemporaries, and no doubt there is something to this. Still, on this score at least, we cannot fairly accuse the apologists of abandoning Scripture for Hellenistic fashion because they were in fact echoing *the Bible's most common way* of portraying God's generation of a divine counterpart before the creation of the world. The thickest seam of such language is found in wisdom literature, which describes the origin of divine Wisdom in a host of impressive ways but never in terms of the kinship vocabulary of Father and Son. True, we do find the procreative verb *gennaō* ("beget"), as when God is said to beget Wisdom "before all the hills" (Prov 8:25) and "before the morning star" (Ps 110:3 LXX). Still, *gennaō* is but one among several verbs that describe the relation of origin and derivation, most of which are verbs outside the sphere of kinship language.[7] Turning to the New Testament writers, they too speak of the preexistent Christ most commonly in the imagery of common nouns inherited from Wisdom literature, as when

---

6. Maurice Wiles, "Eternal Generation," in *Working Papers in Doctrine* (London: SCM, 1976), 18–27, esp. 18. See also Alasdair Heron, "Logos, Image, Son: Some Models and Paradigms in Early Christology," in *Creation, Christ, and Culture: Studies in Honour of T. F. Torrance*, ed. Richard W. A. McKinney (Edinburgh: T&T Clark, 1976), 43–62.

7. Further obscuring matters is the fact that in the ante-Nicene period words derived from the root *gennaō* (beget) were not rigidly distinguished from their equivalent terms derived from the root *ginomai* (become). See G. L. Prestige, *God in Patristic Thought* (London: SPCK, 1952), 37–54.

GENERATIO, PROCESSIO, VERBI, DONUM NOMINIS

they call him "the Word" (John 1:1, 18), "the image of the invisible God" (Col 1:15), "the reflection of God's glory" (Heb 1:3), "the exact imprint of God's very being" (Heb 1:3), "in the form of God" (Phil 2:5), and so on.

Yet however biblical their inspiration, the Logos theologians famously failed to resolve some key questions. Was God's generation of Wisdom inherent in God's very identity as God, and thus as eternal as God himself? Or was it God's first act of creation, and thus temporally subsequent to God himself? In its prolixity of images, wisdom literature could be interpreted in either direction, and it must be said frankly that even the New Testament's Christ hymns are not wholly free of this ambiguity (cf. Christ as "the firstborn of all creation," Col 1:15). This leads us to consider the role played by another vocabulary of divine generation, that of *divine kinship*.

Eternal Generation as Generatio: *Kinship Nouns in Origen and Athanasius*

One the of key breakthroughs in the development of Trinitarian theology in the ante-Nicene period is often said to be the idea of *eternal* generation, which freed the concept of generation from one element of subordinationism, namely, temporal secondariness. The credit for this development usually goes to Origen. While Origen could express the idea of eternal generation in more than one way (as, for instance, the image of Light from Light), he did so quite often by reasoning from the language of Father and Son. His choice of vocabulary was no accident. Unlike most common nouns, kinship terms are inherently reciprocal in character. If God is eternally Father, as Origen held, then the Son too must be eternal, for, as Origen writes, "one cannot be a father apart from having a son."[8] Origen's reasoning remained potent a century later, when Athanasius championed it in his campaign against the Arians. Athanasius sought to sharpen Origen's insight into the eternal relation of Father and Son by emphasizing the distinction between the Father's *begetting* of the Son and the Father and Son's *creation* of the world in the power of the Spirit. The first is an eternal and necessary act of nature; the second a temporal and contingent act of divine will.

Still, even the concept of *eternal* generation as expressed in the language of kinship is not impervious to subordinationist interpretation. After all, fathers are commonly understood to be superior to sons in power and authority, and this might seem especially true in the case of one who is

---

8. Origen, *Princ.* 1.2.10. See Peter Widdicombe, *The Fatherhood of God from Origen to Athanasius* (Oxford: Clarendon, 1994), 69.

137

R. KENDALL SOULEN

eternally Father vis-à-vis one who is *eternally* Son. Perhaps because they sensed this lingering vulnerability, the bishops gathered at the Council of Nicaea sought for yet another way to express the relation of God and Christ, one that would express not only their co-*eternity* but their co-*equality*. And this brings us to the historical role played—and not played—by a third vocabulary.

Eternal Generation as Donum Nominis: *God's Proper Name in the Gospel of John and the Nicene Creed*

I have already pointed out that allusion to the Tetragrammaton is basic to the structure of the Nicene Creed. The Creed's confession of "One God" and "one Lord Jesus Christ" echoes Paul's confession in 1 Corinthians 8:6, which in turn evokes the *Shema*'s confession of the deity who bears the name YHWH. Had the bishops gathered at Nicaea been able to recognize this allusion and its full theological significance, they might have been able to enlist it in their battle against the Arians. Nevertheless, for reasons mostly beyond their control, they couldn't, and so they didn't.[9] Instead the bishops expressed the equal dignity of God and Christ in another way, by means of the extrabiblical terms *ousia* and *homoousios*.

As it happens, the choice was a happy one. The parallel between the oldest dimension of the Creed (its allusion to the Divine Name) and its most novel (*ousia/homoousios*) is really quite extraordinary. Both shore up the vocabulary of divine kinship at exactly the needed point by indicating that the Son is not merely *coeternal* with the Father but *coequal* as well. The Creed's ancient Pauline vocabulary makes this point by implying that God the Father and Jesus Christ jointly bear the Divine Name; the bishops make the same point using the term *homoousios*.

At the same time, it must be conceded that the two forms of expressions are similar in another way: both are concise to the point of obscurity. They affirm *that* God and Christ share a common divine dignity, but neither casts much light on *how* this unity comes to be or how it comports with the fundamental biblical datum that *the Father* is "the one God."

In time, Christian theologians felt compelled to answer such inevitable questions. One way they did so was by elaborating the conceptuality of divine essence already present in the Creed. An example of such elaboration is the scholastic teaching known as "essential communication,"

---

9. For a fuller discussion, see R. Kendall Soulen, *The Divine Name(s) and Holy Trinity*, vol. 1, *Distinguishing the Voices* (Louisville: Westminster John Knox, 2011), 47–60.

138

GENERATIO, PROCESSIO, VERBI, DONUM NOMINIS

according to which the Son is *homoousios* with the Father because the Father communicates or shares the divine essence with him. This event is understood to be identical with the eternal begetting of the Son (*generatio*) or the procession of the Word (*processio verbi*), and I will have more to say about it in the next section.

Long before, however, the New Testament writers had already answered the same question in the Bible's own native idiom of the Divine Name. How can Christ share in the Father's unique dignity as God, as 1 Corinthians 8:6 implies he does? According to one stream of biblical witness, the answer is clear: *God the Father has given him the Divine Name.* We encounter this simple yet profound idea in Philippians 2:5–11, a text virtually as ancient as 1 Corinthians 8:6. There Paul affirms that God gave Jesus Christ "the name that is above every name" (an allusion to the Tetragrammaton), so that all creation would confess that Jesus Christ is "Lord" (another such allusion), to the glory of God the Father.

Still, Philippians seems to portray the giving and receiving of the Divine Name as an event that occurs within created time, not before it. As such, it fails to support the idea that the *donum nominis* is an *eternal* event, analogous to the Father's eternal begetting of the Son. This very idea appears elsewhere in the New Testament, however, in the Gospel of John.[10]

The rich name-theology of the Fourth Gospel defies brief summary. Still, it has two aspects (at least) worth noting: Jesus's explicit references to God's "name" on the one hand, and his "I am" statements on the other. The first are sprinkled across the Gospel, but they come to a climax in John 17 in what is commonly known as "the High Priestly Prayer," but what with equal justification might be called "the Prayer of the Divine Name." Our Lord begins and ends the prayer by invoking God's "name," characterizing it as something that belongs to God alone. He calls it "*your* name" and declares that he has served it throughout his ministry on earth. He has "manifested" and "made known" "your name," and he "will" make it known (17:6, 24). Toward the middle of the prayer, however, Jesus characterizes God's "name" in a remarkably different way. He calls it "your name *that you have given me.*" The phrase is repeated twice, as though to lend it emphasis (17:11, 12). The phrase suggests a new understanding of

---

10. My account of the Tetragrammaton in John has been especially helped by Raymond E. Brown, *The Gospel According to John* (New York: Doubleday, 1966), 2:754–56; Charles A. Gieschen, "The Divine Name in Ante-Nicene Christology," *Vigiliae Christianae* 57, no. 2 (2003): 115–58; and Richard Bauckham, "Monotheism and Christology in the Gospel of John," in *Contours of Christology in the New Testament*, ed. Richard N. Longenecker (Grand Rapids: Eerdmans, 2005).

the words "*your* name." The name is the Father's first, because (presumably) he received it from no one, but it is also and derivatively the Son's, because the Father *has given it to him* (perfect tense, indicating the ongoing result of a completed past action). Thus, as our Lord affirms in the same place, he and the Father are "one" (17:11).

All of this is very suggestive. But are there good reasons to suppose that the *donum nominis* described in John 17 refers specifically to the name God declared to Moses at the burning bush? And that the giving and receiving of this name is an eternal event between Father and Son?

The answer to both questions is a resounding "Yes!" We see this the moment we turn our attention to the awesome "I am" statements that punctuate the Fourth Gospel like lightning in a storm. Clearly, Jesus's words echo God's self-naming at the burning bush. Just so, they set us before a mystery. Is *God's* self-naming on the lips of this *man*?! "The Prayer of the Divine Name" provides the catechesis we need to affirm this mystery with faithful understanding. Yes, Jesus rightly declares *God's* name to us as *his own* name, because it is "*your* name that you have given *me*" (17:11, 12).

But when did Christ receive this name? The question would be intolerably presumptuous were it not raised and answered by Christ himself. "Very truly, I tell you, before Abraham was, I am" (8:58). This extraordinary saying can scarcely mean anything other than that Christ has possessed the divine name from before the foundation of the world. But if so, then God's giving of the divine name to Christ must also precede the work of creation. In short, the giving and receiving of the divine name is an eternal event. Though revealed in time, it characterizes the relation of God and Christ beyond time. Father and Son eternally share in the dignity and unity of the Divine Name because the Father eternally gives it to the Son and so constitutes the Son as its eternal, coequal bearer.[11]

To summarize, Scripture and tradition express the mystery of eternal generation using three different forms of speech: the multifaceted *processio verbi*, *generatio*, and *donum nominis*, the gift of the name. And of the three, it is the last that provides the teaching with its most explicit scriptural support.

---

11. Though affirmed without specific reference to the Tetragrammaton, the idea of the Father's giving his own divine names to the Son is found, for example, in Hilary of Poitiers. "The names (Word, Wisdom, Power) have been transmitted from the Father to the Son (via the birth). This does not mean that the Father loses the name, nor is he in any way diminished by this transmission. The perfect begetting of the Son does not lead to loss in the Father, while it does produce perfection for the one who is born." See Mark Weedman, *The Trinitarian Theology of Hilary of Poitiers* (Leiden: Brill, 2007), 138. On the correspondence between "has been given" and "has been begotten" in St. Augustine, see Keith Johnson, "Augustine, Eternal Generation, and Evangelical Trinitarianism," *TrinJ* 32 (2011): 141–63.

SYSTEMATIC REFLECTIONS

According to Karl Barth, different ways of expressing the mystery of eternal generation do not affirm different truths; they affirm a single inexpressible truth in incomplete but complementary ways.[12] I think Barth was right. Moreover, I think there are probably many legitimate ways to flesh out his intuition. In the rest of this chapter I want to suggest one way.

My suggestion takes its basic steer from one of St. Augustine's illustrative names for the Trinity, "Unity, Equality, Connection," which, in the spirit of friendly paraphrase, I will also dub "Uniqueness, Copresence, and Mutual Blessing."[13] Each member of the triad identifies a divine perfection that the persons of the Trinity share in common. At the same time, each perfection has a special affinity with one person in particular. Similarly, I suggest that the three vocabularies of eternal generation "belong" to all the persons of the Trinity, even though each has a special affinity with one person in particular—for much the same reasons as Augustine's triad.

Eternal Generation as Donum Nominis: *Highlighting Divine Uniqueness*

We have seen that while the first two persons of the Trinity eternally bear one and the same Divine Name, they do so in different ways. While I cannot sufficiently argue the point here, I think the same can be said of the Third Person.

- The First Person eternally bears the divine name (1) by receiving it from no one, (2) by communicating the name to the Second Person in one way, that is, by "giving" it to him, and (3) by communicating the name to the Third Person in another way, namely, by constituting him the Spirit who proceeds from the name's primordial bearer(s).[14] In each case, the First Person does not communicate the name to those who already exist, but the communication of the name constitutes those who receive it, each in a different way.
- The Second Person eternally bears (i.e., has) the divine name by "being given" it by the First Person.
- The Third Person eternally bears (i.e., conveys) the divine name by being constituted the Spirit who proceeds from its bearer(s).

---

12. Barth's own suggestion was that *generatio* emphasizes redemption, while *processio verbi* emphasizes revelation. Barth, *CD* I/1, 496–501.

13. See Augustine, *De Doctrina Christiana* 1.5.5.

14. I leave the question of the *filioque* open for the purposes of this chapter.

Thus each person bears the Divine Name in a distinctive way. Still, the First Person has a special affinity with the name because he bears it *a se*, without receiving it from another. Just as it is impossible to "go behind" the First Divine Person to someone or something more ontologically basic, so it is impossible to "go behind" the Tetragrammaton to some more primordial name. In this respect, the First Person's relation to the Divine Name is similar to his relation to the first member of Augustine's triad, the concept-name "Unity." As Thomas Aquinas observed, we perceive "Unity" in the First Person as soon as we conceive him at all, even if, by an impossible hypothesis, the Second and Third Persons of the Trinity were not. Similarly, we conceive the First Person as the bearer of the Divine Name as soon as we conceive him at all, even if, by an impossible hypothesis, we abstract him momentarily from the Second and Third Persons.

Having noted the analogy, however, we can immediately see that the First Person's affinity with the Tetragrammaton is vastly more intimate than with the concept-name "Unity." However apt, "Unity" cannot distinguish the Living God from the pantheon of putative deities. The Tetragrammaton alone can do that, from among all the names under heaven. The Tetragrammaton is the primordial mark—not merely of the unity but of the *uniqueness* of the one true God. As the primordial bearer of this name, the First Person of the Trinity is not merely *one*; he is *this one*. He is unique (cf. Deut 6:4). When, therefore, we affirm that the First Person eternally gives his name to another and eternally breathes a Spirit that is the Spirit of the LORD, we are declaring something that is inherently good news, an eternal gospel as it were. We affirm that the First Person does not jealously hoard his name but shares it, so that the Son and the Spirit too are uniquely themselves because they share—in equal but different ways—in the unity and uniqueness of the Divine Name.

Let me return briefly to the teaching known as essential communication, according to which the First Person communicates his divine essence so as to multiply the number of those who instantiate it without dividing the essence itself.[15] Opponents of the teaching often accuse it of being a Neoplatonic intrusion into the mind of the church. On the contrary, I have suggested that it is a remarkably faithful paraphrase of a pattern of speech central to the gospel. Insofar as the doctrine has a problem, it is merely

---

15. For an excellent treatment of the subject, together with John Calvin's (idiosyncratic) opposition to it, see Brannon Ellis, *Calvin, Classical Trinitarianism, and the Aseity of the Son* (Oxford: Oxford University Press, 2012). While Ellis favors Calvin's critique of the doctrine, his book is illuminating and fair-minded.

GENERATIO, PROCESSIO, VERBI, DONUM NOMINIS

that its advocates sometimes overlook the fact that it is a *paraphrase*. Misled, perhaps, by the aura of dignity that surrounds the term divine "essence," they overlook the reality it signifies: the Divine *Name*. The remedy is not to reject "essence" talk, but rather to so prioritize the Bible's testimony to the Divine Name that it continuously funds, rules, and chastens what we mean by it.

Eternal Generation as Generatio: *Highlighting Divine Copresence*

Our remaining vocabularies of eternal generation say exactly what the first said but in ways that highlight other dimensions of the same mystery. Consider "Father" as a designation for the First Person. While we could conceive the First Person as bearer of the Tetragrammaton without being required to contemplate any other divine person, we cannot do the same while thinking of the First Person as "Father." The kinship term requires us to think "forward," so to speak, to the one of whom God *is* the Father, namely, the Son. The reciprocity previously signified by verbs ("the One who gives the Name," "the One who receives the Name," etc.) is now implied by the vocabulary itself. For this reason, the terms "Father," "Son," and (by extension) "Spirit" permit simple, unambiguous identification of the three persons, which is possible but more cumbersome in case of our first vocabulary.

Even so, kinship is not an "all-purpose" Trinitarian vocabulary. Instead, like the first terminology we examined, kinship tends to foreground one person in particular, in this instance, the Second Person, the "Son." This is evident from the fact that we call the First Person "Father" with respect to the Son, not the Spirit. "Spirit" is not a kinship term at all, and so stands outside the vocabulary's central idiom. And even when we consider "Father" and "Son" as a pair, "Son" has material priority. The Bible does not use kinship terms of God to pick out who the Father is. That is a foregone conclusion. The Father is the one who bears the divine name *a se*. "You, O LORD, are our Father; our Redeemer from of old is your name" (Isa 63:16). Rather, divine kinship language serves to pick out who among many possible contenders is the *Son*. It is there that the emphasis falls in both testaments: "*Israel* is my first born son" (Exod 4:22). "*This* is my Son" (Matt 3:17). The same accent echoes in the famous adjective μονογενὴς (John 1:18), formerly (and perhaps correctly) translated "only begotten" (KJV) and now translated "only" (NRSV) or "one and only" (NIV).

Augustine proposed "Equality" to signal the divine perfection that comes into focus as we shift our attention from the "priority" of the First

Person to the "centrality" of the Second. I would add, as a friendly gloss, "Presence" or even "Copresence." Generation *per se*, in the sense of (for lack of a better term) ontological origination, is indeed all but inescapably implied by the Bible's language of divine Father and Son, of begetting and being begotten, and occasionally this connotation comes to the fore (e.g., Ps 2:7; Acts 13:33; Heb 1:5–6). Even so, it remains safe to say that the primary theme of divine kinship language is not the movement of origination itself but the personal relationship of mutual availability, copresence, and love to which it gives rise.

I conclude this section by noting what I regard as another happy correspondence between the language of Scripture and the technical nomenclature of the doctrine of the Trinity. Just as the Divine Name provides the biblical original of which "divine essence" is a reasonable conceptual clarification, so the kinship language of "Father" and "Son" (and "Spirit," when taken in conjunction with former) provides the original of which "person" or "hypostasis" is a reasonable redescription. The Divine Name is one, but those who bear it are three.

Eternal Generation as Processio Verbi: *Highlighting Divine Connection*

We conclude by considering a third way we can express the mystery of eternal generation. The last region on our map bears the legend *processio verbi*, for God's utterance of the divine Word (cf. John 1:1; Heb 1:3; etc.). When we examine this region more closely, however, we discover that it is not a homogenous terrain. Beneath the legend "*processio verbi*" we discover a colorful patchwork of names for the Second Person, such as Splendor, Image, Wisdom, and so on. Each of these imparts a distinctive shade of meaning to our idea of eternal procession.[16] At the same time, a moment's reflection confirms the fact that the forms of speech gathered here have something in common. They are all instances of the same *kind* of word, a kind paradigmatically represented by the word "word" (*verbum*) itself: they are *common nouns*.

This fact is relevant for understanding the role that the multifaceted *processio verbi* has played in the development of Christian doctrine. The apologists needed a vocabulary *common* to the Bible on the one hand and their intellectual context on the other in order to expound Christ's divine origin in a way that was faithful to Scripture and intelligible to their

---

16. See Aquinas, *ST* 1.34.2, ad 3.

contemporaries. The translatability (grammatical *and* conceptual) of terms such as Word, Image, Wisdom, and so on belonged to the essence of their appeal in the second century, as it has ever since.

From a systematic point of view, *processio verbi*'s reliance on common nouns suggests an affinity with the Holy Spirit, not in the sense that it refers to the procession of the Spirit (which of course it does not) but in the sense that it refers to the procession of the Son using a *kind* of vocabulary that is characteristic of the Spirit. The Holy Spirit is sometimes called the nameless person of the Trinity, but what this really means is that it is characteristic of the Holy Spirit to be named personally by means of nouns common to the other persons of the Trinity. Each person of the Trinity is "Holy," each person is "Spirit." Still, as Augustine observed, it is especially characteristic of the Third Person to be named personally by words held in common, and in this way to especially manifest the divine perfection of "Connection" in the life of the Trinity.

As a way of speaking about eternal generation, the vocabulary of common nouns extends itself naturally to all three persons in a way that the kinship vocabulary of *generatio* does not. True, "Word," like the "Son," refers uniquely to the Second Person, and not to the First or Third.[17] Nevertheless, when we speak of the Second Person as Word, for example, it comes naturally to speak of the First Person as "God" and the Third Person as "Spirit" or "Breath." The three common nouns connect the persons of the Trinity into a single, unified portrait for the contemplation of faith, one with resonances in both Scripture (cf. Ps 33:6) and daily life. The abundance and plasticity of common nouns makes possible many such portraits, some emphasizing divine oneness ("Light, Light of Light, Spirit of Light"), some divine threeness ("Lover, Beloved, Love"), some somewhere in between ("Memory, Understanding, Will"). In this way, too, the vocabulary of common nouns exhibits the charism of Connection, mediating between *donum nominis*'s emphasis on unity and *generatio*'s on diversity.

Once again, and now for a last time, I wish to register what I regard as a happy correspondence between the mediating vocabulary that we just explored and an aspect of technical Trinitarianism, in this case the teaching that speaks of the persons of the Trinity as three modes of subsistence (*tropos hyparxeos*). The similarity is that both mediate between the emphases of

---

17. In this sense, the common noun "Word" becomes a "personal name" in the technical sense. When it is used in the context of the doctrine of the Trinity, it picks out a single divine person. My point is that it does so by means of a grammatically common noun, in contrast to a kinship term or proper name.

unity and distinction. Just as the motif of *donum nominis* anticipates what later Christian tradition calls *communicatio essentiae*, and *generatio* anticipates the three persons or hypostases, our last vocabulary suggests a kind of mediating path between these two insights. God, Christ, and the Spirit simply are different modes of being of the one divine essence, distinguished by their relations to each other: as God, God of God, and Spirit of God.

CONCLUSION

Barth challenged Christians to speak of the mystery of eternal generation in every available way. I have proposed that in practice this means cultivating three patterns of scriptural speech: one that emphasizes the First Person and the mystery of divine uniqueness at the source of the triune life; one that emphasizes the Second Person and the mystery of divine copresence at the heart of the Trinity; and one that emphasizes the Third Person and the mystery of connection mutual blessing that glorifies the Trinity in eternity and time. My hope is that by cultivating these three forms of speech Christians might speak of the mystery of eternal generation—not adequately, but perhaps a little less inadequately.

PART II

HISTORICAL WITNESS

CHAPTER 8

AT THE ORIGINS OF ETERNAL GENERATION:
Scriptural Foundations and Theological Purpose in Origen of Alexandria

LEWIS AYRES

INTRODUCTION

As many people know, I observe recent debates over the Son's eternal generation in evangelical circles as a bemused outsider. Were someone from my own Catholic tradition to doubt the Son's eternal generation, I hope that a firm swipe of the *Catechism* to the back of the head would be sufficient. If, however, this imaginary miscreant persisted, then the obvious course of action would be for me to return with him or her to the origins of the doctrine and to investigate together the circumstances in which it arose, its exegetical foundations, and its theological purpose. And it is precisely an exercise of this nature that I will undertake in this chapter.[1]

I am going to spend virtually all the space I have with just one author, Origen of Alexandria (ca. AD 185–253). I pick on Origen not because his account can be identified with *the* classical form of the doctrine, if there is

---

1. I have kept the secondary literature in the notes to a minimum. But for further discussions of this theme in Origen other than those noted see Henri Crouzel, *Théologie de l'image de Dieu chez Origène* (Paris: Aubier, 1956), 71–128, esp. 83–98; Marguerite Harl, *Origène et la fonction révélatrice du Verbe incarné* (Paris: Éditions du Seuil, 1958), esp. 123ff.; Michel René Barnes, *The Power of God: Δύναμις in Gregory of Nyssa's Trinitarian Theology* (Washington, DC: Catholic University of America Press, 2001), 111–24; Mark J. Edwards, *Origen against Plato* (Aldershot: Ashgate, 2002), esp. 65–74.

149

such a thing, but because he is the first Christian author from whom survives an extended meditation on why the Son must be born eternally from the Father.[2] This account is part of a broader and complex picture of the Son's relationship with Father and Spirit, not all of which would count as orthodox by the standards of the late fourth century, but his exploration of the Son's eternal generation nevertheless became an integral part of that later orthodoxy.

One of my main goals is to show the network or constellation of scriptural texts from which the notion of eternal generation grew. And, in order to show the character of the exegetical argument involved, I am going to focus mostly on one text: *On First Principles*, book 1, chapter 2. In this chapter Origen offers his initial extended discussion of Christ in order to establish a doctrinal foundation for later discussion of more disputed questions.[3] Even though very little of it survives in anything other than Rufinus's Latin translation, I think we can see quite clearly the contours of Origen's argument—and we can supplement this text with some briefer discussions in the surviving Greek corpus of Origen's works. Through the chapter I hope to draw out two strands of argument. The first is that Origen persistently uses the doctrine as part of a broader attempt to distinguish Creator and creation and to offer an account of the Creator as eternally generative and benevolent. The second is that if we are to understand how Origen defines and defends the doctrine (and by extension any patristic writer), we must take in something of the broader doctrinal and exegetical landscape of which it is part. Methodologically, Origen's manner of bringing different scriptural texts together in his argument needs to be taken seriously and to be understood as foundational in the development and contestation of patristic Trinitarian doctrine. Take away that method of reading, and a great deal of historical Christian doctrine finds itself in a rather precarious relationship to the text of Scripture! We will begin by following his argument for a while and then stop for some reflection on his method.

---

2. It is possible that Clement of Alexandria espoused a similar doctrine. See Mark J. Edwards, "Clement of Alexandria and His Doctrine of the Logos," *Vigiliae Christianae* 54 (2000): 159–77, and R. P. Casey, "Clement and the Two Divine Logoi," *JTS* 25 (1923): 43–56.

3. Although the division of *On First Principles* into four books seems to stem from Origen himself, that division may mask a fundamentally threefold division of the material. Between the beginning of the work and 2.3 we find a series of initial treatments of basic topics, which are followed, starting at 2.4 and running to the end of book 3, by a long discussion of polemical themes and speculative questions. The material we are considering here, then, consists in material that Origen thinks to be basic and established Christian doctrine (however much what we have is also his own articulation of that teaching). This division seems to reflect that found in contemporary philosophical introductions. For this threefold analysis of the text see the original proposals of Marguerite Harl, "Structure et coherence du *Peri Archon*," in *Origeniana*, ed. Henri Crouzel et al. (Quaderni di VetChr 12: Bari, 1975), 11–32, and further comments of Charles Kannengiesser, "Divine Trinity and the Structure of *Peri Archon*," in *Origen of Alexandria: His World and His Legacy*, ed. Charles Kannengiesser and William L. Petersen (Notre Dame, IN: University of Notre Dame Press, 1989), 231–49.

THE PREAMBLE

Origen introduces this chapter of *On First Principles*'s first book by remarking that in Christ are two natures: that which follows from him being the Son of the Father and a human nature that he took on for the divine purpose (*pro dispensatione*). Hence, we must first consider his divine status—in order, I think Origen implies, that we can grasp that divine purpose and so that we can see the full majesty of the incarnation.[4] He then offers some comments that enable two important observations. First, Origen tells us that in order to understand the *unigenitus Filius*, the "Only-begotten" Son of the Father, we need to consider his many titles. What follows, then, has the form of an extended piece of "title exegesis," a commentary on some of the many titles of the Son or Word.[5] As is usually the case in this style of commentary, the titles are gradually interwoven to bring out their mutually informing features. Second, we should note that Origen uses μονογενής as a title, but the term itself receives no discussion or analysis. He does, however, reflect at length on the verb γεννάω, especially where it is used in connection with the Son, and he does reflect on other terms that speak of the Son's coming into being—such as Colossians 1:15's πρωτότοκος—but he does not reflect on μονογενής itself. This nicely bears at the point that Lee Irons makes forcefully in his chapter for this volume: ancient authors frequently and naturally link the compound term μονογενής to other scriptural terms and verses that speak of becoming, generation, and creation.[6] If we are to understand how Origen understands the title μονογενής, we must see something of the broad constellation of scriptural terms of which it is part and to which it sometimes points when used by itself.

Origen's argument begins with a preamble commenting briefly on the three titles of Wisdom (quoting Prov 8:22), Firstborn (quoting Col 1:15), and "Power and Wisdom of God" (quoting 1 Cor 1:24).[7] The organization of the main argument is loose. There are three sections based around the exegesis of, first, Colossians 1:15's description of Christ as "the image of the invisible God" (1.2.5–6), second, Hebrews 1:3's "the brightness of God's glory, and the exact image of his substance" (1.2.7–8), and third, the five

---

4. This is particularly clear when Origen takes up again the question of the Incarnation at *Princ.* 2.6.1–3.

5. Origen's account of the many different title of Christ is related to his account of *epinoiai* or "conceptualizations." See Andrew Radde-Gallwitz, *Basil of Caesarea, Gregory of Nyssa, and the Transformation of Divine Simplicity* (Oxford: Oxford University Press, 2009), 59–66.

6. See chapter 5 of this volume. For an earlier example of such a constellation see Justin Martyr, *Dialogue with Trypho* 105.

7. Origen, *Princ.* 1.2.1–4.

LEWIS AYRES

titles contained in Wisdom 7:25–26 (1.2.9–12). Let us, then, begin with the preamble.

Right at the beginning Origen links exploration of the title Wisdom to exploration of Wisdom's origin.[8] Wisdom, as that which was "created" in Proverbs 8:22, is the same as he who is the "firstborn" in Colossians 1:15 and the power and wisdom *of* God in 1 Corinthians 1:24. Because Wisdom is a title of the Firstborn, the Son, Christ, we must think of this wisdom as nothing "insubstantial," as an *animal quoddam sapiens*, "a wise and living being," as "God's Wisdom existing as a hypostasis." But he immediately issues a warning: "I do not think that our thinking should wander beyond this to what else might be thought." Doing so might lead us to attribute shape, color, or size to the Wisdom of God. He adds a rhetorical question: "Can anyone who knows or thinks about God piously, think or believe that God the Father ever existed, even for a single moment, without begetting his Wisdom?"[9]

This rhetorical question appears, then, as part of a list of transgressive thoughts only entertained by people who do not recognize that God transcends the categories that mark composite, temporal objects. It is also part of Origen's attempt to outline a set of basic boundaries that must govern our interpretation of the Son's scriptural titles. Origen's opponents seem to include both Monarchians, who do not sufficiently recognize the irreducibility of the three *hypostases*, and Valentinians, whose accounts of divine generation seem to Origen to predicate corporeality or temporality of the divine being. Although Origen introduces this theme as a rhetorical question, it gradually becomes clearer that his account of the Son's generation lies at the heart of his account of the divine life and being.

Through the course of this preamble Origen offers two deductive arguments for the necessary eternity of the Son's generation. The first runs as follows: if we do not say that God exists as one begetting his Wisdom, then either we say that God *began* to do so at some point and give in to a temporal account of the divine being, or we say that God could have done so but did not. Origen assumes we would not wish to argue the latter because of the consequences that would follow for our conception of divine being: God would be unwilling to beget his own Wisdom![10] Now, this argument is

---

8. A strong philosophical lineage links understanding a thing's generation to understanding what it is. See e.g., Aristotle, *Metaphysics* 4.2 1003b8; Plato, *Philebus* 26d; and, closer in time to Origen, Galen, *Method of Medicine* 1.5.1 (Kühn, 88): ἡ μὲν γὰρ ἁπλῶς ὀνομαζομένη γένεσις ὁδός ἐστιν εἰς οὐσίαν, ἡ δὲ τοῦδέ τινος γένεσις, εἰς τὴν ὡς ἂν εἴποι τις ὕπαρξιν ἐκείνου.

9. Origen, *Princ.* 1.2.2 (SC 252, 112).

10. Origen, *Princ.* 1.2.2.

AT THE ORIGINS OF ETERNAL GENERATION

extremely important. The same logic that asserts the Father must eternally beget also begins to suggest that the Father's begetting of his Wisdom is a constitutive feature of what it is to be God. It is helpful to note that within a year or two, Origen will speak in his *Commentary on John* of the Father begetting the Son in an eternal "today," in that time which is "coextensive with his unoriginated and eternal life."[11]

Origen's second deductive argument for God's existence as one who generates Wisdom now appears. If the title Father is eternally God's, and if it is so in virtue of the fact that the Son eternally exists—both of which Origen assumes—then the relationship between Father and Son is eternally so. But the relationship between parent and child is one that results from a particular mode of generation, and thus the Father must eternally generate the Son—whatever "generation" means here.[12] The initiating concern of this argument is partly, and once again, the danger of predicating temporality of God—God cannot *become* Father for Origen—but the result is that, once again, the eternity of the relationship reveals to us something about the nature of God as such—God is eternally generative.

In passing, Origen now offers as close to a definition of what he means by eternal generation when he speaks of "[the Father's] only begotten Son, who was born indeed of him and draws what he is from him, but is yet without any beginning. . . . Wisdom, therefore, must be believed to have been begotten beyond the limits of any beginning that we can speak of or understand."[13] Origen's version of the doctrine thus asserts that the Son "draws what he is" from the Father, and yet lacks any beginning, beyond any limit that we can even imagine. Wisdom is also the "beginning of the

---

11. This theme is also explored in some detail in Origen's *Commentary on John* 1.204, in SC 120, 160. English trans. Ronald Heine, *Origen. Commentary on the Gospel According to John. Books 1–10*, (Washington DC: Catholic University of America Press, 1989), 74: "the noble origin of the Son is not presented clearly by all these titles. It is, however, when God, with whom it is always 'today,' says to him, 'You are my Son, today I have begotten you.' There is no evening of God possible and, I think, no morning, but the time, if I may put it this way, which is coextensive with his unoriginated and eternal life, is today for him, the day in which the Son has been begotten. Consequently neither the beginning nor the day of his generation is to be found."

12. Origen, *Princ.* 1.2.4. For an introduction to the importance of this theme see Peter Widdicombe, *The Fatherhood of God from Origen to Athanasius* (Oxford: Clarendon, 1994), 63–92; cf. frg. *Commentary on Genesis* 1, in Eusebius, *Contra Marcellum*, 1.4.22 (GCS 14, 1.11–18, p. 22): οὐ γὰρ ὁ θεὸς πατὴρ εἶναι ἤρξατο κωλυόμενος, ὡς οἱ γινόμενοι πατέρες ἄνθρωποι, ὑπὸ τοῦ μὴ δύνασθαί πω πατέρες εἶναι. εἰ γὰρ ἀεὶ τέλειος ὁ θεός, καὶ πάρεστιν αὐτῷ δύναμις τοῦ πατέρα αὐτὸν εἶναι, καὶ καλὸν αὐτὸν εἶναι πατέρα τοιούτου υἱοῦ, <τί> ἀναβάλλεται καὶ τοῦ καλοῦ ἑαυτοῦ στερίσκει καί, ὡς ἔστιν εἰπεῖν, ἐξ οὗ δύναται πατὴρ εἶναι, οὐ <γίνεται πατήρ>; τὸ αὐτὸ μέντοιγε καὶ περὶ τοῦ ἁγίου πνεύματος λεκτέον.

13. Origen, *Princ.* 1.2.2 (SC 252, 114): Propter quod nos semper deum patrem nouimus unigeniti filii sui, ex ipso quidem nati et quod est ab ipso trahentis, sine ullo tamen initio . . . Extra omne ergo quod uel dici uel intellegi potest initium generatum esse credendum est sapientiam.

153

ways" of Proverbs 8:22. How? Because Wisdom contains "every power and form of the future creation (*omnis virtus ac deformatio future inerat creaturae*)."[14] In other terms, "[Wisdom] fashions beforehand and contains within herself the form (*species*) and causes (*rationes*) of the entire creation,"[15] and thus there is a sense in which *all* that God creates or generates is eternal, though in rather different senses. We do not need to spend any great time with the complexities of reconstructing and interpreting Origen's account of creation here. But we do need to note an important consequence concerning the nature of Wisdom that Origen draws from this assertion about Wisdom's nature: "Wisdom opens to all other beings, that is to the whole creation, the meaning of the mysteries and secrets which are contained within the Wisdom of God, and so she is called the Word, because she is as it were an interpreter of the mind's secrets."[16] The Wisdom of God actively reveals to us the divine reason or nature (*ratio*), conveying to us the meaning of this *ratio*. Here Origen develops his initial hints that the Father's generation of his Wisdom is constitutive of the divine being by suggesting that the eternal coming forth of Wisdom reveals God to be an eternally revealing and loving God. This reading is, I think, reinforced when we notice that only a few sentences later Origen argues that we can now understand why the Son is rightly called the Truth and Life of all things. All things only exist because the Wisdom of God is Logos and life before them. All things may be redeemed and restored because there is life before them—and therefore this "life" is also "the way" because the Wisdom of God draws us toward the Father. Thus clarity that God exists as one who eternally generates his Wisdom provides a foundation for understanding how the creating and saving activity of God stems from God's eternally wise and benevolently willed diffusiveness. Origen's development of "eternal generation" does not only concern the relationship between Father and Son; it is a doctrine through which Origen articulates some of the most central and fruitful aspects of his account of God and God's relationship to the work of creation and salvation.

The end of the preamble confirms something that should be reasonably clear by now. Origen writes,

---

14. Origen, *Princ.* 1.2.2 (SC 252, 114).
15. Origen, *Princ.* 1.2.3 (SC 252, 114).
16. Origen, *Princ.* 1.2.3 (SC 252, 114): hoc modo etiam uerbum dei eam esse intellegendum est per hoc, quod ipsa ceteris omnibus, id est uniuersae creaturae, mysteriorum et arcanorum rationem, quae utique intra dei sapientiam continentur, aperiat; et per hoc verbum dicitur, quia sit tamquam arcanorum menits interpres.

It is impious and shocking to regard the Father in the begetting of his only Son and in the Son's subsistence as being similar to any human being or other animal in the act of begetting. There must needs be something exceptional, worthy of God, to which we can find no comparison whatever, not merely in things, but even in thought and imagination, such that by its aid, human thought could apprehend how the unbegotten God becomes Father of the only-begotten Son.[17]

"Begetting," when used of the Father's "begetting" of the Son, names a unique act about which we can more readily say what it is not than what it is. Origen, of course, has already said quite a bit about what this act is both by differentiating it from other acts and by lighting up some analogical paths down which Scripture calls us. In the very next sentence he points to another: "This is an eternal and everlasting begetting, as brightness is begotten from light." Origen here alludes to both to Hebrews 1:3 and to Wisdom 7:25–6, as he does elsewhere.

Origen ends the ninth of his *Homilies on Jeremiah* with a brief consideration of the savior as Ἀπαύγασμα δόξης ("radiance of glory," Heb 1:3). The Savior has not been begotten just once, and is no longer begotten. Rather, "just as the light is the maker of its radiance, in such a way the radiance of the glory of God is begotten."[18] Origen complements the observation by noting that in Proverbs 8:25 we find that "before the hills he begets me (γεννᾷ με)," not "he has begotten me (γεγέννηκέν με)." Once again, the scriptural language of light and its radiance performs an important function, bolstering not only the bare principle that the Son is eternally begotten but also Origen's wider theology of God's eternally generative nature.

"The Dark Treasures" of the Son's Titles

In *On First Principles*, we have reached the point at which Origen leaves behind his preamble and begins to offer extended reflections on various

---

17. Origen, *Princ.* 1.2.4 (SC 252, 118): Sed necesse est exceptum aliquid esse et deo dignum, cuius nulla prosus comparatio non in rebus solum sed ne in cogitatione quidem uel sensu inueniri potest, ut humana cogitatio possit aprehendere quomodo ingenitus deus pater efficitur unigeniti filii. Est namque ita aeterna ac sempiterna generatio, sicut splendor generator ex luce. Non enim per adoptionem spiritus filius fit extrinsecus, sed natura filius est.

18. Origen, *Homilies on Jeremiah* 9.4: ἀλλὰ ὅσον ἐστὶν τὸ φῶς ποιητικὸν τοῦ ἀπαυγάσματος, ἐπὶ τοσοῦτον γεννᾶται τὸ ἀπαύγασμα τῆς δόξης τοῦ θεοῦ. On the theme of generation in these homilies see the introduction and relevant notes by Erwin Schadel in Origen, *Die griechisch erhaltenen Jeremiahomilien* (Stuttgart: Hiersemann, 1980).

christological themes.[19] Before considering some of that discussion, we need to take a little time to consider Origen's exegetical practice. Most obviously, this form of title exegesis creates a mutually informing constellation of texts and, hence, a constellation of ideas. Origen reads each term from three perspectives: First, he attempts to show how a term or title may tell us something about Christ even as we avoid projecting on to him material or temporal conditions. Second, Origen is attentive to ways in which our reading of a particular term maybe informed by and may inform our reading of other terms or titles. Third, Origen discusses how a term or title may enable reflection on the overall character of God and God's action, a reflection that gradually emerges as we grow in attention to Scripture.

As has been well documented in scholarship over the past thirty years or more, Origen is deeply indebted to a range of Hellenistic literary-analytical techniques adapted by Christians for interpreting both the Old and New Testament with increasing skill during the second century. These techniques push him to read each title within a vision of the whole teaching of Scripture; they push him toward the production of the mutually informing constellation that we are beginning to see. At the same time, these techniques shape Origen's concern to interpret Christ's titles appropriately, given the status of their referent.[20] Finally, the reading culture of which he had imbibed deeply taught him to differentiate various meanings of a term and to use the full resources provided by dialectic and existing philosophical commentary to explore how Christians might interpret a term or phrase.

The verb "explore" in the previous sentence should cause us also to recall that Origen reads in the context of an educational vision parallel to that found in his predecessor Clement.[21] For both authors, one of the ways in which the Scriptures educate and reform is by inviting those so gifted into the providentially ordained labyrinth of imagery and statements, by means of which it reveals the divine being and action. The task of speculative reflection on

---

19. In the section heading, "The Darkest Treasures" refers to Origen's *Commentary on John* 2. 28.173 (SC 120. 324): Ἐὰν δέ τις ταῖς τοιαύταις προσκόπτῃ ἐκδοχαῖς, προαγέσθω ἀπό τε τῶν σκοτεινῶν λόγων καὶ τῶν διδομένων ὑπὸ θεοῦ Χριστῷ θησαυρῶν σκοτεινῶν, ἀποκρύφων, ἀοράτων.

20. There is a very useful introductory discussion of the classical precedents and early Christian use of this notion in Mark Sheridan, "'*Digne Deo*,' A Traditional Greek Principle in Latin Dress," in *L'Esegesi dei padri latini: dalle origini a Gregorio Magno; XXVIII Incontro di studiosi dell'antichità cristina, Roma, 6–8 maggio 1999* (Roma: Institutum Patristicum Augustinianum, 2000): 23–40. Sheridan's focus is the Latin world and, hence, Origen himself is not covered. The fundamental treatment of literary-critical techniques in Origen remains Bernhard Neuschäfer, *Origenes als Philologe*, 2 vols. (Basel: Friedrich Reinhardt, 1987). For a rounded treatment of Origen's work as exegete see Peter Martens, *Origen and Scripture: The Contours of the Exegetical Life* (Oxford: Oxford University Press, 2012).

21. On that vision see, e.g., H. Clifton Ward, "'The Symbolic Mode Is Most Useful': Clement of Alexandria's Scriptural Imagination," *Journal of Early Christian Studies* 25 (2017): forthcoming.

AT THE ORIGINS OF ETERNAL GENERATION

the constellation of texts we have before us is, for Origen, a task to which the Spirit draws us. It is a task that is undertaken both as part of the individual's own growth toward God and for the community of the church. The context of Origen's individual search is seen when we remember that he acted as an invited "expert" in a number of contemporary disputes about Christian belief.

These observations demand of us clarity about the principles that *we* think appropriately govern the interpretation of scriptural texts. I suggest that Origen's method of reflection in this case offers us a model for our own. If it does not, why, and in what ways does he fail? In particular, these observations also point us toward the importance of considering how *we* consider the "implications" of scriptural texts. When we read Origen's discussion of Christ's titles, perhaps it is tempting to identify much of what he offers as secondary "implications" of a text rather than its primary "meaning." Such a perspective can easily slip into methodological naiveté. Origen certainly thinks that what he reads from the christological titles requires careful attention and reflection if it is to be seen, but it is not thereby any less part of what that term is intended to convey. In the same way, Origen certainly thinks that it requires careful labor to place the interpretation of individual terms within the broader constellations of terms that Scripture offers, but this does not mean that we are thereby losing our focus on Scripture! For Origen, God has ordered for us a Scripture whose descriptions of the divine *demand* from us this kind of care and imagination in reading.

THE IMAGE OF THE INVISIBLE GOD

Time constrictions do not allow me to go as thoroughly through the remainder of the argument of book 1, chapter 2, the argument that follows his preamble. But we do have time to see some of the ways in which what follows deepens the account we have seen so far. Three texts are the nodal points in what follows: Colossians 1:15; Hebrews 1:3; and Wisdom 7:25–26. In each case, Origen's treatment slowly bends toward further commentary on the mode of the Son's generation. He begins by reminding us of his conclusions so far, and he does so in striking terms: "Now, as we said above, the wisdom of God has her subsistence nowhere else but in him who is the beginning of all things, from whom also she took her birth. And *because* he himself, who alone is a Son by nature, is this wisdom, he is on this account also called the 'only-begotten.'"[22] Here Origen annexes to his account

---

22. Origen, *Princ.* 1.2.5 (SC 252, 120): Quisque sapientia quia ipse est, qui est solus natura filius, idcirco et unigenitus dicitur.

157

of eternal generation to what was already a developed anti-Monarchian strategy. Because the Wisdom of God is generated without dividing the divine being, that Wisdom exists "in" the one who generates eternally. But because the one who is a distinct and irreducible "Son" is this Wisdom, he is also titled μονογενής. How one translates the title μονογενής is not, I suggest, of immense import here. One might say that the uniqueness of the Son rests on his being the subject of a unique generative act. I think it more likely that the use of "only begotten" quite consciously picks up on that language of the "birth" of Wisdom in the previous sentence. This "summary" sentence thus subtly advances our account by talking of the Son being generated and yet still subsisting "in" the Father.

Origen begins by distinguishing different senses of image. Origen argues that we are concerned here with that sense of "image" that links a Son to a Father—following Genesis 5:3's "Adam begat Seth after his own image."[23] The term "image" defined in this way naturally poses to us questions about the sort of unity that obtains between parent and child, and it poses questions about the modes of generation that result in the existence of the child. In the case of the divine Father and Son there is a unity of nature seen in the fact that the Son does all that the Father does, and "the Father's image is reproduced in the Son, whose birth from the Father is as it were an act of his will proceeding from mind."[24]

God needs no preexisting matter from which to create, and he does not create in any manner that parallels the acts of material beings. The language of mind and will both secures these principles and links the Son's begetting to the activity of the divine being that is for Origen most definitive, the act of intelligence. As may be suspected from this text, invoking the language of generation by will also has implications for Origen's account of the eternal relationship between the Father and his Wisdom, the Word or Son perfectly revealing the eternally communicative nature of the divine goodness. Those implications are spelled out for us in what seems to be a surviving fragment from Origen's John commentary:

One should speak of [the Father] as the mind or heart or thought of God, who abiding unchangeable, producing an offspring of its will, became the Father of the Word. This Word reposing in the bosom of

---

23. Origen, *Princ.* 1.2.6.

24. Origen, *Princ.* 1.2.6 (SC 252, 122): qui utique natus ex eo est uelut quaedam uoluntas eius ex mente procedens. See J. Rebecca Lyman, *Christology and Cosmology: Models of Divine Activity in Origen, Eusebius, and Athanasius* (Oxford: Clarendon, 1993), esp. 47–58, 70–78.

AT THE ORIGINS OF ETERNAL GENERATION

the Father, announces the God whom no one has ever seen, and to those whom the heavenly Father drew to him, he reveals the Father whom no one knows except himself.[25]

Once again, the eternity of the Son's generation helps to secure a developing vision of the triune relationships as constitutive of God's eternal benevolence and self-revelatory care.

Origen comes to Hebrews 1:3. Origen has already used John 1:9 to note that the Son is light, and he now links the Son's status as ἀπαύγασμα ("radiance") to 1 John 1:5 to emphasize that God is light: the radiance of Hebrews 1:3 is also a light shining from light. The Son is the brightness of the light in this sense, coming from the Father without separation and enlightening the entire creation. Origen's expansion of this dual claim again invokes his vision of the divine nature as eternally communicative. Commenting on the first half of the verse, Origen writes, "It is through its brightness that the nature of the light itself is known and experienced . . . it renders [people] capable of enduring the glory of the light, becoming in this respect even a kind of mediator between people and the light."[26] Commenting on the second half of the verse—which speaks of Christ as "the express image of his substance"—Origen suggested that Christ is so described because "he makes God understood and known." He then draws into his argument's orbit the Philippians hymn to suggest that the Son's desire to "empty" himself may be understood as a desire "to display to us the fullness of the Godhead."[27]

At 1.2.9 Origen turns to Wisdom 7:25–6.[28] Origen reads "Solomon" in these two verses as defining God in five ways, each definition centering on one characteristic of the divine Wisdom: "power," "glory," "eternal light," "working," and "goodness." Each of Origen's subsequent discussions paints a few more lines upon our picture, but I will comment on only three aspects of Origen's discussion, not only showing that he continues to develop the theme I have made central but also showing that there is also a real tension between the various principles he interweaves.

---

25. Pamphilus, *Apology for Origen* 106. The text may be from a section of *Commentary on John* 5 (on John 1:18). For translation see St. Pamphilus, *Apology for Origen*, trans. Thomas P. Scheck (Washington, DC: Catholic University of America Press, 2010), 87.

26. Origen, *Princ.* 1.2.7.

27. Origen, *Princ.* 1.2.8 (SC 252, 126): nobis deitatis plenitudinem demonstrare.

28. It is interesting to note that while earlier writers used Wis 7 in various capacities, Origen appears to be the first to focus on Wis 7:25 in such detail. See A. H. B. Logan, "Origen and Alexandrian Wisdom Christology," in *Origeniana Tertia: The Third International Colloquium for Origen Studies*, ed. Richard Hanson and Henri Crouzel (Rome: Edizioni Dell'Ateneo, 1985), 123–29.

159

LEWIS AYRES

First, in discussing the use of power language, Origen reiterates his previous argument that it makes no sense to imagine God having the power to generate and not doing so. But he reiterates this argument in the context of a new discussion of divine power. God's power is that by which he creates and sustains and that "by which he is sufficient for all things."[29] Even though the "breath" of this power comes forth as will from mind, it comes forth as "another power, subsisting in its own nature" (*uirtus altera in sua proprietate subsistens*). But this other power draws all its existence from the one source of the unbegotten power of God. By such language Origen thinks he has secured the principle that there is only one *archē* and rule in the cosmos. But by such language he also raises for us complex questions about how we qualify the Son's power: Is it the same as the Father's? Is it a secondary power, and if so, how does this affect the Son's ability to reveal the Father?[30]

In the second place, when Origen discusses "glory," he considers the term in the context of the whole scriptural phrase "a pure emanation (ἀπόρροια) of the glory of the almighty" (Wis 7:25) and makes the Father's title "almighty" fundamental.[31] He has already argued that the title "almighty" does not precede that of Father, and now he argues that the Son shares the quality of being almighty. Because the Father gives all things to the Son (John 17:10), and because "almighty" is the Father's, the Son must also be "almighty." In a slightly stronger argument, Origen argues that the Father cannot be almighty without something over which to be almighty, that is, the creation. But the Father's dominion is eternally exercised through the Son and on the creation insofar as the creation exists eternally in the Son. The very title "almighty" thus shows that the Wisdom of God is eternally with the Father.

After saying that the Father exercises dominion through his Wisdom, he writes, "It is through Wisdom, that is, by Word and Reason, not by force and necessity, that they are subject . . . and this is the purest and brightest glory of omnipotence, that the universe is held in subjection by reason

---

29. Origen, *Princ.* 1.2.9 (SC 252. 130): qua ad omnia sufficiens est.

30. I only allude here to the complexity of Origen's use of power language. As Barnes shows, *Power of God*, 115–16, Origen uses this language here in a manner perhaps parallel to a Stoic tradition in which the soul's power was a faculty of the soul. It is, then, not surprising that Origen can link power and will so easily. But need also to note that Origen uses this language in different ways. He can, on occasion, use the language of Christ as an image of God's power (not of God) to help indicate Christ's distinction from the Father (see *Commentary on John*, 13.153 and Barnes, *Power of God*, 123); at *Dialogue with Heraclides*, 2.15–27, Origen accepts it is orthodox to confess two Gods but one power (see Barnes, *Power of God*, 113ff). These different positions do not seem clearly to fit a narrative of development so much as to reflect the flexibility of the language for different theological occasions and purposes. That he has this flexibility shows how far we are from the formulations of the late fourth century. On "emanation" here see also Pamphilus, *Apology for Origen*, 99 (Scheck, *St. Pamphilus*, 84–85).

31. Origen, *Princ.* 1.2.10.

160

AT THE ORIGINS OF ETERNAL GENERATION

and wisdom, and not by force and necessity."[32] Here we see yet another dimension of the eternally generated Son as revealing the character of the divine being. The Father's eternal rationality and care is revealed by the existence of an eternally generated governing Wisdom. Origen further tells us that this Wisdom of God is unalterable and unchangeable; there is nothing accidental in it.

Some of the tensions that are apparent in Origen's account may be seen when we turn to his discussion of the phrases "an unspotted mirror of the working of God" and "image of his goodness." His concern here is to show that the Son's distinct existence as a *hypostasis* does not involve presupposing two principles of divine action or goodness.[33] The use of a mirror suggests that the "image," the Son, "moves and acts in correspondence with the movements and actions of him who looks into the mirror"—a statement to which Origen appends John 5:19. This analogy enables the judgment that the Son and the Father do not differ in power: "there is one and the same movement (*opus*; almost certainly ενεργεια in the original Greek), so to speak, in all they do," and is intended to undermine any notion of the Son imitating the Father.[34]

But John 5:19 ends, of course, not simply by saying that the Son does the same things but "the same things *in like manner*." Why? Origen's answer is to assert that the Father is the "original goodness"—"no one is good save one, God the Father" (Mark 10:18). This does not mean that the Son is not good but that he draws his goodness only from the Father and that his goodness has no "dissimilarity or divergence" from the Father's goodness. Rufinus, the fourth-century defender of Origen and the translator of the surviving Latin version, may have made Origen a little more Nicene than he originally was. There is evidence that from this sentence he has excised a clear statement that the Son as Wisdom is in some ways lesser than the Father.[35] So the chapter ends with a clear statement that the Son, because he

---

32. Origen, *Princ.* 1.2.10.

33. This is stated with particular clarity at Pamphilus, *Apology for Origen*, 50 (which may come from *Commentary on Hebrews* 1.2–4). For translation see Scheck, *St Pamphilus*, 66.

34. Origen, *Princ.* 1.2.12.

35. Origen, *Princ.* 1.2.13. Into this paragraph, the GCS editor, Paul Koetschau, inserted a passage that is quoted by Justinian and which may or may not be genuine. He numbers the passage as fr. 6 (in Justinian, *Epistola ad Menam*, ed. Eduard Schwartz, trans. G. W. Butterworth, p. 210): "I consider that in the case of the Saviour it would be right to say that he is an image of God's goodness, but not goodness itself. And perhaps also the Son, while being good, is not yet good pure and simply [καὶ τάχα καὶ ὁ υἱὸς ἀγαθός, ἀλλ᾽ οὐχ ὡς ἁπλῶς ἀγαθός]. So he is the image of the goodness, and yet not, as the Father is, good without qualification [οὕτως ᾽εἰκὼν τῆς ἀγαθότητος, ἀλλ᾽ οὐχ ὡς ὁ πατὴρ ἀπαραλλάκτως ἀγαθός]." On the authenticity of this passage, see Pierre Nautin, *Origène. Sa vie et son œuvre* (Paris: Beauchesne, 1977), annexe 1, pp. 443–48. If this is genuine, Origen actually distinguished the Son as "image of goodness" from goodness itself more clearly.

is uniquely eternally generated, reveals the Father's life, his movement, with reliable clarity. Yet it also ends with Origen struggling to show how the Son is all this and yet not a second ultimate principle in the cosmos. Origen's work was both foundational for later Greek discussion of the Son's eternal generation from the Father, and it contained significant tensions as Origen struggled to bring together all that he wanted to say about the divine life.

CONCLUSIONS

Three brief conclusions will suffice. First, the title μονογενής is, for Origen, not *by itself* the source for the doctrine of the Son's eternal generation. It is part of and points toward a wide constellation of texts that must be read individually and separately in a manner worthy of the divine existence. Second, the doctrine of eternal generation is a central nexus within Origen's account of God as eternal, rational, diffusive, governing, and communicative benevolence. His teaching on eternal generation is not a detachable extra in his theology of God but a vital strand in its cardiac muscle.

Third, and as I noted at the beginning of this chapter, there is much in Origen's account that will not pass the scrutiny of the fourth-century controversies. Origen attempts to show us that the Son's mode of generation reveals the divine nature to be eternally communicative and benevolent, even as the Father is the one principle of all. Origen finds himself somewhat caught between asserting the Son's closeness to the Father—only he knows the Father, only he draws his being directly and eternally from the Father—and arguing that the Son possesses his goodness somehow in a derivative sense.[36] Nicene theologians will eventually reconceive the second of these concerns. They will find ways of presenting the one divine power as either possessed by all, or as shared by the Father with Son and Spirit, such that any "derivation" is the derivation of an equality in power and will. But they will not abandon the first of Origen's principles. Right at the heart of Nicene theology is the principle that as we grow in attention to the Son's eternal generation we see ever more clearly how the triune life is a rational, willed, and benevolent goodness. This principle is one of the foundations of Trinitarian life, and we are forever in Origen's debt for pushing us to consider it more deeply. Perhaps better, we are ever in the Spirit's debt for raising up Origen to do so for us!

---

36. Had we needed to move on and consider Origen's pneumatology, we would see in even more ways how his account does not fit the models of fourth-century orthodoxy.

CHAPTER 9

ETERNAL GENERATION IN THE TRINITARIAN THEOLOGY OF AUGUSTINE

KEITH E. JOHNSON

FEW THEOLOGIANS HAVE HAD a greater impact on our understanding of the Trinity than Augustine of Hippo (354–430).[1] While not everyone views his impact positively,[2] there is no question that Augustine's teaching on the Trinity is by far the most influential in the history of the Western church. It is for this reason that Augustine's teaching on eternal generation—a foundational element of his Trinitarian doctrine—merits careful attention. Although his discussion may lack the theological precision found in later formulations of eternal generation (e.g., medieval theologians like Thomas Aquinas or post-Reformation scholastics like John Owen), his writings offer a helpful window into the biblical and theological basis for eternal generation and shed light on the Trinitarian significance of this doctrine.

---

1. This chapter draws upon an earlier essay. Keith E. Johnson, "Augustine, Eternal Generation, and Evangelical Trinitarianism," *TrinJ* 32 (2011): 141–63.

2. According to critics like Colin Gunton, Cornelius Plantinga, and Catherina LaCugna, Augustine's Trinitarian theology "begins" with a unity of divine substance (which he allegedly "prioritizes" over the divine persons), his Trinitarian reflection is overdetermined by Neoplatonic philosophy, his psychological "analogy" tends toward modalism, and he severs the life of the triune God from the economy of salvation by focusing on the immanent Trinity. Lewis Ayres and Michel Rene Barnes, however, have convincingly demonstrated that these criticisms are based on fundamental misreadings of Augustine. See Lewis Ayres, *Augustine and the Trinity* (Cambridge: Cambridge University Press, 2010); Ayres, "The Fundamental Grammar of Augustine's Trinitarian Theology," in *Augustine and His Critics: Essays in Honour of Gerald Bonner*, ed. Robert Dodaro and George Lawless (New York: Routledge, 2000) 51–76; and Michel R. Barnes, "Rereading Augustine's Theology of the Trinity," in *The Trinity: An Interdisciplinary Symposium on the Trinity*, ed. Stephen T. Davis, Daniel Kendall, Gerald O'Collins (New York: Oxford University Press, 1999), 145–76.

KEITH E. JOHNSON

In this chapter, I will argue that Augustine's teaching on eternal generation arises from substantial engagement with Scripture and plays a crucial
role in explicating both the relations of the divine persons and their work
in creation, providence, and redemption. To this end, we will seek to
answer three questions. First, what is Augustine's understanding of eternal generation? Second, what biblical and theological evidence leads him
to affirm this doctrine? Third, what is the theological significance of the
eternal begetting of the Son in Augustine's theology?

AUGUSTINE'S EXPLANATION OF ETERNAL GENERATION

Augustine writes as a representative of Latin-speaking pro-Nicene theology.[3] He was not the first to articulate a doctrine of eternal generation
as a way of explicating the Father–Son relationship.[4] The begetting of the
Son is a central feature of pro-Nicene theology both in its Latin and Greek
forms. The inclusion of this doctrine in the Nicene-Constantinopolitan
creed bears witness to this reality.[5]

According to Augustine, the Son is constituted as "Son" by virtue of his
eternal relation to the Father.[6] The Father eternally "begets" the Son.[7] While
he uses the active and passive forms of the Latin verb "to beget" (*gigno*) to
describe the eternal generation of the Son,[8] Augustine also speaks about the
Son being "from the Father" (*de Patre*).[9] That the Son is "from the Father" may
represent his simplest description of the mystery of the Son's eternal nativity:
"being born means for the Son his being from the Father."[10] A more formal

---

3. Pro-Nicene theology represents an interpretation of Nicaea that emerged in the second half of
the fourth century. In the context of a clear distinction between "person" and "nature," pro-Nicenes
affirmed that Father, Son, and Holy Spirit share the same power, perform the same works, and possess
the same nature. See Michel R. Barnes, "One Nature, One Power: Consensus Doctrine in Pro-
Nicene Polemic," in *Studia Patristica*, vol. 29, *Historica, Theologica et Philosophica, Critica et Philologica*, ed.
Elizabeth A. Livingstone (Louvain: Peeters, 1997), 205–23; and Lewis Ayres, *Nicaea and Its Legacy: An
Approach to Fourth-Century Trinitarian Theology* (Oxford: Oxford University Press, 2004), 236–40. For
a brief introduction to Augustine's Trinitarian theology, see Keith E. Johnson, *Rethinking the Trinity
and Religious Pluralism: An Augustinian Assessment* (Downers Grove, IL: InterVarsity, 2011), 51–63.
4. The Alexandrian theologian Origen (c. 185–254) is frequently identified as the first to affirm
that the generation of the Son is eternal.
5. The relevant phrases from the Nicene-Constantinopolitan Creed include the following: "And
in one Lord, Jesus Christ, the only-begotten Son of God, eternally begotten of the Father, Light
from Light, true God from true God, begotten, not made, of one being with the Father."
6. English citations of *Trin.* will be taken from Edmund Hill's translation: Saint Augustine, *The
Trinity*, trans. Edmund Hill (Hyde Park, NY: New City, 1991).
7. *Trin.* 1.29 (88): "The Father has begotten the Son as his equal."
8. Augustine also uses the Latin noun *generatio* ("generation")—although this term is used far less
frequently. He only uses *generatio* three times in *Trin.* to refer to the generation of the Son (cf. *Trin.*
15.47–48).
9. Augustine also speaks of the Son's "birth [*nativitas*] in eternity" in *Trin.* 2.3 (99).
10. *Trin.* 4.29 (174).

164

ETERNAL GENERATION IN THE TRINITARIAN THEOLOGY OF AUGUSTINE

description can be found at the end of *De trinitate* where Augustine explains that "generation from the Father [*de patre generatio*] bestows being on the Son without any beginning in time, without any changeableness of nature."[11]

Augustine's discussion of John 5:26 in his *Tractates on the Gospel of John* offers a helpful window into his understanding of eternal generation.[12] "For as the Father has life in himself, so he has granted the Son also to have life in himself" (John 5:26).[13] What does it mean that the Father has "life in himself" (5:26a)? It means that the Father's "life" is completely unlike human "life."[14] Whereas human life is "mutable" and dependent, the life of God is "immutable" and dependent on nothing outside God.[15] In this text, we are told that the Son possesses a form of life identical to that of the Father—namely, "life in himself" (5:26b).[16] However, Father and Son possess "life in himself" in differing ways. The Father possesses "life in himself" that was given by no one while the Son possesses "life in himself" that was "given" to him. How did the Son receive "life in himself"? His answer is both simple and profound: the Father "begat" the Son. In a beautiful turn of phrase, Augustine exhorts his readers to "hear the Father through the Son. Rise, receive life that in him who has life in himself you may receive life which you do not have in yourself."[17]

Augustine's constructive account of eternal generation involves six elements.[18] First, the language of "begetting" is not an essential predication describing God's essence but a relational predication describing the relation of the Father to the Son.[19] Speaking from a relational perspective, we call the

---

11. *Trin.* 15.47 (432).

12. English citations from Augustine's *Tract.* will be taken from Saint Augustine, *Tractates on the Gospel of John, 11–27*, trans. John W. Rettig, Fathers of the Church 79 (Washington, DC: Catholic University of America Press, 1988).

13. Unless otherwise indicated, Scripture quotations in this chapter come from the ESV.

14. It is important to recognize that the Creator–creature distinction provides the context for Augustine's reading of John 5:26. "Life in himself" must be understood on the Creator side of this distinction.

15. See *Tract.* 19.8 (149). Additionally, many contemporary theologians rightly cite John 5:26 as a proof text for self-existence of God. See John S. Feinberg, *No One Like Him: The Doctrine of God* (Wheaton, IL: Crossway, 2001), 242.

16. The phrase "in himself" is crucial. The text does not say that the Father and Son possess "life" but rather that they possess "life in himself" (*Tract.* 22.9 [205]). The fact that the Son possesses "life in himself" rules out the possibility that the Son possesses a mutable form of life: "What does it mean, he might be life in himself? He would not need life from another source, but he would be the fullness of life by which others, believing, might live while they live" (*Tract.* 22.9 [207]).

17. *Tract.* 19.13 (153).

18. It is outside the scope of this chapter to explore how Augustine's understanding of eternal generation matures over time.

19. In books 5–7 of *Trin.*, Augustine reflects critically on the language we use to speak about God. In the context of the Aristotelian distinction between "substance" and "accident," Augustine's opponents argued that terms like "unbegotten" and "begotten" name the substance of God. Since "unbegotten" and "begotten" clearly differ, the substance of the Son must differ from the substance of the Father. Augustine responded by pointing out that while no "accidents" can be predicated of God, not all predications must refer to God's "substance." Some predications (e.g., "begotten" and "unbegotten") are "relational." "With God,

Father "God" while we call the Son "God from God" and "light from light."[20]
Second, the begetting of the Son is not temporal but eternal. Through generation, "the Father bestows being on the Son without any beginning in time."[21]
As a result, the Son is coeternal with the Father.[22] Third, the Son is begotten
in an equality of nature. The Father did not beget a "lesser Son" who would
eventually become his equal. The Father "begot [the Son] timelessly in such a
way that the life which the Father gave the Son by begetting him is co-eternal
with the life of the Father who gave it."[23] Through generation, the Son receives
the "life"—that is, the nature or substance—of the Father.[24] Fourth, the Son
is begotten not by the will of the Father but by the substance of the Father.[25]
Fifth, a created likeness to the eternal begetting of the Son can be found in
the production of a mental "word" by the human mind.[26] This insight may
be inspired, at least in part, by Augustine's reflection on the title "Word" in
John 1:1. Another likeness for the generation of the Son can be found in the
nature of "light." We should not think of the begetting of the Son like "water
flowing out from a hole in the ground or in the rock, but like light flowing
from light."[27] The Son's "light" is equal in its radiance to the "light" of the
Father.[28] Finally, the generation of the Son is beyond human comprehension.[29]

---

though, nothing is said modification-wise [in terms of "accident"], because there is nothing changeable with
him. And yet not everything that is said of him is said substance-wise. Some things are said with reference to
something else, like Father with reference to Son and Son with reference to Father; and this is not said modification-wise, because the one is always Father and the other always Son—not 'always' in the sense that he is
Son from the moment he is born or that the Father does not cease to be Father from the moment the Son does
not cease to be Son, but in the sense that the Son is always born and never began to be Son" (*Trin.* 5.6 [192]).

20. *Trin.* 2.2 (98).

21. *Trin.* 15.47 (432).

22. *Tract.* 19.13 (153): "Before all times he was coeternal with the Father. For the Father never
was without the Son; but the Father is eternal, therefore the Son [is] likewise coeternal."

23. *Trin.* 15.47 (432).

24. It should be noted that the essence of the Son is not "generated" but communicated to him
by the Father.

25. *Trin.* 15.38 (425). To say that the Son is generated by the "will" of the Father is to make
the Son a "creature."

26. Notice how Augustine speaks of the Son as "Word" linking this title to the generation of
the Son: "So the Word of God is sent by him whose Word he is; sent by him he is born of" (*Trin.*
4.27 [172]). In the second half of *Trin.* (books 8–15), Augustine searches for a likeness of the begetting
of the Son in the highest capacities of the human mind—specifically the generation of mental word
through an act of understanding.

27. *Trin.* 4.27 (172). Patristic writers frequently employ "light radiating from light" as an analogy
for the eternal generation of the Son. The ubiquity of this metaphor is reflected by its inclusion in
the Nicene-Constantinopolitan Creed.

28. The Son's light is also equal in "duration" to the Father's: "How does an eternal, someone
says, beget an eternal? As temporal flame generates temporal light. For the generating flame is of
the same duration as the light which it generates, nor does the generating flame precede in time the
generated light; but the light begins the instant the flame begins" (*Tract.* 20.8 [171]).

29. Commenting on the generation of the Son with the context of divine simplicity, Ayres
explains, "Augustine does not imagine that we can grasp the dynamics of such a divine generation at
other than a very formal level—we have no created parallel that offers anything other than a distant
likeness." Ayres, *Augustine and the Trinity*, 226.

The Biblical Basis for Eternal Generation

Critics frequently assert that eternal generation represents a speculative doctrine rooted in a handful of dubious proof texts (e.g., Prov 8:22–25; Ps 2:7; Mic 5:2; John 5:26; Col 1:15; Heb 1:5).[30] In light of this criticism, one might be tempted to assume that Augustine's argument for eternal generation arises from a series of isolated texts strung together like a popcorn string on a Christmas tree. Nothing could be further from the truth. For Augustine, eternal generation arises from integrated reflection on all that Scripture teaches about the person of Christ.[31] It is rooted in a comprehensive christological (and Trinitarian) hermeneutic.[32] Thus, to grasp his argument we need to examine Augustine's christological hermeneutic.

In *De trinitate* Augustine identifies several "canonical rules" to help his community rightly read Scripture in its witness to Christ. His first rule concerns two ways that Scripture speaks about Christ. Drawing on musical imagery, he explains that we must distinguish "two resonances" in Scripture, "one tuned to the form of God in which he is, and is equal to the Father, the other tuned to the form of a servant which he took and is less than the Father."[33] Once we recognize that Scripture speaks about Christ in two ways, "we will not be upset by statements in the holy books that appear to be in flat contradiction with each other."[34] Augustine demonstrates the explanatory power of this distinction through a number of examples.[35] In the form of God, Christ created all things (John 1:3), while in the form of a servant he was made of a woman (Gal 4:4). In the form of God, he is equal to the Father (John 10:30), while in the form of a servant he obeys the Father (John 6:38). In the form of God, he is "true God" (1 John 5:20),

---

30. For an overview of evangelical criticisms of eternal generation, see Keith E. Johnson, "Augustine, Eternal Generation, and Evangelical Trinitarianism," 143–46.

31. For an extended discussion of the importance of this principle for rightly reading the scriptural witness to the Trinity, see Fred Sanders, *The Triune God* (Grand Rapids: Zondervan, 2016), chs. 2–5.

32. This is a characteristically modern way of phrasing it. Augustine (along with all early theologians) did not have a category of "Trinitarian theology" as distinct from "Christology." See John Behr, *The Formation of Christian Theology*, vol. 2, *The Nicene Faith* (Crestwood, NY: St. Vladimir's Seminary Press, 2004), 1–17, 475–81.

33. *Trin.* 1.22 (82). Biblical warrant for this hermeneutical principle is found in Philippians 2:6. "And this rule for solving this question in all the sacred scriptures is laid down for us in this one passage of the apostle Paul's letter, where the distinction is clearly set out. He says: *Who being in the form of God thought it no robbery to be equal to God, yet he emptied himself taking the form of a servant, being made in the likeness of men, in condition found as a man* (Phil 2:6)" (*Trin.* 1.14 [74]).

34. *Trin.* 1.22 (82).

35. See *Trin.* 1.22–24 (82–83).

while in the form of a servant he is obedient to the point of death (Phil 2:8). These two "forms" exist in one "person."[36]

In book 2 of *De trinitate*, Augustine points out that his distinction between the Son in the "form of a servant" and the Son in the "form of God" is inadequate to explain a number of passages that speak of the Son neither as "less" than the Father nor "equal" to the Father but rather intimate that the Son is "from the Father" (*de Patre*). Another "rule" must be applied to these passages: "This then is the rule which governs many scriptural texts, intended to show not that one person is less than the other, but only that one is from the other."[37] We might call this Augustine's "from-another" rule. He explicitly cites John 5:19 and 5:26 as clear examples of this rule: "Truly, truly, I say to you, the Son can do nothing of his own accord, but only what he sees the Father doing. For whatever the Father does, that the Son does likewise" (John 5:19). "For as the Father has life in himself, so he has granted the Son also to have life in himself" (John 5:26). Applying the form-of-a-servant rule to these passages leads to confusion and absurdity.[38] The from-another rule, however, provides the hermeneutical key to rightly reading these texts: "So the reason for these statements can only be that the life of the Son is unchanging like the Father's, and yet is from the Father [5:26]; and that the work of Father and Son is indivisible, and yet the Son's working is from the Father just as he himself is from the Father [5:19]."[39]

It is important to follow Augustine's reasoning. He assumes (rightly) that significant continuity exists between God's immanent life and God's actions in creation, providence, and redemption. As a result, relational patterns in the economy of salvation reflect and reveal patterns in God's inner life. Thus, the reason the Son can do nothing of himself (John 5:19) is because the Son is not "from himself" (John 5:26). This is why the Son's "working" (which is indivisible with the Father) comes *from* the Father.

Combining Augustine's interpretive rules, New Testament references to Christ can be grouped in three categories. First, some texts refer to Son in the "form of God" in which he is equal to the Father (e.g., John 1:3; 10:30;

---

36. *Trin.* 1.28 (86). Although he does not frame the relationship between Christ's two natures in the precise language of Chalcedon, Augustine affirms that Christ possesses two natures and that these two natures are united in one subject. See Brian E. Daley, "Christology," in *Augustine through the Ages: An Encyclopedia*, ed. Allan D. Fitzgerald (Grand Rapids: Eerdmans, 1999), 164–69.

37. *Trin.* 2.3 (99).

38. *Trin.* 2.3 (99). If we try to apply the "form of a servant" rule to John 5:19, then we have to say that the Father walked on water while the Son imitated him and that the Father opened the eyes of a blind man while the Son imitated him.

39. *Trin.* 2.3 (99).

ETERNAL GENERATION IN THE TRINITARIAN THEOLOGY OF AUGUSTINE

16:15; 17:10; Phil 2:6; Col 1:15; 1 John 5:20). Others refer to the Son in the "form of a servant" in which he is "less" than the Father (e.g., Matt 12:32; 26:38; Mark 13:32; Luke 4:18; John 6:38; 7:16; 14:28; Gal 4:4; Phil 2:7; Col 1:18). Finally, some texts speak of the Son as "from" the Father (e.g., John 5:19, 26, 36). The from-another rule does not imply any lack of equality between Father and Son; rather, it intimates the Son's "birth in eternity."[40]

Because John 5:26 represents one of Augustine's most important scriptural witnesses to eternal generation, it will be helpful to examine his reading of this text more closely. As we noted earlier, this text contains two important affirmations: (1) that both Father and Son possess "life in himself" (i.e., self-existent life) and (2) that Father and Son possess "life in himself" in differing ways.[41] The Father possesses "life in himself" from no one while the Son possesses "life in himself" given by the Father.[42] According to Augustine, the phrase "has been given" (v. 26b) is roughly equivalent in meaning to "has been begotten."[43]

Augustine's interpretation of the phrase "has been given" as "has been begotten" may strike some readers as a big leap. It is important to remember that Christian theologians frequently employ terms not found in the biblical text (e.g., Trinity, person, essence, nature) in order to explain what the biblical text teaches.[44] In this case, Augustine appeals to "eternal generation" in order to explain the theological judgment this text renders regarding the Father–Son relation. It is crucial to distinguish the "judgment" this text renders regarding the relationship of the Son to the Father from the "conceptuality" used to express this judgment (i.e., the language of "grant" in the biblical text versus the language of "generation" in the case of Augustine).[45]

There is much to commend Augustine's reading of John 5:26. D. A. Carson offers a compelling case in support of Augustine's reading of this text. It is helpful to quote Carson at length:

---

40. *Trin.* 2.3 (99).

41. John 5:26 includes both "personal" and "essential" predications. The essential predication is "life in himself" while the personal predication includes the names "Father" and "Son" as well as the mode by which Father and Son possess "life in himself."

42. *Tract.* 19.13 (153): "Therefore, the Father remains life, the Son also remains life; the Father, life in himself, not from the Son, the Son, life in himself, but from the Father. [The Son was] begotten by the Father to be life in himself, but the Father [is] life in himself, unbegotten."

43. *Tract.* 19.13 (152).

44. For example, most theologians (including those who reject eternal generation) interpret "life" in v. 26 as referring to God's essence, even though the term "essence" is not found in John 5:26.

45. For more on this important distinction, see David S. Yeago, "The New Testament and the Nicene Dogma: A Contribution to the Recovery of Theological Exegesis," *Pro Ecclesia* 3 (1994): 152–64.

169

KEITH E. JOHNSON

A full discussion of John 5:26 could demonstrate that it most plausibly reads as an *eternal grant* from the Father to the Son, a grant that inherently transcends time and stretches Jesus' Sonship into eternity past. When Jesus says that the Father has "life in himself," the most natural meaning is that this refers to God's self-existence. He is not dependent on anyone or anything. Then Jesus states that God, who has "life in himself," "has granted the Son to have life in himself." This is conceptually far more difficult. If Jesus had said that the Father, who has "life in himself," had granted to the Son to have life, there would be no conceptual difficulty, but of course the Son would then be an entirely secondary and derivative being. What was later called the doctrine of the Trinity would be ruled out. Alternatively, if Jesus had said that the Father has "life in himself" and the Son has "life in himself," there would be no conceptual difficulty, but it would be much more difficult to rule out ditheism. In fact what Jesus says is that the Father has "life in himself" and He has *granted* to the Son to have "life in himself." The expression "life in himself" must mean the same thing in both parts of the verse. But how can such "life in himself," the life of self-existence, be granted by another? The ancient explanation is still the best one: This is an eternal grant. There was therefore never a time when the Son did not have "life in himself." This eternal grant establishes the nature of the eternal relationship between the Father and the Son.[46]

Those who reject eternal generation typically counter that John 5:26b describes the authority the Son received from the Father for his incarnate mission.[47] Two points need to be made in response. First, there is an inconsistency in this explanation. Many theologians who deny that the language of "grant" makes a metaphysical claim about the eternal relation of the Son to the Father nevertheless read "life in himself" as making a metaphysical

---

46. D. A. Carson, "God Is Love," *Bibliotheca Sacra* 156 (1999): 139. See also Marianne Meye Thompson, *The God of the Gospel of John* (Grand Rapids: Eerdmans, 2001), 77–80.

47. "It is entirely possible, indeed, much more likely, that [the words of John 5:26] refer to an aspect of the *incarnate* Son's messianic investiture. John 5:22–23 which precedes the verse refers to his designated authority to judge, clearly an aspect of his Messianic role, and so is the similar thought of 5:27 which follows it. Accordingly, 5:26, paralleling 5:27, seems to be giving the ground upon which the Son is able to raise the dead, namely, it is one of the prerogatives of his Messianic investiture." Robert L. Reymond, *A New Systematic Theology of the Christian Faith*, 2nd ed. (Nashville: Thomas Nelson, 1998), 325, italics original. Although he affirms eternal generation, Calvin (in contrast to many of the Reformers) claims that John 5:26 refers not to the eternal relation of the Son to the Father but rather to the Son's role as mediator: "For there [5:26] he is properly speaking not of those gifts which he had in the Father's presence from the beginning, but of those with which he was adorned in that very flesh wherein he appeared" (*Inst.* 4.17.9 [1369]).

ETERNAL GENERATION IN THE TRINITARIAN THEOLOGY OF AUGUSTINE

claim about the Father and the Son. John Feinberg represents a case in point. On the one hand, he claims that John 5:26 teaches the self-existence not only of the Father but also of the Son.[48] That is to say, he reads both instances of "life in himself" metaphysically. On the other hand, in rejecting eternal generation,[49] he implicitly denies that the language of "grant" makes any metaphysical claims. "Life in himself" is read metaphysically while "grant" is read only economically. This inconsistency begs for some kind of explanation. Second, and more substantially, "messianic investiture"[50] does not capture the meaning of "life in himself." As Marianne Thompson explains, "The life-giving prerogative does not remain external to the Son. He does not receive it merely as a mission to be undertaken. It is not simply some power he has been given. Rather, the Son partakes of the very life of the Father."[51] This is why the incarnate Son is able to raise the dead (v. 25).[52] As Augustine explains, "For the Father has life everlasting in himself, and unless he begot such a Son as had life in himself, then the Son would not also give life to whom he would wish, as the Father raises the dead and gives them life."[53]

Although he offers traditional readings of texts cited by other patristic writers in support of eternal generation (e.g., Ps 2:7; Prov 8:25; Col 1:15),[54] it is Augustine's from-another rule that constitutes the hermeneutical key to his argument.[55] Five lines of biblical evidence support this rule. The first line of evidence includes the numerous "sending" texts scattered throughout the New Testament (e.g., Matt 10:40; Luke 4:43; 10:16; Gal 4:4–6). A high concentration of these passages is found in the Gospel of John (e.g., John 4:34;

---

48. See Feinberg, *No One Like Him*, 212, 242, 258, 462. "Evidence of Christ's deity stems from the fact that NT writers predicated attributes of Christ that belong only to God" (p. 462). In this context, Feinberg claims that John 5:26 explicitly predicates self-existence to Christ: "and possessing life in and of himself, i.e., having the attribute of aseity (John 5:26)" (p. 462).

49. Feinberg, *No One Like Him*, 492: "In sum, it seems wisest to abandon the doctrines of eternal generation and eternal procession. They are shrouded in obscurity as to their meaning, and biblical support for them is nowhere near as strong as supposed."

50. Reymond, *A New Systematic Theology*, 325.

51. Marianne Meye Thompson, "The Living Father," *Semeia* 85 (1999): 24.

52. A causal link between v. 25 and v. 26 is established by the Greek preposition γάρ ("for") at the beginning of v. 26. The Son can raise the dead (v. 25) because he possesses "life in himself" from the Father (v. 26).

53. *Tract.* 19.13 (153).

54. For example, commenting on Psalm 2:7, Augustine explains that while it may sound like the "begetting" spoken of in this text refers to the temporal birth of Jesus Christ, "a divine interpretation is given to that expression, 'Today have I begotten Thee,' whereby the uncorrupt and Catholic faith proclaims the eternal generation of the power and Wisdom of God, who is the Only-begotten Son." Augustine, "Expositions on the Book of Psalms," in *Saint Augustin: Expositions on the Book of Psalms,* ed. Philip Schaff, trans. A. Cleveland Coxe, in *NPNF*[1] 8:3.

55. Although it does not originate with Augustine, his formal explication of this exegetical principle constitutes one of his key contributions to the development of Latin-speaking pro-Nicene theology.

171

KEITH E. JOHNSON

5:23–24, 30–47; 6:29, 38–44, 57; 7:16, 28–29, 33; 8:16–18, 26–29, 42; 9:4; 12:44–50; 13:16; 14:24; 15:21; 16:5, 28; 17:3, 18, 21; 20:21). In these texts, Jesus repeatedly speaks of the Father as "the one who sent me":

- "Whoever does not honor the Son does not honor the Father who sent him" (John 5:23).
- "For the works that the Father has given me to accomplish, the very works that I am doing, bear witness about me that the Father has sent me" (John 5:36).
- "For I have come down from heaven, not to do my own will but the will of him who sent me" (John 6:38).
- "I know him, for I come from him, and he sent me" (John 7:29).
- "I will be with you a little longer, and then I am going to him who sent me" (John 7:33).
- "If God were your Father, you would love me, for I came from God and I am here. I came not of my own accord, but he sent me" (John 8:42).
- "Truly, truly, I say to you, whoever receives the one I send receives me, and whoever receives me receives the one who sent me" (John 13:20).
- "And this is eternal life, that they know you the only true God, and Jesus Christ whom you have sent" (John 17:3).
- "For I have given them the words that you gave me, and they have received them and have come to know in truth that I came from you; and they have believed that you sent me" (John 17:8).

Augustine discusses the sending of the Son at length in books 2–4 of *De trinitate*. He argues that the temporal sending of the Son reflects and reveals the Son's relation of being eternally "from" the Father: "So the Word of God is sent by him whose Word he is; sent by him he is born of. The begetter sends, and what is begotten is sent."[56]

One might wonder how "sending" texts can count as evidence for eternal generation. John the Baptist was "sent" by God (John 1:6), yet we do not infer the divinity of John from the fact he was "sent." This criticism misunderstands the theological significance of the "sending" passages. The passages cited above do not constitute evidence for the "divinity" of Christ

---

56. *Trin.* 4.28 (173). For further discussion of how the temporal mission of the Son reveals his eternal begetting from the Father, see Sanders, *The Triune God*, 93–153.

ETERNAL GENERATION IN THE TRINITARIAN THEOLOGY OF AUGUSTINE

(an essential predication). Rather, they shed light on the Son's relationship to the Father (a personal predication). Returning to John 1, although John the Baptist and Jesus are both presented as "agents," they are not agents in the same way. The agencies of John and Jesus are explicitly contrasted on the basis "of the status or rank of the two."[57] John the Baptist (who is "not the light") functions merely as a human agent (cf. John 1:4–5, 8, 15, 30), whereas Jesus is a divine (and human) agent whose working is identified with the Father (John 1:1–3, 14).[58] Once we recognize that Jesus is a divine agent who is equal to the Father, then we must ask what his unique sending reveals regarding his relationship to the Father. It is precisely in this context that the sending passages point to the Son's eternal relation to the Father.

A second line of evidence represents passages that speak of the Father "giving" and the Son "receiving" (e.g., John 5:19, 22, 26, 27, 36; 10:18; 17:2, 8, 11, 22; 18:11). Although some giving/receiving texts can be explained on the basis of the form-of-a-servant rule (e.g., John 5:22, 27; Phil 2:9), others point to the eternal relation of the Son to the Father.[59] John 5:19 and 5:26 represent passages that should be read in terms of the from-another rule. John 7:16 ("My teaching is not mine, but his who sent me") represents a border-line case.[60] It could be understood either according to the form-of-a-servant rule or the from-another rule (*Trin.* 2.4, 99). If understood in terms of the from-another rule, "'*My teaching is not mine but his who sent me*' (John 7:16) may be reduced to 'I am not from myself but from him who sent me.'"[61]

A third witness to the from-another rule includes passages that reflect an ordered equality that marks the agency of the Father and Son (e.g., John 1:1–3, 10; 5:19, 21; 14:6, 10; Rom 5:1, 11; 1 Cor 8:6; Eph 1:3–14; 2:18; 4:6; Col 1:16; 3:17; Heb 1:1–2; Jude 25). One place this ordered equality can be seen is creation. Reading 1 Corinthians 8:6 alongside John 1:3, Augustine explains that the Father created all things *through* the Son.[62] This reflects a broader scriptural pattern—namely, that the Father works

---

57. Andreas J. Köstenberger and Scott R. Swain, *Father, Son and Spirit: The Trinity and John's Gospel* (Downers Grove, IL: InterVarsity, 2008), 116.

58. Köstenberger and Swain, *Father, Son and Spirit*, 116: "The contrast between John the Baptist and the Word is not that one is an agent of God whereas the other is not. Both are agents of God. . . . The contrast between John the Baptist and the Word concerns, then, their *status* as agents. One is earthly, merely human. The other is divine (and *also* human: see 1:14)."

59. See *Trin.* 1.29 (87).

60. *Trin.* 2.4 (99): "So then, as I started to say, there are some things so put in the sacred books that it is uncertain which rule they are to be referred to; should it be to the Son's being less than the Father because of the creature he took or to his being shown to be from the Father in his very equality with him?"

61. *Trin.* 2.4 (100).

62. *Trin.* 1.12 (72).

all things through the Son (and by the Spirit).[63] This pattern is reflected in the prepositions associated with the agency of the Father and Son. For example, 1 Corinthians 8:6 presents the Father as the one "from whom" all things exist while the Son is named as the one "through whom" all things exist.[64] Augustine offers a Trinitarian reading of Romans 11:36a ("For from him and through him and to him are all things") associating the individual propositions with each of the divine persons. Even if one questions the appropriateness of a Trinitarian reading of Romans 11:36, one cannot deny the broader pattern.

A fourth line of evidence includes the names "Father" and "Son" (e.g., Matt 11:27; 24:36–39; 28:18; Gal 4:4–6). Like the "sending" texts cited above, a high concentration of these passages can be found in the Gospel of John (e.g., John 1:14; 3:35; 5:17–47; 6:40; 14:13; 17:1). Critics of eternal generation assert that the title "Son" only implies the "equality" of the Son to the Father in the New Testament and does not reveal anything regarding the mode by which he eternally exists.[65] This argument, however, commits the fallacy of the excluded middle by claiming that "Son" must refer either to "equality" or "origin," but not both. For Augustine, "Son" implies both equality and origin. In the process of responding to his "Arian" opponents,[66] Augustine argues that "begotten" simply means the same thing as "son": "Being son is a consequence of being begotten, and being begotten is implied by being son."[67] If "Son" only means "equality," then we find ourselves in the odd place where the biblical name "Son" appears to tell us nothing about the relation of the Son to the Father.

A final group of texts supporting Augustine's rule comes from an unlikely source—passages concerning the relation of the Holy Spirit to

---

63. One may wonder where the "equality" is to be found in the ordering described above. Equality is found in the fact that Father, Son, and Holy Spirit act inseparably. The inseparable operation of the divine persons will be discussed below.

64. The word "frequently" is crucial. These patterns are not absolute. Fourth century anti-Nicene theologians appealed to differences among prepositions in order to argue that the Son is ontologically inferior to the Father. Basil of Caesarea responded to this argument by pointing out that flexibility exists in the use of biblical prepositions. See St. Basil the Great, *On the Holy Spirit*, trans. David Anderson (Crestwood, NY: St. Vladimir's Seminary Press, 1980), 15–42.

65. According to Lorraine Boettner, although the terms "Father" and "Son" may communicate ideas of "source of being," "subordination," or "dependence" to contemporary readers, these terms only express "sameness of nature" in their original Semitic context. Lorraine Boettner, *Studies in Theology*, 9th ed. (Philadelphia: P&R, 1970), 112.

66. Augustine's opponents, whom he calls "Arians," were probably Latin Homoian theologians. See Michel R. Barnes, "Exegesis and Polemic in Augustine's De trinitate I," *Augustinian Studies* 30 (1999) 43–52; Barnes, "The Arians of Book V, and the Genre of 'de Trinitate,'" *JTS* 44 (1993) 185–95. Latin Homoian theologians like Palladius and Maximinus emphasized the Father as "true God" over and against the Son (particularly because of the Father's unique status as ingenerate).

67. *Trin.* 5.8 (193).

the Son (and Father). It might be argued that much of the biblical material cited above could be explained away by appealing to the incarnation. This argument, however, cannot be made in the case of the Holy Spirit. One cannot say that Scripture speaks of the Holy Spirit being "sent" because he became incarnate. Similarly, one cannot say that the Holy Spirit "receives" from the Father or Son because he took on flesh. After reminding his readers that the Holy Spirit did not take on the "form of a servant," Augustine cites John 16:13–14. "When the Spirit of truth comes, he will guide you into all the truth, for he will not speak on his own authority, but whatever he hears he will speak, and he will declare to you the things that are to come. He will glorify me, for he will take what is mine and declare it to you" (John 16:13–14). Reading this text alongside John 15:26,[68] Augustine explains that the reason the Holy Spirit does not "speak on his own" is because, like the Son, he is not "from himself."[69] The Holy Spirit speaks as one "proceeding from the Father."[70] Similarly, the reason the Holy Spirit "glorifies" the Son (John 16:14) is because he "receives" from the Son—just as the Son glorifies the Father because he "receives" from the Father.[71] My point is not to attempt to prove the eternal procession of the Spirit from the Father and Son. I simply want to draw attention to the fact that these Holy Spirit passages constitute additional evidence for Augustine's from-another rule. Thus, one cannot dismiss the biblical material cited above merely by appealing to the incarnation.

ETERNAL GENERATION IN AUGUSTINE'S TRINITARIAN THEOLOGY

The eternal generation of the Son plays an integral role in Augustine's Trinitarian theology. First, it provides the basis for affirming the equality of the Son to the Father. One of Augustine's central concerns in *De trinitate*

---

68. "But when the Helper comes, whom I will send to you from the Father, the Spirit of truth, who proceeds from the Father, he will bear witness about me" (John 15:26).

69. Unfortunately, the ESV obscures this point when it says that the Spirit does not "speak on his own authority." The word "authority" is not found in the original text (nor are there any variant readings with "authority" included). The Greek simply reads οὐ γὰρ λαλήσει ἀφ ἑαυτοῦ ("he does not speak from himself").

70. *Trin.* 2.5 (100). Augustine continues, "And just as the Son is not made less than the Father by his saying, *The Son cannot do anything of himself except what he sees the Father doing* (Jn 5:19) (this is not spoken in the form of a servant but in the form of God, as we have already shown, and so these words do not indicate that he is less than the Father but only that he is from him); so here it does not make the Holy Spirit less to say of him, *He will not speak from himself, but whatever he hears he will speak* (Jn 16;13). This is said in virtue of his proceeding from the Father" (ibid).

71. *Trin.* 2.6 (100).

KEITH E. JOHNSON

is affirming the unity and equality of the Son to the Father—particularly in response to Latin Homian denials of the Son's equality. The begetting of the Son constitutes a key element of his argument. Because "the Father has begotten the Son as his equal," Father and Son share one nature.[72] His argument proceeds on the assumption that like begets like: "Thus it is clear that the Son has another from whom he is and whose Son he is, while the Father does not have a Son from whom he is, but only whose Father he is. Every son gets being what he is from his father, and is his father's son; while no father gets being what he is from his son, though he is his son's father."[73]

Second, the generation of the Son constitutes the basis for distinguishing the Son from the Father and Holy Spirit. At the beginning of *De trinitate*, Augustine offers a compact summary of Latin (pro-Nicene) teaching on the Trinity. After affirming that Father, Son, and Holy Spirit are not three gods but one God because they exist "in the inseparable equality of one substance," Augustine turns to the distinction of persons: "although indeed the Father has begotten the Son, and *therefore* he who is the Father is not the Son; and the Son is begotten by the Father, and *therefore* he who is the Son is not the Father."[74] "Begetting" constitutes the basis for affirming the hypostatic distinction between the Father and the Son. Apart from eternal generation, there is no basis for distinguishing the Son from the Father in God's inner life.[75]

Third, building on the previous point, the perichoretic communion that exists among the divine persons is rooted in the Father's act of generating the Son. Lewis Ayres explains that in the decade between 410 and 420, Augustine moves "towards a sophisticated account of the divine communion" in which "the Trinitarian life is founded in the Father's activity as the one from whom the Son is eternally born and the Spirit proceeds."[76] Thus, in his mature theology, Augustine presents Father, Son, and Holy Spirit as "an ordered communion of equals established by the Father."[77] On the one hand, each of the divine persons is "irreducible" and possesses the "fullness of God."[78] On the other hand, Augustine "consistently founds the unity of God in the Father's eternal act of giving rise to a communion in

---

72. *Trin.* 1.29 (88).
73. *Trin.* 1.2 (98).
74. *Trin.* 1.7 (69). Emphasis mine.
75. Interestingly, Augustine does not use the Latin word for "person" (*persona*) in this summary of pro-Nicene teaching on the Trinity. This is not because he is a closet Modalist (contra his critics) but because generation and procession constitute the basis for distinguishing the divine persons.
76. Ayres, *Augustine and the Trinity*, 3.
77. Ibid., 197.
78. Ibid., 230.

ETERNAL GENERATION IN THE TRINITARIAN THEOLOGY OF AUGUSTINE

which the mutual love of the three constitutes their unity of substance."[79]
We might say that eternal generation names the mode of communion that
exists between the Father and Son.[80]

Fourth, the generation of the Son constitutes the ontological basis for his
temporal mission. Augustine's opponents argued that the sending of the Son
reveals his "inferiority" to the Father on the grounds that the one who sends
must be "greater" than the one who is sent.[81] In books 2–4 of *De trinitate*,
Augustine labors to show that "being sent" implies no inferiority on the part
of the Son. It simply reveals that the Son is eternally *from* the Father. Notice
the important role that eternal generation plays in Augustine's explanation:

> If however the reason why the Son is said to have been sent by the
> Father is simply that the one is the Father and the other the Son, then
> there is nothing at all to stop us believing that the Son is equal to the
> Father and consubstantial and co-eternal, and yet that the Son is sent
> by the Father. Not because one is greater and the other less, but because
> one is the Father and the other the Son; one is the begetter, the other
> begotten; the first is the one from whom the sent one is; the other is
> the one who is from the sender.[82]

We might say that the sending of the Son represents a temporal expression
of his generation by the Father in eternity.

Finally, eternal generation shapes the divine agency of the Son. Trinitarian agency includes two elements for Augustine.[83] On the one hand,
because they are one God, Father, Son, and Holy Spirit "work inseparably."[84] Each divine person is involved in every act in creation, providence,
and redemption.[85] Moreover, Father, Son, and Holy Spirit share one will

---

79. Ibid., 319.

80. Although Augustine is speaking about the knowledge of the Father and Son, the following
statement offers a window into this reality: "Therefore the Father and the Son know each other, the
one by begetting, the other by being born" (*Trin.* 15.23 [415]).

81. *Trin.* 2.7 (101).

82. *Trin.* 4.27 (172).

83. For a discussion of the agency of the divine persons in Augustine's theology, see Keith E.
Johnson, "Trinitarian Agency and the Eternal Subordination of the Son: An Augustinian Perspective,"
Themelios 36 (2011): 7–25.

84. *Trin.* 1.7 (70). Among medieval theologians, inseparable operation is expressed though the
axiom *opera ad extra sunt indivisa* ("the external works are undivided"). Although this axiom is faithful to his theology, Augustine prefers to say that the works of the Father, Son, and Holy Spirit are
"inseparable" (*inseparabilis*). For example, Augustine uses the language *patris et filii opera inseparabilia
sunt* ("the works of the Father and Son are inseparable"). See *Tract.* 20.3 (166).

85. *Tract.* 20.3 (166): "The Catholic faith does not say that God the Father did something and
the Son did something else; but what the Father did, this the Son also did, this Holy Spirit also did."

and one power.[86] On the other hand, in this undivided act, the divine persons work in a way that reflects their eternal relations. The Father works with the Son and Spirit according to his mode of being "from no one" (unbegotten). The Son works with the Father and Spirit according to his mode of being "from the Father" (generation). The Spirit works with the Father and Son according to his mode of being "from the Father and the Son" (procession).[87]

The interplay between the Son's eternal begetting and his temporal working can be seen in Augustine's explanation of John 5:19 in his *Tractates on the Gospel of John*. In John 5:19, Jesus explains that he does nothing on his own but only what he sees the Father doing. After noting that Jesus spoke these words in response to criticisms of his Sabbath-healing, Augustine cites John 5:17 ("My Father is working until now, and I am working"). In this verse, Jesus equates his healing work with the divine work of the Father. Augustine reminds his readers that the Father never works apart from the Son nor the Son apart from the Father.[88] The Jewish leaders rightly understood Jesus to be asserting his equality with the Father (v. 18). When Jesus claims that he does nothing by himself but only what he sees the Father doing (v. 19), it was as if he was telling them, "Why were you scandalized because I said, God is my Father, and because I make myself equal to God? I am equal in such a way that he begot me; I am equal in such a way that he is not from me, but I am from him."[89] One might wonder how Augustine infers the eternal generation of the Son from the words of Jesus in v. 19. He rightly recognizes that this verse describes the temporal working of the Son—not his eternal relation to the Father. However, Augustine is attempting to answer the following question: Why does the Son's power to heal come from the Father? His answer is that Son's power to heal comes from the Father because the Son himself is (eternally) from the Father.[90] To employ language that will emerge much later in the Western tradition, the

---

86. Inseparable operation should not be confused with "modalism." Modalism is a heresy that denies hypostatic distinctions among the divine persons.

87. Combining these elements, we might say that the inseparable action of the divine persons is inflected through the intra-Trinitarian *taxis*: every divine action proceeds from the Father, through the Son, and in (or by) the Holy Spirit. This principle is expressed concretely in Augustine's discussion of creation in *Tract*. 20.9 (172): "The Father [made] the world, the Son [made] the world, the Holy Spirit [made] the world. If [there are] three gods, [there are] three worlds; if [there is] one God, Father and Son and Holy Spirit, one world was made by the Father through the Son in the Holy Spirit."

88. *Tract*. 20.3 (166): "The Catholic faith, made firm by the Spirit of God in its saints, holds this against every heretical depravity: The works of the Father and the Son are inseparable."

89. *Tract*. 20.4 (167).

90. That the Son is eternally from the Father is taught a few verses later in John 5:26. Augustine reads 5:19 through the lens of 5:26.

Son's temporal mode of operation reflects his eternal mode of subsistence.[91] To illustrate this principle, Augustine turns to a different miracle—Jesus walking on water. If the Son only does what he "sees" the Father doing, does this mean that the Father walked on water as well? The Catholic faith has a clear answer to this question: the Son walked on the water with the "flesh" walking and the "divinity" guiding its steps.[92] Nevertheless, the Father was not absent. John 14:10 teaches that the Father abiding in the Son does his works.[93] Thus, the Son's water-walking is the joint work of the Father and Son, with the Father working through the Son.[94] Hence, we see that eternal generation provides the key to rightly understanding the agency of the Son. We might say that "generation" names the Son's personal mode of divine action (alongside the Father and Holy Spirit).[95]

CONCLUSION

Like all pro-Nicene theologians, the eternal generation of the Son represents a foundational element of Augustine's teaching on the Trinity. According to Augustine, the Father timelessly "begot" the Son in such a way that the Son is both consubstantial with and hypostatically distinct from the Father. John 5:26 represents an important scriptural witness for Augustine to the eternal begetting of the Son. This text teaches that while Father and Son both possess self-existent life, they possess it in differing ways. The Father possesses "life in himself" from no one while the Son possesses "life in himself" eternally from the Father. Through his Christological hermeneutic, Augustine helps us see that the eternal generation of the Son is rooted not in a handful of questionable proof texts but in a comprehensive reading of Scripture.

---

91. For the Son "to be" and the Son "to act" are not two distinct realities. The Son acts as the Son exists, i.e., in his mode of generation from the Father. Notice the reciprocal relationship between the Son's power and the Son's nature: "Therefore, because the Son's power is from the Father, for that reason the Son's substance also is from the Father; and because the Son's substance [is] from the Father, for that reason the Son's power is from the Father" (*Tract.* 20.4 [168]).

92. *Tract.* 20.6 (169–70).

93. "Do you not believe that I am in the Father and the Father is in me? The words that I say to you I do not speak on my own authority, but the Father who dwells in me does his works" (John 14:10).

94. *Tract.* 20.6 (170): "Therefore, if the Father abiding in the Son does his works, that walking of the flesh upon the sea was by the Father [yet] was done through the Son."

95. The word "mode" is critical. The divine persons do not perform separate actions. It would be inappropriate to speak about a "personal action" of the Son, as if the Son worked apart from the Father and Holy Spirit. For more on the Son's personal mode of action, see Gilles Emery, *Trinity, Church and the Human Person: Thomistic Essays* (Naples: Sapientia, 2007), 115–53.

CHAPTER 10

POST-REFORMATION TRINITARIAN PERSPECTIVES

CHAD VAN DIXHOORN

INTRODUCTION

The Westminster Assembly, meeting from 1643 to 1653, offered a purpose-built arena for the mid-century theological contests of the English-speaking world. The assembly's opening ceremonies were held on July 1, 1643, and from that point forward the gathering was celebrated or hated as the mastermind behind a revolution in the English church—but never ignored. Members of the assembly were paraded down London's streets and feasted at banquets. People across Britain and Europe sought the assembly's patronage and approval. Booksellers promoted the works of assembly members, and newspapers reported their activities or, in the absence of anything to say, simply made something up.

The assembly (what foreigners called the "Synod of London") was in many ways a highpoint of the post-Reformation period, and its formulations carried enormous weight amongst the Reformed orthodox almost immediately upon publication. It also provided a venue for theologians to debate dogmatic formulations, including nuances unsuitable for the pulpit and even for the press. Among other topics, the assembly eagerly discussed the doctrine of the Trinity, and this chapter endeavours to use what we know about the Westminster Assembly's debates and documents in order to provide a window into some post-Reformation Trinitarian perspectives, with a special focus on discussions about the eternal generation of the Son. This study bridges decades not discussed in Brannon Ellis's learned

180

POST-REFORMATION TRINITARIAN PERSPECTIVES

narrative—which in its seventeenth-century discussions moves from the Synod of Dordt to the writings of Roell—and supplements his account of continental sources by noting texts and events of immediate importance to Scottish and English theologians.

While its most public contribution to Trinitarian theology was its brief statements on the doctrine, the assembly is most often remembered by historians for its opposition to anti-Trinitarian ideas. It thus needs to be said up front that this chapter is not another foray into complex dynamic between orthodoxy and heterodoxy. It goes without saying that any consideration of the nuances of anti-Trinitarian teaching requires careful reading of the writings of its advocates and not only its opponents. Orthodox Trinitarian scholars at the assembly read the works of their opposites—more than one member of the synod appears to have amassed an impressive collection of Socinian works.[1] Nonetheless, orthodox divines were never sympathetic, and often not careful, readers of texts written by persons already distrusted for known theological aberrations. Anti-Trinitarians complained that their condemnation took no more than an ordinance from parliament or "decree of a councell, or Assembly of Divines, declaring such or such opinions to be Blasphemous, Heretical, or Schismatical."[2] It was certainly true that many theological judgments—then as now—were crowd-sourced, second hand, and peremptory. Second, in addition to these interpretive challenges, we can add that among the assembly's contemporaries and among historians "the heresy debate had . . . become hopelessly entangled with the toleration controversy"—a generic observation about heterodoxies that applies especially to anti-Trinitarian polemic.[3] Finally, opponents of orthodoxy were often discussed as a collective. This device allowed polemicists to highlight the most offensive statements on each doctrinal subtopic by any given errorist and to then permit the reader to attribute the error to the group, even if persons in that group do not hold to one or more of the charges leveled by the heresiographer. Although John Coffey and Paul Lim find some divines—among them, assembly members—who carefully delineated differences and degrees of heresy, such subtle considerations of heresy were uncommon.[4] John Coffey observes that early modern critics

---

1. See H. John McLachlan, *Socinianism in Seventeenth-Century England* (Oxford: Oxford University Press, 1951), 132–34.
2. Paul C. H. Lim, *Mystery Unveiled: The Crisis of the Trinity in Early Modern England* (Oxford: Oxford University Press, 2012), 63.
3. J. Coffey, "A Ticklish Business: Defining Heresy and Orthodoxy in the Puritan Revolution," in *Heresy, Literature and Politics*, ed. D. Loewenstein and J. Marshall (Cambridge: Cambridge University Press, 2006), 112.
4. Coffey, "A Ticklish Business," 115–17; Lim, *Mystery Unveiled*, 231.

of "orthodoxy" complained that the campaign against heresy was, among other things, "marred by an abundance of polemical vigor and an absence of intellectual rigor."[5] Lim notes the deliberate "blurring the distinction between religious heresies and political sedition," mentioning the case of Obadiah Sedgwick, who "compared heresy to 'a plain Gunpowder-plot, an error which blows up a fundamental truth.'"[6] Thus a study of the writings of Westminster Assembly members will not advance our understanding of the shifting views of sub- or anti-Trinitarians. Nonetheless, even if the views of anti-Trinitarian opponents are not always fairly represented by all assembly members, polemical encounters involving assembly members at least help us to understand the opinions of the early modern narrator, and polemical texts can offer insights into the conviction of the author.

Unfortunately, the importance of the assembly's determinations is matched only by the difficulty of accessing its deliberations. The Westminster Assembly's discussions of the doctrine of the Trinity are among its least well-documented debates. Members of the synod wrote on the subject before, during, and after the assembly,[7] and off stage the assembly's members dealt with Trinitarian debate in other venues, such as the civil courts.[8] Yet the assembly's own discussions on the topic are complicated by lost minutes of some meetings and frustratingly brief accounts of others. This may explain, at least in part, why comments on this particular assembly's debates are limited in number and depth.[9] But this is not the whole story. It is also true that literature on seventeenth-century Trinitarian discussions, like discussions of theology generally, has often been more interested in the politics and personalities involved in the suppression of error than in the disputes themselves. There are exceptions to this general rule: Paul Lim rehabilitates the study of

---

5. Coffey, "A Ticklish Business," 110.

6. Lim, *Mystery Unveiled*, 23.

7. Prior to and during the assembly most writings touching on the doctrine of the Trinity are polemical. Most positive treatments of the subject were authored after the assembly completed its work. For example, see John Arrowsmith, *Theanthropos; or God-Man: being an exposition upon the first eighteen verses of the first chapter of the Gospel according to St John* (London: Printed for Humphrey Moseley and William Wilson, 1660); Samuel Rutherford, *Examen Arminianismi* (Utrecht: Ex Officina Antonii Smytegelt, 1668), ch. 2; Anthony Tuckney, *Praelectiones Theologicae* (Amsterdam: Ex Officina Stephani Swart, 1679), lect. on John 17:3 in sec. 1, and ques. 2 and 39 in sec. 2.

8. Lim mentions a March 1646 case where Francis Woodcock denounced Thomas Hawes before two justices of the peace for his views on the doctrine of God. Lim, *Mystery Unveiled*, 5–6.

9. See Alexander F. Mitchell, *The Westminster Assembly: Its History and Standards* (London: J. Nisbet, 1883), 148; B. B. Warfield, "Calvin's Doctrine of the Trinity," in *Calvin and Calvinism* (Oxford: Oxford University Press, 1932), 279n137; Reymond, *A New Systematic Theology*, 338–41; C. B. Van Dixhoorn, "Reforming the Reformation: The Westminster Assembly and Theological Debate, 1643–1652" (PhD Diss., University of Cambridge, 2005), 1:240–49; Robert Letham, *The Westminster Assembly: Reading Its Theology in Historical Context* (Phillipsburg, NJ: P&R, 2009), 168; J. V. Fesko, *The Theology of the Westminster Standards* (Wheaton, IL: Crossway, 2014), 173–74.

POST-REFORMATION TRINITARIAN PERSPECTIVES

Trinitarian orthodoxy in a historiography more interested in heresy,[10] and Sarah Mortimer gets into the theological weeds in order to debate how closely historians should situate Socinian thought vis-à-vis Protestant thought more generally.[11] Nonetheless the center of this observation still holds.

Thankfully, not all it lost. Where official records of constructive Trinitarian deliberations are lacking, accounts or speeches by assembly members have survived, including some recently rediscovered material and one previously unidentified assembly text that discusses the Trinity (and other topics). It is with these tools, along with better-known texts of the assembly and its members, that this chapter examines three post-Reformation episodes linked to the Westminster Assembly. It proceeds by telling about a late-night visitor to a London home, by recalling the case of an imprisoned theologian, and by moralizing about a bad book endorsement.

Theos ek Theou: THOMAS GATAKER AND THE VISITOR IN THE NIGHT

Thomas Gataker (1574–1654) remembered that it was "at a very unseasonable houre" that he heard a knock at his door. A well-dressed man asked to speak with the lecturer of Lincoln's Inn, and when Gataker let the visitor in, he handed his host "a little scrole, wherein were these words written, 'Whether was the Godhead of Christ begotten of the Godhead of the Father from all eternity?'" The stranger then asked Gataker if the statement was in error.[12]

It was an unusual scene, even by the unusual standards of the time, and so rather than answer the man's question, Gataker asked for a little context. The stranger replied that the statement in question came not from himself but from one who believed what was taught "in the Creed, God of God, light of light." The Creed to which he referred is the one that Gataker called the "Creed of Constantinople" or, as he also put it, what is "commonly called the Nicene Creed."[13] Then the visitor persisted: Was it

---

10. Lim, *Mystery Unveiled*, 7–15.

11. Sarah Mortimer places Socinianism within Protestantism in *Reason and Religion in the English Revolution: The Challenge of Socinianism* (Cambridge: Cambridge University Press, 2010), 14. It was, in the sense that it was against Catholicism. Nonetheless, in disagreeing with most Protestants about the nature of God, in asserting an ethical rather than a redemptive soteriology, and in redrawing Protestant lines between revelation and reason, it is not entirely obvious that what Socinus and other anti-Trinitarians had to offer was not a *tertium quid*.

12. Gataker, *An answer to Mr. George Walkers vindication, or rather fresh accusation* . . . (London: E.G., 1642), 39.

13. Ibid., 38.

an error to speak of "the Godhead of Christ begotten of the Godhead of the Father from all eternity?" In what sense is the generation of the Son to be understood?

Gataker knew it was a setup. Someone had a reason for coming to *him*, and not, say, to George Walker (ca. *bap.* 1582–d. 1651), a fellow London minister who was sure that error lurked in every corner of the church and who ferreted out heretics almost as a hobby. Nonetheless, even if the man was not without guile, Gataker was still willing to play his game. He explained that the sentence (whosesoever it was!) was a poor paraphrase of the Creed, and that properly speaking, "the Godhead was not said, either to beget, or to be begotten." For Gataker, generation did not refer to divinity but to sonship. But perhaps the intention of the person whose words were captured on the scroll meant that "Christ being God was begotten of the Father, who is likewise God from all eternity." In that case the idea was sound, but the "speech" was still "improper." The visitor was pleased with the comment and asked Gataker to write down what he had said and sign it. Gataker asked the man's name. "He told me, I must excuse him for that." Gataker, refusing on such terms to sign anything, "told him, he should likewise excuse me for this" as he showed him the door.[14]

The pieces only came together the following day when Gataker was walking through St. Paul's Cathedral, the ministerial social center of London. He noticed that the Bishop of London was questioning Bartholomew Legate, an English Arian who only accepted "Christ as God by his office rather than his nature" and even then concluded that it was not appropriate to pray to or worship Christ.[15] Gataker quickly surmised that it must have been a well-to-do friend of Legate who had called on him the evening before, equipped with a poorly framed quotation in hand from one of London's less articulate ministers. The stranger was hoping that Gataker would condemn the statement in the scroll in order to show that even orthodox divines sometimes made sloppy statements that were a rough equivalent to Legate's own anti-Trinitarian formulations. But when Gataker refused to categorically denounce the questionable quotation, his visitor realized that Gataker's nuanced answer and generous spirit might nonetheless somehow serve Legate's cause just as well.

From the perspective of the late-night visitor, the doctrine of eternal generation offered a conveniently weak latch in the ancient fortress of

---

14. Ibid., 38–39.
15. Mortimer, *Reason and Religion*, 40.

POST-REFORMATION TRINITARIAN PERSPECTIVES

Trinitarian formulation, and thus an entry point for skeptics to doubt the divinity of Christ. It was no accident that the stranger in the night wished to discuss the phrases "God of God, and light of light." The man was playing off John Calvin's contention, best explained by Brannon Ellis, that a defense of the classical, orthodox doctrine of divine simplicity required a revision of the classical, orthodox doctrine of divine processions.[16] In making this argument Calvin addressed what he saw as lingering vestiges of subordinationism in articulations of Trinitarian theology, and his arguments in turn shaped both post-Reformation discussions of eternal generation and understandings of the Niceno-Constantinopolitan Creed.

Significant church fathers and almost all medieval theologians, some of them without sufficient qualification, had argued that the Father alone was the first principle of the divine essence and that he communicated this essence to the Son and the Spirit. The intention of these formulations was to ensure the unity of the Trinity, with each person essentially united to the Father, and to insist on real distinctions between the persons of the Trinity. Calvin, while affirming unity and distinction in the Trinity, was concerned that this construction undermined the simplicity of God. It predicated something of the Father that was not true, in the same manner, for the Son and the Holy Spirit. Significantly, Calvin's concern for the simplicity of God also entailed a more robust emphasis on the aseity of Christ. Classic statements of the eternal generation of Christ, asserting as they were the generation of divine essence from Father to Son, had promoted an eternal ontological subordination of the Son to the Father.[17] Calvin, in B. B. Warfield's words, moved for the "ascription of 'self-existence' (aseity, *autoousia*) to the Son," Christ as God *a se ipso* in and of himself.[18] Almost incidentally, Calvin demurred from dogmatic assertions that the eternal generation of the Son was a continuous process. Although those who defended the idea did not conceive of it as entailing anything incomplete in God, Calvin thought it an indemonstrable assertion.

Ellis mentions in passing Calvin's one-time "strained relationship with

---

16. Brannon Ellis, *Calvin, Classical Trinitarianism, and the Aseity of the Son* (Oxford: Oxford University Press, 2012), 1–102.

17. The best brief historical-theological treatments of Calvin's thought are provided by Gerald Bray, *The Doctrine of God* (Downers Grove, IL: InterVarsity, 1993), 197–211 and Richard A. Muller, *Post-Reformation Reformed Dogmatics* (Grand Rapids: Baker, 2003), 4:324–26 (hereafter *PRRD*). See also Donald Macleod, *The Person of Christ* (Downers Grove, IL: InterVarsity, 1998), 149–52; and for the fullest account, B. B. Warfield, *Calvin and Calvinism* (New York: Oxford University Press, 1932), 189–284.

18. Warfield, "Calvin's Doctrine of the Trinity," 233. For Warfield this was the main object of Calvin's development of Trinitarian theology; for Ellis this is an important byproduct of Calvin's defense of divine simplicity.

CHAD VAN DIXHOORN

the Nicene creed." Even later in life Calvin would refer to its *"Deum de Deo"* or *"Theos ek Theou"* phrase as "a difficult expression."[19] In English the phrase "God of God" reads like an intensive: *really* God. In Latin and Greek it is more obviously capable of being read as a derivative: *from* God. Calvin's resolution of the difficulty was to insist that the Nicene Creed's "God of God" phrase meant only that the person of the Son was (eternally) generated by the Father; only in this sense is the Son from the Father. Calvin allowed that the Father was the first principle, that the "Son exists from the Father," even that "the beginning of his person is God himself" (referring to the Father).[20] Nonetheless, he insisted that the divine *person* of the Son was generated from the Father and that the Son's divine *essence* was not.

As Ellis observes, this idea has some patristic testimony, but it would be difficult to find anyone prior to Calvin who believed that the Nicene Creed meant *only* that. Calvin, on the other hand, "refused to allow any relative or comparative predication concerning the divine essence per se, even if it meant taking such clear traditional language in an improper way." Not an "unintelligible or disingenuous" way, but an "unnatural" one given its original historic context.[21] So contrary was this to the common reading of the creed that Calvin was taken to be critical of its substance. Calvin's opponents coined a term for his Christology, Christ as *autotheos*, and they criticized the Reformer for undermining the doctrine of the Trinity—particularly with reference to his insistence that the divine essence was "natively" in each person of the Trinity and not principally located in the Father alone.[22]

Calvin could certainly cite church fathers for robust assertions of the aseity of Christ; he cited Augustine and Cyril.[23] Richard Muller sees Calvin swimming in one of two streams of Trinitarianism that wended their way through the medieval period. Tradition A, teaching the kind of theology that Calvin would oppose, held that the doctrine of the Trinity was dependent upon the doctrine of the "eternal generation" of the essence of the Father to the Son. The Father alone was *autotheos*; he was the *principium*, the first

---

19. Ellis, *Calvin, Classical Trinitarianism, and the Aseity of the Son*, 57; see also 141–42.
20. *Inst.* 1.13.25.
21. Ellis, *Calvin, Classical Trinitarianism, and the Aseity of the Son*, 47; see also 33.
22. Calvin's theological position is found throughout his commentaries, extant sermons, and polemical statements, but especially in his 1559 *Institutes*, which contains his latest debate with Gentilis and reserves more than five times the space for the doctrine of the Trinity than his 1536 *Institutes* (see the discussion in Warfield, *Calvin and Calvinism*, 218–24).
23. T. F. Torrance asserts but does not substantiate that Calvin was heavily dependent on Gregory Nazianzen: "The Doctrine of the Holy Trinity in Gregory Nazianzen and John Calvin," in *Trinitarian Perspectives: Toward Doctrinal Agreement* (Edinburgh: T&T Clark, 1994) and Muller's contrary view in *PRRD*, 4:326.

186

POST-REFORMATION TRINITARIAN PERSPECTIVES

principle, and through "eternal generation" the Father communicated his divine essence to the Son. In this tradition, the eternal generation itself was either understood to be a reality that was true of the Father–Son relationship from eternity or, in the writings of John of Damascus, a continuous eternal process. The proponents of Tradition A (such as Gilbert de la Porrée and Joachim de Fiore) held that the essence or divinity of the Godhead needed to reside in one of the persons of the Trinity (the Father) because if it did not, then it became a fourth thing in which all the persons of the Trinity participated and resulted in a kind of quaternity, three persons and divinity. This was the older and more dominant tradition in the church.

Muller's Tradition B (with Lombard, the Fourth Lateran Council, and Durandus of Sancto Porciano), on the other hand, held that "any one of the three persons is that Being (res), namely, substance, essence or divine nature" but denied a quaternity.[24] Their concern appears to be that a denial of aseity to the Second and Third Persons of the Trinity left them less than equal persons in the Godhead, perhaps even less divine than the Father. This was Calvin's concern too.

Muller argues that Calvin's thought reflected an existing tradition. Ellis argues for a sharper contrast between Calvin and his predecessors. At the very least, Calvin heightened awareness of subordinationist tendencies still residing in the dominant stream of Trinitarian theology. And yet regardless of the level of continuity and discontinuity between Calvin and the prior tradition, it is obvious from reading in the later tradition of Trinitarian thought that Calvin single-handedly changed the conversation that followed. In subsequent discussions of eternal generation—or even of the Trinity more broadly—Calvin himself was often mentioned, and friends and foes alike put their own constructions on his statements with widely varying levels of faithfulness to his actual views and concerns. The substance of the discussion might not be as interested in the Niceno-Constantinopolitan Creed as was Thomas Gataker's visitor, but Calvin's concerns are evident.[25]

From the perspective of Gataker, his late-night guest was interesting because it illustrated the care that needed to be taken in conversations about the Trinity. He had told the story in part, he explained, because "it is the humour of old men (such as Mr Walker and my selfe) to be now and then telling of tales."[26] He also thought it important because "a man had need to

---

24. For the medieval background to the debate see Muller, PRRD, 4:17–58, esp. 36, 51, and 58.
25. See for example assembly member Anthony Tuckney's Praelectiones Theologicae, 1–19, 270–79. On p. 14, he argues that his formulation is absolved from alleged quaternity problems.
26. Gataker, An Answer to Mr. George Walkers Vindication, 38.

187

be wary, how he condemne a man of error, of heresie much more, upon a bare relation of words, before he understood what his meaning was."[27] He then illustrated his point with another story! This time it was a story about an uneducated preacher, imprisoned at Newgate, who was asked "whether Christs Deity assumed the person of man or no." The poor man gave confident affirmation to the defective formulation and Gataker's friend, who had posed the question, told the troublemaker that what he had affirmed "was grosse heresie." But as Gataker later recalled, the two ministers did not "hold the silly fellow to be an heretik; no more than those that beare the name of Nestorians in the Eastern parts, are deemed so this day."[28]

Gataker's starting place in debates about eternal generation—or in doctrinal debate generally—was the assumption that people often, accidentally, get it wrong. In his day, there were zealous, uneducated Christians with muddled Christology, as well as orthodox ministers, who offered unhelpful articulations of Trinitarian theology. This made him careful to try as best as possible to understand the meaning and intentions of people's words, and to place the best constructions on them. As it happened, Gataker's late-night visitor was actually devious: he was unsuccessfully attempting to use a record of his conversation to help Legate, who was later burned to death for teaching a form of Arianism. Gataker's visitor was also trying to make hay out of the infelicitous constructions of an unknowing minister who had muddled his explanations of Trinitarian doctrine.

Nonetheless, it almost goes without saying that the incident illustrates how patristic formulations continued to be major reference points in Trinitarian theology. After being assaulted by Arius the church could not return to the innocence of her earliest formulations on the Trinity; she would never feel safe simply by hearing assertions that a preacher believed what the Bible taught. Whatever people in the pews understood, public teachers would be tested through the use of shibboleths that needed to be pronounced correctly. Most of these came from the ancient creeds, for they remained the touchstones of historic orthodoxy as much after the Reformation as they had been before it.

Thomas Gataker was no man's fool. He understood these things, and by 1600 he was already recognized as a notable scholar and controversialist. And as he modestly put it, he could "make a reasonable good sermon."[29]

---

27. Ibid., 39.
28. Ibid., 40.
29. Brett Usher, "Gataker, Thomas (1574–1654)," in *The Oxford Dictionary of National Biography* (Oxford: Oxford University Press, 2004).

He was also an independent thinker, and in a day when unconventional theological systems were all the rage, Gataker's door was an obvious place to knock if one was desperate for a comment that might reveal diversity in the Reformed ranks. By the 1640s Gataker considered himself (and George Walker) to be men of such vintage that they resorted too quickly to telling stories. But he was no doddering old man, and he would become an obvious candidate for the Westminster Assembly. By then one of the oldest members, he would distinguish himself by articulating the most eccentric theological positions held at the gathering, excluding those of Peter Sterry (1613–1672), one of the assembly's youngest members.

Autotheos: DANIEL FEATLEY AND THE PRISON LETTERS

It was not from the story-telling Gataker that the reading public received its first information about the Westminster Assembly's own Trinitarian debates, which began in 1643. The English parliament that had summoned the assembly required secrecy from the assembly's members. No one was permitted to divulge, except to parliament, what the assembly discussed. But when some members of parliament contrived to frame one of the Westminster Assembly's members for treason, he defended himself by publishing his letters from prison—letters that contained his most important assembly speeches (the texts of which were only slight improvements over the words that he actually spoke).[30]

The last of the great post-Reformation synods was meeting during a bloody civil war, and while the English Parliament had told 120 ministers that they must attend the assembly, King Charles I had told them they must not. Dr. Daniel Featley (1582–1645) was a king's man, but since he lived in an area controlled by Parliament, he thought it the better part of prudence to attend. But he had enemies in the House of Commons, and a contractor for the parliamentary army was covertly enlisted to convince Featley that the king was angry with his decision. Feigning friendship, the man told Featley that if he just sent a few of his speeches to the royalist camp, the King would understand why he had disobeyed a royal order. But when Featley surrendered his speeches, they were somehow "intercepted," and the unfortunate theologian was promptly jailed for communicating with

---

30. Working with incomplete copies of both sources, S. W. Carruthers errs in thinking that neither the minutes nor Lightfoot mention Featley's speeches. S. W. Carruthers, *The Everyday Work of the Westminster Assembly* (Philadelphia: Presbyterian Historical Society, 1943), 106–7; curiously, even in discussing Featley's speeches Carruthers does not mention the assembly's *autotheos* controversy.

189

the enemy, his property was seized, and his membership in the Westminster Assembly was terminated. It was a dirty trick, and Featley, in a futile attempt to show that his correspondence was completely innocent, printed his assembly speeches in an anonymous defense of his own conduct.[31]

From Featley's perspective, the original purpose of his speeches in the synod was to ensure that there would be no deviance from Nicene orthodoxy in the assembly. The gathering had been commanded by parliament to examine the Church of England's Thirty-Nine Articles in order to see if they needed any revisions. Featley's speeches confirmed that debate over the first of the Thirty-Nine Articles, on the doctrine of God, sparked a debate about permissible understandings of the eternal generation of the Son, and debate over the eighth of the Thirty-nine articles, which "heartily recommends the three creeds," triggered a debate about whether the "God of God" phrase from the Niceno-Constantinopolitan Creed deserved hearty recommendation or careful qualification.

His spirited offerings quickly zeroed in on the issues of the day. Calvin and his contemporaries were quoted, and Featley, like Calvin, announced that the issue was "easy." Of course it was not. Featley contradicted himself in his two speeches, and he exposed the different lenses through which his fellow members read the debate and the varying positions they held. Some saw the value of Calvin's concerns and queried subordinationist readings ascribed to the "God of God phrase." Others, like Featley, appreciated Calvin's insights but saw no conflict with the creeds. Still others held to traditional formulations and made no reference to Calvin's concerns either because they did not share them or because creedal insistence that the Father and the Son were *homoousion* was sufficient to offset any apprehension about subordination.

Featley's printed speeches have yet to receive the attention they deserve. One study failed to notice the speeches and concluded that the assembly rejected the concept of eternal generation.[32] Another study failed to notice the speeches and concluded that the assembly did not consider the issue.[33] Yet another study noticed the speeches, but not the difference between Featley's own formulations and the quotations that Featley employs. This lack of a careful reading led to a misunderstanding of this aspect of the debate entirely.[34]

---

31. See Daniel Featley, *Sacra Nemesis, the Levites Scourge, or, Mercurius Britan. Civicus disciplin'd* (Oxford: Leonard Lichfield, 1644); Featley, *The gentle lash, or, The vindication of Dr. Featley, a knowne champion of the protestant religion* (n.p., 1644); and Arnold Hunt, "Featley, Daniel (1582–1645)," in *Oxford Dictionary of National Biography* (Oxford: Oxford University Press, 2004).

32. Reymond, *A New Systematic Theology*, 338–41.

33. Letham, *The Westminster Assembly*, 168.

34. Fesko, *The Theology of the Westminster Standards*, 173–74.

On the first day of debate Featley argued that from the idea of God being of God, it does not follow that the "deity" or divinity "of the Sonne is of the deity of the Father." Featley understood the creed to be stating that the Son is of the Father, and since the Father is God, and the Son is God, it is appropriate to say that God is of God. It is a point that Featley would make more than once and it reflected Calvin's views (or Tradition B) closely.[35] Nonetheless, Featley's two speeches on the subject reveal a remarkable inconsistency. As Featley explained (in Latin), one cannot argue from the concrete (by which he means the persons of the Trinity) to the abstract (by which he refers to the deity of those persons), and he offers two examples. The fact that God (i.e., God the Son) suffered does not mean that the deity suffered. Analogously, the fact that Mary is the mother of God (i.e., God the Son) does not entail that she is the mother of deity.[36]

The persons in the assembly to whom he was speaking must have been quoting Calvin, for Featley next states that it is "easie" to reconcile what he just said with Calvin and his insistence that the Son is *autotheos*, God of himself. Like an immigrant who intermittently reverts to his native tongue when speaking with friends, Featley explained to his fellow assembly members in a running mix of English and Latin phrases that, as he saw it, "Christ is God of himself, with respect to his essence, but God of God with respect to his person." But as simple as that solution was to announce, everyone at the assembly knew, and Featley himself admitted, that many theologians (before and after Calvin) considered Christ's divinity to be generated "*per productionem essentiae*" or "*per communicationem essentiae.*"[37]

"Production" or "creation" of a divine essence in Christ was hospitable to Arian readings. So far as I can tell from my reading thus far, among the assembly's theologians only Peter Sterry ever used such language. But Sterry was not an ordinary member; he was the only member in the assembly to be so unclear about the nature of justification that the assembly, alarmed, required him to explain himself.[38] He was the only member to drift towards an increasingly eloquent, mystical, and incomprehensible theology.[39] (Unfortunately, he was also the only member to find himself

---

35. Featley, *Sacra Nemesis*, 15, 17.
36. Ibid., 15.
37. Ibid., 15.
38. C. B. Van Dixhoorn, ed., *Minutes and Papers of the Westminster Assembly, 1643–1652* (Oxford: Oxford University Press, 2012), 2:189 (Oct. 11, 1643; Sess. 72); hereafter *MPWA*.
39. In the earliest reference to eternal generation that I can find in Sterry's work, he writes that "the love that the Father hath to Jesus Christ, is that very love by which he brings out Jesus Christ as the second person in the Trinity," but clarifies that "the eternal generation of the Lord Jesus . . . is the same from eternity to eternity." Peter Sterry, *Free Grace Exalted* (London, 1670), 8. Five years

at a complete loss of words when a woman rushed his pulpit in the middle of a sermon only to expose herself before the congregation.)[40]

Featley himself focused only on the idea of the communication of divine essence, admitting that Beza and others were willing to speak of Christ's divinity "conveyed" or "communicated" to him by the Father. This view was not uncommon. Elsewhere the assembly patriarch William Gouge defined the generation of the Son as "the Father . . . communicating his essence to him" (Muller's Tradition A).[41] Mark Jones argues persuasively that Thomas Goodwin holds a similar view (although he is wrong in thinking Featley entirely opposed it).[42] Jones also asserts that this is a dominant position amongst the post-Reformation orthodox, even at the assembly. This would be difficult to demonstrate because the record of the debate is scanty and most members, at least in their published works, usually did not attempt to comment on the eternal generation of the Son at all. John Arrowsmith, in his book *Theanthropos*, attempts an analogy to eternal generation, arguing that John 1 is discussing eternal generation and offering practical reflections on the doctrine.[43] But Arrowsmith is unusual.

That is not to say that the meaning of eternal generation is never discussed in any depth. Featley's speeches indicate that theologians at the assembly held strong opinions on the subject who had not published on the topic. And assembly members like William Strong (d. 1654) offer clearly articulated stands on the subject of eternal generation. As it happened, Strong strongly opposed the idea of a communicated divine essence from the Father to the Son. He also offers an indirect case in point for the importance of withholding judgments on someone's opinion based on a passing comment. At one point he ambiguously declared, "God doth in the mystery of his eternal generation communicate himself unto his son."[44] But later he clarified what he meant:

---

later he refers to "the first Birth and Production, the eternal Generation of the Son from the Father in the Trinity." Peter Sterry, *A Discourse of the freedom of the will* (London: At the Miter near Temple-Bar, in Fleetstreet, 1675), 43. Eight years later Sterry compares "the Eternal Generation in Heaven" to "the Creation in Paradise," "Regeneration," and other "Love-Births, Love-Unions" in *The rise, race and royalty of the kingdom of God in the Soul of man* (London: Thomas Cockerill, 1683), 310.

40. [David Brown], *The Naked Woman, or a rare epistle sent to Mr. Peter Sterry* (London: At the Angle in Paul's Church-yard, 1652), 8.

41. William Gouge, *A learned and very useful commentary on the whole epistle to the Hebrews* (London: A. M., T. W., and S. G., 1655), 1:33 (sect. 43).

42. Mark Jones, *Why Heaven Kissed Earth: The Christology of the Puritan Reformed Orthodox Theologian, Thomas Goodwin, 1600–1680* (Göttingen: Vandenhoeck & Ruprecht, 2010), 276n114.

43. Arrowsmith, *Theanthropos*, 17, 21, 23–24.

44. William Strong, *A discourse of the two covenants: wherein the nature, differences, and effects of the covenant of works and of grace are distinctly, rationally, spiritually and practically discussed* (London: J. M., 1678), 182.

POST-REFORMATION TRINITARIAN PERSPECTIVES

I conceive, that it were dangerous to say, that as he is God, so he lives
by the Father, though I often find that Divines writing of the eternal
generation of the Son, do speak of the Fathers begetting of the Son by
the communication of the same Essence, that *he is God of God,* &c. But
surely he that is God, must be without cause, he must have his Being
from himself, he must be the first and the last; he that hath his essence
from another must have his sufficiency from another, and he that is from
another must be unto another; for he that is the first cause, he must
also be the last end, *Rom.* 11.36. *For of him, and to him, and through him
are all things,* &c. and therefore he that is not God of himself, is not
God at all. I dare not therefore say, that he hath the Divine Essence
communicated by eternal generation, but rather he is *à seipso Deus, à
Patre filius, essentia ejus principio caret, personae verò principium est ipse Deus:*
it's spoken of Christ, therefore not as he lives in himself, as he is God,
but as he is Mediator made by the Father the fountain of life unto us.[45]

This was a robust restatement of Calvin's own position and perhaps, with his
frank acknowledgement that other divines "often" disagreed, an acknowledgement that Calvin's position was by no means mainstream. Indeed others,
perhaps most others, wanted their Calvin and their creeds too. Featley initially
denied that the communication of divine essence from Father to Son was
entailed by the confession that the Son was "God of God." "It is sufficient"
to say "that his person is generated of the Father" and "safer to say that hee
hath *communum cum patre,* then *communicatum*"—divinity in common with
the Father, not communicated from the father.[46] (Featley is right to flag the
ambiguities in the word communion—in can mean either conveying or
sharing and it is not always clear which meaning divines actually intended.)

And yet on the second day of debate Featley appears to say something
different, even contradictory. He argues that the Son was not "essentiated, or
natured from the Father"—the standard salvo against Arian and Socinians.
But then Featley approves of quotations by Theodore Beza and Josiah Semler:
the one arguing for a pre-Calvinian understanding of the communication
of essence, and the other arguing that through the begetting of the *person*
of the Son there is an ontologically derivative communication (as in a conveying) of *divine essence*—what we might call a "Tradition C," expressed in
the Irish Articles decades before the debates of the 1640s. Curiously, Featley

---

45. Strong, *A discourse of the two covenants,* 328.
46. Featley, *Sacra Nemesis,* 15.

asserts that these statements suggesting an indirect conveying of essence are equivalent to Calvin's own thought, which they are surely not.[47]

Featley's perspective on eternal generation is useful because it captures (among other things) what I call the polemical irenicism that characterized much of post-Reformation Trinitarian debate: within the Reformed world, theologians perhaps argued most vigorously with colleagues unwilling to harmonize variant views on eternal generation or the "God of God" clause. But while peacemaking in the assembly, Featley tips his hand when he comments that Calvin's views are *verissime* and *sanctissime*.[48] What he means is that Calvin passes the muster of patristic orthodoxy and is therefore most true and most right. What Featley refused to understand was that there were some in the assembly who saw Calvin as their standard, and they required the creeds and church fathers to pass Reformational muster.

Featley held that "the Articles of Religion" and their hearty recommendation of the three creeds "need no alterations at all, but onely an Orthodox explication in some ambiguous phrases, and a vindication against false aspersions."[49] Perhaps this was the case, but by his second speech the debate in the assembly had reached the point where Featley thought it better to flatly reject even idea that the creeds contained "ambiguous phrases," an idea that he allowed elsewhere.[50] Of course there were also those outside the camp; errorists who deliberately sabotage doctrine, and they too feature in Featley's addresses to the assembly. To his opponents' objection that creedal "phrases . . . may be taken in an ill sense," Featley retorted that "so may all the Articles of the Creed . . . ; nay so may the whole Scripture, as St Peter teacheth us," when he says that "the ignorant & unstable pervert" them. "What then," Featley asks, "must we weed up all the flowers of Paradise, because hereticks, like spiders, suck such juice out of them which they turn into poyson?"[51]

A Natural Son: Francis Cheynell and the Hasty Book Puff

The assembly debated definitions of the doctrine of the Trinity many times during its meetings, with conversations over the wording of its two

---

47. This reading perhaps betrays that Featley is here following Robert Bellarmine's benevolent conflation of Beza and Semler with Calvin, through which the cardinal deduces that Calvin's Trinitarian theology is not heretical. For a discussion of Bellarmine's reading of Calvin on this point, see Ellis, *Calvin, Classical Trinitarianism, and the Aseity of the Son*, 109–12.

48. Featley, *Sacra nemesis*, 18.

49. Featley, *The gentle lash*, 24.

50. Ibid., 31.

51. Featley, *Sacra Nemesis*, 18.

POST-REFORMATION TRINITARIAN PERSPECTIVES

Catechisms in 1647 bookending the debates begun over the Thirty-Nine Articles. Along the way, the assembly had dealt repeatedly with unorthodox understandings of the doctrine of God.

Lim raises the possibility that the assembly suspected the Arminian theologian Henry Hammond (1605–1660) of anti-Trinitarianism after the publication of his *Practical Catechism*.[52] In November 1645, Francis Cheynell (*bap.* 1608–d. 1665) was one of the members asked to investigate the work. He was alarmed that Hammond avoided discussion of the Trinity and the deity of Christ on the grounds that it was a speculative mystery.[53] The choice of Cheynell to check the work for heresy suggests that the assembly itself was strongly suspicious of Hammond. Cheynell was an inflexible theologian: in 1638 he was suspended for not bowing to the altar, and in 1640 he was refused a Bachelor of Divinity degree for attacking Arminianism.[54] Infamously, in 1644 Cheynell had held a burial service not only for a suspected Socinian, William Chillingworth (1602–1644), but also for Chillingworth's best-known book, *The Religion of Protestants*. At the internment, Cheynell commended the "rotten booke" to the grave, expressing his hope that it would "rot with thy Author, and see corruption."[55] Chillingworth, like Hammond, had pulled up short of a commendation of Trinitarian doctrine, which reticence smelled of heterodoxy. This was distressing in itself, but as Lim points out, it was also problematic because anti-Trinitarianism had rationalist foundations and resulted in an arid piety.[56]

But Hammond and Chillingworth represented the more nuanced cases. There were others that required less discernment. In the autumn of 1644, members reported on Thomas Webb (b. 1624 or 1626) and his blasphemies, one of which seemed to deny the existence of the Holy Spirit, another to minimize the reality of the incarnation.[57] From June 1645 to June 1646, the assembly dealt with Paul Best (1590–1657)—or as the scribe liked to write, Paul "Beast"—an anti-Trinitarian preacher and polemicist from northeast England.[58] In September of that same year, a committee comprised of

---

52. Arminius affirms communication of divine essence, affirming that the Son is God himself but not God of himself. See Ellis, *Calvin, Classical Trinitarianism, and the Aseity of the Son*, 113–20. "While the Remonstrants were heirs to Arminius's theology, their rejection of autothean language reflects a much deeper inclination towards subordinationism" (p. 120); cf. his discussion of Episcopius, 120–27.

53. See *MPWA* 3:705 (Nov. 11, 1645; Sess. 532) and Lim, *Mystery Unveiled*, 175–76.

54. Lim, *Mystery Unveiled*, 174.

55. Cheynell, *Chillingworthi Novissima* (London: At the Brazen Serpent in Paul's Church-yard, 1644), sig., E3.

56. Lim, *Mystery Unveiled*, 172–216.

57. *MPWA* 3:467 (Nov. 22, 1644; Sess. 328).

58. *MPWA* 1:63; for the first mention of Best, 3:614; for the final mention, 4:38–42. The most sympathetic account of Best's beliefs and his trial can be found in McLachlan, *Socinianism*. According to McLachlan, while

195

CHAD VAN DIXHOORN

assembly members was required by the House of Commons to examine John Biddle (1615/16–1662).[59] Biddle held to a mono-personalist construction of the Trinity, and his affirmations of Christ's divinity were open to the *productionem* of essence. He asserted as early as May 1644, "I believe that our Saviour Jesus Christ is truly God, by being truly, really and properly united to the only Person of the Infinite and Almighty Essence."[60]

The assembly itself offered no advice concerning Biddle in 1646 or thereafter. No doubt the gathering was content with the attention that the House of Commons and the London Provincial Assembly were already giving to his case.[61] However, in early 1648, assembly member Cheynell issued a complaint about two books, including a 1647 translation of selections from a 1565 work by Jacobus Acontius (ca. 1520–1566/7). To deal with Acontius, the Westminster Assembly collected a committee, and Cheynell, who thought the book to be "more fit for the fire than for the press" and who was by now considered to be a local expert in Socinianism, was appointed chair.[62] What was so awkward was that fellow member John Dury (1596–1680) had endorsed the offending publication. Dury's anti-Socinian credentials were firmly established by the 1630s and known to many members of the assembly, but as shocking as this may sound, Dury had not read the book carefully prior to puffing it publicly.[63]

Some of the assembly's best minds were appointed to the committee, and four days later, on March 3, four more men were added. Wisely, the assembly also appointed to the committee the thoroughly embarrassed Dury, who, in Cheynell's words, "saw that he had given too faire a testimony" to the book.[64] The account that Cheynell gives of the situation agrees substantially with that of the minutes, save that, if anything, he downplayed his own leadership on the committee and the warmth with which the assembly responded to his work.

Best affirmed the Trinity, he denied that it was "of three co-equall persons" and "that the Godhead of Jesus Christ is co-equal, co-eternal, and co-existent with the Godhead of the Father." McLachlan, *Socinianism*, 154, 158. See also Nigel Smith, "'And if God was one of us': Paul Best, John Biddle, and anti-Trinitarian heresy in seventeenth-century England," in *Heresy, Literature and Politics in Early Modern English Culture*, ed. David Loewenstein and John Marshall (Cambridge: Cambridge Univeristy Press, 2006), 160–84.

59. *MPWA* 4:302 (Sept. 28, 1646; Sess. 719).

60. McLachlan, *Socinianism*, 170. By 1646 he denied the deity of the Holy Spirit, ranking him third after the Father and the Son. McLachlan, *Socinianism*, 172–73.

61. For the assembly's interest in Biddle and the allegation, see Lim, *Mystery Unveiled*, 39–40. There is no evidence that the assembly responded to John Biddle's publications with an attempt to see him executed.

62. *MPWA* 4:737 (Feb 28, 1648; Sess. 1020); Cheynell, *The Divine Trinunity of the Father, Son, and Holy Spirit* (London: T.R. and E.M, 1650), 443; Cheynell, *The Rise, growth and danger of Socinianism* (London: At the Brazen Serpant in Paul's Church-yard, 1643).

63. For Dury's views on Socinianism, see Mortimer, *Reason and Religion*, 54.

64. *MPWA* 4:739 (March 3, 1648; Sess. 1024).

The committee returned with a report to which Cheynell spoke at some length. Acontius had attempted a rapprochement between the Reformed and the Socinians through a minimalistic statement of faith. He didn't mention the divinity of the Son or the Holy Spirit, he acknowledged Christ to be the Son of God but not the "natural Son" of God, and he "cautelously decline[d] the orthodox expressions of the ancient church, in the foure first general synods; and doth deliver his creed in such general expressions, that as we conceive the Socinians may subscribe it."[65]

The assembly accepted Dury's offer of a public retraction, condemned the book, and told Cheynell that if he or another member of his committee were to write against Acontius's errors, it would be acceptable to the body.[66] Cheynell responded two years later with a five-hundred-page tome, *The Divine Trinunity of the Father, Son, and Holy Spirit*. The new term didn't stick.

Philip Dixon judges *The Divine Trinunity* "a remarkable book. It is balanced, clear and still very readable."[67] In fact, Dixon says elsewhere, "The book is so unlike Cheynell's previous works—scholarly, fair, balanced, clear, well written, and so lacking in splenetic polemic—that I suspect it may well be the work of an academic 'ghost-writer' at the university."[68] (There is no real doubt, despite Dixon's conjecture, that Cheynell is in fact the book's author.) Both Lim and Dixon emphasize the significance for Cheynell of the soteriological and sanctifying dimensions of a correct Trinitarian theology.[69] Dixon also notes Cheynell's special emphasis (and optimism!) about grammar: that with the right terms and distinctions the challenges of explaining the fundamental mystery of the Trinity are much reduced.[70] Nonetheless, the book requires careful reading, not least on account of the flexible and often creative vocabulary Cheynell deploys. For example, he equates the "divine life" with the nature or essence of God.[71] He also equates "divine being" with divine subsisting or subsistence,[72] or perhaps "subsisting life,"[73] but he insists that "subsistence" is not "essence"; indeed, "peculiar subsistences" are divine "persons."[74]

---

65. Cheynell, *Divine Trinunity*, [453]–455.
66. *MPWA* 4:741 (March 8, 1648; Sess. 1027); Cheynell, *Divine Trinunity*, 445, [453]–457.
67. Philip Dixon, *"Nice and Hot Disputes": The Doctrine of the Trinity in the Seventeenth Century* (Edinburgh: T&T Clark, 2006), 60.
68. Ibid., 55.
69. Ibid.
70. Ibid., 56, 60.
71. He speaks of the "Son of God, who hath the same divine life, nature, essence with the Father" (Cheynell, *Divine Trinunity*, 194). Nonetheless, when Cheynell writes that "The Son hath life in himself, is life it self, hath life essentially," he only means that the Son is able to give life himself, and that according to John 5:26 he has the ability to pass on life (ibid., 56, 189).
72. Cheynell, *Divine Trinunity*, 54, 55.
73. Ibid., 57, 58.
74. Ibid., 231.

CHAD VAN DIXHOORN

Cheynell often makes his best observations in his extensive Latin notes that run along the margins, the foot, and sometimes the head of the page. Cheynell's doctrine of the Trinity almost offers, as an explanation of Trinitarian unity and distinction, a doctrine that promises something like *perichoresis, circumincessio*, or co-inherence. For he says that the Father, Son, and Holy Spirit "mutually subsist in one another." But Cheynell's full understanding is that they "mutually subsist in one another and all of them subsist in the same glorious Godhead."[75] He also puts it the other way but with the same effect, for instance, "the Godhead subsisting in the Holy Ghost as well as in the Father and the Son."[76]

Some of his creative proposals may well have struck his mainstream readership as awkward. Cheynell speaks of the distinction between persons as not "absolute, but relative only,"[77] or "respective, & *modalis*."[78] Cheynell makes it very clear elsewhere that he believes in a real distinction between person in the Trinity.[79] But with the rise of Socinianism and the radical distinctions between persons of the Trinity, modalism seemed a distant and theoretical threat. This perhaps explains the willingness of some early modern divines to permit Trinitarian language or attempt Trinitarian analogies which are manifestly modalistic.

In discussing the Second Person of the Trinity, Cheynell insists, against Acontius and against the Socinians, that the Son is not God by grace but by "nature."[80] That is to say, "the Son is not begotten of the Fathers seed, or any material substance, because God is a single and pure Act, who doth beget a Son within himself essentially one with himself, and therefore his Sonne doth not subsist out of himself."[81] What he means is that the will of the Father did not precede and produce the Godhead in the Son: "*natura divina in filio est incausata*."[82] In other words, the divinity of the Son is "native" to the doctrine of the Trinity; there was no decision, no decree that initiates the Son into the fullness of the Triune being. Continuing his anti-Arian argument, "the Son is *autotheos*, God of himself, and not God by participation, not a different God from the Father, but the same God with the Father, and therefore an Independent, Eternall God, who did not

---

75. Ibid., 60.
76. Ibid.
77. Ibid., 59–60.
78. Ibid., 59, note g.
79. Ibid., 183–84.
80. Ibid., 231.
81. Ibid., 195.
82. Ibid., 231n57.

POST-REFORMATION TRINITARIAN PERSPECTIVES

begin to be God."[83] The Divine essence of the Son is not begotten, caused, or produced any more than the essence of the Father.[84] It is a point that he asserts often, and at length.

In spite of his insistent language, Cheynell protests not against the idea of *communicationem* but against the heresy of *productionem*. He opposes an explicit form of subordinationism, concluding that this is also Calvin's concern.

> Calvin and Beza did not deny that the Godhead was from all eternity communicated to the Son by the Father; onely they say, 1. That the Godhead which is communicated is in it self, of it self truly, properly, essentially divine. . . . 2. Because the Godhead which is communicated, is not begotten; the unbegotten Godhead is communicated to the only begotten Son by an eternal generation. 3. Because the Godhead which is communicated, is not caused, produced, created by the Father.[85]

But he holds what may be unusual reasons for insisting that the Son is divine by nature. Cheynell thought the production of essence would suggest change (and perhaps temporality) in the Son *and in the Father.* The begetting of the Son, however, requires no change in the Father: it is a begetting "as eternal as the divine nature it self," and as mysterious as the doctrine of the Trinity.[86] The astonishing fact is that "the Father did beget his Son without change or motion" in himself.[87] Contrary to the Socinians, the assertion of the Son's divinity does not in any way take away from the divinity of the Father. Cheynell is adamant: "We deny that there is an active power in the Father, and a passive power in the Son in respect of generation."[88]

Save for a focus on the Father rather than the Son, the concern that there is no active power involved in generation may be the early modern equivalent to the patristic insistence that the Son does not owe his existence to his Father's will (an assertion that focuses primarily on the Son). Why is this lack of change in the Father so important to Cheynell? Because it is the primacy of the Father that Cheynell is anxious to privilege. Only "the self-subsistence of the Father is Incommunicable, it is proper and peculiar to the First Person to have subsistence from none but himself, and to be

---

83. Ibid., 158.
84. Ibid., 231.
85. Ibid., 232.
86. Ibid., 55.
87. Ibid., 195. Elsewhere Cheynell explains, "The Son receives nothing from the Father as from an external cause but as from an intrinsecall principle rather than the cause, for the Son doth not depend upon the Father as an effect upon its cause" (p. 189–90).
88. Ibid., 157. Cf. p. 179, where he explains that this is because the generation of the Son is eternal.

199

the first personal principle which gives subsistence to the other two coessential and coequall persons."[89] Since Cheynell usually uses the language of "subsisting-life," but not "subsistence," to refer to the essence of God, his statement here is not completely clear. But there can hardly be any doubt about his assertion that "the Father did from all eternity communicate the living Essence of God to the Son" and did so "by eternal generation,"[90] or in his explanation that "the Father doth communicate that selfe same divine and entire essence . . . by begetting the personal subsistence of the Son."[91] In other words, while the divine essence is not begotten, the divine person is begotten, and through the generation of the divine person, the divine essence is communicated. It is an indirect communication: "the divine essence is communicated to the Son, but it is not begotten by the Father."[92] This is similar to Tradition C, also stated in the 1615 Irish Articles.[93]

Cheynell's perspective on eternal generation was in essence (if that word may be used in this context) polemical. Elsewhere he complained of Muslims and converts to Islam who denied eternal generation.[94] But as most Muslim contacts with Englishmen were pirates and not imams, Cheynell's main opponents were Socinians. Indeed, this is the key to understanding Cheynell. A case can be made that Cheynell remolds Calvin because Cheynell harbors hope of persuading Socinians that some level of subordination of a divine Son only adds to the glory of the God the Father. Indeed, it appears that Cheynell sees himself scoring an important apologetic point as he indirectly roots the Son's divinity in the Father. The eternal generation of the Son magnifies the glory of the Father, for the Father communicates divine essence without changing in his own essence—which is itself a glorious miracle, if one can misuse the term to make a point.[95]

Cheynell insists that we confess the Son and the Holy Spirit to the glory of God the Father.[96] As he puts it, the Father is the "first personal principle subsisting of himself, and by himself; for he received not his subsistence

---

89. Ibid., 230. Elsewhere: "I call the Father an Intrinsicall principle of the Sons subsistence, because the Father doth beget the Son of, and in himself in the unity of the same Godhead" (ibid., 190). For the Father as "first principle," see ibid., 56, 61, 62, 179.

90. Ibid., 189: "The Son hath life in himself, is life it self, hath life essentially."

91. Ibid., 231.

92. Ibid., 231.

93. "The essence of the Father does not beget the essence of the Son; but the person of the Father begetteth the person of the Son, by communicating His whole essence to the person begotten from eternity." James T. Dennison Jr., ed., *Reformed Confessions of the 16th and 17th Centuries in English Translation* (Grand Rapids: Reformation Heritage, 2014), 4:92 (Art. 9).

94. Cheynell, *The rise, growth, and danger of Socinianisme*, 31.

95. Cheynell, *Divine Trinunity*, 56; cf. a similar comment about Son and Spirit on p. 58.

96. Ibid., 56.

from any other, and he gives subsistence unto two glorious persons equall with himself."[97] The Father's ability to convey divinity without diminution to his being or glory is reason enough, in Cheynell's mind, for those who wish to exalt the Father to also adopt the doctrine of the Trinity.

SAME AND EQUAL: THE ASSEMBLY'S TEXTS

What is so striking is that this polemical perspective and these intricate arguments are entirely missing from the Westminster Assembly's texts. Statements of faith are like military convoys. Some are open-top Jeeps— like the Apostle's Creed, which openly displays a doctrine but makes no effort to defend it. Some are armored cars, sturdy vehicles for conveying concepts that sacrifice elegance in favor of protecting the truths most often targeted by the enemy. The Chalcedonian Definition and Athanasian Creed come to mind: negations outrank assertions; strong adverbs are marched around in squads of four. Other confessions are elegant limousines with protective glass. The Westminster Confession of Faith, and this may be a stretch, is one of these. It contains dignified statements of doctrine, but it is not impregnable. It has some protection from predictable errors, and yet there is no attempt to make its statements as bulletproof as they could be.

The Revision of the Thirty-Nine Articles (1643)

The assembly's seven statements on the Trinity contain careful nuance. But in every case the main effort is to state the doctrine of the Trinity simply and clearly with classic phraseology and without overt polemical comment. The 1643 debate featuring Featley actually left the relevant portions of the Thirty-Nine Articles untouched, save for the addition of proof texts in its support.[98] In the seven statements, we hear an emphasis on unity and the Nicene insistence on the unity of divine substance in the Trinity. "There is but one living and true God, everlasting, without body, parts, or passions, of infinite power; wisdom; and goodnesse; the maker and preserver of all things both visible and invisible. And in unity of this Godhead there be three persons, of one substance, power, and eternity, the Father, the Sonne, & the Holy Ghost."[99]

---

97. Ibid. See also "first personal principle" (p. 61) and "first personal principle of subsisting life" (p. 62, 179).

98. "There is but one living and true God, everlasting, without body, parts, or passions, of infinite power; wisdom; and goodnesse; the maker and preserver of all things both visible and invisible. And in unity of this Godhead there be three persons, of one substance, power, and eternity, the Father, the Sonne, & the Holy Ghost." *MPWA* 5:324 (Doc. 122).

99. *MPWA* 5:324 (Doc. 122).

There is perhaps an emphasis on the One more than the Three in the Thirty-Nine Articles, with the reference to "unity" and the language of "one substance." The assembly, however, was left unresolved about what to do about the eighth article commending the creeds. Indeed, the assembly's debate over the eighth article was the longest running disagreement in the history of the assembly.[100]

The "Shorter Confession" (1645)

The next opportunity to discuss the Trinity came in 1645 when the assembly determined what people needed to believe in order to become communicant members of the church. This statement is particularly important because it is intended to be minimalist rather than maximalist. It states only what someone must know in order for an eldership to reckon that person a Christian worthy of the Lord's table. Here, in what I call the assembly's "Shorter Confession," the assembly emphasized only the equality between the persons as it declared, in the simplest of terms, that "this God is but one, yet three distinct persons, the father Sonne & Holy Ghost, all equally God."[101]

The Draft Catechism (1646)

In 1646 the assembly debated a draft catechism, which dealt extensively with the doctrine of God. Perhaps affirming Calvin's concerns about subordination, but avoiding any finer distinctions, it affirms generation and procession "from all eternity" and has separate questions confessing that Son and the Spirit are "true God equall with the Father."

Ordered: 7 "Q: Are ther many Gods, or is ther but one God?
A: 'Ther is but one God.'"
Ordered: 8 "Q: How many persons are ther in the Godhead? A: Ther are three persons in the Godhead: the father, the son, and the Holy Ghost, and these three are but one God."
Ordered: 9 "Q: Is the sonne equall with the Father in the Godhead? A: The sonne of God who is 'the only begotten of the Father' from all eternity, is true God equall with the Father."
Ordered: 10 "Q: Is the Holy Ghost also God, equall with the Father and the sonne? A: The Holy Ghost who from all eternity

---

100. Chad B. Van Dixhoorn, "New Taxonomies of the Westminster Assembly, 1643–52: The Creedal Controversy as Case Study," *Reformation and Renaissance Review* 6, no. 1 (2004): 82–106.
101. *MPWA* 5:189 (Doc. 67).

Post-Reformation Trinitarian Perspectives

proceeds from the Father and the sonne is also true God, equall
with the father and the sonne."
Resolved upon the Q.: ther shall be severall Questions upon the severall Attributes.[102]

The Confession of Faith, Chapter 2 and Chapter 8 (1646)

The assembly's fourth and best-known statement, polished and delivered
later in the same year, reflects two additional debates. Chapter 8 of the 1646
Confession of Faith discusses the person of the Son simply, but it carefully
deploys the language of begottenness, unity of substance, and equality.

> 8.1 It pleased God, in His eternal purpose, to choose and ordain the
> Lord Jesus, His only begotten Son, to be the Mediator between God
> and man. . . .
> 8.2 The Son of God, the second person in the Trinity, being very and
> eternal God, of one substance and equal with the Father, did, when the
> fullness of time was come, take upon Him man's nature. . . .

Chapter 2 of the confession inserts language redolent of the Father as the
principium of the Godhead, but without the specific details that, say, the
Irish Articles provide. Readers are told that "the Father is of none"—a
statement that is not applied to the other members of the Trinity. And yet
with the insistence on unity of substance, the sentence as a whole is hardly
a statement of eternal ontological subordination, especially as it does not
clarify if the begetting of the "essence" or of "person" is in view, and
probably implies the latter: "In the unity of the Godhead there be three
persons, of one substance, power, and eternity: God the Father, God the
Son, and God the Holy Ghost: the Father is of none, neither begotten, nor
proceeding; the Son is eternally begotten of the Father; the Holy Ghost
eternally proceeding from the Father and the Son."

The Larger Catechism (1647)

In the following year, the assembly issued its Larger Catechism under
the leadership of Anthony Tuckney. As is sometimes the case when the
1647 Larger Catechism and the 1646 Confession are compared, the Larger
Catechism offers a slightly revised doctrinal statement. Questions 8–11 sub-
sume eternal generation and procession under "personal properties." If there

---

102. *MPWA* 4:280, 282 (Sept. 15, 1646; Sess. 708).

was an earlier allowance for the idea that the Father could be the fountain or source of the Godhead, it is gone, and as in the Shorter Confession, the equality between the persons is once again stressed. Equality is not merely asserted, but defended in question eleven.

Q. 8. Are there more Gods than one?

A. *There is but one only, the living and true God.*

Q. 9. How many persons are there in the Godhead?

A. *There be three persons in the Godhead, the Father, the Son, and the Holy Ghost; and these three are one true, eternal God, the same in substance, equal in power and glory; although distinguished by their personal properties.*

Q. 10. What are the personal properties of the three persons in the Godhead?

A. *It is proper to the Father to beget the Son, and to the Son to be begotten of the Father, and to the Holy Ghost to proceed from the Father and the Son, from all eternity.*

Q. 11. How doth it appear that the Son and the Holy Ghost are God equal with the Father?

A. *The Scriptures manifest that the Son and the Holy Ghost are God equal with the Father, ascribing unto them such names, attributes, works, and worship, as are proper to God only.*

The Shorter Catechism (1647)

Finally, the 1647 Shorter Catechism offered a simple sentence, a reduced form of the corresponding Larger Catechism question: "There are three persons in the Godhead; the Father, the Son, and the Holy Ghost; and these three are one God, the same in substance, equal in power and glory."

It was almost as brief a statement as that in the "Shorter Confession." Cheynell had argued that the words "same" and "equal" were important. "Same" emphasized unity, and "equal," in order to be intelligible, assumed diversity: "We do usually say that the Father, the Son and the Holy Ghost are equall in power, to note a distinction of persons; but when we speak strictly, we do not say that the power of the persons is equall, but we say the power of the persons is the same, to note the unity of their essence."[103] The

---

103. Cheynell, *Divine Trinunity*, 183.

Post-Reformation Trinitarian Perspectives

use of these terms, both here and in the Larger Catechism, and the insistence on unity of substance created a crisp (now classic) Trinitarian summary.

Conclusions

In these assembly formulations, we have in microcosm the conundrum of post-Reformation Trinitarian theology, reflected even in this preliminary survey. In the first place, these documents contain one main message that is entirely orthodox, helpful, and in a couple of places even elegant, but with little consistency of expression. Positively, this leaves the impression that there is more than one way to get the doctrine of the Trinity right. Negatively, there is no clear trajectory of development in doctrinal expression.

Second, echoes of Calvin's voice are heard clearly in post-Reformation conversations about the Trinity. Courtesy of Calvin, concerns about aseity and about the eternal subordination of the Son became a standard feature of late sixteenth- and seventeenth-century conversations about the Trinity. This study of Westminster Assembly–related discussion indicates that Calvin's thoughts could not be ignored but that his considerations were not simply accepted as the gold standard. This supports Ellis's contention that Calvin's understanding of Trinitarian procession and the Son's aseity became a minority report in the post-Reformation period. According to Ellis, it was rare to find a theologian who followed Calvin's Trinitarian theology closely.[104] Evidence from the Westminster Assembly and its members would tend to corroborate Ellis's sweeping assertion that "by the end of the seventeenth century there were multiple divergent approaches to advocating the Son's aseity among the Reformed. Remarkably, Calvin's own approach to, and conclusions drawn from, autothean language were represented relatively rarely."[105] The Gataker incident shows that there was a broad awareness of the issues among the learned and among those with a vested interest in opposing the doctrine of the Trinity. But the attempts of a Strong or a Tuckney to defend Calvin's understanding of Christ's aseity— mentioned in passing above—are matched by Featley's or Cheynell's interest in modifying it. As it happens, the published works of most divines who were part of the assembly simply mentioned eternal generation in passing, often as a cause for praise, or to distinguish Christ's sonship from that of

---

104. Ellis, *Calvin, Classical Trinitarianism, and the Aseity of the Son*, 103–68.
105. Ibid., 3.

CHAD VAN DIXHOORN

Christians,[106] or to distinguish Christ's eternal sonship from the sonship of his incarnation.[107] Sometimes the doctrine is mentioned merely as part of a catalogue of the great mysteries of the faith,[108] or simply as a synonym for Christ's deity.[109] But rarely is something more precise is intended, such as an argument that the Father and Son must be of the same substance,[110] or that Christ is divine by communication of the divine essence from the Father.[111] Further research is needed to shed more light on what individual divines might mean in their passing references to generation and communication.

Third, in considering the insistence of many theologians that Calvin be harmonized with the best of patristic Trinitarian theology, one cannot help but notice that Featley's polemical irenicism is not a success. Frankly, Featley's speeches are better than his quotations. His efforts to make his heroes, past and present, speak in unison ultimately lead to a presentation of ideas that is not faithful to any of the figures he admires. Nor is this unique. More than once in this study we encounter a torturous formulation that is intended to conform to both patristic and "Calvinian" statements on

---

106. See William Bridge, *The Works of William Bridge* (London: Peter Cole, 1649), 75; Jeremiah Burroughs, *Gospel-conversation* (London: Peter Cole, 1650), 89; Anthony Burgess, *CXLV expository sermons upon the whole 17th chapter of the Gospel according to St. John* (London: A. Miller, 1656), 264, 293, 584–85; Burgess, *A treatise of original sin* (London, 1659), 198, 389; Burroughs, *Gospel-revelation in three treatises* (London: Printed for Nath. Brook . . . , 1660), 107; Edmund Calamy, *A Compleat collection of farewel sermons* (London, 1663), 54; Joseph Caryl, *An exposition with practical observations upon the three first chapters of the book of Iob* (London: G. Miller, 1643), 80; (repr., London, 1647), 462; Francis Cheynell, *An account given to the Parliament by the ministers sent by them to Oxford* (London: F. K., 1647), 48; Cheynell, *The rise, growth, and danger of Socinianisme*, 31; Daniel Featley, *Clavis mystica: a key opening divers difficult and mysterious texts of Holy Scripture* (London: R. Y., 1636), 455, 475; Featley, *The dippers dipt, or, The anabaptists duck'd and plung'd over head and eares, at a disputation in Southwark* (London: N. Bourne and R. Royston, 1645), 3; William Gouge, *A guide to goe to God* (London: G. M., 1626), 10; Gouge, *A learned and very useful commentary on the whole epistle to the Hebrews*, 1:13 (sect. 15), 1:35 (sect. 47), etc.; Gouge, *Of domesticall duties* (London: John Haviland, 1622), 124–25; William Greenhill, *An exposition continued upon the fourteenth, fifteenth, sixteenth, seventeenth, eighteenth, and nineteenth chapters of the prophet Ezekiel* (London: M. S., 1651), 5; Greenhill, *Sermons of Christ, his last discovery of himself* (London: R. I., 1656), 23; John Lightfoot, *A commentary upon the Acts of the Apostles . . . from the beginning of the Booke, to the end of the twelfth chapter* (London: R. C., 1645), 125; Lightfoot, *The works of the Reverend and learned John Lightfoot* (London: W. R., 1684), 1:672; Edward Reynolds, *Three treatises of the vanity of the creature* (London: W. Hunt, 1631), 452; Lazarus Seaman, *The diatribe proved to be paradiatribe* (London: T. R. & E. M., 1647), 7; Obadiah Sedgwick, *The bowels of tender mercy sealed in the everlasting covenant* (London: E. Mottershed, 1661), 197–98. Frequently comments are associated with Isa 53:8 or Acts 8:33.

107. See G. Walker, *The key of saving knovvledge* (London: Tho. Badger, 1641), 69–70.

108. Lightfoot, *The works of the Reverend and learned John Lightfoot*, 1:576.

109. This is especially true with Anthony Burgess in his anti-Socinian writings. See Anthony Burgess, *An expository comment, doctrinal, controversal, and practical upon the whole first chapter to the second epistle of St. Paul to the Corinthians* (London: A. M., 1661), 136–37; and Burgess, *A treatise of original sin*, 389.

110. William Gouge, *An exposition on the vvhole fifth chapter of S. Iohns Gospell* (London: [H. Lownes, R. Young; and J. Beale], 1630), 24 and perhaps John Wallis, *Three sermons concerning the sacred Trinity* (London: Tho. Parkhurst, 1691), 22.

111. Gouge, *Hebrews*, 1:33 (sect. 43).

eternal generation and results in hair-splitting exercises that, nonetheless, drift toward one of three main positions held in the early modern period. First, the ancient assertion that the Father communicated his divine essence through eternal generation (Tradition A). Second, the contrary insistence, following Calvin, that the divine essence is native to the Son and not communicated at all (Tradition B). And third, the mediating position, seemingly so common in the post-Reformation period, that only the person of the Son is begotten of the Father, but because the person is begotten, the divine essence is thereby communicated (Tradition C).

Herein lies the irony. Statements like the Irish articles have been thought to be closer to Calvin because they discuss the details of *communicatio*, while actually, these, like the statements of Beza and Semler, or Featley and Cheynell, subvert the Reformer's concerns. Oddly enough, in its inability or unwillingness to adjudicate between the three main traditions that appear to have been represented in its debating chamber, the Westminster Assembly's own formulations actually accommodate a broad range of Reformation and post-Reformation Trinitarian perspectives on the meaning and function of the eternal generation of the Son.

CHAPTER 11

JONATHAN EDWARDS AND ETERNAL GENERATION

CHRISTINA N. LARSEN

THAT JONATHAN EDWARDS HELD to a doctrine of eternal generation is without question. Upholding a psychological model of the Trinity
throughout his life, Edwards maintained that the Father eternally generates
the Son as the very image of his glory in order that he might gaze upon
the divine glory in beatific delight. The doctrine is of vital importance
to Edwards insofar as, in his glory-centered theology, it is ultimately as
the eternally generated divine idea that the Son is the visibility of divine
glory both within and without the divine life. Although Edwards offers
no special treatment of eternal generation, his understanding of it is readily grasped in his writings on the Trinity. It stands at the forefront of his
ongoing attempt to confront Enlightenment critiques of God's triunity and
Christ's full divinity, and it perceptibly influences the major contours of
his theological program. It is no exaggeration to say that, in these writings,
Edwards finds the doctrine of eternal generation central to the church's
confession: the Father's eternal happiness in his glorious Son stands at the
beginning and end of all things, and the creature's participation in this
loving apprehension of the divine glory in the Son is that for which she
was made. After offering a brief overview of the basic theological importance of the doctrine of eternal generation in Edwards's early account, then
showing how this entails Edwards's careful qualification of the "fitness"
between the Father's eternal generation of the Son and the relationship
between the Father and the Son in redemption history, this chapter argues
that Edwards's late discussion of Christian religious experience functions
according to a different view of this generation that undermines, however

208

inadvertently, Edwards's early concern with the doctrine. Edwards's early interests are evident in his "Discourse on the Trinity" and Miscellany 1602, and his later discussions appear in *Religious Affections*.

"Discourse on the Trinity"

Written over the course of the 1730s, the unpublished "Discourse on the Trinity" remains Edwards's most thoroughgoing meditation on the Trinity and, consequently, his most substantive articulation of the eternal generation at the center of triune life.[1] The *Discourse* opens in confession of God's infinite happiness:

> When we speak of God's happiness, the account that we are wont to give of it is that God is infinitely happy in the enjoyment of himself, in perfectly beholding and infinitely loving, and rejoicing in, his own essence and perfections. And accordingly it must be supposed that God perpetually and eternally has a most perfect idea of himself, as it were an exact image and representation of himself ever before him and in actual view. And from hence arises a most pure and perfect energy in the Godhead, which is the divine love, complacence and joy.[2]

Here Edwards finds God's infinite happiness central to discussion of the divine life, with the eternal conception of a divine idea—a perfect image of himself engendering infinite divine love—standing at the beginning of Edwards's attempt to speak of it. In fact, the beginning of the "Discourse" takes the form of an *a priori* apologetic, with divine happiness as his argument's presupposition. Given this form, Edwards takes time to elucidate his use of faculty language before any explicit mention of the Son as the person generated. He must first establish that divine happiness necessarily involves God's imaging of himself, if it is as infinitely free as the church confesses, before he goes on to address the Father, Son, and, eventually, Spirit directly. *In nuce*, Edwards first reckons that if God is infinitely happy in himself, God must have self-understanding or an idea of himself as the object of his

---

1. The literature on Edwards's Trinitarianism is vast. See diverse interpretations in (and in the literature cited by) Oliver D. Crisp, "Jonathan Edwards on the Trinity," *Jonathan Edwards Studies* 4, no. 1 (2014): 21–41; Amy Plantinga Pauw, *The Supreme Harmony of All: The Trinitarian Theology of Jonathan Edwards* (Grand Rapids: Eerdmans, 2002); and Kyle C. Strobel, *Jonathan Edwards's Theology: A Reinterpretation* (London and New York: Bloomsbury T&T Clark, 2013), 23–71.

2. Jonathan Edwards, "Discourse on the Trinity," in *WJE* (New Haven, CT: Yale University Press, 1957–), 21:113–44 (113).

delight: "the sum of his inclination, love and joy is his love to and delight in himself" because "the sum of the divine understanding and wisdom consists in his having a perfect idea of himself."[3] For Edwards, the divine happiness is free—entirely independent of causes external to the divine life—because the eternal divine idea is the perfect image of the divine glory.

After establishing that the divine idea's perfect imaging is central for the freedom of divine happiness, Edwards concludes, in a spirit of doxological fervor, that this happy life must consist in the life of at least two equally divine persons within the Godhead. It is in this celebration of equality that Edwards's commitment to eternal generation finally comes to the fore. He finds that God having a *perfect* idea of himself must be the Father's eternal generation of a Son who is his equal in every way, with this equal personhood being basic to the divine idea's ability to image the divine glory perfectly:

> Therefore as God with perfect clearness, fullness and strength understands himself, views his own essence (in which there is no distinction of substance and act, but it is wholly substance and wholly act), that idea which God hath of himself is absolutely himself. This representation of the divine nature and essence is the divine nature and essence again. So that by God's thinking of the Deity, [the Deity] must certainly be generated. Hereby there is another person begotten; there is another infinite, eternal, almighty, and most holy and the same God, the very same divine nature. And this person is the second person in the Trinity, the only begotten and dearly beloved Son of God. He is the eternal, necessary, perfect, substantial and personal idea which God hath of himself.[4]

While not outlined explicitly, Edwards's logic here is rather straightforward. Namely, if God were to behold and delight in an idea of himself that failed to image him in anything (e.g., nature, essence), then God's happiness would not be in himself. It is because the Father eternally generates a second, equally divine person in the Son as his perfect divine idea that the Father eternally delights in beholding his glory made visible in the Son.

---

3. Ibid., 114. In Edwards's psychological model, this "inclination"—or disposition—is none other than the Spirit as the divine love. For a sample of the lively discussion surrounding what might be termed Edwards's pneumatological dispositionalism, see especially Robert W. Caldwell III, *Communion in the Spirit* (Milton Keynes: Paternoster, 2008); Oliver D. Crisp, *Jonathan Edwards on God and Creation* (New York: Oxford University Press, 2012), 14–56; and Sang Hyun Lee, *The Philosophical Theology of Jonathan Edwards* (Princeton: Princeton University Press, 1988).

4. Edwards, "Discourse on the Trinity," *WJE*, 21:116–17. *WJE* editor's brackets.

JONATHAN EDWARDS AND ETERNAL GENERATION

The "Discourse" then offers five scriptural "proofs" in somewhat hurried support of the Son as the eternally generated idea of the Father. First, Scripture finds the Son to be not just "in" the image of the Father but *the* image itself, and on Edwards's reckoning an idea is "the most immediate representation, and seems therefore to be a more primary sort of image." It is for this reason that Christ, the Son incarnate, is the "most immediate representation of the Godhead."[5] Second, identifying the Son as the idea of the Father's glory explains the scriptural references to God's infinite "love to and delight in" the Son because God's delight in his idea is his delight in his Son.[6] Third, the Father's eternal generation of his perfect idea in the Son clarifies scriptural descriptions of Christ as the "face of God" (Exod 33:14) or the "angel of God's presence, or face" (Isa 63:9) because both refer to the way in which God is beheld or looked upon. Edwards cannot think of what "can be so properly and fitly called so with respect to God as God's own perfect idea of himself, whereby he has every moment a view of his own essence" as his own idea, which "is eminently in God's presence."[7] Fourth, Edwards finds this account to "agree with" Scripture's reference to Christ as the "brightness" of divine glory, both because it is by the Son as the divine idea that God delights in his own glory and because, insofar as God is the luminary, it is fitting that it is his idea that is his light: "For what is so properly the light of a mind or spirit as its knowledge or understanding?"[8] And finally, Scripture calls Christ the "wisdom," "logos," and "amen" or "truth" of God, all terms that Edwards believes refer only to God's idea or understanding of himself.[9]

Such is Edwards's basic account of eternal generation in the early pages of the "Discourse." It relies heavily upon a particular psychological model that Edwards finds to illuminate a breadth of scriptural discussion in a time of heated Enlightenment debate.[10] However, even without getting

---

5. Ibid., 117. Here, "Seeing the perfect idea of a thing is to all intents and purposes the same as seeing the thing; it is not only equivalent to the seeing of it, but it *is* the seeing it: for there is no other seeing but having the idea. Now by seeing a perfect idea, so far as we see it we have it; but it can't be said of anything else, that in seeing of it we see another, strictly speaking, except it be the very idea of the other" (ibid., 118; *WJE* editor's emphasis).

6. Ibid., 118.

7. Ibid., 118–19.

8. Ibid., 119.

9. Ibid., 119–20.

10. For an interpretation of Edwards's use of Locke's *Essay* in his model, toward the end of defending Reformed orthodoxy from Enlightenment critiques (specifically, in the "Discourse," those of Samuel Clarke), see Paul Helm, "The Human Self and the Divine Trinity," in *Jonathan Edwards as Contemporary: Essays in Honor of Sang Hyun Lee*, ed. Don Schweitzer (New York: Peter Lang, 2010), 93–106. For discussion of how this model addresses these critques, see Strobel, *Jonathan Edwards's Theology*, 31–71. And for an overview of Edwards's intellectual context that finds "it must

into Edwards's subsequent discussion of the Spirit's procession, it is clear that, dogmatically, what remains critical for Edwards is to establish that the Father's eternal generation of the equally divine Son is integral not merely to the fullness but also to the sufficiency of divine happiness. Ultimately, the irreducible happiness of the divine life centers Edwards's most basic account, and goes on to center Edwards's discussion of the glory of the Son as the very happiness of the creature.[11]

MISCELLANY 1062

Edwards's Miscellany 1062, "[Observations concerning the] Economy of the Trinity and the Covenant of Redemption," is often recognized as a significant *pensée*. It was likely written between 1742 and 1744, not long after the initial parts of the "Discourse." The miscellany begins with the recognition

that there is a subordination of the persons of the Trinity, in their actings with respect to the creature; that one acts from another, and under another, and with a dependence on another, in their actings, and particularly in what they act in the affair of man's redemption. So that the Father in that affair acts as Head of the Trinity, and Son under him, and the Holy Spirit under them both.[12]

---

be questioned whether Edwards's reading of Locke was the central and decisive event in his intellectual life," see Norman Fiering, *Jonathan Edwards's Moral Thought and Its British Context* (Chapel Hill: University of North Carolina Press, 1981), 13–47 (38). However Edwards might have understood himself as a defender of Reformed orthodoxy, his emphasis on the intellective generation of the Son clearly departs from the tradition's general distaste with discussing the difference between the Son and Spirit's processions at length. Chevalier Ramsay's defense of eternal generation appears to bear a greater resemblance to Edwards's psychological model than does the work of Edwards's favored theologians, Francis Turretin and Petrus van Mastricht; see Jonathan Edwards, "1253. Trinity," in *WJE*, 23:184–88. On this general distaste, see Richard A. Muller, *Post-Reformation Reformed Dogmatics: The Rise and Development of Reformed Orthodoxy, ca. 1520 to ca. 1725*, vol. 4, *The Triunity of God* (Grand Rapids: Baker Academic, 2003), 376. For comparison of Edwards's psychological model with Thomas Aquinas's account of divine knowing and loving, see Thomas G. Weinandy, "Jonathan Edwards: 'Discourse on the Trinity,'" in *The Ecumenical Edwards: Jonathan Edwards and the Theologians*, ed. Kyle C. Strobel (Farnham: Ashgate, 2015), 67–80.

11. As the divine image, Christ is "the great prophet and teacher of mankind, the light of the world, and the revealer of God to creatures" (Edwards, "Discourse on the Trinity," *WJE*, 21:120). Edwards frequently meditates on the connection between the Son's imaging of glory for the Father and his economic imaging for creatures. See, for instance, Jonathan Edwards, "321. *Heb. 1:3*," in *The Works of Jonathan Edwards Online*, vol. 49, *Sermons, Series II, 1734* (Jonathan Edwards Center at Yale University, 2008), L. [1r]–17v. It is because Christ images this glory to creatures that Edwards's discussion of the eternal generation does not ultimately occur apart from discussion of Christ in Scripture.

12. Jonathan Edwards, "1062. Economy of the Trinity and Covenant of Redemption," in *WJE*, 20:430–43 (430).

However, after recognizing the equal glory of the Son as the image of the Father's glory, it immediately goes on to insist that, in their subordination,

> the other persons' acting under the Father don't arise from any natural subjection, as we should understand such an expression according to the common idiom of speech; for thus a natural subjection would be understood to imply either an obligation to compliance and conformity to another as a superior and one more excellent, and so most worthy to be a rule for another to conform to, or an obligation to conformity to another's will, arising from a dependence on another's will for being or well-being. But neither of these can be the case with respect to the persons of the Trinity.[13]

The miscellany is relevant to Edwards's understanding of eternal generation insofar as it sets out to distinguish between what is established in the Father's generation of the Son and what is foreign to it, though (in a qualified sense) derivative of this generation because it is "fitting" to this generation. Edwards hopes to both maintain the equality of the Father, Son, and Spirit within the divine life and maintain that the subordination of the Son to the Father in redemption history does not diminish the Son's identity as the perfect image of divine glory and the object of divine happiness. Here, it is Edwards's commitment to the Father's eternal generation of the Son as the perfect image of his glory that grounds Edwards's distinction of what one might call three levels at which the divine life can be discussed: namely, the level of processions, the level of economy, and the level of redemption.

Beginning at the level of processions, Edwards first establishes that the Father's eternal generation of the Son in no way entails the Son's subordination to the Father. Rather, the Son is equal to the Father in every way *because* he is the Father's eternally generated image. Echoing the early "Discourse" (without recourse to the language of "idea"), Edwards finds that it is as the "brightness" of the Father's glory—"the very image of the Father and the express and perfect image of his person"—that the Son exists. As this image, the Son is equal to the Father "in glory and excellency of nature"—so much so that "the way that the Father enjoys the glory of the Deity is in enjoying him." While Edwards does not draw out the Son's significance for the freedom of divine happiness as he does in the early

---

13. Ibid., 430–31.

"Discourse," he nevertheless insists that it is because the Son is this perfect image that "the Father's infinite happiness is in him."[14]

Edwards upholds a sense of the Son's "dependence" on the Father at this level, "because with respect to his subsistence he is wholly from the Father and begotten by him," but he prefers to speak of the "priority" rather than the "superiority" of the Father because the Son's dependence does not include an "inferiority of Deity." As the perfect image, "The whole Deity and glory of the Father, is as it [were] repeated or duplicated: everything in the Father is repeated or expressed again, and that fully, so that there is properly no inferiority." For this reason, Edwards insists that there is not even a qualified sense of "natural subjection" implied in the Father's generation of the Son because this procession "is no voluntary but a necessary proceeding, and therefore infers no proper subjection of one to the will of another."[15] Edwards is quite concerned to safeguard the Son's equal glory and divinity with the Father at the level of natural, unwilled processions, so he finds that the only difference between them is the merely logical priority of the Father as the person who generates the Son for eternity. There is a clear insistence that any other difference—or even a misunderstanding of this difference!—would be catastrophic for the equal glory of the Son.

After establishing the equality of the Father and Son at the level of processions, Edwards distinguishes a second level for discussing their relationship, the level of economy, wherein their "order of acting" in the economic work of divine glorification is determined by their "mutual free agreement."[16] (Given that the divine decision for glorification precedes the divine decision to do so in a work of redemption, this second level is distinct from the order of acting established in the covenant of redemption.) Edwards finds the second level to go beyond the level of processions in two key ways. First, whereas the eternal generation does not involve the Son's subordination to the Father, "decency" to the level of processions "requires" the Son's subordination in his acting "from" and "in a dependence on" the Father in the voluntary, willed "actings" of the economic work of glorification. Such an ordering was unwarranted prior to the decision for self-glorification. However, the ordering embraced to fulfill this glorification is nonetheless in some sense fitting to the processions wherein the Father "is first in the order of subsisting" because it is "fit that the order of the acting of the persons of the Trinity should be agreeable to

---

14. Ibid., 430.
15. Ibid., 430–31. *WJE* editor's brackets.
16. Ibid., 431–32.

the order of their subsisting." Second, this economic level is neither eternal nor a necessary emanation from the level of procession but is initiated by a "mutual free agreement." While "the persons of the Trinity all consent to this order, and establish it by agreement, as they all naturally delight in what is in itself fit, suitable and beautiful" because "decency requires it," it remains an ordering that is freely willed by all three divine persons insofar as none is necessarily subject to another in either will or act: "It is not proper to say decency *obliges* the persons of the Trinity to come into this order."[17] Because of the mutuality of the decision to act according to this order, the equal glory of the persons is maintained.

Edwards's third level for discussing the relationship between the Father and the Son is the level of redemption. In a way, the miscellany is primarily focused on distinguishing the order of acting at this level—the order established in the covenant of redemption—from the order of acting established at the level of economy. Edwards argues for this distinction to support his fundamental concern that the Son's humiliation is not seen as naturally following from his procession from the Father but as befitting the end of divine glorification.[18] While the covenant is designed to establish the fitting means of achieving divine glorification, it goes far beyond the level of economy by introducing a subordination that includes an inequality of glory between the Father and Son. Given Edwards's continued support of their equality, it is hardly surprising that his talk of this subordination proceeds with remarkable caution.

Edwards admits that the ordering of this third level is "in several respects agreeable" to the order of economy because the logically prior Father is not subject to the Son. However, Edwards finds he "must distinguish between the covenant of redemption, that is an establishment of wisdom wonderfully contriving a particular method for the most conveniently obtaining a great end," and the prior "establishment that is founded in fitness and decency and the natural order of the eternal and necessary subsistence of the persons of the Trinity" because it is the work of redemption that requires an "obedience that implies an humiliation below his [the Son's] proper divine glory."[19] Moreover, such a humiliation is not a mere byproduct of this covenantal ordering; rather, humiliation lies at the center of it: "no other subjection or obedience of the Son to the Father arises properly from the covenant of redemption" except for "that which implies humiliation, or a state and

---

17. Ibid., 431. Edwards's emphasis.
18. See especially ibid., 433–35.
19. Ibid., 437, 432, 438.

relation to the Father wherein he descends below the infinite glory of a divine person."[20] Edwards is clear that the only reason such an inglorious ordering finally achieves divine glorification is because it is only the Son's freely chosen humiliation of glory that merits for those he redeems. The Son's humiliation is befitting of the work of glorification because it is not directly befitting of his procession from the Father within the divine life.[21]

Because of this, although the covenant of redemption is similar to the agreement of the second level in its free inauguration of a further level of Trinitarian ordering that is in some sense fitting to the level that precedes it, the covenant is qualitatively different: the subordination of glory it introduces into the relationship between the Father and the Son is not directly grounded in the "fitness and decency and the natural order" of the eternal generation.[22] Any sense of fitness between the Son's subordination of glory and his eternal generation from the Father is derivative. Insofar as this subordination is "agreeable" to the level of economy, it is derivatively agreeable to the level of processions. But it remains distinct from the fitness at the level of economy because it ultimately takes its shape in fitness to the redemptive work that glorification requires. Edwards's refusal to find the Son's humiliation as fitting to the divine processions is no less than his attempt to acknowledge the paradox at the heart of this affair: the notion that the Son might somehow be less than the Father at any point of the work of glorification verges on denying the eternal happiness of the divine life from whence it flows.

There is plenty to say about the concept of fitness that pervades Edwards's theology.[23] However, in the miscellany it is critical to discern how Edwards deploys the concept toward the end of maintaining a rather difficult dialectic. Consider the carefulness with which Edwards finds the Father–Son relationship at the levels of economy and redemption to be fitting to the

---

20. Ibid., 437.

21. See ibid., 436–38.

22. Ibid., 432. Edwards finds that "if there were any such thing as a way of redemption without the humiliation of any divine person, the persons would act in man's redemption in their proper subordination, without any covenant of redemption" (ibid., 437) and that, because of the close connection between humiliation and covenant, the covenant of redemption is between the Father and the Son alone given that the Spirit does not undergo a further humiliation at the level of redemption. However, what is perhaps most interesting is that Edwards finds both that everything the Son does in his obedient fulfillment of the covenant before or after his humiliation is established at the level of economy, and that the Son's temporary ruling on behalf of the Father, along with the Spirit's temporary twofold subjection to the Son, are established at the level of redemption (ibid., 435, 438–43).

23. For discussion of Edwards's aesthetics—wherein Edwards's appeal to "fitness" facilitates his theological aims in light of his characteristically seventeenth- and eighteenth-century aesthetic, ethical, and metaphysical concerns—see especially Roland Delattre, *Beauty and Sensibility in the Thought of Jonathan Edwards: An Essay in Aesthetics and Theological Ethics* (New Haven and London: Yale University Press, 1968); and Fiering, *Jonathan Edwards's Moral Thought and Its British Context.*

Father's eternal generation of the Son at the level of processions because they are only in a qualified sense derivative of this generation (though fitting because they are truly derivative in this qualified sense!).

On one hand, both of the Son's freely willed subordinations to the Father go beyond the equality that is eternally the Son's as the perfect image of the Father's glory, yet both are celebrated as "fitting" or "agreeable" because, either directly (at the level of economy) or by derivation (at the level of redemption), they pattern their shape after the logical priority of the Father in his eternal generation of the Son, and are ultimately taken towards the end of declaring the divine glory *ad extra*. Because the Father's eternal generation of the Son is the ground for the Father's logical priority in the Son's subordinations, the Son's obedience does not in the end obscure or, worse, collapse the generation at the heart of this glory. Instead it reveals the glory of the divine life wherein the Son is in no way subordinate to the Father. On the other hand, it is only because these subordinations are freely willed that Edwards finds them truly fitting. While these subordinations are either directly or derivatively befitting to the eternal generation, both must be freely willed by the Father and the Son. If either subordination were to be included in this generation, then the Son's equality with the Father would be compromised, he would not perfectly image the Father, and the divine happiness would not find its object in him.

For this reason, the good news for Edwards is that the Father and the Son, not by necessity but as the very wisdom of God, have freely willed these subordinations for the free display of the divine glory abroad! That Edwards goes to great lengths to establish a level of economy prior to the level of redemption only stresses how foreign the Son's full subordination is to the fullness of the divine life, even if it is, in a qualified way, fitting to it towards the end of divine glorification.[24] Throughout the miscellany, what remains essential and *essential* to the Son's identity is established at the level of unwilled processions in the eternal generation wherein the Son, as the perfect image of the Father, is the Father's equal and, consequently, is the brightness of the Father's glory in which he eternally delights. Only this Son can shine forth this brightness into the world.[25]

---

24. This is underlined by Edwards's insistence that the level of redemption ceases as soon as the Son's humiliation is complete, while the level of economy continues for eternity (see Edwards, "1062. Economy of the Trinity and Covenant of Redemption," *WJE*, 20:434, 438–40). For Edwards's further discussion of the Son's subordination given his full equality with the Father, see especially Jonathan Edwards, "On the Equality of the Persons of the Trinity," *WJE*, 21:146–48; and Edwards, "Of God the Father," *WJE*, 25:144–54.

25. There is certainly significant debate surrounding the extent to which Edwards embraces an emanationism in his discussion of the divine disposition to pour forth of the divine glory. Some

CHRISTINA N. LARSEN

Religious Affections

Published in 1746 after being preached as a sermon series in 1742–43—a few years after Edwards's work on the Trinity in the initial pages of the "Discourse," and more or less contemporaneous with his composition of Miscellany 1062—*Religious Affections* offers Edwards's mature reflections on Christian religious experience in response to the New England awakenings. One of Edwards's most important texts, its discussion of the creature's apprehension of divine glory in redemption history contrasts with the miscellany's discussion insofar as *Religious Affections* is more concerned with unfolding redemption history's evocative significance than with exploring its constitutive significance as the working out of divine glorification in the Son's humiliation. Here, it is the Son's identity as the image of divine glory that grounds the possibility of the creature's sight of this glory, true Christian experience consisting in the creature's loving apprehension of the divine image in the incarnate Son.[26] While *Religious Affections* relies implicitly upon a psychological model of the Trinity wherein the Son images the divine glory within the divine life as the Father's eternally generated idea, in its concern to address the Son's evocative significance it relies upon a view of this generation that is markedly different from Miscellany 1062 and the early parts of the "Discourse." *Religious Affections* finds a different psychological logic at work—a logic that does not obviously satisfy the concerns of Edwards's early account.

Edwards's underlying stress throughout *Religious Affections* is that it is ultimately a loving apprehension of the glory of divine holiness in Christ that constitutes the genuine religious affection in which true Christian

---

even identify a tendency in Edwards's work to speak of the Father's eternal generation of the Son as in some sense the first emanation of the divine disposition to pour forth of the divine glory through which the glory then emanates *ad extra* (see Michael David Bush, "Jesus Christ in the Theology of Jonathan Edwards" [PhD diss., Princeton Theological Seminary, 2003]). It is no doubt true that Edwards finds the divine decrees fitting to the divine happiness in the pouring forth of the divine glory *ad extra*, however it seems significant that Edwards does not dispose of the language of decree in this discussion. Despite his language of emanation, his focus on the fitness of the divine decrees appears fixated on stressing the happiness of divine glorification—a happiness that a crude voluntarism might eclipse, yet a necessary emanationism might render inconsequential. Edwards's commitment to the voluntary nature of the decrees is clearly pronounced in this very discussion of the Son's humiliation wherein the divine freedom to choose is decisive: "For 'tis only that obedience which the Son voluntarily and freely subjected himself to from love to sinners . . . that merits for sinners" (Edwards, "1062. Economy of the Trinity and Covenant of Redemption," *WJE*, 20:438). Perhaps Katherine Sonderegger's recent use of disposition to knit more closely together the concepts of divine will and divine nature is not entirely dissimilar to Edwards's approach (I owe this comparison to Philip Ziegler). See Katherine Sonderegger, *Systematic Theology*, vol. 1, *The Doctrine of God* (Minneapolis: Fortress, 2015), 249–54, 309–26, 474–90.

26. See, for instance, Jonathan Edwards, *WJE*, 2:270–74, 297–300, 324–28, 392–96.

218

JONATHAN EDWARDS AND ETERNAL GENERATION

experience consists. However, to make this claim he distinguishes creaturely apprehension of the divine glory in God's natural attributes from
apprehension of the divine glory in God's moral attributes, aligning each
kind of attribute with a distinct part of the divine image in the creature:

> As there are two kinds of attributes in God, according to our way of
> conceiving of him, his moral attributes, which are summed up in his
> holiness, and his natural attributes, of strength, knowledge, etc. that
> constitute the greatness of God; so there is a twofold image of God
> in man, his moral or spiritual image, which is his holiness, that is the
> image of God's moral excellency (which image was lost by the fall); and
> God's natural image, consisting in men's reason and understanding, his
> natural ability, and dominion over the creatures, which is the image
> of God's natural attributes.[27]

While the creature cannot apprehend the moral attributes apart from the
natural attributes, as the locus of divine holiness it is the glory of God's
moral attributes that evokes the creature's loving apprehension, restoring
the diving image within her and, consequently, enabling her creaturely
participation in the glory of the divine life. Fundamentally, this is because
"a love to divine things for the beauty and sweetness of their moral excellency, is the first beginning and spring of all holy affections."[28]

In this account of Christian experience, Edwards distinguishes between
a natural and graced apprehension of the divine glory in order to address
the importance of love and delight in God in such a way that accounts for
the total difference the Spirit's regenerative work makes for the creature's
experience of God. Here, a full, graced apprehension of the divine glory in
Christ is a loving apprehension made possible by the indwelling of the Spirit
as a vital principle of love patterned after the Spirit's procession within the
divine life. Beyond a mere intellectual assent, this full apprehension of the
divine glory in Christ consists in a "*sense of the heart*, wherein the mind don't
only *speculate* and *behold*, but *relishes* and *feels*."[29] Such an apprehension transforms the creature because, once the will is inclined, the creature's entire
being turns toward God in love; her previously hardened heart is exchanged

---

27. Ibid., 256.
28. Ibid., 253–54. On the creature's end as her economic participation in the divine glory poured
forth, see especially Jonathan Edwards, *Dissertation I: Concerning the End for Which God Created the
World*, in *WJE*, 8:404–36. On Edwards's innovations in Reformed discussion of the beatific vision
wherein this participation is fully realized, see especially Strobel, *Jonathan Edwards's Theology*, 149–33.
29. Edwards, *Religious Affections*, *WJE*, 2:272, Edwards's emphases.

for the heart of flesh whereby she shares in the divine glory, united to him in heart and mind by his own understanding and love of himself.[30]

An apprehension of the divine glory in the natural attributes is possible apart from an apprehension of the moral attributes whereby the beauty of divine holiness is seen, but such a natural apprehension condemns precisely because it does not perceive the beauty by which the hearts of fallen creatures are transformed. For Edwards, only a graced apprehension is inescapably transformative due to its involvement in the creature's heart—where the Spirit's regenerative work takes place. And then only a graced apprehension engenders the creature's participation in the divine glory because this participation is mediated by the Spirit's unition of the creature and Christ in a bond of love.[31]

Throughout *Religious Affections*, Edwards stresses that both the manifestation of the natural attributes and the beauteous manifestation of the moral attributes (divine holiness) are found in Christ alone and therefore can be apprehended in him alone—he is the image of divine glory after all. However, it is difficult to reconcile the psychological logic operative in *Religious Affections* with the psychological logic assumed in the early "Discourse" and Miscellany 1062 because, in the later logic, the Son is the eternally generated divine image wherein the divine glory is apprehended, but it appears that he is this image as something like a *natural* divine image that locates something like a *moral* divine image in the Spirit.

Consider the way in which Edwards's later additions to the "Discourse" insist that the Son is the attribute of divine understanding that locates the Spirit as the attribute of divine love. Nearing the end of the "Discourse," Edwards suggests that the totality of divine attributes is best understood as the communion of two truly distinct person-attributes, the Son as the divine idea summarizing the attribute of understanding and the Spirit as the divine love summarizing the attribute of love:

---

30. For discussion of the central role this spiritual sense of the heart holds in Edwards's anthropology, see especially John E. Smith, "Religious Affections and the 'Sense of the Heart,'" in *The Princeton Companion to Jonathan Edwards*, ed. Sang Hyun Lee (Princeton: Princeton University Press, 2005), 103–14; and Strobel, *Jonathan Edwards's Theology*, 153–90, 214–24.

31. Edwards draws out this distinction sharply: "But the saints and angels do behold the glory of God consisting in the *beauty of his holiness*: and 'tis this sight only, that will melt and humble the hearts of men, and wean them from the world, and draw them to God, and effectually change them. A sight of the awful greatness of God, may overpower men's strength, and be more than they can endure; but if the moral beauty of God be hid, the enmity of the heart will remain in its full strength, no love will be enkindled, all will not be effectual to gain the will, but that will remain inflexible; whereas the first glimpse of the moral and spiritual glory of God shining into the heart, produces all these effects, as it were with omnipotent power, which nothing can withstand" (Edwards, *Religious Affections*, WJE, 2:264–65). For Edwards's discussion of these two apprehensions, see especially ibid., 253–66.

There are but these three distinct real things in God; whatsoever else can be mentioned in God are nothing but mere modes or relations of existence. There are his attributes of infinity, eternity and immutability: they are mere modes of existence. There is God's understanding, his wisdom and omniscience, that we have shown to be the same with his idea. . . . There is God's holiness, but this is the same—as we have shown in what we have said of the nature of excellency—with his love to himself . . .

It is a maxim amongst divines that everything that is in God is God, which must be understood of real attributes and not of mere modalities . . . if it be meant that the real attributes of God, viz. his understanding and love, are God, then what we have said may in some measure explain how it is so: for Deity subsists in them distinctly, so they are distinct divine persons. We find no other attributes of which it is said that they are God in Scripture, or that God is they, but Λογος and Αγαπε, the reason and the love of God (*John 1:1* and *1 John 4:8, 1 John 4:16*).[32]

In this passage, Edwards hopes to establish that creaturely discussion of the divine attributes is not a discussion of God's qualities but of God himself, given that God is his attributes. However, the way in which Edwards allows for a distinction between attributes pertaining to the divine idea and attributes pertaining to the divine love is quite odd. Rather than denoting the one divine essence directly, here the attributes fall into two distinct categories denoting one or other of two distinct divine persons. And so, while the attributes are properly predicated of the divine essence (and, consequently, each of the divine persons) because "they have communion with one another,"[33] there remains a sense that, as the eternally generated divine idea, the Son is the person-attribute who summarizes the natural attributes, and as the divine love, the Spirit is the person-attribute who summarizes the moral attributes.[34]

---

32. Edwards, "Discourse on the Trinity," *WJE*, 21:131–32. Kyle Strobel argues that Edwards's views develop over the course of the "Discourse," presenting a compelling case for reading the divine attributes as the divine persons at this juncture (see Strobel, *Jonathan Edwards's Theology*, 23–71, 234–42).

33. Edwards, "Discourse on the Trinity," *WJE*, 21:133. See also 21:132–34.

34. For discussion of the relationships between the divine attributes, divine essence, and divine persons in Edwards, and how Edwards's quite unusual commitment to divine simplicity compares to that of his favorites Turretin and Mastricht and others, see especially (and the literature cited by) Crisp, "Jonathan Edwards on the Trinity"; Phillip Hussey, "Jonathan Edwards's God: Simply Relational or Relationally Simple?" (unpublished paper, 2016), 1–27; Sabastian Rehnman, "Is the Distinction Between Natural and Moral Attributes Good? Jonathan Edwards on Divine Attributes,"

CHRISTINA N. LARSEN

Because of this, when *Religious Affections* speaks of the creature's full apprehension of divine glory in Christ's manifestation of moral and natural attributes, it seems as if Christ's significance as the incarnate Son is to supply a locus for the visibility of the divine glory *in the Spirit* (who summarizes the moral attributes) in order to restore the creature's moral image. While it is possible to apprehend Christ without apprehending the Spirit (the apprehension that condemns), it is only possible to apprehend the divine holiness or other moral attributes in Christ by apprehending the Spirit within him. As the Son, Christ is the manifestation of the divine natural attributes (attributes of greatness) that provides the magnitude for the Spirit's manifestation of the divine moral attributes, because the moral attributes have no magnitude of their own. Consequently, although it is true that all the attributes are predicable of all three divine persons, the creature ultimately looks upon the incarnate Son to see the glory of the natural attributes that he images as the divine idea as well as the glory of the moral attributes in the Spirit within him.[35]

Although it is as the divine idea and the divine love within a psychological framework that these attributes denote the Son and Spirit respectively, the eternal generation within this psychological logic is clearly different insofar as the Spirit perfects what appears to be the Son's partial imaging of the Father's glory. In the eternal generation, the Son, as the divine idea, images the glory of the natural attributes as something like a natural image that enables the Spirit, as something like a moral image of the glory of the moral attributes, to shine. While in his manifestation of the Spirit the Son might be said to reflect perfectly the image of the Father, this is unlike Edwards's earlier account wherein the Son's perfect imaging of the divine glory is in some sense the origin of the Spirit's procession. Here, the Father's happiness in the Son is not grounded in the Son's perfect imaging, but the Son's perfect imaging is grounded in the Father's happiness in the Son.

Whether or not the latter pages of the "Discourse" attempt to move beyond Edwards's initial understanding of the Son's eternal generation, when the latter pages of the "Discourse" are read alongside Edwards's discussion of moral and natural attributes in *Religious Affections*, the logic

---

History of Philosophy Quarterly 27, no. 1 (2010): 57–78; and Strobel, *Jonathan Edwards's Theology*, 234–42. Seng-Kong Tan argues that Edwards adopts Turretin's "mediating" understanding of the Son as *autotheos* (Seng-Kong Tan, *Fullness Received and Returned: Trinity and Participation in Jonathan Edwards* [Minneapolis: Fortress, 2014], 5-7, 357-58).

35. For further discussion of how the Son functions as the divine greatness for the goodness of the Spirit throughout the scope of Edwards's theology, see Joseph C. Williamson, "The Excellency of Christ: A Study in the Christology of Jonathan Edwards" (PhD diss., Harvard University, 1968), 67–119.

at work in *Religious Affections* certainly seems to conflict with Edwards's initial view (of course Edwards's recognition of this is impossible to know). Similar to Edwards's initial view, his account in *Religious Affections* seeks to highlight a fitness between the Son's eternal procession from the Father and the Son's fulfillment of the work of glorification; by locating what is effectively the imaging of the moral attributes in the Spirit, Edwards demonstrates a tremendous fitness between the psychological underpinnings of the creature's renewal and the Son–Spirit relationship at the level of processions. However, insofar as the Son perfectly images the Father by his Spirit in a manner very different from the early "Discourse" and Miscellany 1062, Edwards undermines his earlier concern to regard the Son as the eternally generated object of divine happiness that ensures the eternal freedom of divine delight.

CONCLUSION

This brief overview of eternal generation in Edwards's "Discourse," Miscellany 1062, and *Religious Affections* shows how central the doctrine is to his theological program. The Father's eternal generation of the Son is basic to Edwards's understanding of the glorious happiness of divine life—as the eternally generated image of divine glory, the Son completes his work of glorification as the very happiness of the creation. Edwards's glory-obsessed theology is not able to speak of God or his works without speaking about the eternal generation in which God knows his own glory, or the Son's mission (that critically follows from this generation) in which God, in his wisdom, freely gives his glory to be known. Not least because, without speaking about the eternal reality of this generation at length, the irreducible happiness of the glorious divine life—and the possibility of creaturely happiness!—that stands at the heart of who God is would not weight his creaturely confession of God's glory as it ought.

Edwards's initial understanding of eternal generation in the "Discourse" is vital to his discussion about God because it establishes that the Son is the divine idea who, as the Father's equal in all things, perfectly images the divine glory and grounds the total freedom of the divine happiness that remains at the center of divine life. And then Miscellany 1062's careful delineation of three levels for speaking of this life is vital to his discussion because it establishes the wisdom of God in the fitness of the work of divine glorification, while at the same time establishing the utter gratuity of the Son's freely willed subordination given the foreignness of any inequality in his eternal generation from the Father. The slightest inequality in this generation would cause the glory at the beginning and end of this glorification to vanish.

Finally, while *Religious Affections* functions according to an account of the Son's imaging in the eternal generation that is quite opposed to Edwards's early view, even this points toward the end of insisting that it is because the Son's mission is befitting to his eternal imaging of the Father's glory that the work of glorification succeeds. Here, Edwards's understanding of eternal generation is vital to his discussion of God's works because the Spirit's evocative application of salvation to creatures is achieved by the Spirit as the Spirit of the eternally generated Son. In other words, it is in Christ alone as the eternally generated natural image that the Spirit's moral imaging of the Father's glory provides its transformative vision.

Clearly, for Edwards the doctrine of eternal generation is central to the church's confession. Nonetheless, the conflict between his early and late writings is real. And given the centrality of the doctrine to his theological program, this is devastating to the ability of his program—as it stands—to speak intelligibly about the singular glory of divine life that stands at the beginning and end of all things. Insofar as the logic implicit in Edwards's later writings undermines his initial grounding of the freedom of divine happiness in the Son's perfect imaging, it not only alters his understanding of the Son as the visibility of divine glory in redemption history, but it also unravels his understanding of the ground of this freedom and, with it, his context for understanding the perfect equality of the Son.

While the later logic might appear to facilitate Edwards's lifelong hope to elevate the Spirit as the "sum of all good things," it is not obviously a cogent enough view to illuminate another way of understanding the freedom of divine happiness (the memorable starting point of Edwards's theology).[36] What does it mean that the Son and Spirit function as person-attributes within a divine faculty psychology when the strongly volitional person-attribute provides the object for divine understanding instead of the intellective person-attribute? Regardless of whether Edwards's distribution of the creature's apprehension of glory between the imaging persons is finally guilty of separating inseparable operations, or fails to escape any manner of ills to which psychological models are prone, because Edwards allows another account of eternal generation to function behind the scenes of his discussion of Christian experience, his doctrine of God does not evolve but evaporates.

---

36. Edwards, "Discourse on the Trinity," *WJE*, 21:136.

JONATHAN EDWARDS AND ETERNAL GENERATION

The lamentable tragedy of Edwards's untimely death is often rehearsed by appreciative critics who wish to see how his anticipated masterworks might have developed—or withdrawn—his embryonic innovations. It is not fair to say that, in the end, Edwards's theology fails because it is not internally consistent. While admitting the mystery of which he writes, he was himself far from satisfied with where he left things in the "Discourse":

> I don't pretend fully to explain how these things are, and I am sensible a hundred other objections may be made, and puzzling doubts and questions raised, that I can't solve. I am far from pretending to explaining the Trinity so as to render it no longer a mystery . . . but in time, with reason, may [be] led to say something further of it than has been wont to be said, though there are still left many things pertaining to it incomprehensible.[37]

We have a copious number of occasional writings that belie the underlying conviction that the doctrine of God in his glory must, however implicitly, structure all creaturely talk about him and his works. But we do not have a mature masterwork, so we do not know whether Edwards might have modified his psychological speculation and pulled together a better-ordered discussion of this glorious God in the end. What can be said is that, for Edwards, the eternal generation is central to the church's confession because, in one way or another, the Father's eternal happiness in his glorious Son stands at the beginning and end of all things.[38]

---

37. Ibid., 134. *WJE* editor's brackets.
38. I am grateful to Ivor Davidson, the late John Webster, and Steven Duby for their conversations during the writing of this chapter.

CHAPTER 12

ETERNAL GENERATION AFTER BARTH

MICHAEL ALLEN

INTRODUCTION

In this chapter I will examine two ways in which Karl Barth's doctrine of Christ prompts further theological exploration in significant and challenging directions. His doctrine of eternal generation is, in and of itself and strictly construed, especially uninteresting, which I would argue is not a bad thing.[1] But the systemic manner in which he connects this doctrine to ancillary topics or themes is remarkable and well worth our attention. First, we will consider the ways in which Barth connects this doctrine to *theologia*, the exploration of God's inner life and works. Second, we will examine the path by which Barth relates this doctrine to *oikonomia*, the scope and sequence of the Gospel of the triune God.

Before turning to those topical and thematic connections, however, two preliminary matters are worthy of attention. First, I should comment briefly on how this exploration relates to contemporary debates regarding Barth's doctrines of election and of the Trinity. Second, I will briefly note the location of Christological material within the structures of dogmatic theology, noting its distributed nature and its interrelated connection to other key topics. Having considered those issues, we will be in a good position to reflect upon Barth's contributions and promptings to contemporary

---

1. For recent assessment of classic accounts by which one might make a judgment regarding the nature of Barth's doctrine of eternal generation as compared to, say, that of various patristic or later medieval figures, see the following helpful studies: Keith Johnson, "Augustine, Eternal Generation, and Evangelical Trinitarianism," *TrinJ* 32 (2011): 141–63; John Webster, "Eternal Generation," in *God Without Measure: Working Papers in Christian Doctrine*, vol. 1, *God and the Works of God* (London: T&T Clark, 2016), 29–41.

226

reflection on the doctrine of eternal generation. My goal is not to offer exposition of Barth's text so much as to note areas where his trajectory might lead, thus making good on my title: thinking *after* Barth about eternal generation.

PRELIMINARY MATTER 1: RELATIONSHIP TO THE DEBATE ON ELECTION AND THE TRINITY

How does my exploration relate to the suggestive account of evangelical historicism as developed in recent years by Bruce McCormack?[2] His account has implications, of course, for the doctrine of eternal generation, and he has begun to gesture toward that significance with some specificity by riffing in a Barthian manner of appropriating the Thomistic claim that that "the [divine] processions contain the [divine] missions."[3] I do not have time to mount any case for or against McCormack's proposal, but I should offer a couple of comments regarding its influence and its viability.

First, regarding its influence, I regularly observe that Barth interpretation often occurs in situations markedly different than Barth's. They take his material claims and put them to unintended functional uses. For example, several American and Canadian students of Barth take him to be

---

2. There are precursors to much of McCormack's argument in the German literature. For example, key elements can be found in this passage from Jüngel: "As the 'sum of the Gospel' and the 'very essence of all good news' God's election of grace is the beginning of 'all the ways and works of God.' In his ways and works God sets himself in relation. In speaking of a beginning of these ways and works, we mean a relation of God to that which he is not. For God himself 'has indeed no beginning.' It is thus a question of the beginning of God's *opera ad extra* [external works]. But as the beginning of all the ways and works of God, God's election of grace is not only an *opus Dei ad extra* [external work of God] or, more precisely, an *opus Dei ad extra externum* [external work of God directed outwards]; it is at the same time an *opus Dei ad extra internum* [external work of God directed inwards]. For election as such is not only a decision made by God and in so far an election which also certainly concerns him; it is equally a decision which affects God himself 'because originally God's election of man is a predestination not merely of man but of Himself.' If, then, the decision of the election of grace not only affects elect humanity but also at the same time affects God in a fundamental way, then it is dogmatically consistent to treat the doctrine of predestination as a part of the *doctrine of God*" (Eberhard Jüngel, *God's Being Is in Becoming: The Trinitarian Being of God in the Theology of Karl Barth*, trans. John Webster [Grand Rapids: Eerdmans, 2001], 82–84).

3. Bruce L. McCormack, "Processions and Missions: A Point of Convergence between Thomas Aquinas and Karl Barth," in *Thomas Aquinas and Karl Barth: An Unofficial Catholic-Protestant Dialogue*, ed. Bruce L. McCormack and Thomas Joseph White (Grand Rapids: Eerdmans, 2013), 99–126. Thomas Aquinas distinguished between the acts of nature and of will in his account of the triune being of God. Bruce McCormack has made much of the Thomistic claim that the divine processions and divine missions are one act with two terms. This is true. But Thomas also says—elsewhere in his doctrine of God—that there is a distinction between God's necessary, characteristic acts and his freely willed, creative acts (*ST* 1.41.2). McCormack has read one statement apart from its wider Trinitarian context. See further Matthew Levering, "Christ, the Trinity, and Predestination: McCormack and Aquinas," in *Trinity and Election in Contemporary Theology*, ed. Michael T. Dempsey (Grand Rapids: Eerdmans, 2011), 244–73.

MICHAEL ALLEN

a beacon of a leftward-leaning version of evangelical theology, and he is viewed as an intellectual symbol of viability for a continuing evangelicalism shorn of its more mindless fundamentalisms. In my Presbyterian context, he has sometimes been taken to represent an orthodox but nonconfessional theology upon which this tradition might venture forward. Of course, it is worth noting that Barth was responding to a very different context than American fundamentalism or to a traditional Presbyterianism (based on, for example, confessing the Westminster standards). He was responding to Harnack and later to Bultmann and to what they represented, which was, above all else, the liberal theology of the European churches. It is ironic when a figure who fought to bring a confession-less church back toward orthodoxy becomes a symbol of a movement to dial down the confessional standards of a very different denominational setting.

Something similar is occurring with regard to Barth's Christology and Trinitarian theology. For example, take this statement from Paul Dafydd Jones in his response to Paul Molnar regarding Barth's theology of the *logos asarkos*:

> Molnar's mistake, then, is to suppose that Barth epitomizes what he presumes to be dogmatically needful in the present day, namely, "*a clear and sharp distinction* between the immanent and economic Trinity," the corollary of which is an affirmation of the *logos asarkos*. This dogmatic claim inflates regulative claims about the independence and provenience of God to the point at which they distract from Barth's own convictions about the divine being. The plain (and assuredly critical) fact of divine freedom tells only one part of the divine story. Barth's focus is on what God *does* with God's freedom. His suggestion is that the economic event of Christ ramifies in the time and space of God's immanent life.[4]

Jones is right. Barth's focus—his rhetorical passion—is to emphasize that God wills to be with us and not apart from us and, thus, can only be known as he makes himself known amongst us. Barth is a Christ-centered theologian, if ever there was one, and the driving argument of the *Church Dogmatics* hits its high points in affirming what Barth elsewhere calls the "humanity of God." But Molnar is right: Barth affirms the *logos asarkos*, he speaks of the economy as "correlating" to (and not constituting) the inner

---

4. Paul Dafydd Jones, *The Humanity of Christ: Christology in Karl Barth's Church Dogmatics* (London: T&T Clark, 2008), 93.

ETERNAL GENERATION AFTER BARTH

life of God, and he locates the roots of God's willed decision to elect the Christ-story as his own in God's own inner loving freedom. Viewing the two together requires a contextual sensitivity, namely, Barth was responding in a time and to an intellectual milieu of cultural Christianity with a Christ-centered focus on the electing God. We do not live in such a time, at least not in the mainline religious traditions of North America. Our culturally compelling presuppositions about God are psychologistic and historicist, not anything driven by the categories of classical theism. While Barth contextually and rhetorically emphasized the economic focus of theology upon the Christ event (which Jones rightly attests), I can only imagine that his concern today would regard God's freedom, transcendence, and holiness (which Molnar champions). So our thinking about Barth's doctrine of God and any utility it might have for contemporary thinking needs to be mindful of changing contexts.

Second, regarding its viability as a historical and a systematic proposal, I wish to suggest a thesis directly regarding Barth interpretation: Barth overtly teaches a fundamentally traditional doctrine of the Trinity and extensively provides a doctrinal matrix within which that traditional doctrine might be radically retooled. If one looks at his overt Trinitarian claims in I/1 and even later in his occasional comments in his final years, he upholds a classic approach to the doctrine of eternal generation, specifically, and the eternal character of the triune God, broadly speaking. But attention to his historicized Christology—in particular, to the way he reconfigures the two states of Christ and moves away from operative use of the language of "natures"—suggests a line of reasoning that might well lead elsewhere. "Two roads diverged" in the corpus of Karl Barth—I think honesty compels that we acknowledge this reality.

I suggest we call an end to this focus upon the historical question and move instead to the dogmatic query. Is election an act of the divine will or an instance of divine self-constitution? Is God's triune being an object or implicate of God's free election of Jesus Christ? More specifically, can we speak of the antecedence of eternal generation to the Son's faithful embrace of his Father's sending? There remains a place for Barth studies as such, but the historical question is far less interesting and important than the theological question: which rubric better provides categories to keep us alert to the way Holy Scripture schools us regarding the character of the God of the gospel, evangelical historicism or reformed catholicity?

Paul Nimmo has mounted a provisional defense of McCormack's Barth with respect to its constructive value. Against the charge that McCormack's

MICHAEL ALLEN

view of the doctrine of God leaves us with a hidden God behind the decree of election and, thus, the decree to be triune, Nimmo states,

> One might note initially that it betrays a very substantialist mode of thinking, wherein substances are complete and definable in themselves above any historical action or relation. The corollary to this is that in order for there to be an action, there must be a subject. This might be intuitively satisfying (and perhaps even true) for contingent beings such as human agents; but to assume that it holds for God without further analysis is nothing less than anthropomorphic speculation without biblical foundation.[5]

The terminology of substance is beside the point here, inasmuch as it is an accidental reference to the doctrinal point made by McCormack's detractors (likely few of whom, if any, would defend Aristotelian substance metaphysics as such). Ultimately Nimmo's defense suggests that with respect to creatures a subject precedes action, while with respect to God a subject may not need to precede action.

Without employing the language of substance, we can restrict ourselves to fundamental doctrinal terminology and convey the point. The perfect God acts to make himself present to others. Presence necessarily implies (logically) prior perfection. One might scroll through the divine economy to trace acts that demonstrate this rhythm: creation *ex nihilo*, unilateral covenant initiation, and, of course, the incarnation of the preexistent Son. In fact, I think the logic of the gospel requires us to say the exact opposite of that which Nimmo suggests. It is only with respect to creatures that acts precede a stable subject, for ours is a pilgrim existence. But with respect to God, any action flows forth from God's settled identity. Again, this is not the result of a substance metaphysics so much as it is simply an attempt to honor the logic of basic doctrines like the aseity of God, on the one hand, and creation *ex nihilo*, on the other hand.

All this is to say that my sympathies are with the classical rendering of Barth's Christology and Trinitarian theology, though it will soon be seen that some of Barth's most significant insights involve new or freshly rearticulated applications or implications of those classical teachings.[6]

---

5. Paul T. Nimmo, "Election and Evangelical Thinking: Challenges to Our Way of Conceiving the Doctrine of God," in *New Perspectives for Evangelical Theology: Engaging with God, Scripture, and the World*, ed. Tom Greggs (London: Routledge, 2010), 36.

6. Evangelical historicism does present a particular approach to the doctrine of eternal generation,

PRELIMINARY MATTER 2: CHRISTOLOGY IN THE STRUCTURE OF DOGMATIC THEOLOGY

A second preliminary observation warrants our attention. Christology—in particular, the doctrine of eternal generation—occurs at numerous locations in the *Church Dogmatics*. Having been addressed in volume I/1 as a part of the doctrine of "God the Son," it reappears in I/2 with other christological material before surfacing yet again (at great length, both explicitly and implicitly) in volume IV/1 amidst the doctrine of reconciliation, specifically the section on "the way of the Son into the far country."

John Webster addresses "the place of Christology in systematic theology" in a recent essay. He notes that "in much modern (and notably, but not exclusively, Protestant) systematic theology these matters have acquired a special prominence, because discrete teaching about the person and work of Christ has often annexed the fundamental role which earlier theologies more naturally recognized in teaching about the Trinity, and so has come to speak as the hallmark of the genuineness, purity and distinctiveness of Christian doctrine."[7] Webster notes this tendency but observes that the distinctiveness of the Christ cannot be glibly elided into the primacy of Christology, in as much as attesting the Christ requires a whole spate of categories already at work with which the Christ is identified (e.g., God, the human, the covenant). Thus Webster prompts us to begin further back and address God himself (*theologia*) and all things "relative to him as their origin and end" (*oikonomia*).[8]

Does this distinction and order not privilege the abstract? Does it not make the incarnation and the mission of the Son a secondary or accidental matter? Webster notes such concerns and offers three clarifying comments to this schematic of theology and economy as the subjects of this intellectual and spiritual discipline. First, although theology is primary and economy is secondary, the distinction is not a separation. In other words, "the preeminence of theology does not mean that economy is an accidental or

---

but in doing so it does not actually present a novelty. Centuries ago, Wilhelmus à Brakel reflected upon such an approach. In his analysis of eternal generation, he addressed a number of "evasive arguments," the third of which was: "The second Person is called the Son because He agreed to assume the human nature in the Counsel of Peace, and for the accomplishing of the work of redemption was manifested in the flesh as the visible image of the invisible God" (Wilhelmus à Brakel, *The Christian's Reasonable Service*, vol. 1, *God, Man, and Christ*, ed. Joel Beeke, trans. Bartel Elshout [Grand Rapids: Reformation Heritage, 1992], 150).

7. John Webster, "Christology, Theology, Economy: The Place of Christology in Systematic Theology," in *God Without Measure*, 44.

8. Ibid., 45–46, citing Aquinas, *ST* 1.1.7, ad. For further analysis of Thomas on this point, see Gilles Emery, "*Theologia* and *Dispensatio*: The Centrality of the Divine Missions in St. Thomas's Trinitarian Theology," *The Thomist* 74 (2010): 515–61.

MICHAEL ALLEN

inessential element of systematic theology."[9] He goes on: "A treatment of faith which did not proceed beyond the divine essence and triunity to the effects of God would be Christianly unthinkable. But these effects, including the incarnation of the Word, are just that: effects, only intelligible when their cause is grasped."[10] Second, while theology precedes economy materially, economy communicates or reveals theology. Further, "the outer works of God are his works, not some remote operation which is not proper to him, and this continuity of acting subject means that God's economic acts elucidate his inner being, even though they do not exhaust it."[11] Third, this talk of the material order and the epistemological order need not be matched necessarily by the pedagogical order. In other words, one could begin with the economy, if one does so in a way that clarifies that the economy is secondary in the order of being. Pedagogy may be shaped by various needs of the time, place, and setting; the metaphysical primacy of God's inner life, however, must be attested in one way or another.

Barth illustrates these principles in the architectonics of the *Church Dogmatics*. While he does cycle back to address the doctrine of God amidst his Christology, he has already reflected upon God's inner life in *CD* I/1–2 and again in II/1. Still further, he locates election as an act of will rather than nature in II/2. One need not be convinced of the precise nature of his Christocentrism to appreciate the systemic application of his Christology consistently across the *CD*. I remain broadly unpersuaded that he has provided a coherent and viable way beyond natural theology and what he views as its two forms, Protestant liberalism and Roman Catholicism. And yet I marvel at the way in which he puts Christology to use by exploring how the Trinitarian relations of origin must be extended in the direction of relations of ongoing intra-Trinitarian communion and by showing how the mission of the incarnate Son corresponds to the eternal life of the Son. And how, in so doing, he continues to honor this distinction and ordered relation between theology and economy. It is to these connections that we now turn.

Theologia: THE OBEDIENCE OF THE ETERNAL SON

Barth had already begun with and dealt with God—yet theology continued to haunt the *Church Dogmatics*. Quite literally, the doctrine of God had been addressed in volume two, and yet there is no getting around the fact that

---

9. Webster, "Christology, Theology, Economy," 46.
10. Ibid., 48.
11. Ibid., 46.

ETERNAL GENERATION AFTER BARTH

volume four, addressing the doctrine of reconciliation, returns to *theology*. In speaking this way, I am not making the obvious judgment that Barth continues to speak on matters that concern religious issues or regard divine things, as the term "theology" is employed in North America, nor do I make the slightly more particularly Christian claim that Barth addresses matters of Christian principle, as the term "theology" would be put to use in Great Britain; rather, I use the term theology in its classic, scholastic sense (*theologia*) to refer specifically to affirmations of God's own being (over against his relations to others). And I do so to note the startling reality that in this extended account of the incarnation, that central hub of God's involvement with others (when another nature is assumed by the Second Person of the Trinity), *theologia* returns as a matter for our consideration.

Why this? Why here? Barth's theological principles compel him to think theology whenever and wherever God reveals himself and, we might add, nowhere else. In this vein, Barth continues the Reformed tradition's antispeculative, iconoclastic approach. He adds his own spin to it, of course, in the way he articulates its Scripture principle and in the distinctive Christocentrism that flavors his hermeneutical appropriation of that text.[12] Such matters, however, are not my concern in this chapter. I do not want to consider where he draws theological matters from, but instead where he takes them to. In other words, it is worth highlighting the way in which God's self-revelation in the incarnation and in the reconciling work of the incarnate Son is apparently an event (or a narrative cycle of such events) that tells us of God (his being in and of himself). So right in the vortex of his exposition of the gospel narrative—the nexus of divine economic activity—Barth turns back to *theologia*.

And Barth's application of that methodological return to theology is also noteworthy. In *Church Dogmatics* IV/1, §59.1, he turns to the obedience of the Son to the Father in the Son's incarnational life and death as well as his perfect life in the Godhead.[13] This discussion occurs amidst chapter fourteen of the *Church Dogmatics*, on "Jesus Christ, the Lord as Servant," in other words, on the humiliation of the Son. More specifically this paragraph focuses upon "the obedience of the Son of God," to which later part-volumes will offer contrasting and paired reflections upon "the exaltation of the Son of Man" (§64) and "the glory of the mediator" (§69). It is followed in this chapter and part-volume by reflections upon pride

---

12. See esp. Barth, *CD* IV/1, 177.
13. Barth, *CD* IV/1, 192–210.

(§60), justification (§61), the Spirit and the gathering of the community (§62), and the Spirit and faith (§63). But the most pertinent material for our purposes is specifically found in §59.1, amidst his exposition of the "way of the Son of God into the far country."

What *theologia* is found in this reference to and rumination upon the incarnate Son's trek into the wilderness? Some say that Barth historicizes Christology and, in so doing, the Godhead.[14] And to the extent that he fails to do so consistently, we might press on further. For example, Bruce McCormack claims that §57, specifically its attention directed to the methodological or epistemological rule played by God's self-disclosure as willed in the covenant of grace, "is significant for the treatment of the doctrine of the incarnation which will follow in §59.1 in that the door is closed firmly on the thought of the incarnation of a Logos understood along the lines of an abstract metaphysical subject."[15] Thus the economy is predicated of God, and, more strikingly, God is subject only of this economy and in no other way (though not only *in* this economy). In McCormack's rendering, this will lead to an unease with a number of pieces of classical Christian divinity: divine impassibility and divine simplicity, for starters. His iconoclasm here stems not from a philosophical aversion to such ideas but from an exegetical and hermeneutical conviction that they fail to be coherently confessed of the one whom the gospel narrative names as the eternal Son.[16] This one suffered—this one cannot be construed along the lines of simplicity—this one reveals the Father—and thus, the Godhead cannot be impassible or simple.[17]

As mentioned above (regarding the first preliminary matter), I will not be addressing this claim about genetic development within and beyond Barth. It is worth noting, however, that McCormack's approach has been followed by or, perhaps we might say, paralleled by a number of significant

---

14. Bruce L. McCormack, "Karl Barth's Historicized Christology: Just How 'Chalcedonian' Is It?," in *Orthodox and Modern: Studies in the Theology of Karl Barth* (Grand Rapids: Baker Academic, 2008), 201–34.

15. Ibid., 219.

16. Barth, *CD* IV/1, 192.

17. Admittedly, McCormack continues to develop his constructive arguments (as well as the historical excurses that relate to them, at least with regard to figures beyond Barth and movements deeper in the tradition), and thus any judgments regarding his project remain provisional. Thus far the widest portrait he has sketched in a publicly accessible way is his series of Kantzer Lectures delivered at the Henry Center of Trinity Evangelical Divinity School in 2011 (available online: http://henrycenter.tiu.edu/kantzer-lectures-in-revealed-theology/past-lectures-publications/bruce-mccormack/). For an assessment of his project to this point (noting some modifications that have already been undertaken regarding the notion of divine freedom), see Scott R. Swain, "Grace and Being: Bruce McCormack on the Gospel's God," in *The God of the Gospel: Robert Jenson's Trinitarian Theology* (Downers Grove, IL: IVP Academic, 2013), 208–27.

ETERNAL GENERATION AFTER BARTH

figures doing constructive work downstream from volume four of the *Church Dogmatics*. Jüngel, Pannenberg, Moltmann, and Jenson each approach this kind of historicizing (albeit they tend to tilt either towards protology or eschatology). To each of them, one might respond in many ways, perhaps most pointedly by noting that in IV/1 Barth insistently uses the language of "correspondence" to speak of the link between *theologia* and *oikonomia*, a term that notes a distinction within a unity.[18] The route of reading divine eternity in or within history may not fit Barth's structural rhetoric here.

Another way might be pursued, however, which sought to honor Barth's theological principle—that the incarnation reveals the Father and so our Christology must again return us to *theologia*—without discarding a classical Trinitarian theology and its (at least classically adjoined) complex of divine attributes.[19] In another place Scott Swain and I have sought to make good on this sort of project.[20] In that argument, we contend that "the obedience of the eternal Son in the economy of salvation is the proper mode whereby he enacts the undivided work of the Trinity 'for us and our salvation.' More fully, the obedience of the Son is the economic extension of his eternal generation to a Spirit-enabled, creaturely life of obedience unto death, and therefore the redemptive foundation for his bringing 'many sons to glory' (Heb. 2:10)."[21]

A number of objections can be raised to such an approach, arising from both classical and modern motivations. First, can the idea of the Son's obedience, within the realm of *theologia* and not merely the incarnate *oikonomia*, be held alongside the conviction that the Godhead shares a single will? Second, would the Son's obedience in any way render his omnipotence (as the Almighty) problematic? Third, does any attempt to affirm the eternal Son's obedience within a classical Trinitarian theology not fall afoul of a wider problem, namely, the essentialism of a substance ontology? These questions would not exist, at least not in that form, for anyone taking

---

18. See, e.g., Barth, *CD* IV/1, 187; IV/2, 43–44. Paul Jones uses the language of the incarnate Christ's election being "coincident" and "coordinate" with the inner life of the Trinity rather than being "constituted" by it, which appears to be a shrewd judgment of what is being implied with this terminology (*The Humanity of Christ*, 81n51).

19. It was Gregory of Nyssa, after all, who said that "obedience is part of his nature" (*Against Eunomius*, in *NPNF²* 5:122 [2.11]).

20. Scott Swain and Michael Allen, "The Obedience of the Eternal Son," *International Journal of Systematic Theology* 15, no. 2 (April 2013): 114–34. See also Swain and Allen, "The Obedience of the Eternal Son: Catholic Trinitarianism and Reformed Christology," in *Christology, Ancient and Modern: Explorations in Constructive Dogmatics*, ed. Oliver D. Crisp and Fred Sanders (Grand Rapids: Zondervan, 2013), 74–95. Some significant parallels can be seen in Bruce D. Marshall, "The Unity of the Triune God: Reviving an Ancient Question," *The Thomist* 74 (2010): 1–32.

21. Swain and Allen, "The Obedience of the Eternal Son," 117.

MICHAEL ALLEN

Barth's Christology into a historicizing trajectory. These queries necessarily arise, however, for someone who remains committed to the attributes and Trinitarian metaphysics of classical Christian divinity and who seeks to honor the epistemological rule of the incarnation—*à la* Barth.[22]

Oikonomia: THE FAITH OF THE INCARNATE SON

Barth's doctrine of eternal generation, and his wider Christological approach, not only leads to a methodological return to *theologia* in considering the obedience of the eternal Son, but it also prompts further attention to the particularity of the Son's economic course. Specifically, we will see that the eternal receptivity of the Son, who is marked by filiation, flows forth out of his divine fullness into an economy not only of incarnation but of a life of trust and obedience to his Father's will.

As mentioned above, the obedience of the eternal Son extends the eternal generation of the Son into the economy. Thomas Aquinas taught that the missions contain the processions or, to put it otherwise, that the processions extend outward to the missions. Yet this axiom precedes even that high medieval distinction, for Cyril of Alexandria elaborated on the manner in which the eternal generation of the Son necessarily shaped the revelation bestowed by the Son in his gracious economy of making the Father known.[23]

Might we press further and suggest that eternal generation not only finds extension in the reality of the incarnation but also in the patterns of that incarnate life? Barth's Christology prompts us to relate the humble and dependent manner of the lordly servant to his eternally receptive character in the Godhead.

Ought we to go this route? Barth's exegesis suggests that the New Testament—particularly the Pauline writings—do point toward this kind of economic specificity. Barth was well ahead of his time, as it were, in rendering the Pauline phraseology *pistis christou* in the manner of a subjective genitive ("Christ's faith") rather than an objective genitive ("faith in the Christ").[24] Whereas New Testament studies would come around to this

---

22. Significant concern has been raised in a thoughtful way by Thomas Joseph White in the essay "Intra-Trinitarian Obedience and Nicene-Chalcedonian Christology," *Nova et Vetera* 6, no. 2 (2008): 377–402. Swain and Allen have attempted to address his concerns, however, in their essay.

23. See especially his Commentary on John 12:49–50. For analysis, see Matthew R. Crawford, *Cyril of Alexandria's Trinitarian Theology of Scripture* (New York: Oxford University Press, 2014), 20–21.

24. This phraseology occurs in the following Pauline texts: Rom 3:22, 26; Gal 2:16 (2x), 20; 3:22; Phil 3:9; Eph 3:12.

translational and interpretive move only in the 1980s, Barth anticipated this move by decades.[25] Owing to his efforts, theologians were talking about the faith of the Christ (at least in oblique ways) long before Richard Hays and others led the charge to rethink Pauline studies in the 1980s and 1990s.[26] The notion had, by that point, already been mentioned or even discussed in the works of Gerhard Ebeling, Thomas Torrance, James Torrance, John Murray, Wolfhart Pannenberg, Jon Sobrino, and the United Presbyterian Church of the United States of America's "Confession of 1967."[27]

Exegetical reflection upon those *pistis christou* phrases remains debated. I confess that I remain convinced by the more traditional rendering of them as objective genitives ("faith in Christ"), for specific syntactical and rhetorical reasons and not due to any dogmatic presuppositions that would render the subjective genitive questionable or problematic. Yet while I remain convinced by more traditional exegesis, it seems equally significant to note that Barth's broader point may find surer footing on other biblical grounds.[28] For example, the Epistle to the Hebrews addresses the incarnate life of the Messiah with greater pointedness than any of those Pauline texts (see Heb 2:10–3:6; 4:14–5:10). This may be a case of bad texts being employed to prompt a good doctrine, if the Christ's faith is a significant facet of Christology that was rediscovered by questionable Pauline exegesis but finds better scriptural warrant in Hebrews and possibly the Gospels. Elsewhere I have explored the coherence of claims that the incarnate Son did exercise faith—anthropologically, covenantally, metaphysically—as well as the soteriological significance and ethical implications of such an attestation.[29] In that initial study on *The Christ's Faith*, I only hinted at the way in which the economic form of the Son's earthly life as a life of "ec-centric" dependence mirrored or extended in a new way that intra-Trinitarian life of the eternally begotten Son. In a comparative dogmatic analysis of the

---

25. See, e.g., Karl Barth, *The Epistle to the Romans*, trans. Edwyn C. Hoskyns, 6th ed. (London: Oxford University Press, 1968), 96; Barth, "Gospel and Law," in *Community, State, and Church: Three Essays*, trans. G. Ronald Howe (Garden City, NY: Anchor, 1960), 74. But note that Barth seems to render Phil 3:9, at least, with the relevant phrase as an objective genitive: Barth, *The Epistle to the Philippians*, 40th anniv. ed., trans. James W. Leitch (Louisville: Westminster John Knox, 2002), 99–103.

26. The key work here is Richard B. Hays, *The Faith of Jesus Christ: The Narrative Substructure of Galatians 3:1–4:11*, 2nd ed. (Grand Rapids: Eerdmans, 2001).

27. Full bibliography can be found in Michael Allen, *The Christ's Faith: A Dogmatic Account* (London: T&T Clark, 2009), 17–22.

28. For accounts that are more deferential to the exegetical claims of a few recent New Testament scholars (e.g., Richard Hays), see David Stubbs, "The Shape of Soteriology and the *Pistis Christou* Debate," *Scottish Journal of Theology* 61, no. 2 (2008), 137–57; Douglas Harink, *Paul among the Postliberals: Pauline Theology beyond Christendom and Modernity* (Grand Rapids: Brazos, 2003).

29. Allen, *The Christ's Faith*.

place that the Christ's faith might hold within the theological schemas of Thomas Aquinas, the federal theologians, and Karl Barth, I noted that each had their own way of sustaining "this axiomatic claim that the works *ad extra* reveal the life *ad intra*," more specifically, that the "faith of the Christ would be construed by each of these dogmatic systems as the economic echo of eternal filiation which marks the Son in relation to his Father."[30] I noted that Aquinas uses the language of processions and missions, the federal theologians employ the doctrine of the covenant of redemption (*pactum salutis*), while Barth turns to the obedience of the Son of God and its relation to eternal generation at this axiomatic point.

I noted in that initial study that these three dogmatic systems each offered greater testimony of the immanent life of God than is currently on offer in many of the most notable approaches of the supposed Trinitarian renaissance of the last century. Each approach—Thomas, the federal tradition, and, yes, Barth—compels us to speak not only of the evangelical history of the triune God, but of the fullness of that God's life from which that history receives its movement. And reflection upon the way in which the shape of that economy—specifically, the Son's obedience of faith before his Father and ours—can inform our account of that immanent triune life. Thus, I pressed forward in a more recent article to explore this connection between *oikonomia* and *theologia* still further.[31] In that account an attempt was made to note the widespread import of the Son's receptivity or fidelity. Thus, "the earthly fidelity of Jesus is a distributed doctrine in as much as it manifests itself in every part of his earthly sojourn: the willingness of the eternal Son to assume human nature, the virgin birth, the patient apprenticeship of a Son being brought to perfection, the ministry, and, finally, the passion and bruising at the behest of his neighbors."[32] I also argued there, with Barth, that Christology must lead to a return to our doctrine of God. Thus, soteriology must be rooted in Christology, and I made the effort to "show that the Christological account flows forth from the eternal relations of the Trinity." In so doing, a thesis was unpacked: "In the eternal life of the perfect God, the divine Son pleases the Father in the Spirit and, therefore, the divine Son trusts the Father by the Spirit's power during his earthly pilgrimage."[33]

---

30. Ibid., 180–81.

31. Michael Allen, "'From the Time He Took the Form of a Servant': The Christ's Pilgrimage of Faith," *International Journal of Systematic Theology* 16, no. 1 (2014): 4–24.

32. Ibid., 5.

33. Ibid., 6.

ETERNAL GENERATION AFTER BARTH

Much of that argument proceeded by way of engaging the biblical exegesis, not of Karl Barth but of the early church fathers (especially Athanasius and Gregory of Nyssa), Thomas Aquinas, and some sixteenth- and seventeenth-century Reformed theologians (Bullinger, Ursinus, Polanus, Perkins, and Turretin play key roles in the argument). And more surely needs to be said than that which was expressed regarding the ways in which Spirit Christology's attempts to construe the incarnate action of the Son must be further rooted in a Logos Christology, whereby the single subject acts according to his Spiritually graced human nature *and* his divine personhood and nature as the Word incarnate. Here Cyril of Alexandria could further enhance the argument, particularly by drawing on his anti-Nestorian polemic regarding the lived significance of the Son's divine nature during his earthly sojourn.[34] But all that patristic, medieval, and reformational conversation aside, it remains the case that Barth has prompted such attention. For this reason, Kevin Vanhoozer has spoken of a need to engage the doctrine of God in terms of a "post-Barthian Thomism."[35]

CONCLUSION: TOWARD A REFORMED CATHOLIC CONFESSION OF ETERNAL GENERATION

This exploration has been brief and suggestive, noting ways Karl Barth's theological ruminations prompt doctrinal development in matters regarding the life of God in himself as well as the economy of the gospel. While his doctrine of eternal generation is remarkably unremarkable in and of itself, his attempt to show its systematic vitality must be described as both vivid and provocative. I have tried to offer the briefest of descriptions of ways my own reflections on *theologia* and *oikonomia* have alike been stirred by his methodological and material concerns, even though I neither consider myself a Barthian nor wind up agreeing with many of his most central doctrinal moves.

Nonetheless, as a systematic and historical theologian, I must note with Vanhoozer that any Thomism or Augustinianism or Scotism or any other classical articulation of God's character today will benefit from being reiterated in a "post-Barthian" fashion. For Barth's central reminder and prompt is one deep at the core of biblical, patristic, and, yes, Reformed theology, namely, that all speculation must be tethered to and tested by God's

---

34. See Crawford, *Cyril of Alexandria's Trinitarian Theology of Scripture*, 35–42.
35. See Kevin J. Vanhoozer, *Remythologizing Theology: Divine Action, Passion, and Authorship* (Cambridge: Cambridge University Press, 2010), esp. pt. 2.

self-revelation, most centrally in the person and work of the incarnate Son. We do well, as we think about the classical doctrine of eternal generation, to think forward to its connections with the specific shape of the gospel economy as well as backward toward its wider theological significance in the immanent life of God. In both facets of Christological reflection, while Barth may not provide the answers, he does prompt the right questions.

CONTEMPORARY STATEMENTS

CHAPTER 13

PHILOSOPHICAL MODELS OF ETERNAL GENERATION

MARK MAKIN

THE DOCTRINE OF ETERNAL GENERATION has fallen on hard times of late. Critics of eternal generation dwell overwhelmingly on whether the doctrine finds support in Scripture, and this is as it should be. If no biblical warrant exists for eternal generation, then Christians should simply reject the doctrine. In the end, the doctrine of eternal generation, like all other doctrines, stands or falls with Scripture. Yet several critics have gone beyond disputing the doctrine's biblical warrant, raising philosophical-theological objections to eternal generation. Eternal generation, critics charge, is unintelligible and entails subordinationism by robbing the Son of necessary existence and self-existence (aseity). Heavy charges, indeed, that would undoubtedly undermine the doctrine of eternal generation if true.

While some progress has been made against these philosophical-theological objections, proponents of eternal generation have been hampered by their inability to produce philosophical models of eternal generation that withstand the unintelligibility and subordinationism objections.[1] In this chapter I defend eternal generation by developing three viable philosophical models of the doctrine that withstand these objections: a causal model, a grounding model, and an essential dependence model. Although these models cannot provide a positive case for the doctrine of eternal generation, they demonstrate

---

1. William Hasker admirably defends eternal generation against philosophical-theological objections, but he does not propose a philosophical model of the doctrine. See William Hasker, *Metaphysics and the Tri-Personal God* (Oxford: Oxford University Press, 2013), ch. 26.

that eternal generation is philosophically coherent and theologically sound. Eternal generation cannot be dismissed on philosophical-theological grounds.

I begin by presenting a minimal statement of the doctrine of eternal generation, rehearsing the unintelligibility and subordinationism objections, and laying out desiderata for philosophical models of eternal generation. I then develop a causal model, a grounding model, and an essential dependence model in turn. With each model, I show how it meets the minimal statement of the doctrine, satisfies the desiderata, and withstands the unintelligibility and subordinationism objections. Potential drawbacks of each model are noted along the way.[2]

THE DOCTRINE, OBJECTIONS, AND DESIDERATA

According to the doctrine of eternal generation, the Father eternally begets the Son. But what does this mean? What exactly does affirming that the Father eternally begets the Son commit proponents of eternal generation to, minimally? Begetting suggests dependence. The Father's begetting of the Son implies that the Son *depends on* the Father for his existence or, equivalently, the Son exists *in virtue of* the Father. Much like my son depends on me for his existence, the Son somehow depends on the Father for his existence. The begetting of the Son is eternal at least in the sense that the Son exists *eternally*. Whether God exists in time or not, there was never a time at which the Son was not. At minimum, then, proponents of eternal generation seem committed to the following statement:

> *Eternal Generation*: Necessarily, the Son depends on the Father for his existence, yet the Son exists eternally.

In other words, eternal generation requires necessary eternal existential dependence. Whatever it means for the Father to eternally beget the Son, it means at least this.[3]

This minimal statement of the doctrine of eternal generation must be interpreted with two crucial constraints in mind. As the ancient church

---

2. I defend my own essential dependence model of eternal generation over against causal and grounding models in "God from God: The Essential Dependence Model of Eternal Generation," in *Religious Studies* (forthcoming). There, I take a "half-empty" view of causal and grounding models of eternal generation; here, I take a "half-full" view.

3. To prevent the Father from "deifying" the Son, less minimal statements of the doctrine add that the Father "communicates" the divine essence (*ousia*) to the Son. In contrast, the Father "generates" the personal subsistence (*hypostasis*) of the Son. See, for example, Hasker, *Tri-Personal God*, 220; and Keith Johnson, "What Would Augustine Say to Evangelicals Who Reject the Eternal Generation of the Son?," *Southern Baptist Journal of Theology* 16 (2012), 26.

PHILOSOPHICAL MODELS OF ETERNAL GENERATION

stressed, the Father begets the Son "of necessity" and the Son is "begotten, not made." The Father begetting the Son "of necessity" prohibits eternal generation from being contingent. The necessity of eternal generation entails that the Father and the Son are mutually inseparable. Just as the Son cannot exist without the Father, the Father cannot exist without the Son; necessarily, the Father exists if and only if the Son exists. The necessity of eternal generation, however, does not entail that the Father begets the Son against his will. Nothing forces the Father to beget the Son; rather, the Father willingly affirms the betting of the Son. Moreover, the Son is "not made" or created. Eternal generation cannot amount to eternal creation. The relation between the Father and the Son must differ importantly from the relation between the Father and creation.

Despite these constraints, critics of eternal generation have sought to undermine the doctrine on philosophical-theological grounds. According to the *unintelligibility objection*, eternal generation is simply unintelligible. Erickson, for example, maintains that the doctrine "does not make sense philosophically," deriding it as "meaningless."[4] He elaborates:

> Philosophically, [eternal generation] has been deemed by many to draw
> a distinction that does not make sense: to insist on some sort of eternal
> derivation of being from the Father, or the Father being eternally the
> source of the subsistence of the other two persons, yet in such a way
> that they are not at all created by him.[5]

Driscoll and Breshears similarly complain that "the term 'begotten' could never be defined with any clarity, so it was of little use."[6] Eternal generation falls on an unhappy spectrum somewhere between philosophically incoherent, at worst, and unclear, at best. Wherever it may fall, eternal generation is unintelligible, and so untenable.

Another, more sophisticated objection to eternal generation is the *subordinationism objection*. Critics who level this objection allege that the doctrine of eternal generation entails subordinationism, the view that the Son is less than fully divine. Eternal generation, they contend, robs the Son of two divine attributes: necessary existence and self-existence (aseity). The doctrine robs

---

4. Millard Erickson, *Who's Tampering with the Trinity? An Assessment of the Subordination Debate* (Grand Rapids: Kregel, 2009), 251.

5. Ibid., 184.

6. Mark Driscoll and Gerry Breshears, *Doctrine: What Christians Should Believe* (Wheaton, IL: Crossway, 2010), 28.

the Son of *necessary existence* because eternal generation cannot but render the Son's existence contingent. Although proponents of eternal generation insist that the Father begets the Son "of necessity," some argue the doctrine entails that it is possible for the Father to exist without the Son. If the Father causes the Son to exist, and causation is contingent, then the Son could have not existed.[7] Thus, the Son lacks necessary existence. Eternal generation robs the Son of self-existence or *aseity* because the Son exists in virtue of the Father. According to Yandell, aseity is "the property *existing without being caused by anything else.*"[8] On the doctrine of eternal generation, Yandell claims the Father acts and the Son results, implying that the Father causes the Son to exist. Since the Father causes the Son's existence, the Son lacks aseity. At best, the Son possesses a kind of knockoff aseity or what he dubs "'next door to aseity'—aseity regarding every being but one."[9] Craig raises the same worry but conceives of aseity more broadly. Aseity, for Craig, is the property of existing without depending on anything else: "God is not dependent upon any other being for His existence. . . . God does not exist through another or from another. He just exists in and of Himself, independent of everything else."[10] On this broader conception of aseity, if the Son's existence depends in any way (causal or otherwise) on the Father, then the Son lacks aseity. "Even if [eternal generation] takes place necessarily and apart from the Father's will," reasons Craig, "the Son is less than the Father because the Father alone exists *a se*, whereas the Son exists through another (*ab alio*)."[11] Eternal generation thus robs the Son of the divine attributes of aseity and necessary existence, rendering the Son less than fully divine. In this way, the doctrine of eternal generation entails subordinationism.

Any viable philosophical model of eternal generation must meet the minimal statement of eternal generation and withstand the unintelligibility and subordinationism objections. Every model will involve some sort of dependence relation between the Father and the Son. But what more

---

7. Paul Helm pushes this line of reasoning against Richard Swinburne's view of eternal generation in *Eternal God: A Study of God without Time* (Oxford: Oxford University Press, 2010), 280–81. On a related note, William Lane Craig claims that the Son "becomes an effect contingent upon the Father" (Craig, "A Formulation and Defense of the Doctrine of the Trinity," http://www.reasonablefaith.org/a-formulation-and-defense-of-the-doctrine-of-the-trinity.) He could mean by this that the Son exists only contingently and lacks necessary existence, but more likely he means that the Son's existence depends on the Father.

8. Keith Yandell, "Review of Metaphysics and the Tri-Personal God," in *Notre Dame Philosophical Reviews*, https://ndpr.nd.edu/news/48755-metaphysics-and-the-tri-personal-god/, 2014. Emphasis in original.

9. Ibid.

10. William Lane Craig, *God Over All: Divine Aseity and the Challenge of Platonism* (Oxford: Oxford University Press, 2016), 1.

11. Craig, "A Formulation and Defense."

PHILOSOPHICAL MODELS OF ETERNAL GENERATION

should we look for in a philosophical model of eternal generation? More specifically, what features must the dependence relation between the Father and the Son have? I submit four desiderata.

The first and most obvious desiderata is that the dependence relation must be able to *relate persons*. After all, eternal generation is a relation holding between two persons, the Father and the Son. So, for instance, if a proposed model involves a dependence relation that can only hold between events, then the model is not viable.

Second, the dependence relation between the Father and the Son must be *nondiachronic*. A diachronic relation holds across time; one of the relata is temporally prior to the other. If the relation between the Father and the Son were diachronic, then the Father's existence would be temporally prior to the Son's existence. There would be a time at which the Son does not exist. But there was never a time at which the Son was not. His existence is eternal. So the dependence relation cannot be diachronic. The relation between the Father and the Son can be nondiachronic by being simultaneous or timeless. Either way ensures that there was never a time at which the Son was not.

Third, a viable model of eternal generation must involve an *asymmetric* dependence relation between the Father and the Son. On the classical Christian doctrine of the Trinity, the Father eternally begets the Son—but not vice versa. Eternal generation is a one-way street. Demanding that the dependence relation be asymmetric rules out the possibility that the Son eternally begets the Father.

Fourth and finally, the dependence relation must *preclude spurious eternal generation*. The Father eternally begets the Son, but nothing else besides the Father should be said to do so. A viable model of eternal generation needs a dependence relation fine-grained enough to eliminate unwanted eternal generation. For example, a model entailing that any necessary existent, such as the number two, eternally begets the Son should be rejected out of hand.[12]

To sum up, a viable model must involve a dependence relation between the Father and the Son that can relate persons, is nondiachronic, is asymmetric, and precludes spurious eternal generation. Though perhaps not exhaustive, these four desiderata establish a sensible standard by which we can assess the

---

12. This precise problem dooms a modal dependence model of eternal generation. On a modal dependence model, eternal generation is a form of modal existential dependence. To say that the Father eternally begets the Son is just to say that necessarily, the Son exists only if the Father exists, and the Son exists eternally. Modal existential dependence, however, is not asymmetric and cannot preclude spurious eternal generation. I expand on these criticisms in my "God from God" (forthcoming).

viability of proposed models of eternal generation.[13] In what follows I argue that a causal model, a grounding model, and an essential dependence model each satisfy all four desiderata, meet the minimal statement of eternal generation, and withstand the unintelligibility and subordinationism objections.

CAUSAL MODEL

On a causal model of eternal generation, eternal generation is a form of causation. In its most basic form, it states:

> *Causal Model*: The Son is eternally begotten of the Father =$_{df.}$
> Necessarily, the Father causes the Son to exist eternally.

To say that the Father eternally begets the Son is just to say that necessarily, the Father causes the Son to exist eternally. Not just any old conception of causation will do, however. A causal model of eternal generation will require a more permissive conception of causation. Causation is widely assumed to relate events. A causal model needs causation to relate persons as well, not just events involving persons. Causation is likewise typically thought to be diachronic; the cause always precedes the effect in time. A causal model needs simultaneous or timeless causation to be possible. So for a causal model to be viable, one needs a conception of causation that allows for simultaneous or timeless causation between persons. This is not a popular conception of causation, but it's not crazy either.

Given this more permissive conception of causation, a causal model of eternal generation meets the minimal statement of the doctrine and satisfies all four desiderata. Necessarily, the Father causes the Son to exist (perhaps because causing the Son's existence is part of the Father's essence), and simultaneous or timeless causation allows for the Son to exist eternally. The more permissive conception of causation can relate persons and is nondiachronic, and causation is generally regarded to be asymmetric. Spurious eternal generation poses no threat since causation is sufficiently fine-grained; for instance, the model does not entail that the number two eternally begets the Son because the number two, while a necessary existent, does not cause the Son to exist.[14]

---

13. A potential fifth desiderata, which I discuss later when considering a grounding model of eternal generation, is that a model should account for the difference between generation and procession.

14. One might wonder how eternal generation differs from eternal creation on a casual model. Though the Son and creation are both caused by the Father, the Father causes creation out of nothing (*ex nihilo*), whereas the Father causes the Son out of himself (*ex Patre*).

248

PHILOSOPHICAL MODELS OF ETERNAL GENERATION

A causal model can also withstand the unintelligibility and subordination-ism objections. The more permissive conception of causation is meaningful and arguably philosophically coherent.[15] Causation remains compatible with necessary existence. God causes necessary existents like the number two to exist, yet the number two nonetheless exists necessarily. Similarly, the fact that the Father causes the Son to exist in no way undermines the Son's necessary existence. The Son's existence is caused, but it needn't be contingent.

That a causal model of eternal generation can preserve the Son's aseity is less obvious. Recall that Yandell defines aseity as the property of existing without being caused by anything else. The Father clearly causes the Son's existence on a causal model of eternal generation, so how can the Son still possess aseity? One way to mitigate the aseity worry emphasizes the familiar distinction between the divine essence (*ousia*) and the person (*hypostasis*) of the Son. Following John Calvin, we can maintain that the Son possesses aseity with respect to the divine essence, but not with respect to his person:

> Therefore we say that the deity in an absolute sense exists of itself; whence likewise we confess that the Son since he is God, exists of himself, but not in respect of his Person; indeed, since he is the Son, we say that he exists from the Father. Thus his essence is without beginning; while the beginning of his person is God himself.[16]

Unlike the Father, who possesses aseity with respect to the divine essence and his person, the Son only possesses aseity with respect to the divine essence. The Son differs from the Father in that he does not possess aseity with respect to his person, but it is not at all obvious that this difference entails that the Son is less than fully divine. That the Son must also possess aseity with respect to his person in order to be fully divine demands further argumentation, argumentation that critics of eternal generation have not provided.

Another way to mitigate the aseity worry invokes a distinction between things existing "inside" God and things existing "outside" God. Divine aseity, one might think, only precludes God from depending (causally or otherwise) on things existing "outside" God. Depending on things existing "inside" God does not violate divine aseity. Even Craig concedes that this

---

15. Immanuel Kant famously cites a ball resting on a pillow as an example of simultaneous causation in *The Critique of Pure Reason*. For a defense of simultaneous causation, see Myles Brand, "Simultaneous Causation," in *Time and Cause: Essays Presented to Richard Taylor*, ed. Peter van Inwagen (Dordrecht: D. Reidel, 1980), 137–53.

16. *Inst.* 1.13.25 and 1.13.19.

qualification on divine aseity is plausible. In another context, while discussing whether God depends on his thoughts, Craig observes, "Still, I think that we have to admit that there remains intuitively a sense, difficult to articulate, in which divine thoughts existing 'inside' God do not seem to violate divine aseity as do uncreated, Platonic, abstract objects existing 'outside' God."[17] The distinction between things existing "inside" and "outside" God is a murky one, to be sure. That said, if anything counts as existing "inside" God, it is the divine persons! On a causal model of eternal generation, the Father causes the Son's existence, and the Father exists "inside" God. Because the Son's existence is not caused by anything existing "outside" God, the Son possesses aseity *tout court*. Therefore, a causal model of eternal generation does not violate divine aseity. (The same reasoning holds for any model of eternal generation. If divine aseity only precludes the Son from depending on things existing "outside" God, then eternal generation cannot rob the Son of aseity.)

The drawbacks of a causal model of eternal generation are twofold. First, it requires a controversial, some might say incoherent, conception of causation. Someone who has independent philosophical reasons for rejecting simultaneous and timeless causation between persons will consider a causal model a nonstarter. Second, withstanding the subordinationism objection requires qualifying divine aseity. If divine aseity requires unqualified causal independence, then saying that the Son possesses aseity with respect to the divine essence or that the Son's existence is not caused by anything existing "outside" God will not be enough. The Son still lacks aseity with respect to his person, and the Father still causes the Son's existence. For those who think aseity requires unqualified causal independence, the Son simply cannot possess aseity on a causal model. The Son must settle for a kind of knockoff aseity. Even so, other plausible conceptions of aseity remain on which the Son fully possesses aseity.

Grounding Model

Although likely unfamiliar to anyone not immersed in contemporary analytic metaphysics, the past decade has witnessed burgeoning philosophical interest in a dependence relation called grounding.[18] Complete consensus

---

17. Craig, *God Over All*, 81.

18. For helpful introductions to the notion of grounding, see F. Correia and B. Schnieder, "Grounding: An Opinionated Introduction," in *Metaphysical Grounding: Understanding the Structure of Reality*, ed. Fabrice Correia and Benjamin Schnieder (Cambridge: Cambridge University Press, 2012), 1–36; and Ricky Bliss and Kelly Trogdon, "Metaphysical Grounding," in *The Stanford Encyclopedia of Philosophy*, ed. E. Zalta (Winter 2014 Edition), http://plato.stanford.edu/archives/win2014/entries/grounding/.

PHILOSOPHICAL MODELS OF ETERNAL GENERATION

on grounding has proven elusive, but grounding is generally taken to be an asymmetric relation of noncausal dependence. Grounding is widely regarded to be a necessary relation—that is, necessarily, if the grounds are present, then the grounded is present. Considerable disagreement surrounds the relata of grounding; for present purposes, however, I assume that grounding relates things from any ontological category, including persons such as the Father and the Son. Putative examples of grounding abound in philosophy: sets are grounded in their members, truths are grounded in their truthmakers, wholes are grounded in their parts, determinable properties are grounded in determinate properties, and so on. Consider a specific case of a determinate property grounding a determinable property: my navy blue sweater. The navyness of my sweater grounds its blueness. Notice that the blueness of my sweater asymmetrically depends on its navyness. My sweater is blue because it is navy; it is not navy because it is blue. The dependence relation here is taken to be noncausal largely because it is nondiachronic. The navyness of my sweater is not temporally prior to its blueness; these properties are instantiated simultaneously. This grounding relation is also necessary in that necessarily, if my sweater is navy, then it is blue. In this way, the blueness of my sweater necessarily, asymmetrically, and noncausally depends on its navyness. Every case of grounding will have these features.

These features of grounding bode well for a grounding model of eternal generation. According to a grounding model of eternal generation:

Grounding Model: The Son is eternally begotten of the Father =$_{df.}$
The Father grounds the Son.

A grounding model of eternal generation easily meets the minimal statement of the doctrine and satisfies all four desiderata. Because grounding is a necessary relation, it is necessary that if the Father exists, then the Son exists. And since the Father exists necessarily and eternally, it follows that necessarily, the Son depends on the Father for his existence and exists eternally. Every possible world is one in which the Father grounds the Son and the Son exists eternally. Grounding can relate persons because it relates things from any ontological category. It is asymmetric, nondiachronic, and fine-grained enough to preclude spurious eternal generation.

A grounding model also withstands the unintelligibility and subordinationism objections. To defend grounding's intelligibility, grounding enthusiasts point to putative examples of grounding and describe its formal features (e.g., irreflexivity, asymmetry, and transitivity). Grounding remains compatible with the Son's necessary existence and aseity. For example, the set that contains the number two as its sole member, {2}, is grounded in the number two, yet {2} still exists necessarily. Because grounding is noncausal, the Son possesses aseity because his existence is not caused by anything else. Even if one conceives of aseity more broadly as the property of existing without depending on anything else, the Son's existence still does not depend on anything existing "outside" God.

Suppose critics of eternal generation press further, insisting that aseity requires unqualified independence. Aseity demands that the Son cannot depend in any way on anything whatsoever, regardless of whether it exists "inside" or "outside" God. On a grounding model (or, for that matter, any model of eternal generation!), the Son still depends on the Father, so the Son does not possess unqualified independence. At this point, proponents of eternal generation ought to question such a sweeping conception of aseity. Why think that aseity requires unqualified independence? Why should divine aseity preclude the Son from depending on anything existing "inside" God (namely, the Father)? Eternal generation is a dependence relation located entirely "inside" God. As long as the dependence relation stays "inside" God, God is self-existent. God's existence does not depend on anything existing "outside" his triune self.[19] Furthermore, why should aseity preclude all forms of dependence? Aseity may rightly preclude causal dependence, but why should it preclude every form of dependence? After all, some dependence relations seem perfectly innocuous, posing no threat to divine aseity. Take modal existential dependence, for instance. One thing modally existentially depends on another just in case necessarily, the former exists only if the latter exists. God modally existentially depends on the number two, since necessarily, God exists only if the number two exists. Perhaps God modally existentially depends on the number two because numbers necessarily exist in virtue of God's nature. One could object to this picture for many reasons (for example, because it subverts God's freedom with respect to creation)—but not for the reason that modal existential dependence violates divine aseity.[20] If divine aseity is compatible with modal existential dependence, why can't it be compatible with grounding or essential dependence? Without additional argumentation, we have no

---

19. Craig in his more recent work regrettably refrains from discussing whether he still believes eternal generation robs the Son of aseity. At one point Craig remarks that the divine Persons "exist acceptably *a se*," but the context does not explicitly mention eternal generation. The suggestion seems to be that the Son possesses aseity in an acceptable sense because the Son's existence does not depend on anything existing "outside" God. Hedging with the adverb "acceptably" ostensibly indicates that the Son does not possess aseity in its fullest sense. See Craig, *God Over All*, 81–82, for the remark in context.

20. Tellingly, Craig (*God Over All*, 57–58) objects to this picture because it restricts God's freedom, not because it violates divine aseity.

PHILOSOPHICAL MODELS OF ETERNAL GENERATION

good reason to think that aseity requires unqualified independence. Such a sweeping conception of aseity is unmotivated.

A few drawbacks accompany a grounding model of eternal generation. The first drawback is that, unlike causation, the very notion of grounding is controversial. A number of philosophers reject the grounding relation, deriding it as useless and unintelligible.[21] As far as critics of eternal generation are concerned, a grounding model may simply swap one unintelligible relation for another unintelligible relation. A second drawback is that grounding, at least according to some, is a type of causation. Grounding and what we ordinarily call causation are two sides of the same coin. Grounding just is metaphysical causation.[22] If this is right, then the drawbacks of a causal model carry over to a grounding model of eternal generation. The third drawback is that a grounding model, when extended to the eternal procession of the Holy Spirit, has difficulty accounting for the difference between eternal generation and eternal procession. Generation and procession hold between different persons on a grounding model, yet there is no qualitative difference between the relations of generation and procession. Especially on the single procession view of eternal procession, the grounding relation between the Father and the Son and the grounding relation between the Father and the Spirit will be qualitatively identical. Generation and procession will differ in name only.[23]

ESSENTIAL DEPENDENCE MODEL

Before developing an essential dependence model of eternal generation, the notions of essence and essential definition need some introduction.[24] As I understand it, essence is a primitive; essence cannot be analyzed.[25]

---

21. Grounding skeptics include Christopher Daly ("Scepticism about Grounding," in Correia and Schnieder, *Metaphysical Grounding*, 81–100), Jessica Wilson ("No Work for a Theory of Ground," *Inquiry* 57 [2014], 535–79), and Kathrin Koslicki ("The Coarse-Grainedness of Grounding," in *Oxford Studies in Metaphysics*, vol. 9, ed. Karen Bennett and Dean Zimmerman [Oxford: Oxford University Press, 2015], 9:306–44). For a reply to Daly's accusation that grounding is unintelligible, see Paul Audi's "A Clarification and Defense of the Notion of Grounding" in Correia and Schnieder, *Metaphysical Grounding*, 101–21.

22. Alastair Wilson argues that grounding just is metaphysical causation. See "Metaphysical Causation" in *Noûs* (2017), doi:10.1111/nous.12190.

23. To be fair, grounding comes in varieties; for an inventory, see Kit Fine, "Guide to Ground," in Correia and Schnieder, *Metaphysical Grounding*, 37–80. Nevertheless, generation and procession will be instances of the same variety of grounding on the single procession view of eternal procession.

24. For present purposes, I omit many technicalities surrounding an essential dependence model of eternal generation. Those who desire a more philosophically rigorous development of the model should see my "God from God" (forthcoming).

25. I presuppose a definitional account of essence, which elucidates essence using the notion of essential definition. Accounts of essence generally divide into definitional accounts and modal

The essence of a thing is simply *what the thing is*, or *what it is to be the thing*. Or as John Locke, emulating Aristotle, puts it, the essence of a thing is "the very being of any thing, whereby it is, what it is."[26] The essence of a thing is not a further thing (e.g., a collection of properties) mysteriously related to the thing in question. Things *have* essences. Essences are not themselves things.[27] Although primitive, essences are expressed by essential definitions. An essential definition is a proposition representing the essence of a thing. In an essential definition, the definiens will characterize the essence of the definiendum; the definiens will characterize what the definiendum is, or what it is to be the definiendum. Essential definitions are typically of the form "To be X is to be Y," where "X" is the definiendum and "Y" is the definiens. For example, consider the Aristotelian essential definition of a human being: To be a human being is to be a rational animal.[28] Notice that the definiens specifies both a genus and a differentia or differentiating feature. In this case the definiens specifies the genus, animal, and the differentia, rationality. Taken together, the genus and differentia characterize the essence of the definiendum. What it is to be a human being is just to be a rational animal; that's the essence of humanity, for Aristotle.

Essential dependence, like essence, is best understood in terms of essential definition. Essential dependence holds when the essence of one thing involves another thing; one thing is part of what it is to be another thing.[29] In terms of essential definition, essential dependence holds when one thing is a constituent of an essential definition of another thing.[30] Where "Y" and "X" represent things from any ontological category, essential dependence may be formulated as follows:

---

accounts. Following Kit Fine ("Essence and Modality," in *Philosophical Perspectives* 8 [1994], 1–16), David Oderberg (*Real Essentialism* [New York: Routledge. 2007]), and E. J. Lowe ("Two Notions of Being: Entity and Essence," in *Royal Institute of Philosophy Supplement* 62 [2008]: 23–48; and "The Rationality of Metaphysics," *Synthese*, 178 [2011]: 99–109), I reject modal accounts of essence, which analyze essence in terms of *de re* modality, as deeply flawed.

26. John Locke, *An Essay Concerning Human Understanding*, ed. Peter H. Niddich (Oxford: Oxford University Press, 1979), 3.3.15.

27. Here I follow Lowe, "Two Notions" and "Rationality of Metaphysics."

28. Example adapted from Kathrin Koslicki ("Varieties of Ontological Dependence" in Correia and Schneider, *Metaphysical Grounding*, 197–98). For similar characterizations of essential definition, see Kit Fine, "Essence and Modality," *Philosophical Perspectives* 8 (1994): 1–16, and "Ontological Dependence," *Proceedings of the Aristotelian Society* 95 (1995): 269–90; and David Oderberg, "Essence and Properties," *Erkenntnis* 75 (2011): 85–111.

29. For an opinionated introduction to essential dependence, see Kathrin Koslicki's "Ontological Dependence: An Opinionated Survey," in *Varieties of Dependence: Ontological Dependence, Grounding, Supervenience, Response-Dependence*, ed. Miguel Hoeltje, Benjamin Schnieder, and Alex Steinberg (Munich: Philosophia, 2013), 31–64.

30. I use the indefinite article "an" so as to leave open the possibility that a thing may have multiple equally accurate essential definitions.

PHILOSOPHICAL MODELS OF ETERNAL GENERATION

Essential Dependence: Y essentially depends on X =$_{df.}$ X is a constituent of an essential definition of Y.

For example, smiles essentially depend on mouths. Take Mona Lisa's smile. Mona Lisa's smile essentially depends on her mouth. The essence of Mona Lisa's smile involves her mouth; her mouth is part of what it is to be her smile. In other words, her mouth is a constituent of an essential definition of Mona Lisa's smile. To be Mona Lisa's smile is to be her mouth with the corners turned upward. Mona Lisa's smile, in this way, essentially depends on her mouth.

On an essential dependence model of eternal generation, eternal generation is a form of essential dependence. To say that the Son is begotten of the Father is just to say that the Son essentially depends on the Father. To put it more formally:

Essential Dependence Model: The Son is eternally begotten of the Father =$_{df.}$ The Father is a constituent of an essential definition of the Son, and the Son exists eternally.

According to the essential dependence model, the essence of the Son involves the Father. The Father is part of what the Son is, or what it is to be the Son. An essential definition of the Son will be of the form "To be the Son is to be the divine person who _____ the Father," where the blank is filled in by some description characterizing the Son's essence. Note that the Son, like the Father and the Spirit, falls under the genus divine person; once filled in, the blank will help specify the differentia, what differentiates the Son from the other persons.

The best way to fill out the Son's essential definition is by consulting what God has revealed in Scripture. Of all the descriptions of the Son in the Old and New Testaments, the following verses seem to me to characterize the Son's essence, or what it is to be the Son:[31] "The Son is *the image of the invisible God*, the firstborn over all creation" (Col 1:15); "the Son is the radiance of God's glory and *the exact representation of his being*" (Heb 1:3); and "Christ, who *is the image of God*" (2 Cor 4:4). Without getting into exegetical tangles about whether these verses refer to the eternal Son, these excerpts suggest that to be the Son is to be the divine person who *is the image of the Father*. The essence of the Son involves being the image of the Father; being the image of the Father is part of what it is to be the Son. In this way, the Father is a constituent of an essential definition of the Son, and so the Son essentially depends on the Father.

---

31. All translations are taken from the NIV. Emphasis added.

255

For the essential dependence model to succeed, the Father cannot essentially depend on the Son. There must be an essential definition of the Father in which the Son is not a constituent to show that the Father's essence does not involve the Son. The form of such an essential definition will be "To be the Father is to be the divine person _____," where the blank is to be filled in by some description characterizing the Father's essence. Once again we consult Scripture to fill out the essential definition of the Father: "God, for whom and *through whom everything exists*" (Heb 2:10); "for *from him* and through him and for him *are all things*" Rom 11:36); and "yet for us there is but one God, *the Father, from whom all things came* and for whom we live; and there is but one Lord, Jesus Christ, through whom all things came and through whom we live" (1 Cor 8:6). Together these verses suggest that to be the Father is to be the divine person *on whom all things ultimately depend*.[32] Alternatively, the Father may be defined as the divine person who is the ultimate source (*principium*) of all things. However, the term "source" is misleading, suggesting that the Father is the *causal* source of all things. All things, created or not, ultimately depend on the Father. Creation causally depends on the Father, but not all things depend on the Father causally. Most notably, the Son does not causally depend on the Father, yet the Son still depends on the Father. That is, the Son essentially depends on the Father. To be the Father is to be the divine person on whom all things ultimately depend, causally or otherwise.[33]

The essential dependence model of eternal generation just outlined easily meets the minimal statement of the doctrine and all four desiderata. Because the Son's essence involves the Father, it is necessary that the Son depends on the Father for his existence, and essential dependence is compatible with eternal existence (imagine an eternal smile, for instance). Essential dependence can relate things from any ontological category (including persons) and is nondiachronic. The essential dependence relation between the Son and the Father is also asymmetric. On the proposed essential definitions above, the Son's essence involves the Father, but the Father's essence does not involve the Son; thus, the Son essentially depends on the Father but not vice versa. An essential dependence model also precludes spurious

---

32. The quantifier "all" is restricted only to exclude the Father so that the Father doesn't essentially depend on himself.

33. One might think that the Father should be defined as the divine person who eternally generates the Son. This essential definition of the Father implies that the Father essentially depends on the Son, making the relation between the Father and the Son symmetrical. But this essential definition of the Father is not at all satisfactory. It presupposes the very relation (namely, eternal generation) that an essential dependence model seeks to illuminate and does nothing to answer the unintelligibility and subordinationism objections.

PHILOSOPHICAL MODELS OF ETERNAL GENERATION

eternal generation, since necessary existents like the number two are not constituents in any plausible essential definition of the Son.

The essential dependence model likewise withstands the unintelligibility and subordinationism objections. Essential dependence has been widely regarded as intelligible for millennia, dating as far back as Aristotle. Examples like Mona Lisa's smile demonstrate essential dependence's intelligibility, and nothing prevents essential dependence between the Son and the Father from being similarly intelligible. Moreover, essential dependence is perfectly compatible with necessary existence. Consider again the number two and {2}. Both the number two and {2} exist necessarily, yet {2} essentially depends on the number two. The number two is a constituent in an essential definition of {2}: To be {2} is to be the set that contains the number two as its sole member. Essential dependence is thus entirely consistent with the Son's necessary existence. Essential dependence also poses no threat to the Son's aseity. On an essential dependence model, the Son's existence is not caused by anything else because essential dependence is a noncausal form of dependence. Nor does the Son depend on anything existing "outside" God. The Son admittedly does not possess unqualified independence, but this sweeping conception of aseity lacks motivation. Therefore, an essential dependence model preserves the Son's aseity.

One likely objection to the essential dependence model is what I call the *different essences objection*. Some might argue that the essential dependence model entails that the Father and the Son are not *homoousious*—that is, they do not share the same divine essence. The Father and the Son have different essential definitions, after all, so they must have different divine essences. But on the classical doctrine of the Trinity, there is only one divine essence (*ousia*). Hence, an essential dependence model contradicts the classical doctrine of the Trinity.[34]

The problem with the different essences objection is that it conflates two different senses of the term "essence." Although I have been speaking as if "essence" is univocal, the term can be used to refer to a thing's *individual essence* or its *general essence*. Every individual object is an instance of some kind K. "If X is something of kind K," Lowe explains, "then we may say that X's *general* essence is *what it is to be a K*, while X's *individual* essence

---

34. The different essences objection is raised against eternal functional/role subordinationism by Erickson, *Tampering*, 172; Keith Yandell, "How Many Times Does Three Go Into One?" in *Philosophical and Theological Essays on the Trinity*, ed. Tom McCall and Murray Rae (Oxford: Oxford University Press, 2009), 159–60; and Tom McCall, *Which Trinity? Whose Monotheism? Philosophical and Systematic Theologians on the Metaphysics of Trinitarian Theology* (Grand Rapids: Eerdmans, 2010), 179–80.

is *what it is to be the individual of kind K that X is*, as opposed to any other individual of that kind."[35] For example, Eli Manning is an instance of the kind human. Eli's general essence is *what it is to be a human*, while Eli's individual essence is *what it is to be Eli*, as opposed to some other human. The individual-general essence distinction similarly applies to the Son. The Son is an instance of the kind divine. The Son's general essence is *what it is to be a deity* or *what it is to be a divine person*, while the Son's individual essence is *what it is to be the Son*, as opposed to some other divine person.

In general, every person has an individual essence, and if two persons are numerically distinct, then they must have different individual essences (*what it is to be this person* and *what it is to be that person*). Because the Father and the Son are numerically distinct persons on the classical doctrine of the Trinity, they must have different individual essences. There can be no distinction between the Father and the Son without a difference in their individual essences. The Father's individual essence is *what it is to be the Father*, as opposed to the Son or the Spirit, and the Son's individual essence is *what it is to be the Son*, as opposed to the Father or the Spirit. Now, on an essential dependence model, the Father and the Son have different essential definitions. But these essential definitions characterize the Father's and the Son's *individual* essences—not their general essence. In fact, the Father and the Son have the same general essence on an essential dependence model. Essential definitions of the Father's and the Son's general essence will be identical, both specifying *what it is to be a divine person*. Thus, the Father and the Son share the same general essence—that is to say, they share the same divine essence. On an essential dependence model, therefore, there are two individual essences (setting aside the Spirit) but only one general or divine essence.

The sole drawback of an essential dependence model of eternal generation is that it may require reconceiving Fatherhood. One might hope that the Father's essence involves the Son in some way, that the Son is somehow a constituent in an essential definition of the Father. How could the Father be the Father without the Son? Though the Father cannot exist without the Son on an essential dependence model, the Son is still not part of the Father's essence. The Son cannot be a constituent in an essential definition of the Father if the essential dependence relation between the Son and the Father is to be asymmetric. Instead, an essential dependence model returns to a conception of Fatherhood common in the ancient church: Fatherhood

---

35. Lowe, "Two Notions," 35. Emphasis in original.

PHILOSOPHICAL MODELS OF ETERNAL GENERATION

as being the ultimate source (*principium*) of all things. This alternative conception of Fatherhood has historical precedent and, more importantly, finds support in Scripture, as evidenced by the verses cited earlier.[36]

CONCLUSION

A viable philosophical model of eternal generation, I have argued, must meet the minimal statement of the doctrine, satisfy all four desiderata, and withstand the unintelligibility and subordinationism objections. My aim here has been to present three such models: a causal model, a grounding model, and an essential dependence model. While each model of eternal generation has its drawbacks, the viability of these models shows that philosophical-theological qualms about the doctrine of eternal generation have been overblown. The doctrine of eternal generation has proven philosophically coherent and perfectly compatible with the Son's necessary existence and aseity. Critics of eternal generation, I hope, will heed this philosophical "alter call" and embrace the eternally begotten Son.

---

36. It's worth noting that an essential dependence model has the virtue of illuminating Calvin's claim that the Son possesses aseity with respect to the divine essence, but not with respect to his person. Additional virtues include the model's natural extension to the eternal procession of the Holy Spirit and its account of the difference between generation and procession. I laud these virtues of an essential dependence model and more in my "God from God."

CHAPTER 14

ETERNAL GENERATION AND SOTERIOLOGY

FRED SANDERS

THE GOAL OF THIS CHAPTER is to draw a very close connection between the doctrine of eternal generation and the doctrine of salvation so that the two theological loci may mutually illuminate each other. Although it is almost always valuable to juxtapose any two doctrines within the Christian theological system, the motivation in this case is deeper than mere curiosity about what sparks may fly when any two doctrines collide. Eternal generation and soteriology are not just two randomly selected doctrines. These two doctrines presuppose each other in a special way. In other words, the mutual illumination of eternal generation and soteriology is not so much a matter of two distinct light sources held close to each other, but two topics suffused with the radiance of the one light source of all proper theological reasoning: the God of our salvation.

This claim, that soteriology and some element of Trinitarian theology have a uniquely close relationship, would not be sustainable if the soteriology in question were a relatively low one or if the Trinitarian theology in question were a relatively thin one. But the claim's warrant applies to a high soteriology and a conceptually rich Trinitarianism. What this chapter commends is a correlation between a high view of salvation and a conceptually rich doctrine of the Trinity. By "a high view of salvation" we mean one that is explicit about salvation's origin in God's self, stemming from the divine self-determination, self-revelation, self-communication, self-donation, and self-impartation. Soteriology is often presented in a highly abbreviated form that investigates its results and articulates its processes, but pays scant attention to its abiding and constantly present source in God.

Such treatments of soteriology can be all foreground and no background, to the doctrine's diminishment. The appropriate background for the gospel message is an elaborate, or conceptually rich, doctrine of the Trinity. By "conceptually rich" we mean a doctrine of the Trinity that, in line with the great, central tradition of Christian thought, has made explicit the biblical dynamic of how the one God reveals himself in a way that corresponds to the manner of his existence in eternity: as the begetting Father, the begotten Son, and the proceeding Spirit. A contemporary articulation of the doctrine of the Trinity, if it is indeed to be articulate, ought to make extensive use of the traditional categories of eternal relations of origin within the divine essence. The doctrine of eternal relations of origin teaches that there are two processions in God which have been revealed in temporal missions of the Son and the Holy Spirit among us (the incarnation and Pentecost). This revelation happened at the level of the economy of salvation, resulting in adoption, reconciliation, and indwelling at the level of personal experience in the church. Eternal processions ground temporal missions, which ground full salvation. To trace the same logic backwards, believers are fully saved because in the fullness of time the Father sent the Son, from whose fullness we have received. This Son is he who was sent because he had eternally proceeded from God the Father in the life of the blessed Trinity.

A Supporting Witness

The fact that the doctrine of the eternal generation of the Son enjoys a good fit or close correlation with soteriology may rank highest among the reasons why it is a theologically and spiritually satisfying doctrine. It shows that the doctrine of eternal generation has systematic and existential advantages. Most of these advantages can be traced in the way that the doctrine provides a norm and a form for Trinitarian soteriology. This belongs on the credit side of the ledger for eternal generation. However, the doctrine of eternal generation must not be based on its benefits for, or its alignment with, the doctrine of salvation. The only argument capable of establishing the doctrine of eternal generation is a biblical argument, and real warrant for believing eternal generation must be the warrant of a right interpretation of Scripture.

The demand for recourse to scriptural revelation of eternal generation has been widely shared in the Christian tradition. The reason for this is that eternal generation is an integral part of the doctrine of the Trinity, and all things Trinitarian are made known by God alone. They do not belong among the invisible things understood by what is seen, nor to the truth which can be demonstrated by arguing back from creaturely effects. The same Thomas Aquinas who had at least five ways to prove God's existence resolutely denied that God's triunity could be proven demonstratively by argument. Rather, if we are to become aware of the truth that God has an eternal Son, God will have to tell us. John of Damascus begins his doctrine of God with a florilegium of three New Testament quotations: first from John, then from Jesus (according to Matthew), and finally from Paul:

> No one hath seen God at any time; the Only-begotten Son, which is in the bosom of the Father, He hath declared Him (John 1:18). The Deity, therefore, is ineffable and incomprehensible. For no one knoweth the Father, save the Son, nor the Son, save the Father (Matt 11:27). And the Holy Spirit, too, so knows the things of God as the spirit of the man knows the things that are in him (1 Cor 2:11).[1]

The harmonious witness of the apostles, then, testifies that knowledge of the Father, Son, and Holy Spirit is something only brought about by those three persons who have the requisite insider knowledge. Hilary of Poitiers similarly said that "the divine sonship of Jesus Christ . . . we prove by the witness of the Father, by the preaching of the apostles, and by the faith of believers."[2] Knowledge of the Trinity is a secret locked up in the Trinity until the Trinity crosses over to spread it abroad among us. "Why," asks question 25 of the Heidelberg Catechism, "do you speak of three, Father, Son, and Holy Spirit . . . since there is only one divine being?" Answer: "Because that is how God is revealed in God's own word . . . these three distinct persons are one true eternal God."[3] The seventeenth-century Lutheran theologian Johann Gerhard put it more combatively in one of his theses on the revelation of the Trinity: "The mystery of the Trinity should and also can be proved not from the streams of the fathers, nor from the murky pools of the scholastics, but from the utterly clear springs of the Holy Scriptures."[4]

For these reasons, we must give decisive priority to clear biblical revelation of the identity of God the Son and his relation to God the Father,

---

1. John of Damascus, *On the Orthodox Faith* I.1, in *Saint John of Damascus: Writings*, trans. Frederic H. Chase Jr. (New York: Fathers of the Church, 1958), 165.
2. Hilary of Poitiers, *De trinitate* 1.18.
3. *Heidelberg Catechism*, Q. 35.
4. Johann Gerhard, *Theological Commonplaces: On the Nature of God and On the Trinity* (St. Louis: Concordia, 2008), 274.

ETERNAL GENERATION AND SOTERIOLOGY

and avoid the temptation of reverse engineering a savior to fit a salvation. The theological task cannot be reduced to seeking after whatever doctrine of God satisfies the demands of soteriology. The doctrine of God takes normative theological precedence over the doctrine of salvation that hangs from it, and any warrants drawn from soteriology are retroductive at best.[5]

JUSTIFICATIONS FOR AN APPEAL TO SOTERIOLOGY

There are nevertheless three justifications for an appeal to soteriology as an important supporting witness in the case for eternal generation: first, as we have said, a relation of fittingness obtains between them; second, the two doctrines are already entangled as revealed doctrines; and third, contact with soteriology has motivational force.

First, although the eternal generation of the Son could not initially be established on the basis of our adoptive sonship—which would be a case of the soteriological tail wagging the Christological dog—it is valid to reason a posteriori about the fittingness that links the triune God of salvation and the Trinitarian work of salvation. Speaking of the role of rational argument, Aquinas puts it this way: we do not use it "to prove a root [of doctrine] sufficiently . . . [but to] show that consequent situations are in harmony with the root already posited."[6] There is thus some persuasive force to the insight that our salvation is a blessedly "consequent situation" that is "in harmony with" the Son's eternal generation "already posited." Salvation by adoption is the salvation than which nothing more fitting can be imagined by a triune God.

The second justification is that a truly biblical doctrine of salvation is itself a matter of revelation, so appeal to it is not an appeal to any source other than God's own self-witness. In fact, we might even say that soteriology is the native biblical soil of Trinitarian theology because it is conspicuously true that God did not make these things known as merely verbal announcements ("I have a Son") but as explanations accompanying the accomplishment of salvation ("This is my Son"). It is not the case that we had an intact doctrine of the Trinity and then waited expectantly to see how that triune God would save us. It is the case that the one God of Abraham, Isaac, and Jacob fulfilled his promises by sending forth his Son,

---

5. For "retroductive warrants" in theological method, see Francis Schussler Fiorenza, "Systematic Theology: Task and Methods," in *Systematic Theology; Roman Catholic Perspectives*, ed. Francis Schussler Fiorenza and John Galvin (Minneapolis: Fortress, 1991), I:77.

6. Aquinas, *ST* 1.32.1.

a Son he apparently already had, so that the New Testament retroactively adjusted the Old Testament doctrine of God to accommodate what must always have been true if Jesus is Lord and God is unchanging. Thus to appeal to the doctrine of salvation is to take recourse to the same subject matter that funds our canonical doctrine of God. It is of course a matter of decorum and accountability with respect to the opinions of other theologians that when we argue from soteriology, we keep our chain of reasoning as short as possible, our scaffolding of presuppositions as evident as possible, and our network of inferences as modest as possible.

The third justification for making an appeal to soteriology is that if the doctrine of eternal generation is to thrive within the intellectual culture of systematic theological today, it requires more than just demonstration. Retrieving it will also be a motivational and persuasive undertaking. Rhetoric, in the tradition of Aristotle, is the art of finding the available means of persuasion. "Available" refers to those elements which are at hand for, or are able to avail with, a particular audience. Considered in itself, the truth has a superabundant panoply of persuasiveness. But persuasion is the art of matchmaking between certain elements of the truth and the receptivity of a particular audience. We are living through a fraught and awkward era for Trinitarian biblical interpretation. For good reasons and for ill, the passages our forebears taught us to consult on this doctrine do not function for us as they did in previous centuries. The Johannine Comma, which launched a thousand Trinitarian sermons with its "three that bear witness in heaven," has gone missing. Fair enough; the text-critical case for it is far too weak to support its evidential use. The interpretation of the word *monogenēs* bristles with footnotes and hesitations, and is rarely rendered "only-begotten." This is peculiar but not in itself a matter of great doctrinal weight. Proverbs 8, whatever it means, is not a key player in Trinitarian theology now as it manifestly was in the fourth or sixteenth centuries. The hermeneutical issues around this fact begin to seem more significant. These are just a few examples at the text-critical, lexical, and allegorical levels. Battalions of Trinitarian verses have gone down under heavy fire from the steady Socinianizing forces of historical criticism. Scholarly reinforcements for traditional doctrines like eternal generation, such as those gathered in this volume, are beginning to make themselves known. It seems that after all the besieged fortress of biblical Trinitarianism may in fact give proof through the night that the creed is still there. In the interim, many defenses of eternal generation have been based on temporizing tactics, such as letting church tradition carry the weight that the Bible has seemed unable to bear.

ETERNAL GENERATION AND SOTERIOLOGY

This is sometimes propped up with a robust account of doctrinal development, wherein the Bible provides some raw materials, but the early church makes something actually Trinitarian out of them. This is a short-sighted and inadvisable strategy. If we are to believe in the Trinity, we ought to do so on the same grounds as the church fathers did: because it is a biblical doctrine, not because it is a patristic doctrine. It would not have become the latter if it had not been the former, at least if we believe the testimony of the fathers. To help motivate the present generation to gather its wits for a more robust biblical doctrine of eternal generation, a galvanizing strategy is to show eternal generation's deep resonance with the gospel. About eternal generation the apostles have much to say, but if we are too sluggish to hear it, it has become, in a literal rendering of Hebrews 5:11, dyshermeneutical: hard to speak in interpretation. During this dark age of dyshermeneutical Trinitarianism, we will gather strength to go forward into Scripture from a vivid apprehension of salvation.

THREE CONNECTING THEMES
FOR TRINITARIAN SOTERIOLOGY

With these motivations clarified, we turn now to three themes that illuminate the close connection between eternal generation and the gospel: first, metaphysical sonship; second, being from the Father; and third, considering God relatively.

"See what kind of love the Father has given to us, that we should be called children of God; and so we are" (1 John 3:1).[7] The Christian experience of adoption to be children of God is founded on a reality, rather than ventured from a figure of speech. Speaking in terms of literary craftsmanship, the concept of sonship may be thought of as a powerful metaphor, one that serves especially well to integrate and focus the entire semantic domain of biblical language about family, household, and inheritance. But sonship is also more than a metaphor, because naming the Christian experience of salvation by the name adoption (whether as "son-making" or as "placing in the position of a son") is not an exercise in evocative metaphorical description. It instead descends from that Father [pater] from whom every fatherhood [patria] in heaven and on earth has its name.[8] The relation of Father to Son is a relation in God, which is brought down to,

---

7. Unless otherwise noted, English Scripture quotations come from the ESV.
8. See Eph 3:14.

FRED SANDERS

or given over to, us; or to say the same thing, into which we are exalted and incorporated. "Multitudes of us," says Hilary of Poitiers, "are sons of God; He is Son in another sense. For he is God's true and own Son, by origin and not by adoption; not in name only but in truth; born and not created."[9] Or as the *Heidelberg Catechism* asks and answers: "Why is He called God's only begotten Son, since we also are the children of God? Because Christ alone is the eternal, natural, Son of God; but we are children of God by adoption, through grace, for his sake."[10] The relation of sonship is his by definition and ours by a polite extension, or rather by a gracious and costly exchange. If we are to call soteriological sonship metaphorical in any sense, it would be in a sense that demands metaphysical grounding in Trinitarian sonship. The doctrine of eternal generation specifies the metaphysical foundation behind the metaphorical extension.

At some points in the history of Trinitarianism, theologians have considered whether it might be adequate to stop at the assertion of mere sonship—coeternal, coequal, metaphysical sonship—instead of going on to the language of begetting or eternal generation. The proper response is that much would be lost, obscured, and rendered inarticulate by stopping short of generation. Nineteenth-century Methodist theologian William Burt Pope put it this way:

> Those who would efface the interior distinctions of generation and procession in the Godhead surrender much for which the earliest champions of orthodoxy fought. They take away from the intercommunion of the divine persons its most impressive and affecting character; and they go far toward robbing us of the sacred mystery which unites the Son's exinanition in heaven with his humiliation as incarnate on earth.[11]

Pope is speaking circumspectly, but his point is that the Son stands eternally in a relation of origin to the Father, which explains his sending. The Father sends the Son and not vice versa. This is not because the Father has more authority than the Son, but because the Father eternally Fathers the Son. To call the Son a Son without going on to confess the "interior distinctions

---

9. Hilary, *De trinitate* 3.11.

10. *Heidelberg Catechism*, Q. 33.

11. William Burt Pope, "Methodist Doctrine," *The Wesley Memorial Volume*, ed. J. O. A. Clark (New York: Phillips and Hunt, 1881), 176. "Exinanition" is an obscure English word for emptying; it seems to be Pope's way of using Latin word roots to avoid the connotations that had built up around the Greek word *kenosis* in nineteenth-century theology.

ETERNAL GENERATION AND SOTERIOLOGY

of generation" is to truncate the filial relation in a way that is immediately registered by a less potent account of soteriology.

Confronting a similar reticence to pursue eternal sonship all the way up into eternal generation, W. G. T. Shedd took another line of argumentation. Shedd was concerned about theologians who were so cautious to stay within the bounds of scriptural terminology that they embraced the word "Son" but refused to extend it to some antecedent process of the production of the Son. Shedd pointed out that this truncation was an inconsistent one because the eternal relations of origin are analytically contained in the Biblical names, properly understood.

> These trinal names, Father, Son, and Holy Spirit, given to God in Scripture, force upon the theologian the ideas of paternity, filiation, spiration, and procession. He cannot reflect upon the implications of these names without forming these ideas and finding himself necessitated to concede their literal validity and objective reality.[12]

Shedd draws from the proper names their corresponding verbs: the theologian "cannot say with scripture that the First Person is the Father and then deny or doubt that he 'fathers.' He cannot say that the Second Person is Son and then deny that he is 'begotten.'"[13] In fact, he goes one further grammatical step while insisting that it is not really a further step at all: "Whoever accepts the nouns Father, Son, and Spirit as conveying absolute truth must accept also the corresponding adjectives and predicates—beget, begotten, spirate, and proceed—as conveying absolute truth."[14]

Confessing eternal generation is the consequence of grounding adoptive sonship in a higher sonship that belongs to the essence of the living God. It is especially when considered in relation to salvation that we see why that relation must be solidly grounded in a conceptually rich confession of what makes sonship. As Ivor Davidson says, "At the heart of the *beneficia Christi* of which the gospel speaks lies a specific blessing: the opening up of the eternal Son's native sphere to others, the drawing of contingent beings into the realm of his intimate, eternally secure relation to his Father."[15]

The second theme that connects eternal generation to soteriology is

---

12. William G. T. Shedd, *Dogmatic Theology*, 3rd ed., ed. Alan W. Gomes (Phillipsburg, NJ: P&R, 2003), 245.

13. Ibid., 246.

14. Ibid.

15. Ivor Davidson, "Salvation's Destiny: Heirs of God," in *God of Salvation: Soteriology in Theological Perspective*, ed. Ivor Davidson and Murray Rae (London: Routledge, 2010), 161.

the notion of being from the Father. "Every good and perfect gift is from above, coming down from the Father of lights" (Jas 1:17). Not only do all created gifts come from the Father, but creation itself comes from the Father. The Son, too, comes from the Father. But the Son comes from the Father in a wholly other way than the way the world comes from the Father. Clearing up the desperate confusions over these two ways of being from the Father was the urgent business of the pro-Nicene theology of the early church. There are four ways of being from the Father, or of coming from God, and it is crucial to distinguish them.

In the first way, the Son comes from the Father by filiation, or by eternal generation. "Begetting is not an event of time, however remote, but a fact irrespective of time."[16] This is a relation of from-ness or of-ness that is part of the definition of God, as the Son is God of God, light of light.

In the second way, the world comes from God by creation, and the difference is marked in the Nicene Creed's phrase that the Son is "begotten, not made" because, as Athanasius says, "a man by craft creates a house, but by nature begets a son."[17] Here Christology and cosmology are distinguished and creation *ex nihilo* begins to be more clearly articulated because of Trinitarian theology. The Creator–creature distinction must be recognized even though our concern is not primarily with the doctrine of creation but with soteriology.

In the third way, when the Son is sent into the world, he comes from God in yet another way, a new way. The eternally generated one (first way) takes to himself a created nature (second way) and is the subject of an economic sending, a temporal mission that reveals his eternal generation as he brings metaphysical sonship into the realm of creatures. When he comes from God in this new and unique way, he is not two sons, as if he added a created sonship to the uncreated Sonship. There is one Son, who always came from the Father in the first way, and took up a nature created in the second way to be the instrument of his coming in the third way.

In the fourth way, when he who comes from God the first way is sent among those who come from God the second way in this unparalleled third way, is the Creator–creature distinction transgressed? May it never be! But it is infiltrated, spanned, and surprisingly fulfilled as the eternal generation of the Son reaches its "strangely logical final conclusion"[18] in the way of the Son of God into the far country. And it establishes a fourth

---

16. H. C. G. Moule, *Outlines of Christian Doctrine* (London: Hodder and Stoughton, 1902), 59.
17. Athanasius, *C. Ar.* 3.62.
18. Karl Barth, *CD* IV/1, 203.

ETERNAL GENERATION AND SOTERIOLOGY

way of being from the Father, or of coming from God. When creatures, fallen and atoned for, are joined to the eternally begotten one, these who come from God as creatures are given their share in the Trinitarian way of coming from God as sons. Eternal generation grounds regeneration. "See what kind of love the Father has given to us, that we should be called children of God; and so we are" (1 John 3:1).

The final theme that connects soteriology and eternal generation is the notion of God considered absolutely and relatively. Systematic theology has traditionally distinguished the doctrine of God into two treatises: the doctrine of God's unity of being and the doctrine of God's trinity of persons (or *de deo uno* and *de deo trino*). There is plenty of material content to discuss under each heading, and as long as the treatises adequately inform and presuppose each other, it is a fine distinction. Another title for that distinction is "God considered absolutely" and "God considered relatively." This was a common way of handling the distinction in the period of Protestant scholasticism. For example, in Johannes Quenstedt's theological system, he titles chapter 9 "On God Relatively Considered; that is, on the Most Holy Trinity." He elaborates on the distinction:

> The consideration of God is twofold, one absolute, another relative. The former is occupied with God considered essentially, without respect to the three persons of the Godhead; the latter, with God considered personally. The former explains both the essence and the essential attributes of God; the latter describes the persons of the Holy Trinity, and the personal attributes of each one.[19]

The distinction could be paraphrased less precisely as "God from the outside, God from the inside." In more current theology, Scott Swain says, "The truth of the Trinity does not concern relations external to God's most excellent being; for example, the relation of creator to creature or of divine king to creaturely subject. The truth of the Trinity concerns relations internal to God's being . . . the truth of the Trinity is internal to the hidden depths of God's being."[20] The point is that knowledge of the Trinity is knowledge of God from within. Gerald Bray says that "Christians have been admitted to the inner life of God . . . The God who appears as One to those who

---

19. Quenstedt, as cited in Heinrich Schmid, *The Doctrinal Theology of the Evangelical Lutheran Church* (Minneapolis: Augsburg, 1889), 134.

20. Scott Swain, "Divine Trinity," in *Christian Dogmatics: Reformed Theology for the Church Catholic,* ed. Michael Allen and Scott R. Swain (Grand Rapids: Baker Academic, 2016), 82.

view him on the outside, reveals himself as a Trinity of persons, once his inner life is opened up to our experience."[21] It is a striking claim, but it is the one we have been moving toward in our entire argument that a high soteriology and an elaborate Trinitarianism cohere.

Trinitarian theology arises from the biblical conviction that Jesus Christ must be described as internal to God, as something to be considered under the heading "God, relatively or relationally considered." That is why confessing the deity of Christ has never been considered "good enough." The Nicene formula is not that Jesus Christ is God but that he is "God of God, light of light" and is of one substance with the Father, which is a relational statement. In his life among us, we have not just beheld God, but the glory of the only begotten. To omit the begottenness is to omit internal relation that is the secret of salvation, the deep link between God and the gospel. Trinitarian soteriology, then, stands on eternal generation. Eternal generation is implicit as the background of salvation as the Bible presents it. It only needs attention, unfolding, or paraphrasing. For the sake of salvation, then, let us attend, let us unfold, and let us paraphrase. Confessing processions and missions, let us proceed with our mission.

---

21. Gerald Bray, "Out of the Box: The Christian Experience of God in Trinity," in *God the Holy Trinity: Reflections on Christian Faith and Practice*, ed. Timothy George (Grand Rapids: Baker Academic, 2006), 45–46.

CHAPTER 15

ETERNAL GENERATION:
Pro-Nicene Pattern, Dogmatic Function, and Created Effects

JOSH MALONE

You, oh God, are a fountain of life, and in Your light we see light.
Psalm 36:9[1]

PRO-NICENE THEOLOGICAL REASONING

The doctrine of eternal generation is the church's attempt to specify the origin of Jesus Christ in the eternal life of the one God.[2] Our received formulations of the doctrine were developed and refined around the Arian controversy in the fourth century, and a form of the doctrine is confessed in the Creed of Nicaea (325) and the Nicene Creed (381). Plainly stated, the doctrine teaches that the Son is from the Father, and God has always been this way and did not become this way. Yet in its confession, the church was acutely aware that familiarity of language could threaten to obscure the fact that we speak of the ineffable. The pre- and post-Nicene fathers are united concerning the danger inherent in improper speech about God's inner life. Irenaeus chastens the Gnostics for speaking of the Son's generation "as if they themselves had assisted at His birth, thus assimilating Him to the word

---

1. Author's translation. Unless noted otherwise, the remaining English Scripture translations come from the ESV.

2. This chapter is written in memory of my Doktorvater, John Webster, and it indelibly bears his mark. Working under his supervision was a true joy—a brilliant man shrouded in humble self-forgetfulness in imitation of Christ. His great work remains unfinished, but he left a legacy of students. We are your "letter, written on our hearts, known and read by everyone," and may God "show that [we] are a letter from Christ, the result of our ministry, written not with ink but with the Spirit of the living God" (2 Cor 3:2–3).

of mankind formed by emissions."[3] Origen warns that we must not "regard God the Father in the begetting of his only-begotten Son as being similar to any human being or other animal in the act of begetting."[4] Athanasius contends, "It is not holy to venture such questions concerning the generation of the Son of God."[5] Likewise Gregory of Nazianzus claims, "The begetting of God must be honored by silence."[6] Such cautionary impulses occur with regularity across the great tradition pre- and post-Nicaea.

Even so, pro-Nicene theology has insisted on the necessity of affirming the Son's eternal generation. Why? The answer is bound to a pattern of theological reasoning that holds scriptural language as primary in dogmatic discourse.[7] Central to the pro-Nicene approach was securing the biblical name(s) of the one God: Father, Son, and Spirit. This pattern can be observed in the threefold structure of the Creed of Nicaea (325): "We believe in one God *Father* . . . and in one Lord Jesus Christ, the *Son of God* . . . and in the *Holy Spirit*." By privileging the name "Father, Son, and Spirit," pro-Nicenes elevated the language of Scripture—giving it primacy over derivative concepts like ingenerate (*agenētos*), unbegotten (*agennētos*), or *Monad*—which they judged to be inadequate to describe the Godhead *in toto*. Instead, they carefully reflected on the divine name and titles, given in Scripture, to rationally wrestle with the divine mystery of the Father–Son relation, illumined by the Spirit.

From this emerged a very carefully crafted theological grammar, albeit one with a set of technical terms rife for misunderstanding. The danger is such that theologians (both historical and contemporary) have questioned if we should simply avoid making such explicit creaturely reference and eschew speaking in animalistic terms like substance (*ousia*) and beget

---

3. Irenaeus, *Against Heresies* 2.28.5–6 (*ANF* 1:401).

4. Origen, *On First Principles*, trans. George William Butterworth and Paul Koetschau (repr.; Eugene, OR: Wipf & Stock, 2012), 1.2.4 (17).

5. Athanasius, *C. Ar.* 2.36 (*NPNF*[2] 4:367).

6. Gregory of Nazianzus, *Or. Bas.* 29.8 (*NPNF*[2] 7:303).

7. The broader pro-Nicene pattern of exegesis from which the doctrine of eternal generation emerged is explored in Josh Malone, "God from God: The Origin, Function, And Meaning of the Doctrine of Eternal Generation" (PhD diss., University of Aberdeen, 2014). In sum, the exegetical reasoning starts from the one God declared in the Hebrew Scriptures; gathers the exalted titles ascribed to that one God (title-exegesis); notes how these titles are ascribed to Christ; explores scriptural use of those titles, making a distinction between all other titles and the name "Son"; uses the name "Son" (and relatedly the title "only-begotten") to collect this constellation of texts, explicating the meaning of the analogical language of "Father" and "Son"; and draws on the analogy, titles, intertextual witness (disambiguating voices through prosopological exegesis), and the acts of Christ to explicate the meaning of "only-begotten Son." Emerging from this reading strategy, pro-Nicenes refined the proper dogmatic use of language of "will" and "being" to relate Father and Son, and located the origin of the Son in the eternal life of God informing the analogical interval between Creator and creation.

ETERNAL GENERATION

(*gennaō*). Certainly these terms could be replaced with others, far less freighted with corporeality. Yet, the pro-Nicene tradition has refused any such alternative. Trenchantly, it has clung to the primacy of the scripturally given divine names "Father" and "Son" (and "Spirit"), which by analogy were inextricably linked to the concept and language of "generation." Why? For all the difficulties with human language, the inadequacy of analogy, and the limitations of our creaturely intellect, the language of "generation" names a personal, fecund relation central to the biblical witness to God's perfection. The divine name was not seen to be merely metaphorically informative but rather metaphysically proper to God's perfect life. Aquinas states plainly and profoundly, "The names signify procession."[8] In light of this reality, the pro-Nicene tradition came to confess that fatherhood (paternity) and sonship (filiation) are originally true of God (*archetype*) and only secondarily true of us (*ectype*).[9] This exercise in wise theological reason offered a way to think and speak of the Father and Son that maintained unity of nature, enabled distinction of persons, and echoed the relationally ordered movement from Father to Son (and Spirit) given in the gospel. Now, we turn to an explication of these three themes in Trinitarian dogmatics and then to a few ways that eternal generation is echoed in the created effects caused by the external work of the triune persons.

DOGMATIC FUNCTION

In our dogmatic reflection, we must strike a careful balance between the pro-Nicene pattern of scriptural reasoning and the divine ineffability included in that pattern. The words of the prophet Isaiah provide spiritual disciplinary measures against saying too much: "To whom will you compare me? Or who is my equal?" (Isa 40:25 NIV). The answer is "no one." "God is not human" (Num 23:19 NIV). God is *not* like us. Yet God, so *unlike* us in his uncreated being, has made us in his *likeness*, and he condescends to make himself known—the fullness of deity hypostatically dwelling in the fullness of humanity (Col 2:9). So John the evangelist proclaims, "No one has ever seen God, but the only begotten Son, who is in the bosom of the Father, has made him known" (John 1:18).[10] This Son is the very radiance

---

8. *ST* 1.27.1. English translation from Aquinas, *Summa Theologiae*, vol. 6, *The Trinity (1a. 27–32)*, trans. Ceslaus Velecky O.P. (Cambridge: Cambridge University Press, 2006).

9. Provocatively Paul writes that God is "the Father, from whom every family in heaven and on earth is named" (Eph 3:14–15).

10. Author's translation.

of the Father's glory and the exact imprint of his nature (Heb 1:3). Thus God from God means Son from Father, scripturally expounded as Light (1 John 1:5) from Light (John 8:12), True God (John 17:3) from True God (1 John 5:20).

Sanctified reason recognizes the dogmatic task is carefully ordered: first we listen, and only then do we speak. We speak *as* spoken to. Yet we are compelled by the Spirit to bear joyous witness to the divine reality that the eternal Father and Son have drawn us into familial fellowship by the power of the gospel (Gal 4:6), while simultaneously we are reminded not to overexplain the very same triune God who dwells in unapproachable light (1 Tim 6:16). In faith and mystery, we hear the pattern of the prophetic and apostolic witness, and thus we speak of the doctrine's dogmatic function in theology proper considered under three headings: essential unity, personal distinction, and relational order (*taxis*).

Essential Unity

First, in what way does eternal generation speak of essential unity? Initially, it appears as though the confession of the Son as the only begotten of the Father must strike against the doctrine of essential unity (divine simplicity). How can the one God be both Father and Son? The pro-Nicene answer can be seen by looking at the language of the two councils of Nicaea (325) and Constantinople (381). Both confess that the Son does not proceed from the Father as a creature from the Creator: he is begotten, not made. The Son is not part of the created order; begetting is not the first act of creation. However, neither council attempts to fully explain what it means to be begotten. In fact, they carefully avoid doing so, respecting the ineffability of this act. Rather, they assert there is a way to be "from" that is outside all beginnings (recalling John 1:1). This generation is conceived as an act internal to God.[11] "For as the Father has life *in himself*, so he has granted the Son also to have life *in himself*" (John 5:26).[12] And it subsists within God: "I am *in* the Father and the Father is *in* me" (John 14:11). Theologically, the Father generates the Son of his substance, *ek tēs ousias tou Patros* (325), and as such, the Son is consubstantial or *homoousion* (325, 381) with the Father.

---

11. The description of generation as an *internal act* that is "within God himself" is seen most clearly in Aquinas (*ST* 1.27.1; against the Arians and Sabellians), but the concept appears as early as Origen, who claims the Son is not Son "by any outward act, but by his own nature," *Princ.* 1.2.4 (*ANF* 4:247).

12. Emphasis added. This text was important in Augustine's Trinitarian thought; see Augustine, *Tractates on the Gospel of John, 11–27*, trans. John W. Rettig, Fathers of the Church 79 (Washington, DC: Catholic University of America Press, 1988).

ETERNAL GENERATION

Two things should be noted concerning this strange language, rooted in divine mystery. On the one hand, the word *homoousion* is not employed to indicate some sensible and detachable metaphysic; the language offers no objective referent on its own. Instead the term *homoousion* functions as a conceptual summary of the scriptural affirmation of the Son's unity with the Father, grounded in his ineffable generation.[13] On the other hand, this articulation of the Son's generation is a denial that Begetter and Begotten are related as externally opposed realities. The one God (Father) and one Lord (Son) are truly *one* (cf. 1 Cor 8:6). Accordingly, generation is conceived as the mode of sharing of the one undivided essence between Father and Son.

Can we say more? Should we? With trepidation, the pro-Nicenes conceived of generation as a communication of the whole undivided essence, or "whole participation," as Athanasius puts it.[14] Reformed scholastic Francis Turretin summarizes the analogy: "All generation indicates a communication of essence on the part of the begetter to the begotten."[15] Notably, these affirmations include the denial that we truly know what the divine essence is. To secure this, the Nicene Creed (381) specifies the qualitative difference between creaturely and divine begetting and being by adding the corresponding clause that the Son is "begotten of the Father before all ages." Generation is eternal, wholly contained in the indivisible life of God, and incorporeal, since God is Spirit (John 4:24). These guard against any unfitting metaphysical speculation about the one who is *sui generis*. Dogmatically, begetting is a mode of divine unity, an affirmation of eternal essential unity rather than a denial of it.[16]

Personal Distinction

Second, in what way does eternal generation speak of personal distinction? To confess eternal generation is to deny that Jesus is Son of God by means of his miraculous virgin birth, no less his baptism or resurrection. Instead, he is begotten of the Father before all ages. That this entails personal distinction seems rather straightforward, but it is crucial for securing this reality as true in God.

---

13. Khaled Anatolios, *Retrieving Nicaea: The Development and Meaning of Trinitarian Doctrine* (Grand Rapids: Baker Academic, 2011), 128.

14. Athanasius, *C. Ar.* 1.14 (*NPNF*² 4:315).

15. Turretin, *Institutes of Elenctic Theology*, ed. James T. Dennison, trans. George Musgrave Giger (Phillipsburg, NJ: P&R, 1992–94), 1:292–93.

16. Historically there was a simmering debate about whether the manner of eternal generation is properly conceived as a communication of essence. The majority of patristic, medieval, and Reformation authors do affirm it as such. For an account of the minority report and incisive contribution to this debate see Brannon Ellis, *Calvin, Classical Trinitarianism, and the Aseity of the Son* (Oxford: Oxford University Press, 2012).

JOSH MALONE

The appearing of the Son incarnate evoked wonder and praise as Christians slowly began to articulate both a confession of the one God, creator and redeemer, and simultaneously a confession that Christ, the Son of God the Father, is himself God. And while the Son is not the Father, they share the same life together with the Spirit. The doctrine of eternal generation is the pro-Nicene pathway by which this mystery is conceptually traversed. It asserts that Father and Son are eternally related by origin alone, Begetter and Begotten, not by essential difference (since they share the same undivided essence). This is what makes a divine person, a person.[17] In doing so, the doctrine specifies that the two are not primarily differentiated by historical accomplishment; rather, history is an echo of their eternal relation.[18] Jesus "was *declared* to be the Son of God in power according to the Spirit of holiness by his resurrection from the dead" (Rom 1:4). Nor are Father and Son eternally differentiated by their "roles," for these are willingly undertaken in the economy.[19] The Son's external work is willed, temporal, particular to the incarnation, and rooted in his eternal begetting. As such, the state of humiliation is the first movement in the incarnational career of the Son, followed by his present exaltation. Scripture stubbornly resists collapsing Christ in the "form of a servant" backwards to explicate the Son's filial identity "in the form of God" (Phil 2:6–11).

Instead, eternal generation affirms both the Father and Son's complete unity in all things pertaining to deity and their personal distinction in all things pertaining to their uniqueness as Father and Son, that is, with respect to one another. In this way, eternal generation attempts to follow the language of Scripture, which affirms that before the beginning the Word who is with God, as God (John 1:1), is none other than the only begotten in the bosom of the Father (John 1:18). Dogmatically, begetting is the eternal ground of personal distinction, an affirmation of the eternal uniqueness of Father and Son without severing the divine essence.

Relational Order

Third, in what way does eternal generation speak of relational order (*taxis*)? The pro-Nicene tradition has taught that eternal generation speaks of a

---

17. Like the careful grammar above—*ousia, gennaō, homoousion*—the term *hypostasis* came to be used technically by the Cappadocians as theological shorthand for this reality. Gregory Nyssa, *On the Difference Between Ousia and Hypostasis*. In Basil's canon, *Letter 38* (*NPNF²* 8:137–41).

18. For recent competing accounts that make history constitutive to the Son's divine identity, see Wolfhart Pannenberg, Robert Jenson, and the continuing work of Bruce McCormack.

19. As some recent theologians have suggested with competing formulations of Eternal Functional Subordination (EFS), Eternal Submission of the Son (ESS), or Eternal Relationship of Authority and Submission (ERAS).

ETERNAL GENERATION

correlative relation between Father and Son; paternity and filiation are mutually specifying, yet they are relationally ordered and not flatly symmetrical. What does this mean?

Today one might confess the eternal Sonship of Christ yet deny that this implies *taxis* in the Godhead. Or, as above, one might confess the obedience of the incarnate Son to his Father in the economy and infer a certain form of *taxis* in the Godhead that could be articulated as authority-submission. In contrast, the doctrine of eternal generation teaches that the Father–Son relation is fundamentally ordered, asymmetrical, and yet by origin alone. The Son is Son because he is begotten by the Father, and the Father is Father because he is from no one, and thus the Father begets his Son.[20]

This order of personal subsistence is *established* by an eternal relation of origin, and nothing else, and *manifest* in the saving economy in the order and manner of the Son's working from the Father. Indeed, many incarnational texts bear witness to this: "I have come down from heaven, not to do my own will but the will of him who sent me" (John 6:38). The meaning of this obedience must remain a matter of theological interpretation.[21] Pro-Nicene theology has understood the temporal obedience of the eternal Son as an economic extension of his eternal generation, in the Spirit's power, for us and our salvation. Later pro-Nicenes have expressed this by noting that the Son's earthly mission reveals his eternal procession, while never collapsing the two nor "reading back" unfitting features of the created economy into the divine life.

Carefully articulating the mystery of divine *taxis* is a continuing challenge for the church. Insightfully, Matthew Levering notes that perhaps our modern concerns about *taxis* arise from viewing the Trinity through a lens of *power* (or *authority* in gender debates) rather than as divine *wisdom*.[22] Here, more than anywhere, the balance of holding the pro-Nicene pattern of theological reasoning together with divine ineffability is central. Doing so enables us to resist the temptation to make eternal relational order a superordinate form of human relational order. Dogmatically, begetting (and spiration) is the root of relational order, an affirmation that eternal personal subsistence describes the very *taxis* echoed in the saving economy.

---

20. So Aquinas reasons, "Because he is Father, he begets (*quia Pater est, generat*)," and not the inverse proposition: Because he begets, he is Father. See *ST* 1.40.4, ad 1.

21. Scott R. Swain and R. Michael Allen. "The Obedience of the Eternal Son," *International Journal of Systematic Theology* 15, no. 2 (2013): 114–34.

22. Matthew Levering, *Scripture and Metaphyiscs: Aquinas and the Renewal of Trinitarian Theology* (Oxford: Blackwell, 2004), 172.

CREATED EFFECTS

With respect to God's life in himself, the doctrine of eternal generation functions to elaborate the Father–Son relation. With respect to God's external works, the begetting of the Son is revealed in *created effects*. Thomas Aquinas offers a cogent ground for this mode of theological reflection. Briefly, our theological language employs human speech and words that reflect upon created effects caused by the external work of God. Whatever divine goodness is echoed in these effects can be traced back to God whose perfect life is the source of each created effect.[23] What follows is a conceptual meditation on a series of created effects observed to mirror the generation of the Son within the external divine works of creation, redemption, and consummation.[24]

Creation: Divine Gift and Triune Movement

The act of creation is a movement of divine generosity and life. How might we look back along the act of creation into its ground in God's life in himself? Gilles Emery explores this trajectory in Aquinas, noting that God's creative and redemptive activity is "not the first element in the order of speculative exposition, but it can be useful to consider first the influence of the Trinitarian faith."[25] Emery notes that both East and West have maintained a "rule of unity" in the activity of the divine persons.[26] This "rule of unity" is a coordination between theology and economy—God's life in himself and God's work. In addition to this rule of unity, Emery highlights Aquinas's coordinating principle: "the processions of the divine persons are the cause of creation."[27]

Such a coordination of theology and economy is stunning to consider. For Aquinas this serves to link divine activity *ad extra* (creation, redemption, and consummation) to divine act *ad intra* (eternal generation and spiration). Divine act governs and directs divine activity. This brings together essential unity (seen in coordination of action *ad extra*, rooted in coessentiality),

---

23. *ST* 1.13.2, ad 2.

24. For an insightful comparison of Aquinas and Barth (with deference to Barth) coordinating Trinity, Christology, and creation, see Keith L. Johnson, "Natural Revelation in Creation and Covenant," in *Thomas Aquinas and Karl Barth: An Unofficial Catholic-Protestant Dialogue*, ed. Bruce L. McCormack and Thomas Joseph White (Grand Rapids: Eerdmans, 2013). I hope some of the paths traced here provide additional trajectories picking up Johnson's concluding suggestions.

25. Gilles Emery, "Essentialism or Personalism in the Treatise on God in Saint Thomas Aquinas," *The Thomist* 64 (2000): 527.

26. *Opera ad extra trinitatis indivisa sunt*—the external works of the Trinity are undivided. This rule itself is rooted in the affirmation of the coessentiality of the divine persons.

27. *ST* 1.45.6, ad 1. Emery notes this is present in all of Aquinas's works: "Outside the commentary on the Sentences (which contains more than ten passages developing this thesis), cf. notably *De Potentia*, q. 10, a. 2, arg. 19, sed contra 2, and ad 19; *ST* 1.45.6 and 7, ad 3." Emery, "Essentialism or Personalism," 528n23.

ETERNAL GENERATION

personal distinction (seen as acts of personal agents in the economy, rooted in the processions), relational order (seen in the movement from Begetter to Begotten), and "motive" for divine action in the economy. Why is there a creation rather than nothing at all? Because the eternal God "spoke" rather than remained silent. Creation is a freely created overflow of the eternal movement between Father, Son, and Spirit. This eternal movement is an act of nature concomitant with divine will, and its temporal repetition is an act of divine willing fitting to and free for the divine nature. By an act of divine generosity God wills to establish a reality beyond himself as a further object of his love.

Augustine, too, considers the underpinnings of God's creative act within his triune perfection. In *Confessions*,[28] he reflects on how God made the world in Genesis 1. He reasons that it could not have been identical to a human worker who envisions a product and then shapes it (e.g., out of wood, stone, or metal). Rather, God made workers and his creative work stands above theirs. Instead, "You spoke and they were made, and by your word you made them."[29] Yet Augustine ponders—what does this mean? Is it parallel to God saying "this is my beloved Son" from the clouds over Jesus's transfiguration in Matthew 17:5? It is a voice that uttered sound through syllables at one moment and then passed away a moment later? No, Augustine reasons, because God's Word is together with God before the beginning of creation in John 1:1. Furthermore, if that Word was just like the words uttered at his transfiguration, how is it the Word by which heaven and earth were made?

Here Augustine recognizes what God's creation by his Word means: the Father creates through the Son.[30] Through a freely willed extension of the creative power that God is (that is, God's eternal life of begetting and spirating), the world comes to be. Creation out of nothing is the Father working through the Son (by the Spirit). No preexisting materials (contra Plato). No eternal creation (contra Aristotle). No emanation (contra the Gnostics). Simply the triune God, working in power as Father, Son, and Spirit. And creation through God's Word (by the Spirit) is the biblical way of speaking of creation *ex nihilo*—or creation from God, through God, by God alone. "By the word of the LORD the heavens were made, and by the breath of his mouth all their host" (Ps 33:6). The triune God needs no material to create from because he is the fountain of life.

---

28. Augustine, *Confessions*, trans. Henry Chadwick (Oxford: Oxford University Press, 1991), 11.5–7.

29. Ibid., 11.5.

30. Ibid., 11.9.

But creation is not simply making; rather, it is the beginning of the history of the triune God's loving care. Consequently, the doctrines of creation and providence are inseparable. The Christian doctrine of providence is an extension of the Christian doctrine of creation, where the Creator governs the works of his hands revealing continued created effects. As John Webster writes, "God is triune . . . his works . . . manifest the persons . . . The Father determines the course of created time (Eph 1:3, 5); the Spirit causes creaturely causes (Eph 1:13); the Son intervenes to draw back creation from ruin so that it may attain its end (Eph 1:7, 10). Only because God is thus does creation issue in providence."[31] The inner acts of divine procession manifest in the external activity of faithful care, "that work of divine love for temporal creatures whereby God ordains and executes their fulfillment in fellowship with himself."[32] And this fulfillment in fellowship is none other than a temporal extension of the eternal fellowship God is in his triune perfection.

Image as Sonship: From Creation to New Creation

In what way are the eternal relations of origin, specifically the generation of the Son, seen in the history of divine fellowship with human creatures?[33] Astonishingly, Scripture bears witness to a deep resonance between the eternal Son who is the image of the Father and created sons and daughters made in the divine image. Irenaeus of Lyons powerfully draws on the connection between image and filiation when refuting the Gnostics in *Against Heresies*. In an ambitious, synthetic retelling of the biblical narrative, Irenaeus sketches how embodied humans are created in the image of the Son of God, himself the true image of the Father—created images of *the* image: "For in times long past, it was said that man was created after the image of God, but it was not [actually] *shown*; for the Word was as yet invisible, after whose image man was created."[34] The Son as true image is made manifest and revealed in the incarnation, and we come to see Adam himself is a type of the image of Christ. For Irenaeus, this means the ultimate archetype for humanity is Christ, not Adam.[35] It also means that creation was "fitted"

---

31. John Webster, "On the Theology of Providence," in *The Providence of God: Deus habet consilium*, ed. Francesca Aran Murphy and Philip G. Ziegler (London: T&T Clark, 2009), 167.

32. Ibid., 158.

33. A fuller form of the argument traced below, linking image and sonship, is in progress for future publication.

34. Irenaeus, *Against Heresies* 5.16.2 (*ANF* 1:544). Emphasis and brackets original.

35. A parallel theme in patristic Christology is explored in Alasdair Heron, "Logos, Image, Son," in *Creation, Christ and Culture Studies in Honour of T. F. Torrance*, ed. Richard W. A. McKinney (Edinburgh: T&T Clark, 1976).

ETERNAL GENERATION

for incarnation: "God shall be glorified in His handiwork, fitting it so as to be conformable to, and modelled after, His own Son."[36]

The scriptural ground for Irenaeus's argument can be sketched in brief.[37] In the beginning, God created humanity in his "image and likeness" (Gen 1:26–27).[38] In the Genesis account, this language is used of both God and Adam as models. First God creates Adam in his "image and likeness" (Gen 1:26–27), then Adam fathers a son according to his "image and likeness" (Gen 5:1–3). Adam, who is made in the divine image, in turn, *images* through human begetting. Provocatively, Luke the evangelist draws on this connection in his genealogy, tracing the lineage of Christ back to Adam and calling him not "image" but "son of God" (Luke 3:38). In Genesis 3, sin defaces the image in humanity, yet the image is not erased (Gen 9:6; cf. Jas 3:9). Instead, the longing for deliverance through a "son" is now echoed both inside (Gen 3:15) and outside the garden (Gen 5:29). The language of "sonship" is appropriated to Israel in the Exodus, "my firstborn son" (Exod 4:22; Hos 11:1), and continues in the Pentateuch as the Lord carries (Deut 1:31) and disciplines his "sons" (Deut 8:5). The hope for a true "son" is prophetically present throughout the history of Israel, reaching a crescendo in the Davidic promise: "I will be to him a father, and he shall be to me a son" (2 Sam 7:14).

In the New Testament, the reclamation of the sonship of humanity is achieved by Israel's hope and consolation, Jesus Christ. John the evangelist reveals that the incarnate Son is always the reflection of his Father—he only does what he sees the Father doing (John 5:19) such that if you have seen the Son, you have seen the Father (John 14:9). The apostolic preaching about the Son draws this connection more explicitly. Jesus Christ *is* the perfect image of the Father (2 Cor 4:4; Col 1:15). In these last days, God has spoken through his Son (Heb 1:2), the exact imprint of the Father's nature (Heb 1:3). Central to the saving work that the true image and Son accomplishes is relational restoration, a restoration with familial import via Paul's language of adoption (treated below). Accordingly, the continuing renovation of adoptive sons and daughters entails being "transformed into his image" (2 Cor 3:18)—this language echoing the glorious transfiguration of the "beloved Son" (Matt 17:5). The eternal plan of God is that his created and redeemed children be "conformed to the image of the Son"

---

36. Irenaeus, *Against Heresies* 5.6.1 (*ANF* 1:531).

37. Irenaeus does not trace his full scriptural reasoning in one place, but reference to a number of the texts cited here are distributed throughout *Against Heresies*.

38. For Irenaeus, unlike most modern exegetes, the terms image (*tselem*) and likeness (*demuth*) each have a different sense.

(Rom 8:29a), where Christ himself is "firstborn among many brothers and sisters" (Rom 8:29b NIV). In the eschaton, resurrected children of God will be remade to "bear the image of the man of heaven" (1 Cor 15:49).

In the Irenaean account, thinking from the incarnation backward, divine begetting—perfect imaging—in eternity is freely extended in time through the incarnation of the Son, such that Christ, the last Adam, is the true pattern of the *imago Dei* in humanity. Thinking from creation forward, the first *imago Dei* in the temporal order, Adam our progenitor, stands in primal history as type of the archetype who is to come, Christ the true Son and image. While admittedly dizzying to comprehend, such an approach offers significant explanatory power for dogmatics.[39]

Here we note that a great deal hangs on our dogmatic articulation of the image. As archetype, the eternally begotten Son's relation to his Father is "wholly unique and incommunicable. As Son, he stands at the head of many brothers and sisters among whom he is the firstborn (Rom. 8.29); he is, indeed, the first-born of all creation (Col. 1.15). But *prototokos* denotes his relation to creatures, not his relation to the Father."[40] However, the absolute analogical interval between Christ's sonship and ours does not imperil his fraternal fellowship with humanity; rather, it marks the infinite depth and immeasurable power that grounds his saving efficacy. The success of Christ's mediatorial priesthood is not founded upon a preexisting creaturely possibility but on the power of an indestructible life that both creates creaturely possibilities and completes them (Heb 7:16). This life is none other than the life of the Son, who is eternally begotten from the Father.

Prodigals Return: Adoption and Resurrection

Tracing a final movement in the saving economy surfaces two additional created effects: adoption and resurrection. How do the doctrines of adoption and of resurrection bear created effects that witness to the Son's eternal begetting? John Calvin illuminates both in his treatment of Jesus Christ, the Mediator.

---

39. Col 1:15–18 bears witness to this pattern *in nuce*. Paul begins with the Son's eternal begetting (Col 1:15), next weaving together all created effects under the *creational* work of Christ (Col 1:16). From this vantage he looks backward to Christ's ground in God's eternal life (Col 1:17a) and forward to his work in *all creation* (Col 1:17b). Importantly, we see that Christ's *creational* work is distinct from, and prior to, his *redemptive* work as the head of *the church* (Col 1:18a). In his redemptive work he is the beginning of new creation, firstborn in the resurrection (Col 1:18b), ultimately manifesting his supremacy in all things (Col 1:18c). The distinction and order here is critical, and the dogmatic possibilities offered by grounding creational work in eternal generation and viewing redemptive work as its outflow might form a rapprochement for Thomists and Barthians about how to Christologically relate creation and covenant.

40. John Webster, "Eternal Generation," 33. Webster notes that Turretin exerts great energy here to secure the dogmatic import of this difference in *Elenctic Theology*, 298–300.

ETERNAL GENERATION

Calvin spends a good deal of effort explicating the meaning, reality, and spiritual grace of our adoption as sons and daughters in the gospel. He does not treat it as a discrete theme, instead distributing his discussion throughout his *Institutes*.[41] Broadly, divine Fatherhood is the faithful care by which God sustains all humans and angels by virtue of their created relation to him. "At their creation angels and men were so constituted that God was their common father."[42] More narrowly, another kind of divine Fatherhood comes as a benefit of adoption by grace (not by created relation), which is "the free benevolence of God."[43]

Calvin's understanding of our humanity is twofold: we were originally created in a state of integrity due to our creation in the *imago Dei*, but the image is pervasively corrupted (either entirely or almost entirely) in the fall.[44] Because of the fall, we are no longer sons in any real sense because "our sin [is] just cause for his disowning us and not regarding or recognizing us as his sons."[45] Our only hope for returning to God's fatherly care is through the preaching of the cross, "if we desire to return to God our Author and Maker from whom we have been estranged, in order that he may again begin to be our Father."[46] This redemptive sonship is the matter to which our adoption refers. For Calvin, it is qualitatively different than created sonship, which pales by comparison, since "to neither angels nor men was God ever Father," but he becomes so to us only "by free adoption because Christ is the Son of God by nature."[47]

Here especially Calvin carefully safeguard the distinction between Christ's sonship and ours. God is the Father of Christ as "only-begotten Son."[48] Our sonship by adoption is "free benevolence." Son by *nature* and son by *grace* are the key qualifiers that distinguish eternal begetting from temporal created effect.[49] With this distinction in place, Calvin can see the incarnation as the event upon which our adoption is founded: "Who could have done this [restored us] had not the self-same Son of God become the

---

41. For a helpful synthetic treatment of Calvin on adoption, see Nigel Westhead, "Adoption in the Thought of John Calvin," *Scottish Bulletin of Evangelical Theology* (13 Aug 1995): 102–15.

42. *Inst.* 2.14.5 (1:489).

43. *Inst.* 3.1.3 (1:540).

44. *Inst.* 1.15 (creation) and 2.1–4 (fall). Calvin's later work seems to soften on this point. See Randall Zachman, *Image and Word in the Theology of John Calvin* (Notre Dame: University of Notre Dame Press, 2007), 64–68.

45. *Inst.* 2.6.1 (1:341).

46. *Inst.* 2.6.1 (1:341).

47. *Inst.* 2.14.5 (1:488).

48. *Inst.* 2.14.5 (1:488).

49. The same careful distinction is seen in the Heidelberg Catechism written around the same time, "Christ alone is the eternal, natural Son of God; but we are children of God by adoption, through grace, for his [Christ's] sake," (Heidelberg Catechism, Q. 33).

JOSH MALONE

Son of man, and had he not so taken what was ours as to impart what was his to us, and to make what was his by nature ours by grace?"[50]

Notice that the approach Calvin uses to weave the scriptural account together mirrors what we saw in Irenaeus. The story of salvation is that from eternity: "[the Father] predestined us for adoption to himself as sons through Jesus Christ" (Eph 1:5). Our creation as the divine image is parallel to the relation of created sonship. The fall distorts this relation in the sense that the image is essentially gone; this means we have been disowned by the Father. Yet, "when fullness of time had come, God sent forth his Son . . . so that we might receive adoption as sons" (Gal 4:4–5). Christ, the Son incarnate, enters into our predicament, bearing true Sonship as the true image. In the gospel we are drawn into vital relation with God, through union with Christ, reclaiming us as sons in the Son—redemptive sonship—and imparting "the Spirit of adoption . . . [who] bears witness with our spirit that we are children of God" (Rom 8:15–16). Westhead aptly summarizes Calvin, "In a word, the climax of this grace of adoption is renewal in God's image. This image, as we have seen, is the ground of our being children of God by creation."[51]

Eschatologically, the Spirit who begins the renovation of the image in our adoption completes this work in our resurrection. "We ourselves, who have the firstfruits of the Spirit, groan inwardly as we wait eagerly for adoption as sons, the redemption of our bodies" (Rom 8:23). In a glorious final created effect, our fraternal union with Son is consummated in resurrection. The fountain of life that the Son *is* as eternally begotten necessarily remakes us by virtue of our union with him (John 11:25). He "will transform our lowly body to be like his glorious body, by the power that enables him even to subject all things to himself" (Phil 3:21), and that power is the power of his eternally begotten divine life. Calvin sees this final phase of our adoption as essential, for without the redemption of our bodies, "the sacrifice of the death of Christ would be in vain and fruitless." Accordingly, our future inheritance is found precisely in resurrection as conformity to Christ, "all whom he has adopted should bear the image of Christ."[52] While we are "God's children now," what we will be has "not yet appeared," but in the glorious *visio Dei* when "he [Christ] appears we shall be like him, because we shall see him as he is" (1 John 3:2).

---

50. *Inst.* 2.12.2 (1:465).
51. Westhead, "Adoption in the Thought of John Calvin," 112.
52. John Calvin, *Commentary on Romans* (Albany, OR: Ages Software, 1998), Logos electronic edition, on Rom 8:29.

ETERNAL GENERATION

In sum, our God is a fountain of life, and the church confesses this mystery to entail that the Father begets, the Son is begotten, and the Spirit proceeds. These eternal acts are temporally manifest in love and grace in the missions of the Son and Spirit. Before all ages, the Father has life in himself and grants the Son life in himself (John 5:26), and in creaturely time the Son gives life to whom he will (John 5:21). The wonder of the gospel is that the eternal Son, for whom and through whom are all things, has in these last days come from the Father to the far country to bring many sons to glory (Heb 2:10).

Trinity and Retrieval

Here are three things by way of conclusion. First, faithful theological reasoning is biblical reasoning. Retrieving the pro-Nicene pattern traced here matters precisely because it claims to be faithful to Scripture. Namely, it offers the most compelling reading of the God of the gospel delivered by prophetic and apostolic emissaries.

Second, faithful dogmatic reasoning entails a conceptual meditation on God in his inner and outer movements: paternity, filiation, and spiration, as well as creation, redemption, and consummation. The order is nontrivial; without a firm grasp on the Trinity we will have a dangerously impoverished understanding of the created economy.

Third, faithfully meditating on God's created effects, centered on Christ in his filial identity, is promising for a synthetic reading of Scripture, which is critical to theology's constructive task. In this vein, we see the biblical story is about Christ: last Adam, architect, and archetype. At the center of creation itself is Christ: Logos, Image, and Son. And precisely because he is the eternal Son of the Father, he is fitted to mediate redemption by becoming the firstborn among many brothers and sisters (Rom 8:29).

For from him and through him and to him are all things. To him be the glory forever. Amen.

Romans 11:36

SUBJECT INDEX

Abraham, 34, 86, 88, 90, 108–9, 128, 140, 263

Acontius, Jacobus, 196–98

Adam, 38, 39, 41, 158, 280–82, 285

Adonai, 75

adoption, 25, 87, 123, 261, 263, 265–66, 281, 282–84

adoptionism (or, adoptionist Christology), 49, 117, 130

Aelius Herodianus, 112

Agamemnon, 109

Alexander, 50

Anchor Bible commentary, 76–77

angels, 40, 42, 86, 97, 120, 121, 123, 124–25, 126, 127, 220, 283

anti-Nicenes, 45, 49–52, 55, 65, 174

anti-Trinitarians (or, anti-Trinitarianism), 181–83, 195

Aquila of Sinope, 108

apologists, 47–48, 136, 144

Apollonius Dyscolus, 112

Apostles' Creed, 201

Arianism (or, the Arian heresy), 59, 87, 100, 102–3, 188

Arminianism, 195

Articles of Religion, 194. *See* Irish Articles; Thirty-Nine Articles

aseity, 56, 171, 185, 186–87, 205, 230, 243, 245, 246, 249–50, 251–53, 257, 259

Asterius, 45, 49, 51

Athanasian Creed, 201

autotheos, 186, 189, 191, 198, 222

begetting, discontinuity and continuity between human and divine, 116

Bethlehem, 21, 68, 70, 72, 76

biblical theology, 32, 33

biblical warrant, 20, 56, 59, 61–62, 64–66, 167, 243

Byzantine text-type. *See* Majority Text

"canonical rules," 54–55, 167

Cappadocians, 52, 53, 54, 276

Catholic faith, 171, 177–79

Catholicism, 183, 232

causation, 248–49, 250, 253, 246

Chalcedonian Definition, 201

Charles I, 189

Christology, 36, 54, 81, 103, 117, 123, 130, 167, 186, 188, 228–32, 234–39, 268, 278, 280

church fathers, 21, 30, 67, 73, 91, 98, 99–100, 106, 116, 185, 186, 194, 239, 265

Codex Vercellensis, 100

common nouns for God, 134, 135–37, 144–45

communicatio essentiae, 146

copresence, 141, 143–44, 146

Council of Constantinople. *See* First Council of Constantinople; Third Council of Constantinople

created effects, 25, 273, 278, 280, 282, 285

creating, relation of fathering to, 38

Subject Index

creation, 25, 29, 30, 39, 40, 49, 50, 56,
57, 58, 60–63, 74, 76, 83, 85, 91,
103, 111, 119, 136–37, 139, 140,
150, 151, 154, 159–60, 164, 168,
173, 177, 178, 191, 192, 223, 230,
245, 248, 252, 255, 256, 268, 272,
274, 278–85
a divine gift and triune movement,
278–80
from creation to new, 280–82
ex nihilo, 230, 248, 268, 279
Creed of Constantinople. *See* Nicene
Creed
Creed of Nicaea (325), 271–72
dependence, 81, 83–86, 93–96, 174,
214, 237, 244, 246–59
ditheism, 79, 83, 85, 170
divine essence. *See* essence
divine names (or, the Divine Name),
20, 23, 31–36, 42–43, 52–53, 55,
63, 66, 126, 134, 138–44, 272, 273
how the persons of the Trinity bear
the, 141
the ontological basis of the, 35
two broad categories of, 36–37
divine nature, 82
divine simplicity, 166, 185, 221, 234, 274
donum nominis, 133, 138–42, 145, 146
draft catechism (1646), 202–3
Durandus of Sancto Porciano, 187
economic argument, 51, 64
economic Trinity, 63, 86, 93, 94, 228
egalitarian/complementarian debate,
92–93
election, 226, 227, 229–30, 232, 235
emanation, 160, 215, 218, 279
emanationism, 49, 217–18
"equality" (Father and Son), 143–44,
174
essence, 24, 46, 50, 52, 55, 60, 67, 70,
71, 72, 73, 74, 82, 96, 98, 103,
119, 138–39, 142–43, 144, 146,

165, 166, 169, 185, 186–87, 189,
191–94, 195, 196, 197, 199, 200,
204, 206, 207, 209, 210, 211, 221,
232, 244, 248, 249, 250, 253–59,
261, 267, 269, 275–76
essential communication, 138–39, 142–43
essential unity, 25, 274–75, 278
ESV (*English Standard Version*), 101,
113, 114–15, 175
eternal begetting 43–44, 61, 116, 118,
139, 164, 166, 172, 178–79, 276,
282, 283
eternal functional subordination (EFS),
62–63, 65, 66, 93, 276
eternal grant, 43, 82, 85, 96, 170
eternal procession, 29, 46, 52, 98, 144,
171, 175, 223, 253, 259, 261, 277
Eusebius of Nicomedia, 45, 49, 51
evangelical historicism, 227, 229, 230
evangelicalism, 228
exinanition, 266
faith of Christ, 236–39
fall, the, 219, 283, 284
fallacy of the excluded middle, 174
family resemblances, 33, 35–36, 37, 40–41
Fatherhood, ancient church's conception
of, 258–59
fathering, 38–39
Father of lights, 29, 38–39, 41, 268
father–son relationships, three analogous
patterns of, 37–42
Creator to creature, 38–39
creature to creature, 37–38
divine Father to divine Son, 40–42
Featley, Daniel, 189–94
figures of speech, 133, 265
filiation, 17, 37, 94, 236, 238, 267, 268,
273, 277, 280, 285
"firstborn," 125–26, 137, 151, 152, 255,
281, 282, 282
First Council of Constantinople (381),
100–101, 102, 274

First Council of Nicaea (325), 100, 118, 138, 274

Fourth Lateran Council, 187

from-another rule, 55, 56, 168, 169, 171, 173, 175

fundamentalism, 228

Gataker, Thomas, 183–84

generatio, 132, 133, 139, 140, 145, 146

genre, 53, 54, 55, 66, 112

gennaō (beget), 136, 272–73, 276

Gnostics, 271, 279, 280

God–Adam relation, 38

Goodwin, Thomas, 192

Gospel of John, name-theology of the, 139–40

grammar, a theological account of, 77–78

Greek–English Lexicon, A. See LSJ

grounding, 250–53, 266

grounding skeptics, 253

Hammond, Henry, 195

hapax legomenon, 53, 75

Heidelberg Catechism, 262, 266, 283

High Priestly Prayer. *See* "Prayer of the Divine Name"

homoousios, 47, 55, 65, 116, 119, 138–39

Hugh of St. Victor, 68

hypostasis, 67, 144, 152, 161, 244, 249, 276

hypostases, 46, 146, 152

"I am" statements, 139, 140

image of God, 42, 160, 161, 219, 255, 280

"image of the invisible God" (Col. 1:17), 137, 151, 157–58, 255

imago Dei, 282, 283

incarnation, 29, 45, 48, 51, 54, 55, 56, 63, 64, 73, 77, 93, 96, 151, 175, 195, 206, 230, 231, 232, 233–36, 261, 276, 280–82, 283

inseparable operation, 174, 177, 178, 224

Irish Articles (of 1615), 193, 200, 203, 207

Isaac, 34, 88, 90, 108–9, 163

Ishmael, 88, 90, 108

Jewish monotheism, 55, 58, 61

kenosis, 266

King James Version (and "only begotten"), 100

kinship term(s), 133, 134, 135, 137, 143, 145

kinship nouns in Origen and Athanasius, 137–38

last Adam, 282, 285

Legate, Bartholomew, 184, 188

Liddell and Scott. See LSJ

"life in himself," 42, 79–82, 85, 92, 96, 165, 168–71, 179, 197, 200, 274, 278, 285

light(s), 29–30, 38–42, 97, 118, 119, 133, 134, 137, 145, 155, 159, 164, 166, 173, 183, 185, 212, 268, 270, 271, 274

"likeness" of God, 39

literal exposition, three levels of, 68

Logos, 50, 51, 52, 54–55, 56, 58, 60, 61–62, 64, 70, 73, 82, 123, 154, 234, 239, 285

Logos theologians, 136–37

LSJ (*Liddell and Scott*), 103–4, 111, 112

Majority Text, 113, 115

Manichaeism, 49

Marcellus of Ancyra, 51, 53

Mary, 118, 191

Mediator (Christ as), 170, 193, 203, 282

modalism, 46, 63, 163, 178, 198

modes of subsistence, 98, 145–46

Molnar, Paul, 228–28

Monarchianism, 49, 96

Monarchians, 65, 152

Monobazus, king of Adiabene, 90, 108

monogenēs, 22, 59, 89, 99–116, 264

etymology of, 103–5

SUBJECT INDEX

examples of the scientific usage of, 111

history of interpretation of, 99–10

lexical argument for "only begotten," 105–12

technical uses, 112

three nonliteral extensions, 108–12

various Bible translations' rendering, 101

monothelite/dyothelite controversy, 96

monothelitism, 96

natural theology, 232

Nestle-Aland, 113

NIV (*New International Version*), 100, 114

Nicene controversy, 49–56

Nicene Creed (381, Nicene-Constantinopolitan Creed), 62, 118, 135, 138–39, 164, 183, 185–86, 187, 190, 268, 271, 275

NIDOTTE (*New International Dictionary of Old Testament Theology and Exegesis*), 76

Novum Testamentum Graece. See Nestle-Aland

obedience of the Son, 95–96, 215, 232–33, 235, 236, 238, 277

oikonomia, 51, 226, 231, 235, 236, 238, 239

'*olam*, 75–76

"only begotten." See chapter 10, (98–116). *See also* 22, 59, 87–90, 118, 129, 143, 151, 153, 155, 157–58, 164, 171, 199, 202–3, 210, 262, 264, 266, 270, 272, 273, 274, 276, 283

in John 1, 112–15

use by ecclesiastical writers (table), 99–100

ontological subordination, 46, 94, 185, 203

Paraklētos, 95. *See* eternal procession

paroimia, 53

paternity, 37, 94, 267, 273, 277, 285

Paul of Samosata, 49

perichoresis (co-inherence), 198

personal distinction, 275–76

personal properties among the persons of the Trinity, 94

Philoxenus, 112

phoenix (as an example of *monogenēs*), 111

pistis christou, 236–37

predestination, 227

Presbyterianism, 228

principium, 186–87, 203, 256, 259

procession(s), 23, 29, 46, 52, 72–74, 78, 87, 94, 95, 98, 132, 139, 144–45, 171, 175, 176, 178, 185, 202, 203, 205, 212, 212–17, 219, 222, 223, 227, 236, 238, 248, 253, 259, 261, 266, 267, 270, 273, 277–80

processio verbi, 132–33, 139, 140, 141

eternal generation as, 136–37, 144–45

production (or, *productionem*) of divine essence, 191–92, 196, 199

pro-Nicene

theological reasoning, 271–73

understanding of the temporal obedience of the Son, 277

use of the term, 100–101

pro-Nicenes, 55, 65, 103, 164, 275, 277

prosopological exegesis, 54, 120, 123

providence, 40, 164, 168, 177, 280

qedem, 76

Qumran, Micah fragment at, 75

Racovian Catechism, 69–70

"radiance" of God's glory, the Son as the, 29, 40, 90–91, 119, 155, 159, 255, 273–74

"rationalistic reductionism," 71, 72

"recapitulation," 48

redemption, 74, 141, 164, 168, 177, 208, 212, 213, 214, 215–17, 218, 224, 231, 238, 278, 284, 285

289

Reformed orthodoxy, 211, 212
Reformed theologians, 30, 239
Reformers, 24, 82, 170
relational order (*taxis*), 25, 274, 276–77, 279
RSV (*Revised Standard Version*), 101
"rule of unity," 278
Sabellianism, 49, 87
Sarah (daughter of Raguel), 109
Sarah, 90, 108
self-existence, 79–80, 82, 165, 170–71, 185, 243, 245, 246. *See also* aseity
Septuagint (LXX), 53, 60, 75, 106–8, 110, 125, 136
Seth, 38, 39, 41, 158
Shema, 135, 138
Similitudes of Enoch, 76
social Trinitarianism, 46, 65, 66
Socinianism, 69–70, 183, 196, 198
Socinians, 71, 193, 197, 198, 199, 200
"sons of God," 125–26
sonship, 17, 18, 25, 86–87, 91–92, 100, 112, 114, 115, 121, 122–23, 126, 170, 184, 205–6, 262–63, 265–68, 273, 277, 280–84
soteriology, 25, 183, 238, 260–70
    justifications for an appeal to, 263–65
    three connecting themes for Trinitarian, 265–70
speculative theology, 68–69, 76
spiration, 37, 267, 277, 278, 285
Stoic tradition, 160
submission, 65, 86, 93, 94, 95, 276, 277
subordination, 46, 59, 62–66, 83, 93–94, 96, 174, 185, 190, 200, 202–3, 205, 212–17, 223
subordinationism, 18, 19, 46, 137, 185, 187, 195, 199, 243, 244–46, 257
subordinationism objection (to eternal generation), 245–46, 248, 249, 250, 251, 256, 257, 259

subordinationists, 49, 51
subsistence, 98, 145, 155, 157, 179, 197, 199–201, 214, 215, 244, 245, 277
substance (divine), 40–42, 48, 94. 98, 118, 119, 151, 159, 163, 165, 166, 176–77, 179, 187, 198, 201, 201–2, 203, 204–5, 206, 210, 270, 272, 274
Symmachus, 108
Synod of London. *See* Westminster Assembly
systematic theology, 19, 231, 232, 269
taxis, 63, 94, 95, 96, 178, 274, 276–77
Tetragrammaton, 134–35, 138, 139, 140, 142, 143. *See also* YHWH
Theodore of Mopsuestia, 72
theologia, 226, 231, 233–34, 235–36, 238, 239
theological reflection, the nature of, 47
Thesaurus Linguae Graecae. *See* TLG
Third Council of Constantinople, 96
Thirty-Nine Articles, 190, 195, 201–2
Thomism, 239
TLG (Thesaurus Linguae Graecae), 89, 99, 104, 106
Trinitarianism, 17, 21, 25, 46, 49, 65, 66, 145, 186, 209, 260, 264–66, 270
    Tradition A, 186–87, 192, 207
    Tradition B, 187, 191, 207
    Tradition C, 193, 200, 207
Trinity
    common nouns for the persons of the, 134, 135–37, 144–45
    doctrine of the (defined), 17
    divine uniqueness of the persons of the, 141–42
    personal properties among the persons of the, 94
triunity, 208, 232, 262
tropos hyparxeos, 145–46

SUBJECT INDEX

typology, 48, 61
unintelligibility objection, 243, 244,
    245, 246, 248, 249, 251, 256,
    257, 259
United Presbyterian Church United
    States of America's "Confession
    of 1967," 237
unity, 25, 46, 52, 63, 65, 67, 98, 138,
    140, 142, 145, 146, 158, 163,
    176–77, 185, 198, 200, 201–5,
    235. 269, 273, 274–75, 276, 278
    of divine substance, 48, 94, 118,
        163, 176–77, 201–2, 203, 204,
        205, 206, 270
    of the Scriptures, 33, 48, 49, 51,
        64, 72
Unity, Equality, Connection (Trinity),
    141, 142
Valentinians, 152
virgin birth, 238, 275

Virgin Mary, 118, 191
Vorlage, 53
Vulgate, 75, 100, 102
Westminster Assembly, 24, 180–83,
    189–92, 194–97, 201–5, 207
Westminster Confession of Faith, 201,
    203
Westminster Larger Catechism, 203–4
Westminster Shorter Catechism, 202,
    204–5
Wisdom (personified), 21, 42, 47–49,
    52, 54–55, 57–62, 64, 66, 110,
    129, 136, 140, 144–45, 151–55,
    158–61, 171
word-concept fallacy, 21–22
words, the twofold potential of, 77
YHWH, 33, 122, 127, 134, 135, 138.
    See also Tetragrammaton
Zerubbabel, 72, 73
Zeus, 105

SCRIPTURE INDEX

Genesis

1 . . . . 61, 279
1–2 57
1:1 61
1:1–2 36
1:26–27 281
3 281
3:15 281
5:1 38
5:1–3 . . . . 37–38, 281
5:3 . . . . 38, 158
5:29 281
6:1–4 125
6:2 124
6:2, 4 124
9:6 281
21:10–12 . . . . 90, 108
22:2 108
22:2, 12, 16 108
22:12 108
25:1–2 . . . . 88, 90

Exodus

4:22 . . . . 143, 281
33:14 211

Numbers

23:19 273

Deuteronomy

1:31 281

4:4 130
6:4 . . . . .36, 135, 142
8:5 281
32:18 . . . . 38, 134
33:27 76

Judges

11:34 107

2 Samuel

7 . . . . 122, 127
7:11–14 126
7:13 75
7:14 . .91, 120, 122, 124, 125, 128, 281

2 Kings

10:27 75

1 Chronicles

17:13 125
22:10 125
28:6 126

Tobit

3:15 . . . . 107, 109
6:11, 15 107
8:17 107

Job

1:6 124
2:1 124

SCRIPTURE INDEX

15:7 38
38:7 .124

Psalms

2 . . . . 22, 122, 126, 127, 128, 131
2:6 . . . . 91, 92, 122, 129
2:6a 91
2:7 . . . . 44, 70, 91, 117, 120, 121, 122,
         125, 128, 130, 144, 167, 171
2:8 . . . . 122, 127
8 128
21:21 110
22:20 110
24:16 110
25:16 110
28:1 124
33:6 . . . . .36, 145, 279
34:17 110
                      35:17
36:9 271
88:7 . . . . 124, 125
89:23 126
89:26–29. 126
89:27 125
90:2 . . . . 35, 38, 76
95:7–11. 128–29
102:26 39
102:27 .130
110. . . . . 124, 128
110:1 121
110:3 136
145:3 34

Proverbs

8. . . . . .21, 44–66, 264
8:22 . . 45, 53, 54, 58, 61, 66, 151, 152,
                          154
8:22–25. . . . . 51, 167
8:22–31. . . . . 44, 55, 56, 60, 61
8:23 . . . . 61, 70
8:25 . . . . 54, 56, 61, 66, 110, 136,
                        155, 171

8:30 . . . . 57, 58, 61, 64, 66
9:1 53

Wisdom of Solomon

7:22 110
7:25 160
7:25–26. . . . . 152, 155, 157, 159

Isaiah

8:11 126
9:6 75
11:1 75
33:17 29
40:25 273
42:1 121
53:8 206
54:5 134
63:9 211
63:16 . . . . 133, 143

Jeremiah

6:26 110

Daniel

7:9 . . . . 72, 76

Hosea

11:1 281

Amos

8:10 110
9:11 75

Micah

4:1–4 75
4:14 75
5:1 67
5:2 . . . . 21, 67–78, 167

Zechariah

12:10 110

293

Matthew

2:4–6	73
3:17	143
5:9	91
10:40	171
11:25	36
11:27	174, 262
17:5	279, 281
12:32	169
20:20–28	95
22:42–45	123
24:36–39	174
26:38	169
28:18	174
28:19	36
28:20	95

Mark

10:18	161
13:32	169

Luke

3:38	38, 39, 281
4:18	169
4:43	171
7:12	89, 106
8:42	89, 106
9:38	89, 106
10:16	171
11:13	37

John

1	87
1:1	87, 114, 137, 144, 166, 173, 221, 274, 276, 279
1:1–3	30, 36, 61, 173
1:1–5	83
1:1–14	62
1:1, 14	86
1:1–18	40, 42
1:3	36, 61, 62, 167, 168, 173
1:4	30, 173
1:5	173
1:6	172
1:8	173
1:9	30, 159
1:10	173
1:14	30, 100, 102, 112–15, 173, 174
1:14, 18	88, 99
1:15	
173	
1:18	40, 42, 88, 89, 99, 100, 102, 112, 113, 114–15, 119, 137, 143, 159, 262, 273, 276
1:30	173
3:16	81, 87, 88, 99, 100, 101, 113, 114
3:17	86, 91
3:18	88, 99, 100, 114
3:35	84, 174
4:34	171
5:1–9	83
5:8–13	83
5:16	83
5:17	83
5:17–47	174
5:18	41, 83, 84, 178
5:19	55, 56, 83, 84, 161, 168, 169, 173, 178
5:19–30	83, 85, 86
5:20	84
5:21	81, 84, 173
5:22	84, 170, 173
5:23	85, 170, 172
5:24	170
5:24–30	83
5:25	171
5:26	21, 36, 41, 42, 55, 56, 79–96, 165, 167–71, 173, 274
5:26a	165
5:26b	165, 169, 170
5:27	85, 170, 173
5:30	85
5:36	169, 172, 173
5:30–47	172

294

Scripture Index

6. 80
6:29, 38–44, 57 172
6:38 . . . . .167, 169, 172
6:40 174
6:53 80
6:57 80
7:5 61
7:16, 28–29, 33 . . . . 172, 173
7:29 172
7:33 172
8:12 274
8:16–18. . . . . 26–29, 172
8:29 . . . . 86, 172
8:42 172
8:44 91
8:58 . . . . 86, 140
9:4 172
10:18 .173
10:30 . . . . 167, 168
12:44–50. 172
13:16 .172
13:20 .172
14:6, 10. 173
14:9 86
14:11 .274
14:13 .174
14:16, 26. 95
14:24 .172
14:31 . . . . 84, 86
15:21 .172
15:26 95
16:5, 28. 172
16:15 .169
16:33 81
17. . . . . 139, 140
17:1 174
17:2 173
17:3 . . . . 172, 274
17:6, 24. 139
17:8 . . . . 172, 173
17:10 . . . . 160, 169
17:11 . . . . 41, 43, 139, 140, 173

17:11, 12. . . . . 139, 140
17:12 . . . . 41, 43, 139
17:21 .172
17:22 .173
18:11 .173
20:21 .172
20:28 . . . . 36, 86
20:31 81

Acts
5:3–4 36
8:33 206
13:33 .144

Romans
1:4 276
1:20 29
3:22, 26. 236
5:1, 11. 173
8:15–16. 284
8:23 284
8:29 . . . . .282, 284, 285
8:29a. .282
8:29b. .282
8:32 41
11:36 . . . . 174, 193, 256, 285
11:36a. 174

1 Corinthians
1:24 . . . . 50, 52, 151, 152
1:24, 30. . . . . 60, 61, 62
2:10–11. 36
2:11 262
8:6 . . . . . . 36, 135, 138, 139, 173–74,
                                      256, 275
11:3 . . . . 62, 63, 93
15:20–28. 94
15:24 95
15:25 94–95
15:27 95
15:28 . . . . 62, 63, 94, 95
15:49 .282

2 Corinthians

3:2–3 271
3:17–18. 36
3:18 .281
4:4 . . . . 255, 281

Galatians

2:16, 20. 236
3:22 .236
4:4 . . . . 167, 169
4:4–5 284
4:4–6 . . . . .36, 171, 174
4:6 274

Ephesians

1:3–14 173
1:3, 5 280
1:5 284
1:7, 10. 280
1:13 .280
2:18 .173
3:12 .236
3:14 .265
3:14–15. 273
3:15 35
4:4–6 .36
4:6 . . . . 35, 173
5. 93

Philippians

2:5 137
2:5–11 139
2:6 . . . . 167, 169
2:6–11 276
2:7 169
2:8 168
2:9 173
3:9 . . . . 236, 237
3:21 .284

Colossians

1:15 . . . . .137, 151–52, 157, 167, 169,
171, 255, 281, 282

1:15–17. 61
1:15–18. . . . . 42, 282
1:15–20. 40
1:16 . . . . 173, 282
1:17a. 282
1:17b 282
1:18 .169
1:18a. 282
1:18b 282
1:18c. 282
2:9 273
3:17 .173

1 Timothy

6:16 .274

2 Timothy

1:15 .105
2:23 .107

Hebrews

1. . . . . .22, 61, 117–31
1:2 90
1:1–2 173
1:1–3a. 119
1:1–4 . . . . 40, 61, 62
1:1–5 117
1:2 . . . . 90, 91, 127–28, 281
1:2–3 .40
1:3 . . . . 29, 37, 39–40, 41, 90–91,
119, 121, 126, 137, 144, 151,
155, 157, 159, 255, 274, 281
1:4 126
1:5 . . . 91, 92, 117, 118, 120, 121, 122,
124, 127, 130–31, 167
1:5–6 144
1:5ff 91
1:6 . . . . 121, 125
1:8–9 . . . . 126, 130
1:8, 10. 40
1:8, 13. 40
1:10–12. 127

Scripture Index

1:11–12 40
1:12 .130
1:13 .121
2 . . . . 120, 128
2:9 128
2:10 . . . . .235, 256, 285
2:10–3:6 237
3–4 128
3:13 .129
4, 12 .120
4:14–5:10 . . . .
237 . . . .
5 128
5:11 .265
7 130
7:16 .282
7:24 .130
11 128
11:17 . . . . . .88, 89–90, 106, 108, 109
11:39 .128
12:9 37
12:23 .125
13:8 . . . . 128, 129

James

1:5, 17 .35

1:17 . . . 29, 34, 35, 37, 38–39, 41, 268
3:9 281

2 Peter

1:17 134–35

1 John

1:1–3 30
1:5 . . . . 39, 159
1:15 274
3:1 . . . . 265, 269
3:2 284
4:8 221
4:9 . . . . 88, 99, 100, 113, 114
4:16 221
5:20 . . . . .167, 169, 274

Jude

25 173

Revelation

3 61
3:14 . . . . 50, 61, 64
22:16 .104

AUTHOR INDEX

Abbot, Ezra, 89, 103
à Brakel, Wilhelmus, 231
Abramowski, Luise, 53, 54
Aeschylus, 106, 107, 109
Aesop, 107
Allen, Michael, 13, 24, 31, 42, 45, 89, 96, 226–40, 269, 277
Ambrose, Aurelius, 82
Ammonius of Alexandria, 111
Anatolios, Khaled, 49, 50, 65, 275
Andersen, Francis I., 77
Anderson, David, 174
Andresen, Carl, 120, 123
Antoninus Liberalis, 107
Apion, 107
Apollonius Rhodius, 107
Aquinas, Thomas, 24, 35, 56, 68–69, 73–74, 142, 144, 163, 212, 227, 231, 236, 238, 239, 262, 263, 273, 274, 277, 278
Aristotle, 111, 152, 254, 257, 264, 279
Arius, 45, 49, 50, 51, 52, 58, 65, 66, 188, 195
Arminius, Jacobus, 195
Arrian, 106, 107
Arrowsmith, John, 182, 192
Athanasius, 51, 52–54, 62, 66, 89, 99, 106, 119, 137, 239, 268, 272, 275
Audi, Paul, 253
Auerbach, Erich, 77
Augustine, 23–24, 51–56, 59, 63, 69, 77, 82, 85, 87, 91, 94, 129–30, 140–43, 145, 163–79, 186, 274, 279

Ayres, Lewis, 13, 23, 31, 73, 100–101, 150, 149–62, 163, 164, 166, 176
Bakon, Shimon, 57
Barker, Kenneth, 88, 101
Barnes, Michel René, 11, 149, 160, 163, 164, 174
Barrett, C. K., 113
Barth, Karl, 24, 68, 69, 73, 74, 132–33, 141, 146, 226–30, 232–40, 268, 278, 282
Barth, Markus, 120
Bartholomew, Craig, 32
Barton, John, 118
Basil of Caesarea (Basil the Great), 51, 52–54, 99, 106, 174, 276
Bates, Matthew W., 54, 120, 123, 127
Bauckham, Richard, 40, 55, 58, 125, 139
Bauer, Walter, 119
Bauks, Michaela, 61
Baumann, Gerlinde, 61
Beasley-Murray, George R., 81
Beeke, Joel, 231
Beekes, Robert, 103
Behr, John, 167
Bellarmine, Robert, 194
Bennett, Karen, 253
Best, Paul, 195–96
Beza, Theodore, 192, 193, 194, 199, 207
Biddle, John, 69–72, 196
Bliss, Ricky, 250
Boehmer, Julius, 134
Boettner, Lorraine, 174

AUTHOR INDEX

Bonaventure, 42
Bowden, John, 51
Brand, Myles, 249
Bray, Gerald, 96, 185, 269–70
Breshears, Gerry, 245
Bridge, William, 206
Bromiley, Geoffrey W., 132
Brown, David, 192
Brown, Raymond, 81, 139
Brown, William P., 57
Brownlee, William Hugh, 123
Bulman, James M., 102, 107
Bultmann, Rudolf, 81–82, 228
Burgess, Anthony, 206
Burkholder, Benjamin J., 103
Burroughs, Jeremiah, 206
Bush, Michael David, 218
Butner, D. Glenn, Jr., 96
Butterworth, George William, 161, 272
Caird, George B., 125
Calamy, Edmund, 206
Caldwell, Robert W., III, 210
Calvin, John, 30, 56, 68, 74, 76, 82, 142,
　　170, 185–87, 190–91, 193–94, 199,
　　200, 202, 205–7, 249, 259, 282–84
Caneday, Ardel B., 125
Carruthers, S. W., 189
Carson, D. A., 13, 21–22, 79–97, 169–70
Caryl, Joseph, 206
Casey, R. P., 150
Chadwick, Henry, 279
Chambry, Aemilius, 107
Chantraine, Pierre, 103, 104
Chase, Frederic H., Jr., 262
Cheynell, Francis, 194–201, 204–7
Childs, Brevard S., 67
Clark, J. O. A., 266
Clarke, Samuel, 211
Clement of Alexandria, 49, 110, 111,
　　150, 156
Clifford, Richard J., 57
Cockerill, Gareth Lee, 121, 122

Coffey, J. (John), 181–82
Collins, John J., 57, 127
Colson, F. H., 130
Cornutus, Lucius Annaeus, 110
Correia, Fabrice, 250, 253, 254
Corrigan, Felicitas, 129
Cousins, Ewert, 42
Coxe, A. Cleveland, 171
Craig, William Lane, 59, 246, 249–50,
　　252
Crawford, Matthew R., 236, 239
Crisp, Oliver D., 11, 96, 209, 210, 221,
　　235
Croft, William, 106, 107
Cross, F. L., 99
Crouzel, Henri, 149, 150, 159
Crowe, Brandon D., 37
Cruse, D. Alan, 106, 107
Cyril of Alexandria, 73, 99, 186, 236,
　　239
Cyril of Jerusalem, 100, 106
Dabney, Robert Lewis, 98
Dahms, John V., 102, 105
Dahood, Mitchell, 57
Daley, Brian E., 168
Daly, Christopher, 253
Davidson, Ivor, 225, 267
Davidson, Richard M., 45, 47, 57–58, 61
Davis, Stephen T., 163
DelCogliano, Mark, 53, 54, 106
Delattre, Roland, 216
de Lubac, Henri, 56
Dempsey, Michael T., 227
Dennison, James T., 42, 200, 275
de Savignac, Jean, 57
Dinda, R. J., 74
Diodorus Siculus, 106, 107
Dionysius the Arapagite, 34, 35
Dionysius of Halicarnassus, 106, 107
Dixon, Philip, 197
Dodaro, Robert, 163
Dodd, C. H., 113

Donceel, J., 94
Driscoll, Mark, 245
Driver, Daniel R., 40
Duby, Steven, 225
Dunn, James D. G., 121
Dury, John, 196–97
Ebert, Daniel, 60, 61
Eckstein, Hans-Joachim, 120
Edwards, Jonathan, 24, 208–25
Edwards, Mark J., 149, 150
Ellis, Brannon, 30, 56, 82, 142, 180–81,
    185–87, 194, 195, 205, 275
Elshout, Bartel, 231
Emery, Gilles, 24, 56, 68–69, 73–74,
    179, 231, 278
Epiphanius of Salamis, 99, 107
Erickson, Millard, 64, 245, 257
Eudemus of Rhodes, 107
Eunomius (of Cyzicus), 52, 53, 89,
    103, 106
Euripides, 104
Eusebius of Caesarea, 99, 111, 153
Evans, C. F., 57
Evans, G. R., 56
Emerson Matthew Y., 11, 13, 21, 44–66
Falls, Thomas B., 48
Farley, B. W., 74
Farmer, Craig S., 82
Featley, Daniel, 189–94, 201, 205, 206,
    207
Feinberg, John, 59, 61, 62, 65, 165, 171
Fesko, J.V., 182, 190
Fiering, Norman, 212, 216
Fine, Kit, 253, 254
Fiorenza, Francis Schussler, 263
Fitzmyer, Joseph A., 122
Fockner, Sven, 125
Fox, Michael V., 57, 118
Frame, John, 94
Fraser, Peter M., 104
Freedman, David Noel, 76–77
Frisk, Hjalmar, 103

Galen (Aelius Galenus), 111, 152
Galvin, John, 263
Gasquet, Francis A., 100
Gataker, Thomas, 183–84, 187–89, 205
Geeraerts, Dirk, 107
Gerhard, Johann, 262
Gieschen, Charles A., 139
Giger, George Musgrave, 42, 275
Gignilliat, Mark S., 13, 21, 67–78
Giles, Kevin, 18–19, 44, 46, 56, 59, 93,
    101
Gomes, Alan W., 63, 267
Gouge, William, 192, 206
Granerød, Gard, 122
Greene, Colin, 32
Greenhill, William, 206
Greggs, Tom, 230
Gregory of Nazianzus, 42, 51, 53, 100,
    272
Gregory of Nyssa, 52, 53, 89, 99, 103,
    106, 186, 235, 239, 376
Grillmeier, Aloys, 51
Grudem, Wayne, 59, 61, 62, 64–65
Gunton, Colin, 163
Hammond, Henry, 195
Hanson, R. P. C. (Richard), 57, 159
Hardy, Edward R., 42
Harink, Douglas, 237
Harl, Marguerite, 149, 150
Hart, Trevor A., 40
Hasker, William, 243, 244
Hastings, James, 101
Hausrath, August, 107
Hays, Richard B., 237
Hebgin, Scholastica, 129
Heen, Erik M., 119
Heine, Ronald, 153
Helm, Paul, 59, 211, 246
Herbert, George, 132
Herodotus, 106, 107
Heron, Alasdair, 136, 280
Hesiod, 105–6, 107

Author Index

Hilary of Poitiers, 82, 87, 140, 262, 266
Hill, Edmund, 54, 164
Hill, Robert C., 73
Hillers, Delbert R., 76
Hippolytus, 107
Hoeltje, Miguel, 254
Holmes, Michael W., 111
Holmes, Stephen, 34, 35, 46, 52
Horrell, J. Scott, 46
Hort, F. J. A., 101, 113
Hoskyns, Edwyn C., 237
House, H. Wayne, 94
Howe, G. Ronald, 237
Hübner, Hans, 120
Hunger, Herbert, 107
Hunnius, Aegidius, 82
Hunsinger, George, 69
Hunt, Arnold, 190
Hurst, L. D., 118, 121
Hussey, Phillip, 221
Irenaeus, 48–49, 51, 102–3, 271, 272, 280–81, 284
Irons, Charles Lee, 11, 13, 22, 64, 88–90, 98–116, 151
Issler, Klaus, 46
Jaeger, Werner, 106
Jenson, Robert, 235, 276
Jeremias, Jörg, 76
Jipp, Joshua W., 121
John of Damascus, 187, 262
Johnson, Keith E., 11, 13, 23–24, 46, 54, 55, 59, 90, 94, 140, 163–78, 226, 244, 278
Johnson, Luke Timothy, 122
Jones, Mark, 192
Jones, Paul Dafydd, 228, 229, 235
Josephus, Flavius, 89–90, 106, 107, 108
Jowers, Dennis W., 94
Jüngel, Eberhard, 227, 235
Justinian, 161
Justin Martyr, 47–48, 102, 151

Kaegi, Adolf, 105
Kannengiesser, Charles, 51, 54, 61, 150
Kant, Immanuel, 249
Kattenbusch, Ferdinand, 101
Kapic, Kelly M., 35
Keener, Craig S., 94
Kendall, Daniel, 163
Kidd, James, 18
Kidner, Derek, 62
Koester, Craig, 129
Koetschau, Paul, 161, 272
Koslicki, Kathrin, 253, 254
Köstenberger, Andreas J., 173
Krey, Philip D. W., 119
Kries, Douglas R., 51
Ku, John Baptist, 39
LaCugna, Catherina, 163
Landmesser, Christof, 120
Lang, C., 110
Langacker, Ronald W., 106
Larsen, Christina N., 13, 24, 208–25
Lawless, George, 163
Lee, Sang Hyun, 210, 220
Leitch, James W., 237
Leithart, Peter J., 54, 89
Lenzi, Alan, 57
Letham, Robert, 182, 190
Levering, Matthew, 24, 73, 227, 277
Lichtenberger, Hermann, 120
Lightfoot, J. B., 82
Lightfoot, John, 189, 206
Lim, Paul C. H., 181–83, 195, 196, 197
Lincoln, Andrew T., 45
Lindars, Barnabas, 113
Livingstone, E. A. (Elizabeth), 99, 164
Locke, John, 211, 212, 254
Loewenstein, D., 181, 196
Logan, A. H. B., 159
Longenecker, Richard N., 88, 101, 139
Lowe, E. J., 254, 257–58
Luibheid, Colm, 34
Luther, Martin, 74, 97

301

Lyman, J. Rebecca, 158
MacDonald, Nathan, 40
Macierowski, E. M., 56
Macleod, Donald, 185
Makin, Mark, 13, 25, 243–59
Malone, Joshua, 11, 13, 25, 271–85
Marg, W., 110
Marshall, Bruce D., 235
Marshall, John, 181, 196
Martens, Peter, 77, 156
Martínez, Florentino G., 122
Mason, Eric F., 122
Maspero, Giulio, 31
Mastricht, Petrus van, 212, 221
Mays, James Luther, 75
McCall, Tom, 257
McCormack, Bruce L., 35, 73, 74, 227,
    229–30, 234, 276, 278
McDonough, Sean M., 134
McKinney, Richard W. A., 136, 280
McLachlan, H. John, 181, 195–96
Megasthenes, 107
Meier-Brügger, Michael, 105
Melanchthon, 74
Mettinger, Tryggve N. D., 122, 123
Metzger, Bruce M., 113
Michaels, J. Ramsey, 80
Mitchell, Alexander F., 182
Möller, Karl, 32
Moo, Douglas J., 38
Moody, Dale, 88, 101, 102, 103, 109
Mortimer, Sarah, 183, 184, 196
Moule, H. C. G., 268
Muller, Richard A., 71, 185, 186–87,
    192, 212
Murphy, Francesca Aran (also F. A.),
    56, 280
Murphy, Roland E., 45
Nautin, Pierre, 161
Neuschäfer, Bernhard, 156
Newman, J. O., 77
Niddich, Peter H., 254

Nimmo, Paul T., 229–30
O'Collins, Gerald, 163
Oderberg, David, 254
O'Keefe, John, 48
Origen, 23, 49, 77, 100, 103, 137, 149–62,
    164, 272, 274
Oswald, H. C., 74
Outler, Albert Cook, 130
Ovey, Michael J., 85, 87, 96
Owen, John, 68, 69–73, 74, 163
Paddison, Angus, 45
Pamphilus, 159, 160, 161
Pannenberg, Wolfhart, 235, 237, 276
Parvis, Sarah, 45, 50, 51
Pauw, Amy Plantinga, 209
Peeler, Amy L. B., 125
Pelikan, Jaroslav, 60
Pendrick, Gerard, 105, 111
Pentiuc, Eugen J., 53
Petersen, William L., 150
Peterson, Robert A., 60
Philo of Alexandria, 108, 130
Philoponus, Joannes, 110, 111
Pierce, Madison N., 13, 22, 40, 117–31
Pietersma, Albert, 109
Plantinga, Cornelius, 163
Plato, 106, 107, 110, 152, 279
Plutarch, 106, 107, 110
Polanyi, Michael, 77
Pope, William Burt, 266
Posidonius, 107
Prestige, G. L., 104, 136
Quenstedt, Johannes, 269
Radde-Gallwitz, Andrew, 106, 151
Rae, Murray, 257, 267
Rahner, Karl, 94
Ramsay, Chevalier, 212
Rehnman, Sabastian, 221–22
Reno, R. R., 48
Rettig, John W., 165, 274
Reuss, J., 111
Reymond, Robert L., 170, 171, 182, 190

AUTHOR INDEX

Reynolds, Edward, 206
Rheaume, Randy, 86, 93
Rhee, Victor, 121, 122
Robinson, J. Armitage, 49
Rogers, Cleon L., III, 57
Rondeau, Marie-Josèphe, 120, 123
Rotelle, John E., 54
Rusch, William G., 48, 49
Rutherford, Samuel, 182
Sandbach, F. H., 107, 110
Sanders, Fred, 13, 17–26, 46, 96, 123, 167, 172, 235, 260–70
Savignac, Jean de, 57
Schadel, Erwin, 155
Schaff, Philip, 171
Scheck, Thomas P., 159, 160, 161
Schenck, Kenneth, 121
Schmid, Heinrich, 269
Schnieder, Benjamin, 250, 253, 254
Schwartz, Eduard, 161
Schweitzer, Don, 211
Scott, R. B. Y., 58, 61
Seaman, Lazarus, 206
Sedgwick, Obadiah, 182, 206
Semler, Josiah, 193, 194, 207
Seng-Kong Tan, 222
Shedd, William G. T., 63, 267
Sheridan, Mark, 156
Shillaker, Robert, 94
Simonetti, Manlio, 47
Slusser, Michael, 48
Smith, John E., 220
Smith, Nigel, 196
Smyth, Herbert Weir, 109
Sommerstein, Alan H., 109
Sonderegger, Katherine, 218
Soulen, R. Kendall, 13, 23, 41, 132–46
Spinoza, Baruch, 71, 72
Steinberg, Alex, 254
Steiner, George, 69, 77
Sterry, Peter, 189, 191–92
Steyn, Gert Jacobus, 122

Still, Todd D., 82
Strobel, Kyle C., 209, 211, 212, 219, 220, 221, 222
Strong, William, 192–93, 205
Stubbs, David, 237
Svensson, Manfred, 31
Swain, Scott R., 14, 17–26, 29–43, 89, 91, 96, 173, 234, 235, 236, 269, 277
Swinburne, Richard, 246
Tanner, Kathryn, 34
Tertullian, 102
te Velde, Rudi, 35, 37
Theiler, Willy, 107
Theobald, Michael, 119
Theodoret of Cyrus (or Cyrrhus), 73, 99
Theophilus, Michael P., 119
Theophilus of Antioch, 136
Theophrastus, 106, 111, 112
Thompson, Marianne Meye, 80–81, 170, 171
Timaeus (Locrus), 110
Tkacz, Catherine Brown, 51
Torrance, Iain, 34
Torrance, James, 237
Torrance, Thomas F. (also T. F.), 132, 186, 237
Treier, Daniel J., 11, 45, 89
Trogdon, Kelly, 250
Trueman, Carl R., 37, 71
Tuckney, Anthony, 182, 187, 203, 205
Turner, Denys, 34
Turretin, Francis, 42, 212, 221, 222, 239, 275, 282
Usher, Brett, 188
Van Dixhoorn, Chad, 13, 24, 180–207
VanDrunen, David, 31
Vanhoozer, Kevin J., 239
van Inwagen, Peter, 249
Van Pary, Michel, 54
Vawter, Bruce, 57

303

Velecky, Ceslaus, 273
Waaler, Erik, 135
Walker, George, 184, 187, 189, 206
Wallis, John, 206
Wallis, N. Hardy, 100
Ward, H. Clifton, 156
Warden, Francis Marion, 88, 101, 102, 103
Ware, Bruce, 59, 62–63, 64–65
Warfield, B. B., 182, 185, 186
Watson, Francis, 118
Webb, Thomas, 195
Webster, John, 34, 40, 41, 225, 226, 227, 231–32, 271, 280, 282
Weedman, Mark, 140
Weeks, Stuart, 57
Wehrli, F., 107
Weinandy, Thomas G., 94, 212
Weinrich, William C., 125
Westcott, Brooke Foss, 88, 100–102, 103, 113
Westhead, Nigel, 283, 284
Whitaker, G. H., 130

White, Thomas Joseph, 227, 236, 278
Whybray, R. N., 57
Widdicombe, Peter, 137, 153
Wiles, Maurice, 136
Williams, Daniel H., 57
Williamson, Joseph C., 222
Wilson, Alastair, 253
Wilson, Jessica, 253
Witherington, Ben, III, 82
Wolff, Hans Walter, 75
Wolters, Al, 32
Wozniak, Robert, 31
Wrede, G. F. E. William, 118
Wright, Benjamin G., 109
Wright, N. T., 118
Yandell, Keith, 246, 249, 257
Yeago, David, 47, 61, 72, 169
Yee, Gale, 57
Yonge, C. D., 130
Zachman, Randall, 283
Zalta, E., 250
Ziegler, Philip, 218, 280
Zimmerman, Dean, 253